Collector's Encyclopedia of Stangl DINNERWARE

Robert C. Runge, Jr.

COLLECTOR BOOKS
A Division of Schroeder Publishing Co., Inc.

The current values in this book should be used only as a guide. They are not intended to set prices, which vary from one section of the country to another. Auction prices as well as dealer prices vary greatly and are affected by condition as well as demand. Neither the author nor the publisher assumes responsibility for any losses that might be incurred as a result of consulting this guide.

Front cover clockwise from top left:
Jack and Jill musical mug, $300.00 – 350.00; Blue Melon 6" plate, drilled for a handle, $8.00 – 10.00; Fulper Fayence #1007 Ritz pitcher, Oxblood, $55.00 – 65.00; Assorted Stangl paper napkins, $1.00 – 2.00 each; Blue Caughley 3 quart casserole, $125.00 – 150.00; Fulper Fayence #1009 teapot, Persian Yellow, $150.00 – 175.00; Fruit 11½" oval platter, $110.00 – 140.00; Fruit cup & saucer, $16.00 – 22.00; Fruit sauce boat, $50.00 – 60.00; Fruit mug, 2 cup, $40.00 – 50.00.

Cover & book design by Michelle Dowling

Searching For A Publisher?

We are always looking for knowledgeable people considered to be experts within their fields. If you feel that there is a real need for a book on your collectible subject and have a large comprehensive collection, contact Collector Books.

Contents

Dedication

This book is dedicated to the memory of my great-grandmother, Olga Javes; the first person to take me to the Flemington Outlet.

To my grandmother, Dot Javes, for being my lifelong friend and inspiration.

Also to my parents, Robert and Linda Runge, for their unfailing encouragement and support.

Acknowledgments

First and foremost, I thank Diana Bullock, my colleague in research, best friend, partner, and wife, for her steadfast support of this project from its inception over 10 years ago through its completion. She has been with me every step of the way and has provided me the lasting encouragement, time, and support necessary to accomplish this work.

All this work would certainly never have been possible without the assistance of a number of extraordinarily generous individuals. I am genuinely grateful to Martin Stangl's daughters and sons-in-law for their tremendous assistance. I thank Christl (Stangl) and Merrill Bacheler for sharing their time and loaning their dinnerware. I wish to acknowledge Betty (Stangl) and Dave Thomas for patiently indulging my many letters and telephone calls, and for offering an abundance of detailed Stangl production knowledge.

I would like to express heartfelt thanks to the following Stangl employees. The vast amount of information and personal insight each graciously shared adds great depth and detail to this book.

Edward Alvater, Flemington Outlet manager, 1972 – 1978

Christl Stangl Bacheler, demonstrator, cataloging, decorator, 1935 – 1964

Martha Stangl Bacheler, Flemington Outlet showroom decorator, 1936 – 1943

Merrill Bacheler, demonstrator, Flemington Outlet manager, 1938 – 1964

Gloria Cardone, decorator, 1956 – 1978

Helen Orashan Cervenka, Flemington Outlet secretary, museum curator, 1965 – 1968

Agnes Douglass, Flemington Outlet sales clerk, 1948 – 1953

Norma (Nonny) Stockwell English, designer, 1944 – 1945

Edith Gambi, personnel, switchboard, 1950 – 1972

Florence Gardner, decorator, 1949 – 1978

Florence Dunn Glenn, decorator, 1948 – 1960

Kathleen (Kay) Kastner Hackett, designer, 1941 – 1965

Teresa Hawryluk, decorator, 1945 – 1978

Rose Herbeck, designer, 1967 – 1972

Rose Jacobs, decorator, 1946 – 1970s

Charles Jankowski, ceramic engineer, 1964 – 1968

Mary Myers Jones, Martin Stangl's secretary, 1929 – 1944

Paul Kavulic, kiln operator, 1960 – 1978

Rudolf Kleinebeckel, designer, modeler, 1968 – 1978

Ruth Klenk, decorator, 1952 – 1956

David Koch, production control and shipping manager, 1973 – 1976

Gerrie Majeski, decorator, 1954 – 1968

Alice Maple, Flemington Outlet sales clerk, 1968 – 1978

Anné Fritsche Martin, Flemington Outlet potter/decorator, 1965

Walter McBride, jiggerman, supervisor, 1949 – 1978

Enez Mitzkewich, Flemington Outlet assistant manager, 1969 – 1978

Richard Nerges, jiggerman, 1963 – 1967

James Paul, general manager, 1964 – 1971

Clinton Peterman, accountant, 1942 – 1973

Irene Podayko, Flemington Outlet assistant manager, 1949 – 1964

Anne Pogranicy, office manager, 1946 – 1978
Jean Taylor Polasek, Flemington decorator, 1946 – 1948
Denise Rehl, Flemington Outlet sales clerk, 1976 – 1978
Cleo Crawford Salerno, designer, 1942 – 1947
Alice Samsel, decorator, 1951 – 1978
Irene M. Sarnecki, designer, forelady of decorating, 1948 – 1978
William Smith, engineer's assistant, 1949 – 1956
Shirley Thatcher Spaciano, Flemington Outlet sales clerk, decorator, demonstrator, 1942 – 1962
David Thomas, general manager, engineer, 1945 – 1956
Betty Stangl Thomas, decorator, 1939 – 1941
Rosa Veglianetti, decorator, 1938 – 1976
Fred Walker, jiggerman, 1948 – 1971
Geraldine Walker West, engobe sprayer, 1951 – 1967
Ethel Weyman, decorator, 1947 – 1954

I am especially indebted to the many fine Stangl collectors and dealers who enthusiastically shared information or loaned items for photography. Through the combined efforts of all, this project has been possible. Thanks to: Flossie and Bennett Avila, Muriel Brannon, Diana Bullock, Scott Creighton, Jim Davidson, Natalie Del Vechio, Lynn Dezmain, Agnes and Manning Douglass, David and Deb Gainer, Gordon Gray, Nora Godown, Ruth Godown, Dolores and Skip Hager, Patrick Harmon, Loretta Javes, Lennie and Vernon Javes, Sandra Klawson, Nancy and Kevin Klein, Beatrice and Larry Levine, Elaine and Jim Martin, Johann and Chris McKee, Judy and Dan Meck, Curtis and Peggy Meissner, Barbara Miller, Donna and Bob Miller, Jim and Barbara Nelson, Mary Ann Null, Carrolyn Pearson, Nancy and Bob Perzel, Carolyn Pyatt, Tom and Donna Rago, Charity and Mark Rinker, Dottie Ritter, Nancy and Luke Ruepp, Julie Sferrazza, David Solomon, Lowell Snare, Ed Stump, Anna Todd, Judy Vianden.

Special thanks to Roxanne Carkhuff of the Hunterdon County Historical Society, Charles Webster of the Trentoniana Collection at the Trenton Public Library, Gay Taylor and Elizabeth Wilk of Wheaton Village Museum of American Glass, and Gary Shaner, district manager of Pfaltzgraff, for all their kind assistance.

I am very grateful to my dearest friend Kay Hackett for sharing her memories of Stangl, and inspiring me to write this book. I wish to thank several outstanding friends whose help was invaluable: Patricia Walther for her editing and getting this project started; and Frank and Liz Kramar for their unending support and cherished friendship. I am indebted to my parents, Linda and Robert Runge, for allowing their dining room to become a photography studio for three years; my brother Ralph for all his technical assistance; to my daughter Heather for her enthusiasm and support.

Photos processed by Direct Photo, owners Diana Bullock and Robert Runge.

For more information or specific questions regarding Stangl Dinnerware or Stangl Pottery, please feel free to contact the author at:

Robert C. Runge Jr.
PO Box 5427
Somerset, NJ 08875

For information concerning Country Life or Kiddieware patterns, please contact:
Luke and Nancy Ruepp
PO Box 349
Lake Hiawatha, NJ 07034

Stangl Sources & Dinnerware Matching Services:

Ben and Floss Avila
157 Kingwood-Locktown Rd.
Stockton, NJ 08559-1221

Judy and Dan Meck
229 Hogestown Road
Mechanicsburg, PA 17055

BullRun Unlimited
Diana Bullock, Rob Runge
PO Box 5427
Somerset, NJ 08875

Pinecone Antiques
Barbara Miller
150 Greenbrook Road
North Plainfield, NJ 07060

Lynn Dezmain
106 Garrett Circle
Ephrata, PA 17552

Julie Sferrazza
144 Tanglewood Drive
Somerville, NJ 08876

Grandpa's Trading Company
Jim and Barbara Nelson
5403 15th Street East
Bradenton, FL 34203

Introduction

Between 1924 and 1978 Stangl Pottery produced a great assortment of earthenware lamps, artware, dinnerware, and utilitarian lines. It was Stangl's dinnerware, however, that was manufactured in the greatest quantities. Stangl's hand-carved, hand-painted fruit and floral decorated dinnerware patterns were renowned. Martin Stangl was quite innovative and influential in directing the course of the American ceramics industry. The Stangl company, under the name Fulper at that time, was the first American pottery to introduce a full line of nationally distributed solid-color glazed dinnerware in 1924. Stangl also was a major American ceramics and dinnerware supplier when European imports were not available during World War II. Additionally, Stangl continually developed and introduced new and varied dinnerware patterns in an effort to keep abreast of the latest popular trends. Examples of this were the brushed-gold patterns introduced during the 1950s and the sponge decorated patterns of the 1960s and 1970s.

This book lists nearly all of Stangl's dinnerware patterns and dinnerware related items in the order in which they were introduced. This chronological order effectively reflects the progression of Stangl dinnerware. It also demonstrates the prominent role that American home-decorating styles played in the development of many Stangl patterns. Listed with each pattern are all known pieces with a price range and brief description of the pattern. When known, production details and history of the pattern are also included.

The prices listed are average values for each piece in each pattern. Several factors that will always affect Stangl pricing include a particular pattern's availability, collectibility, and regional area. Recently, there has been very strong activity in the Stangl categories of Internet auctions, such as eBay. Although this has affected retail values to a certain extent, the extreme high and low prices sometimes realized on Internet auctions do not represent the retail values of Stangl items offered for sale at antiques shops, shows, and markets and through mail-order. Please remember that the values published here are examples only and are not the standard for Stangl dinnerware pricing.

"In our world of automation, there are few industries that specialize in hand-crafted items. Stangl Pottery, one of America's oldest potteries, still takes the time to hand-craft and hand-paint each and every piece of dinnerware ... Stangl dinnerware is still, and will continue to be, a work of art. We are proud of Stangl hand-crafted dinnerware and artware ... those who own it also experience this pride of possession."
— J.M. Stangl, 1965

Foreword quoted from *Stangl, A Portrait of Progress in Pottery.*

Recently employed as ceramic chemist and technical superintendent, a young Johan Martin Stangl works on developing Vasekraft glazes at Fulper Pottery Co. in 1910. Photo courtesy of the Fulper and Stangl Museum Collection.

Fulper Pottery

Stangl Pottery Company's earliest beginnings were as Hill Pottery on Mine Street, Flemington, New Jersey. Hill Pottery was founded by Samuel Hill in 1814 and produced utilitarian items from Flemington area clays. Although Fulper and Stangl used the founding date 1805 in trademarks and advertisements from 1900 onward, local historians had determined as early as the 1940s that 1814 is a more accurate date.

After Samuel Hill's death in 1858, Hill Pottery employee, Abram Fulper, purchased the pottery business, known thereafter as Fulper Pottery. During the late nineteenth century, Fulper Pottery became increasingly important as a manufacturer of utilitarian earthenware and stoneware articles and architectural tile for the metropolitan New York/New Jersey area.

During the 1890s and early 1900s, William Hill Fulper II, then president of Fulper Pottery Company, began experimenting with, and ultimately producing, several lines of artware. Most notable was the Vasekraft artware line, introduced in 1909. This line was made of heavy stoneware clays and featured magnificent glaze effects in many color and texture combinations. This line was acclaimed for its arts and crafts styling and historically accurate Oriental forms and glazes.

Although the Vasekraft line was discontinued by 1920, Fulper Pottery continued to produce high-quality stoneware bodied artware through 1934.

On September 22, 1910, Fulper hired 22-year-old Johan Martin Stangl as ceramic chemist and technical superintendent. Stangl, originally of Hof, Germany, had studied ceramic design and ceramic engineering in Bunzlau, Germany, and had earned a master's degree in both those subjects. William Fulper II felt that Stangl's experience at Bunzlau with mirrored glazes could enhance the Vasekraft line of artware.

A portion of the contract dated September 22, 1910, between Fulper and Stangl states: "In consideration of this contract between you and ourselves for three years of your service from this date as Superintendent of Technical Department of our Pottery you are to work up glazes and bodies for the best results to the company, use your best endeavors in all departments of Ceramics for the good of the company ... we agree to pay you a yearly salary of seven hundred eighty dollars ($780) per year, payable weekly fifteen dollars ($15) per week and a commission on art ware equal to 5% on actual sales and a commission of 2% on actual sales of Guaranteed Fire Proof Cooking Ware."

Fulper Pottery buildings, Mine Street, Flemington, New Jersey, 1909.

On October 19, 1911, Martin Stangl was promoted to superintendent of Pottery, with control over all men, including foremen. From October 1911 until April 1914, Martin Stangl was to supervise all aspects of Fulper production and continued to be responsible for developing new shapes, glazes, and bodies. According to a contract between Stangl and Fulper, dated September 26, 1913, Stangl's salary for this position was fifteen dollars per week plus a four percent commission on actual sales of all Vasekraft artware. This contract states: "In consideration of this salary and commission, you are to work up new glazes and bodies as needed; assist in designing and overseeing the general factory work, all for the benefit and advancement of the company."

In April 1914, Stangl left Fulper and was employed by Edmund H. Haeger of the Haeger Brick & Tile Company at Dundee, Illinois. At Haeger, Martin Stangl developed a line of earthenware artware with multicolor and solid-color glazes. The Haeger artware line bore some similarities to Fulper's Vasekraft, but was actually designed as an inexpensive alternative to the costly artware lines of that era.

In 1918, Martin Stangl resigned at Haeger and returned to Fulper. Stangl again became Fulper's factory superintendent, and was instrumental in developing the Fulper Porcelaine doll heads and novelties. William Fulper II appointed Martin Stangl vice president of Fulper Pottery in 1924. By 1926, Stangl had assumed presidency. William Fulper II continued as secretary/treasurer and retained partial ownership of the company until his death in 1928. It was in 1924, therefore, when Martin Stangl's control over the Fulper product lines becomes distinctly evident, that the history of Stangl Pottery actually began.

Fulper Fayence, 1920s

Because of the economic depression of the early 1920s and the declining demand for stoneware utilitarian articles, Fulper Pottery introduced an inexpensive line of solid-color glazed earthenware products in 1924. This line consisted of lamps, vases, ashtrays, and dinnerware and was cumulatively known as Fulper Fayence. Fulper Fayence articles were made of a lightweight, but durable, earthenware body and were available in four bright colors. These colored glazes were Colonial Blue, Silver Green, Persian Yellow, and Chinese Ivory. The classic shapes and attractive glazes of Fulper Fayence dinnerware were well received, which prompted the development of additional solid-color dinnerware patterns and glazes throughout the 1920s and 1930s.

To acquire the space needed to produce the Fulper Fayence line, a second manufacturing facility was purchased in February 1924. This modest concrete-block structure had originally been built for the D. & H. Confectionery Company in 1922 and was located on Mine Street, Flemington, about one block west of the original Fulper Pottery works. Martin Stangl promptly added two kilns and several production rooms to the building at this site. The new facility became known as Plant #2, while the original Fulper buildings were called Plant #1. Plant #2 was in full operation by the end of 1924.

Fulper Pottery Plant #2, 1935.

Fulper/Stangl

When Martin Stangl became president of Fulper Pottery in 1926, he instituted the Fulper/Stangl logo. This was an effective way to connect the Stangl name with the Fulper Pottery reputation for outstanding high quality. Although the Fulper/Stangl trademark was used to designate solid-color glazed earthenware products, it did not replace the Fulper Fayence brand name. The Fulper Fayence trademark continued to be used on neoclassic and Oriental styled products until 1930. Items bearing the

Fulper/Stangl trademark were customarily very modern or very primitively styled. Both logos were used simultaneously on solid-color glazed earthenware products until 1930 when both were replaced with the Stangl trademark.

In order to expand production facilities and meet the continued demand for Stangl's bright dinnerware, Fulper Pottery Company leased a small portion of the former Anchor Pottery in 1926. The Anchor Pottery buildings were located on New York Avenue in Trenton, New Jersey, 23 miles south of Flemington. Martin Stangl used the Trenton site to manufacture the expanded Fulper Fayence and Fulper/Stangl dinnerware lines. In January 1928, Fulper Pottery purchased the Anchor Pottery buildings and promptly made full use of this facility.

Anchor Pottery buildings, New York Avenue, Trenton, New Jersey, rear view, 1900.

The popularly held explanation for Stangl's move to Trenton in 1926 was because of William Fulper's supposed dislike for solid-color dinnerware. He personally may not have liked it, but being a sound businessman, Fulper recognized a lucrative product. The Trenton facility was acquired for practical reasons more than anything else. Fulper Fayence and

Anchor Pottery buildings, Trenton, New Jersey, front view, 1900.

Fulper/Stangl dinnerware patterns had become increasingly popular, and it was more economical to relocate the dinnerware manufacturing to the existing Anchor Pottery buildings than to expand at either of the cramped properties in Flemington. The Anchor buildings were already equipped with fourteen kilns and all of the fixtures necessary for dinnerware production. This facility also had three rail sidings and a canal slip, serviced by two separate railroad companies and an active canal. This greatly facilitated the receiving of raw material and coal, and the shipping of finished products. Both Plant #1 and Plant #2 in Flemington required supplies to be trucked to and from rail platforms, incurring greater handling expenses.

As an incentive for employees living in the Flemington area to transfer to the Trenton plant, Martin Stangl supplied a jitney-bus to convey them from Flemington to Trenton and back. During the 1950s, as many as three station wagons were making the daily trips to and from Flemington.

According to the New Jersey State Chamber of Commerce, in 1928 only dinnerware was produced at the Trenton plant. The Fulper and Stangl artwares were manufactured at the two facilities in Flemington. The Fulper stoneware lines were produced at Plant #1, while the Fulper/Stangl earthenware articles were produced at Plant #2. Also at Plant #1 were showrooms where Fulper and Stangl first- and second-quality products were displayed and sold.

On September 19, 1929, an electrical fire completely destroyed Plant #1. Lost were the Fulper artware production rooms, kilns, and showrooms. Also lost were the finished wares, packed and ready for shipment. By a stroke of great fortune, product orders and the highly

Stangl Pottery buildings, Trenton, New Jersey, front view, 1935.

Courtesy of the Wheaton Village Museum of American Glass.

valuable Fulper glaze formulas were saved from the fire. Martin Stangl decided not to rebuild Plant #1 on the small original lot. Instead, he expanded at Plant #2 by adding a third kiln and enlarging the production area. A fourth kiln was planned but never built. A small showroom was also added to Plant #2 at this time.

Once production was resumed, only Fulper artware and Stangl's hand-thrown lines were produced at the remaining Flemington Plant #2. All production of Stangl dinnerware and cast artware was transferred to the Trenton plant. Thanks to the generosity and support from the residents of Flemington and surrounding communities, the Fulper Pottery Company was again fully operational in time for Christmas, 1930.

Stangl, 1930s

In 1930, Martin Stangl purchased William Fulper's share of Fulper Pottery from his estate. Also in 1930, the Fulper Fayence and Fulper/Stangl brand names and logos were completely replaced with the Stangl trademark, for which a patent had been granted in 1929. A 1930 Stangl catalog states, "Because of the increasing demand for brightly colored table ware and for low priced art pottery, The Fulper Pottery Company has perfected and offered to the public the now popular Stangl Ware which

successfully meets both demands. The large variety of Stangl pottery consisting of useful articles of practical design offers an unusual selection of ware successfully combining art, utility and moderate price." Stangl products were advertised at this time as "Stangl Pottery, made by Fulper Pottery." The name Fulper Pottery Company was not legally changed to Stangl Pottery Company until December 28, 1955.

Fulper artware sales had been diminishing during the early 1930s, while demand for inexpensive solid-color dinnerware and artware bearing the Stangl trademark increased. Fulper brand artware products continued to be manufactured until 1935, but production of Stangl dinnerware ultimately became the backbone of the Fulper Pottery Company.

During the early 1930s, sales at the Flemington showroom had increased substantially, and it became apparent that operating two production facilities 23 miles apart was very inefficient. Martin Stangl therefore decided to relocate Flemington's remaining production operations to the larger facility at Plant #3 in Trenton and devote the whole Flemington building to retail sales. During 1934 the Plant #2 building in Flemington was renovated and by 1935 had become the Fulper Pottery Company showroom and retail outlet.

Courtesy of the Wheaton Village Museum of American Glass.

Aerial view of Flemington Plant #2, or Flemington Outlet and Showroom, 1949.

The only pottery production conducted at Flemington after 1935 was during World War II, when a large portion of the retail showroom was set up for decorating bird figurines. Demand was so great for Stangl's bird figurines at that time that approximately 40 decorators were added to the staff at Flemington just to help fill outstanding orders. Following World War II until Stangl's close, however, small-scale pottery production for tourist demonstrations was carried out at the Flemington Outlet at various times.

Hand-Painted Dinnerware

Until the late 1930s, Stangl produced underglaze decorated dinnerware in very limited quantities for special orders only. Large scale production of mass-produced, hand-decorated dinnerware was begun in 1937. During the late 1930s, the hand-decorated dinnerware was only a small portion of Stangl's vast assortment of solid-color dinnerware and artware lines.

The mass-produced, hand-decorated dinnerware patterns introduced in 1937 featured easily decorated silk-screened motifs with accents applied by hand. These silk-screened patterns were on the #1388 and #2000 shapes and utilized the same white earthenware body as the solid-color glazed patterns. Because the silk-screened patterns were cheaply mass produced, they lack the depth and brilliance found in many of Stangl's later hand-decorated patterns.

During 1938, Stangl introduced several dinnerware patterns with motifs that were wholly hand painted. These motifs were stenciled onto each piece with powdered charcoal, and decorators applied the underglaze colors by following the charcoal outlines. Not one of Stangl's dinnerware patterns was ever decorated freehand.

1940s

Because of the impending war in Europe, by 1939 American distributors and department stores were no longer able to supply customers with the imported, hand-painted pottery popular at that time. Aware of this ceramics void, Stangl began producing bird and animal figurines, and greatly expanded the hand-painted dinnerware lines. Many of the newly added dinnerware patterns were similar to those which had been available overseas. These patterns utilized Stangl's white earthenware body and were decorated with hand-painted underglaze motifs. Also developed at this time was Stangl's Terra Rose glaze finish. Combining boldly brushed metallic oxides with a semi-opaque glaze, the Terra Rose finish imparted a look of antiquity to whatever it was applied. Stangl utilized this glaze on several lines of artware and dinnerware throughout the 1940s and 1950s.

Martin Stangl escorting Carole Stupell of Carole Stupell, Ltd., through the Trenton factory in August 1940. The potter is creating casseroles for the handmade #3506 Pie Crust dinnerware line.

Courtesy of the Wheaton Village Museum of American Glass.

Private Label Accounts

As early as the 1920s, Stangl Pottery would contract with various distributors and retailers to manufacture exclusive dinnerware patterns for them. "Private label" is the term Stangl used to describe such patterns. During and immediately after World War II Stangl produced more private label patterns than at any other time. Depending on the distributor, private label patterns were marked with a distributor's logo in conjunction with a Stangl mark or the distributor's logo only. Several companies commissioned private label Stangl patterns during the 1950s, 1960s, and 1970s. But it was throughout the 1940s that Stangl produced the greatest number of private label patterns. Some of the

distributors that Stangl supplied with specialty items or dinnerware on a continuing basis were:

Black, Star, & Gorm
Boston, MA

Jordan Marsh
Boston, MA

Marshall Field & Co.
Chicago, IL

B. Altman & Co.
New York, NY

Henri Bendel
New York, NY

L.D. Bloch Co.
New York, NY

Bloomingdale's
New York, NY

Carole Stupell, Ltd.
New York, NY

Daison
New York, NY

Davart
New York, NY

Frederik Lunning
New York, NY

R. Levin Co.
New York, NY

R.H. Macy
New York, NY

Nieman-Marcus
New York, NY

Rafco
New York, NY

Rena Rosenthal
New York, NY

Ritz Mfg. Enterprise
New York, NY

Sak's Fifth Avenue
New York, NY

Simon Jay-Willfred
New York, NY

Tiffany & Co.
New York, NY

Bamberger's
Newark, NJ

E.W. Murphy
Roselle, NJ

Fisher, Bruce & Co.
"Della-Ware"
Philadelphia, PA
New York, NY

S. S. Kresge
Detroit, MI

Hand-Carved Dinnerware

By the early 1940s, several other American potteries had also begun to manufacture hand-painted, white-bodied dinnerware. Martin Stangl desired to produce something saleable, different from what other potteries were doing. For this reason Stangl began experimenting with sgraffito-decorated dinnerware patterns. He believed designs similar to Pennsylvania Dutch redware pottery would coordinate with the Early American style of home furnishings popular at that time.

In October 1941, Kay Hackett was hired as a dinnerware designer. Her experience with engobes and sgraffito decoration was a factor in her obtaining this position. After several weeks of learning the operating procedures of Stangl Pottery and researching authentic Pennsylvania Dutch decoration, Kay Hackett began designing what would become Stangl's extremely popular hand-carved, hand-painted dinnerware.

The first of the sgraffito-decorated patterns were introduced in January 1942. These patterns utilized a red-colored clay body with a thin coating of white clay, called engobe, brushed over the surface of each piece. The motifs were carved into the engobe, then hand painted with bright underglaze colors. The sgraffito-decorated dinnerware required much labor and handling of each piece, so was more costly, but became increasingly popular throughout the 1940s.

Stangl's dinnerware shapes were formed using two different methods. Hollow ware pieces, such as teapots, coffee pots, creamers, and sugars were slip cast. In slip casting, liquid clay, commercially known as slip, was poured into plaster molds. As the plaster mold absorbed water from the slip, a coating of solid clay lined the interior surface of the mold. This lining of solid clay ultimately formed the walls of the cast item. When enough water was absorbed and the walls were of an appropriate thickness, the excess slip was poured off and the cast item allowed to dry. When the molded piece was dry and firm enough to stand on its own, the mold was opened and the piece removed to dry further.

Plates, cups, and bowls were jiggered; that is, formed of soft clay on a spinning plaster mold on a "vertical lathe," similar to the way a woodworker uses a wood lathe. Two men were usually involved in the jiggering process. These would be the "batter out man" and the "jigger man."

Clay was brought to the jiggering room as cylinders of soft clay, called pugs. The batter out man would slice a small section from the pug and place it on a plaster mold then "bat" or flatten the clay over the mold. The jigger man then put the mold on the spinning jigger and lowered a steel template over the clay to form the back of a plate or bowl. The plaster mold would shape the face of the piece. Jiggered pieces were dried on the molds until stiff enough to handle.

The batter out man on the left prepares the plaster mold and soft clay for the jigger man, on the right, who then forms the back of the piece.

Jiggering cups. Pugs of clay are on the left, plaster cup molds are behind the jigger man, and stacks of greenware cups are on the conveyor at right.

After jiggering or casting, each piece of unfired dinnerware was in the "green" state or "greenware." When dry enough to handle, greenware was taken to the finishing department where edges were trimmed and mold seams were smoothed.

A finisher "finishing" edges of greenware plates.

Stangl's finishing department during 1952.

After finishing, engobe was applied to the surface of each piece of hand-carved dinnerware. Originally, engobe was hand brushed on each piece. In 1950 Stangl began spraying engobe on most pieces but a few patterns continued to be produced on brushed engobe. By 1952 engobe was sprayed on all pieces, no longer were any brushed.

Following engobing, the design motif would be stenciled on each piece. Stangl's stencils were made of parchment-like architect's tracing paper. For each stencil, the outline of the pat-

Saucers being sprayed in one of the engobe spraybooths. Each piece of dinnerware was sprayed at booths such as this. In the background are wareboards stacked with greenware waiting to be sprayed.

tern motif was formed by tiny perforations in the paper. The stencil was placed where the motif was to be on a piece of greenware, then a small cloth bag of powdered charcoal was "pounced" over the motif on the stencil. When the stencil was lifted, charcoal that had been forced through the perforations formed a "dot-to-dot" outline of the motif.

Stenciled pieces of greenware were then sent to the carving department where the design was carved through the engobe, into the red body by following the stenciled outline. Originally, the designs were carved with a sharp stylus. In later years, stylus carving tools were replaced with automatic pencils that held disposable steel phonograph needles.

Stangl's carving department.

Close-up of a carver hand carving the motif on a
Star Flower teapot.

One of Stangl's carvers working on plates.

Several of Stangl's carvers during 1952.

Following carving, each piece was cleaned and sort-
ed before being packed into the bisque kiln. This
woman is vacuum cleaning clay "crumbs" from
carved greenware.

A loaded kiln car just out of the bisque kiln. Large
fans were used to cool the pieces so they could be
handled quickly.

One of Stangl's several bisque sanders.

One of the "wheels" used in the decorating department.

After bisque firing, imperfections were sanded and the bright underglaze colors were hand painted on each design. A few of Stangl's simpler patterns were decorated by a team of decorators on a device known as the "wheel." Developed by Stangl's engineer, Dave Thomas, the "wheel" was a three-tier revolving table, around which sat several decorators. Each decorator applied certain colors or brush strokes to a piece, then passed the piece on to the next decorator. By the time a piece traveled completely around the table, it was on the top shelf and fully decorated.

There were three of these wheels in Stangl's decorating department. Pieces decorated on the wheel were usually marked with an "X" or an "XE," indicating that the piece was decorated by a team of decorators. Some of the patterns decorated in this manner were Five-Petal Flower, Golden Harvest, and Amber-Glo.

At first, Stangl's hand-carved patterns were produced by a very small decorating department, headed by Kay Hackett. By 1946, the red-bodied, hand-carved patterns had become so popular that the earlier white-bodied solid-color and hand-decorated patterns were completely discontinued. At this time, all production was turned over to the manufactur-

An overview of Stangl's decorating department during 1964. In this area, Stangl's more complex patterns were decorated by one decorator only.

ing of red-bodied articles. Only bird figurines and a few special items made exclusively for the Flemington Outlet were still produced with an all white body. Stangl's distinctive "hand-carved, hand-painted" dinnerware remained a strong seller throughout the 1940s, 1950s, and 1960s, and was distributed to nearly 4,000 retailers across the nation.

Hand-carved patterns introduced during the early part of the 1940s utilized the #3434 rim shape. In 1947, patterns on the modern #3774

A group photo of Stangl's carvers and decorators, 1952.

Stangl's shipping and sorting department, 1952.

Stangl's firing capability. Also with the tunnel kilns, firings were better controlled, which resulted in fewer "misfires" and flawed glazes.

Inactive Patterns

Stangl's hand-carved patterns were rarely discontinued. Instead, when popularity waned, most patterns became "inactive." Complete sets of inactive patterns were not available, but fill-in pieces could be ordered directly from Stangl. Inactive patterns were never available year-round. At first they were produced only during slow periods, but in later years were available during specifically scheduled times of the year.

1950s

The 1950s were probably the most productive and innovative years for Stangl Pottery. During that decade 60 new dinnerware patterns were introduced and several manual operations in the factory were eliminated by the addition of conveyors and other modern equipment. The three most notable changes made in the production of Stangl dinnerware during the 1950s were the conversion from hand brushing engobe to spraying; the introduction of colored engobes in 1952, and gold-decorated dinnerware in 1956. While many other American potteries were foundering at this time, due to imports and the increasing popularity of plastic dinnerware, Stangl was not only weathering the storm, but was prospering as well.

coupe shape were introduced. Stangl designers liked to use the coupe shape as it gave them greater freedom in designing. The designers often felt their motifs were confined by the wide rim of the #3434 shape.

Between 1944 and 1947, Stangl replaced the coal-fired "bee hive" kilns with large gas-fired tunnel kilns. This greatly increased

Aerial view of Stangl Pottery buildings, Trenton, 1949. Missing are the distinctive brick "bee hive" kilns that formerly dominated the roof line. Courtesy of the Wheaton Village Museum of American Glass.

Salad Sets

From the 1920s onward, one of the methods Stangl used to determine whether or not a new dinnerware

Stangl designer Kay Hackett (seated on right) with assistant trying out Stangl's newly constructed "demonstration table" in 1949. This table was used at department store demonstrations and trade shows to illustrate the processes involved in the handcrafting of Stangl dinnerware.

pattern was marketable was to offer it as a salad set. This was a short set, having a limited number of pieces. Stangl's primary dinnerware patterns were composed of between 20 and 45 individual shapes. A Stangl salad set usually consisted of a chop plate, salad bowl, and 8" plates. This varied, however, as different pieces were used to suit different needs.

Larger department stores that carried Stangl patterns often offered salad sets in addition to the regular dinnerware lines. If enough interest was shown in a particular salad set pattern, it was then expanded into a full set. Examples of this are the Fruit, Kumquat, and Lime patterns. These motifs were originally available only on the three basic salad set pieces. By 1948, however, these patterns had become popular enough to warrant the production of additional shapes in each pattern.

Many of the salad set patterns introduced during the 1950s were never expanded and were only available on the chop plate, salad bowl, and 8" plate shapes. The 8" plates are usually easiest to find simply because there were six 8" plates sold for each chop plate and salad bowl. Whenever a Stangl pattern is referred to as a salad set, it means that only a limited number of shapes were produced with that particular motif.

Sprayed and Colored Engobes

Dave Thomas, Martin Stangl's son-in-law, manager, and engineer of the Trenton plant from 1946 through 1956, with the assistance of William Smith, developed a process that enabled engobe to be sprayed on each piece instead of hand brushed. The spraying technique was perfected and put into use as early as 1950. This immediately lessened the amount of hand labor required for each piece. Hand brushing of engobe was diminished, but was not completely discontinued until mid-1952. Because of this, pieces belonging to certain patterns that were made through 1952 can be found with either brushed or sprayed engobe.

Although Martin Stangl realized spraying engobe saved the company money, he felt that the swirl of hand-brushed engobe in the center of each piece represented handcraftsmanship. He was afraid consumers would no longer be interested in buying Stangl dinnerware if it were not completely handmade. This turned out not to be true, for Stangl patterns became even more popular throughout the 1950s, partly due to the smooth white background created by sprayed engobe.

The engobe spraying process also made it possible to use colored engobes. A green engobe was introduced in 1952 on the Star Flower and Magnolia patterns. In 1953 gray engobe was introduced on Golden Harvest and Song Bird. The colored engobes were very novel at that time, so Stangl was able to charge more for those patterns, even though they cost no more to produce than similar patterns with white engobe. Other colored engobes that were used in later years were light gray on Bella Rosa and Garland, and dark yellow on the Rooster and Yankee Doodle patterns.

Gold-Decorated Dinnerware

In 1953, Stangl installed an electric kiln for the low-temperature firing of red overglaze on bird figurines such as cardinals and tanagers. In 1956, a second electric kiln was added, and Stangl began using both kilns for firing metallic lusters. These electric kilns were not stationary as were the large tunnel kilns. Ware was

Stangl Trenton plant, 1959. This photo was taken from the newly completed Trenton Freeway (US Route #1).

1960s

If the 1950s were the most productive years for Stangl Pottery, the 1960s were certainly the most innovative. New shapes and new methods of decoration were introduced. During the 1960s, patterns with molded decorations were developed, as were patterns with sponged motifs. The new styles and shapes were created in an effort to compete with the imported dinnerware products that continued to flood the American marketplace during that time.

Flemington Outlet

The Flemington Outlet played a major role in maintaining cash flow for Stangl Pottery. Martin Stangl threw nothing away; firsts, seconds, flawed pieces, tests, samples, and experiments were all sold through the outlet. By selling all of these various items that most potteries destroyed, Stangl was able to survive difficult times, such as the Great Depression during the 1930s, the recession following World War II, and the tremendous influx of imported dinnerware during the 1960s.

Because Flemington was on the direct route from Manhattan, New York to the celebrity getaway area of Bucks County, Pennsylvania, Stangl's Flemington Outlet was often visited by many notable personalities. Playwrights George Kaufman and Moss Hart were known to have stopped at the Flemington showroom at least once, as

The newly installed electric kiln loaded for its first test firing in July 1953.

stacked on stationary firebrick tables, and the whole kiln was then rolled over the table and sealed for firing.

In 1956, several dinnerware patterns were introduced with platinum and 22 karat gold luster decorations. Ultimately, Stangl's dry-brushed gold finishes became very popular and were their most widely distributed artware decoration during the 1960s and 1970s. During the late 1970s, the electric kilns were also used for the firing of decals on the decal-decorated Christmas patterns produced at that time.

View of the front doors of the Flemington Outlet, 1955.

were Clark Gable, Kitty Carlisle, Helen Hayes, and Damon Runyon. There were also a few noted celebrities with permanent or vacation homes in the Flemington area who purchased Stangl products on a regular basis. Some of the outlet's frequent luminaries during the 1940s and 1950s were band-leader Paul Whiteman, television and movie actor Ralph Bellamy, and comic actress Zasu Pitts. Anne Elstner Mathews, "Stella Dallas" on radio during the 1940s and 1950s, decorated her River's Edge restaurant in Lambertville, New Jersey, with Stangl dinnerware purchased at the Flemington Outlet.

In addition to Stangl's regular lines of dinnerware and giftware, a variety of items sold at the Flemington Outlet were not available to Stangl retailers. Some of these items were simply inexpensive pieces designed to generate cash flow, market tests, or merely second-quality merchandise. During the 1940s and early 1950s, badly flawed seconds were often decorated with French green, Blue #95, Orange, or no color at all. Artware green was used as a seconds treatment throughout the 1950s and early 1960s. These single color and brushed color seconds-treatments were quickly and inexpensively produced, but not wildly popular. Stangl's bestselling seconds, naturally, were decorated with their most popular dinnerware motifs.

settings at the Flemington Outlet showroom. Each table setting featured the appropriate flatware and linens for the dinnerware used and was not complete until it was graced by an arrangement of flowers grown by Martin Stangl himself. An avid gardener, Mr. Stangl cultivated several large plots of flowers and even had a greenhouse constructed at the Flemington Outlet property to continually supply the showroom with fresh blooms.

Bargain conscious shoppers had been aware of Flemington's Flemington Fur, Flemington Cut Glass, and Stangl Outlet for many years. During the 1950s and 1960s, however, more and more weekend shoppers were visiting the Flemington area to take advantage of an increasing number of shops and outlets. Up to 3,000 customers per day had been known to shop at the Stangl outlet during busy weekends and holidays.

In order to capitalize on the increasing number of tourists visiting the outlet during this time, numerous "Flemington Exclusives" were produced. Many of these exclusive items were designed to coordinate with Stangl's best-selling dinnerware patterns. Others were simply novelty items or short-run dinnerware patterns. Often, the "Flemington Exclusives" were inexpensively decorated, with little or no carving and marked with the simple "second" mark and no pattern name.

Aerial view of the Flemington Outlet (originally Plant #2), 1972.

During the late 1930s and early 1940s, Martin Stangl's eldest daughter, Martha Stangl Bacheler, arranged all the displays and the table

Interior view of the Flemington Outlet in 1974. Stacks of dinnerware are in the foreground with the sample board showing all available and inactive patterns in the background.

A favorite Flemington item was the handled tidbit tray. These were produced at the Flemington Outlet by drilling holes in plates to accommodate standard inexpensive handles. In 1958, Merrill Bacheler (Martin Stangl's son-in-law, and manager of the Flemington Outlet during the 1950s and early 1960s) instituted the practice of producing handled tidbits as a means to

In 1950, the interior of this Flemington Outlet kiln was set up with a display showing the steps involved in the manufacture of Stangl dinnerware. This 1974 photo shows the kiln surrounded by some of the non-Stangl wares available at the Flemington Outlet during the latter 1970s.

unload stacks of plates that were otherwise not selling. Any items that sat too long at the outlet were candidates for a handle, but 10" plates were most often used. Usually the tidbits were advertised at very low prices in order to draw additional customers to the Flemington Outlet. Sometimes tidbits were simply given to outlet customers during special promotions. Because of the vast quantities of tidbits produced at the Flemington Outlet, they are very common items at this time.

In addition to the handled tidbits, many 10" plates were also converted into clocks during the 1960s and 1970s. Clinton Peterman, Stangl Pottery accountant, would drill the appropriate sized hole and affix the clock movements and numerals in addition to his duties as accountant.

From the 1940s onward, prices for second-quality items were hand written on the back of each piece with green china markers. Many seconds can still be found with the original price scrawled across the back in green wax. First-quality pieces were always priced using paper price tags and Stangl paper labels. The Stangl paper labels were only applied to firsts and

Aerial view of Stangl's Trenton factory immediately following the fire in August, 25 1965.

Interior view of the Trenton factory showing extensive fire damage.

Stangl decorator Florence Dunn Glenn standing midst debris and toppled kiln cars on the day after the great blaze.

Courtesy of the Trentoniana Collection, Trenton Public Library, Trenton, New Jersey.

Trenton factory during reconstruction, 1965.

Flemington exclusives. Paper labels were rarely applied to seconds.

In 1965 there occurred two momentous events in Stangl's history. The first was the celebration of the 160th anniversary of Stangl-Fulper-Hill Pottery Company in conjunction with Martin Stangl's 55th anniversary with the firm and the 50th anniversary of Fulper Pottery winning the Award of Merit, the highest award, at the 1915 Panama Pacific Exposition. For the occasion, a Stangl Museum of Stangl products was opened to the public in a newly constructed building at the Flemington Outlet. Also, the booklet *Stangl, A Portrait of*

Progress in Pottery was published. This booklet outlined the history of the company and included a detailed account of Stangl's manufacturing procedures.

The second event was much more tragic. On August 25, 1965, a fire destroyed nearly half of the Trenton facility. Ironically, this fire, like the 1929 fire in Flemington, was electrical in origin and had nothing to do with the extreme temperatures created by the kilns. It was later determined that an old freezer in the factory kitchen caused a short circuit that started the blaze. Fortunately, the buildings housing the main kiln and clay processing equipment were unaffected. However, the kiln used for specialty glazes, such as Satin White and Ivory Satin, was ruined. Patterns requiring these glazes were out of production until May 1966, when this kiln was again operable.

In order to speed up production immediately following the fire, certain hollow ware shapes were cast of white clay instead of red. This eliminated some of the steps necessary for the spraying of engobe. The white-bodied shapes produced during late 1965 were pitchers, creamers, and sugars. All other shapes continued to be made of red clay. Total red-body dinnerware production was resumed in early 1966.

During the 1960s, there was a shift toward using less carved decoration on most of the newly introduced patterns. This was done for two primary reasons. First was rising labor costs. If some manufacturing steps could be eliminated, such as carving, the final cost of the product could remain competitively priced. The second reason was for a problem that had plagued Stangl's carved dinnerware patterns since the early 1940s. Whenever carved areas were not sufficiently glazed, they were prone to absorb any liquid the piece came in contact with, such as salad dressings, butter, and especially dishwater. Liquids absorbed by the porous dinnerware caused a permanent stain under the glaze. The use of fewer hand-carved dinnerware motifs was an effort to eliminate the staining problem.

In an attempt to add more strength to the relatively soft earthenware body of Stangl dinnerware, the temperature used in the bisque firing was raised. This process helped somewhat but did not entirely prevent the problems of cracking and chipping. Beginning in 1963, pieces fired at this higher temperature were marked with the word "Durafired." Stangl continued to raise kiln temperatures and improve the clay body throughout the 1960s. By the 1970s, Stangl was actually producing a stoneware product fired at stoneware temperatures but continued referring to most of the product line as "earthenware."

1970s

The decade of the 1970s saw significant changes in Stangl Pottery, both in operations at the Trenton plant and in the dinnerware itself. During the early 1970s, there was an ongoing endeavor to improve upon the Stangl lines and lower production costs as well.

In 1971, a series of dinnerware patterns was introduced on a true, high-fired, stoneware body. This line was advertised as Stangl Stoneware. Stangl Stoneware was a heavy, durable product line with bold motifs decorated with fashion colors popular during the early 1970s. This dinnerware should have been more popular than it was. The initial high price tag on these patterns may have been a contributing factor to their lack of public approval.

In spite of failing eyesight and the general infirmities tolerated by an individual of 84 years, Martin Stangl continued personally to oversee Stangl operations until a heart attack caused him to be hospitalized in October 1971. Never fully recovering from this, Martin Stangl died February 13, 1972.

The Wheaton Era

After Mr. Stangl's death, the whole Stangl Pottery operation was put up for sale. In June 1972, Stangl Pottery was bought by Frank Wheaton of Wheaton Industries. Frank Wheaton had planned to use Stangl's Trenton plant for the production of pottery bottles for Avon but later found he could have them produced more cheaply in Mexico.

Frank Wheaton had planned to continue manufacturing a first rate product line in keeping with the Stangl reputation. However, by the mid-1970s, rising production and labor costs were putting a strain on the company. In order to reduce labor, an increasing number of inexpensively produced patterns with little or no carved decoration were introduced. Also at this time, Stangl management was exploring such economical production methods as white bodies, transfer print motifs, silk-screen designs, and overglaze decals.

White-Bodied Patterns

By the beginning of 1975, all of Stangl's patterns were converted to a high-quality, white-colored body, and red clay was no longer used at Stangl. The use of a white body eliminated the need to apply engobe and speeded the greenware finishing process. For a short time after the body color transition, many patterns on the white body were still hand carved. This added depth to the designs, but was soon stopped in order to eliminate labor-generated costs.

By the late 1970s, Wheaton found it difficult to manufacture Stangl products economically at the antiquated Trenton plant. The oldest part of the factory dated from the 1860s and all the clay processing equipment had been installed by Anchor Pottery during the early 1900s.

Frank Wheaton was faced with two choices: either invest an enormous amount of money to replace completely all the archaic production equipment and modernize the whole facility, or cease production altogether. Because of the bleak market for American ceramics and dinnerware during the late 1970s, the decision was made to close Stangl.

In July of 1978, Pfaltzgraff Pottery purchased the Flemington Outlet property, all inventory, and legal right to the Stangl trademark. By November 1978, all remaining Stangl wares had been liquidated from the Flemington Outlet, and Stangl Pottery was officially closed. The closing of Stangl Pottery signaled the end of a truly unique American product.

1920s SOLID-COLOR DINNERWARE

Fulper Fayence and Fulper/Stangl Patterns

Although Fulper Pottery had produced novelty tea sets and utilitarian kitchenware and cooking vessels for some years prior to the 1920s, it was not until 1924, when Martin Stangl became vice president of the company, that dinnerware manufacturing was begun in earnest. Fulper Fayence and Fulper/Stangl were brand names introduced by Martin Stangl to designate certain lines of earthenware products throughout the 1920s. These were quality wares, designed to be both affordable and popular.

Fulper Fayence #901 Dinnerware

Introduced: 1924
Designer: Martin Stangl
Colors: Colonial Blue, Persian Yellow, Silver Green, Chinese Ivory, Grey, Tangerine

Known Pieces:

ashtray, 4½" . . . . $15 – 20	plate, 10" . . . . $25 – 30
bowl, fruit . . . . $10 – 12	plate, 8¾" . . . . $15 – 20
bowl, lug soup 5½" . . . . $15 – 20	plate, 7" . . . . $12 – 15
bowl, lug nut 3½" . . . . $15 – 20	plate, 6" . . . . $10 – 12
bowl, 8" tea . . . . $45 – 55	platter, 11" oval . . . . $40 – 50
bowl, 6" tea . . . . $15 – 20	saucer, after dinner . . . . $10 – 12
bowl, 4" tea . . . . $10 – 15	saucer . . . . $10 – 12
coffee pot, after dinner . . . . $135 – 165	sugar, individual . . . . $30 – 35
coffee pot, musical . . . . $200 – 250	sugar . . . . $20 – 25
creamer, individual . . . . $30 – 35	tea tile, round . . . . $20 – 25
creamer . . . . $15 – 20	tea tile, square, with ball feet . . . . . . $50 – 60
cup, after dinner . . . . $15 – 20	teapot, individual . . . . $110 – 135
cup . . . . $12 – 18	teapot . . . . $100 – 130
pitcher, 1 quart, hot water . . . . $65 – 75	teapot, musical . . . . $200 – 250
cover for pitcher . . . . $15 – 20	toast cover . . . . $60 – 75

Fulper Fayence dinnerware pattern #901 has been credited as being America's first solid-color dinnerware to be distributed nationwide. Fulper Fayence #901 was also the first complete dinnerware pattern with "open stock" availability produced by Fulper Pottery.

This pattern was originally glazed in Colonial Blue, Persian Yellow, Silver Green, and Chinese Ivory. However, the Chinese Ivory glaze was discontinued by 1926. The Grey glaze was tried on this pattern for a very short time during the latter 1920s. Stangl's Tangerine glaze was used on the Fulper Fayence #901 shapes very briefly after 1929, when that glaze was introduced. The Chinese Ivory, Grey, and Tangerine glazes are very rare on this shape.

Fulper Fayence #901 shapes were sometimes marked with the number 901 in-molded on the bottom. Usually, the only identification on Fulper Fayence pieces was a Fulper Fayence paper label.

During the mid-1920s, shape #901 teapots and coffee pots were produced with music box movements in the bottoms as special-order products for Ritz of New York. These musical items are extremely rare.

Most of the Fulper Fayence #901 was produced during the 1920s. Although some production of this pattern continued into the early 1930s, very little was made at that time. Any pieces of #901 manufactured after 1930 were marked with Stangl paper labels or STANGL die-pressed into the bottoms. The Fulper Fayence designation was no longer used after 1930.

Fulper Fayence #901: teapot, Persian Yellow; 11" oval platter, Persian Yellow; individual sugar, Colonial Blue; individual teapot, Silver Green; individual creamer, Persian Yellow; hot water pitcher with cover, Colonial Blue.

Fulper Fayence #901: after dinner coffee pot, Colonial Blue; after dinner cup & saucer, Silver Green; 8¾" plate, Persian Yellow; lug soup, Silver Green; 4" tea bowl, Colonial Blue; round tea tile, Persian Yellow; cup & saucer, Silver Green.

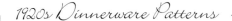

Fulper Fayence #926 Service Pitchers

Introduced: 1924
Colors: Colonial Blue, Persian Yellow, Silver Green, Chinese Ivory, Tangerine, Rust, Blue of the Sky

Known Pieces:

mug "M," 1 pint . . . . $25 – 35	pitcher "EL," 1 quart. . . . . $30 – 40
mug "S," ½ pint . . . . $20 – 30	pitcher "L," 1½ pint . . . . $25 – 30
pitcher, waffle, 2 qt. . . . . $45 – 55	pitcher "M," 1 pint . . . . $20 – 25
cover, waffle pitcher . . . . $20 – 25	pitcher "S," ½ pint . . . . $15 – 20

The letter designation indicating size was sometimes, but not always, molded into the bottom of each of the #926 shapes. This line was available in the Fulper Fayence glaze colors throughout the 1920s. After 1929 the Blue of the Sky, Tangerine, and Rust glazes were applied to these shapes. The #926 mugs and waffle cover are very uncommon, as are pieces glazed with Tangerine, Rust, or Blue of the Sky.

Beginning in the 1940s, the #926 pitcher shapes were used with the #3434 Rim dinnerware shapes for Stangl's hand-carved dinnerware patterns.

Service pitchers #926: ½ pint, Persian Yellow; 1 pint, Colonial Blue; 1 quart, Silver Green; 1 pint mug, Rust.

Fulper Fayence #956 Rena Rosenthal Oval Jam Jar

Introduced: 1924
Colors: Colonial Blue, Persian Yellow, Silver Green, Oxblood
Made For: Rena Rosenthal

Known Pieces:
jar, oval 3½" x 6" x 3½" with cover .. $45 – 65   underplate, oval with indent for jar . . $30 – 45

From 1924 through 1928, Fulper Pottery Company produced many special-order Fulper Pottery and Fulper Fayence exclusive items for Rena Rosenthal's specialty gift shop in New York. One of these items was the #956 Fulper Fayence oval jam jar. This jar and underplate set was available in the Fulper Fayence glazes of Silver Green, Persian Yellow, Colonial Blue, and Oxblood. By the late 1920s, Rena Rosenthal's contract with Fulper ended, thus discontinuing production of many of the Rena Rosenthal articles.

#956 Rena Rosenthal Fulper Fayence oval jam jar, Silver Green.

Fulper Fayence #988 E. C. Rich Six-Sided Jars

Introduced: 1924
Colors: Colonial Blue, Persian Yellow, Silver Green
Made For: E. C. Rich Inc.

Known Pieces:
jar, "L," 7½" x 5" with cover . . . . $60 – 75   jar, "M," 5" x 3½" with cover . . . . . . $45 – 50
jar, "S," 4" x 3¼" with cover . . . . $30 – 35

In 1924, these geometric jars in three sizes were designed for E. C. Rich Inc. of New York, an importer of Oriental spices and food products, most notable of which was their "Crystallized Canton Ginger" which was usually packed in tins. E. C. Rich filled the brightly glazed Fulper Fayence jars with their better grade of food products. These jars were affixed with gold foil labels, tied with bright ribbons, and sold only in exclusive specialty shops.

#988 E. C. Rich six-sided jars small, Colonial Blue; large, Silver Green; medium, Colonial Blue; and small, Silver Green with original foil label.

Fulper Fayence #1007 Ritz Pitchers

Introduced: 1925
Colors: Colonial Blue, Persian Yellow, Silver Green, Oxblood, Rose
Made For: Ritz Mfg. Enterprise

Known Pieces:

pitcher "EL," 2 quart. . . . . $130 – 175	pitcher "M," 1 pint . . . . $65 – 75
pitcher "L," 1 quart. . . . . $100 – 125	pitcher "S," ½ pint . . . . $55 – 65

This series of classically shaped pitchers was produced for the Ritz Manufacturing Enterprise of New York. The shapes were typical of the Neoclassic styles popular during the mid-1920s. The #1007 pitchers are quite rare and seldom seen.

#1007 pitchers: 2 quart, Silver Green; ½ pint, Oxblood.

Fulper Fayence #1009 Tea Set

Introduced: 1925
Colors: Colonial Blue, Persian Yellow, Silver Green

Known Pieces:

creamer . . . . $30 – 35	
cup. . . . . $15 – 18	
plate, 7" . . . . $25 – 30	
saucer . . . . $10 – 12	
sugar . . . . $30 – 40	
teapot. . . . . $150 – 175	

A #1009 teapot in Persian Yellow glaze.

The #1009 tea set shows the Neoclassic styling popular during the Colonial Revival period of the 1920s. Production of this pattern was very short lived, causing pattern #1009 to be especially scarce.

Fulper Fayence #1076 Rena Rosenthal Hors d'Oeuvres Pig

Introduced: 1926
Colors: Colonial Blue, Persian Yellow, Silver Green, Oxblood, Satin White, Rust, Tangerine
Made For: Rena Rosenthal

Known Pieces: pig, 6" figural hors d'oeuvres server . . . . $175 – 225

During the mid-1920s, Fulper Pottery Company produced several variations of the #1076 Pig shape for the gift company Rena Rosenthal. The most abundant versions of the #1076 Pig were the piggy bank and planter shapes. Of very limited production were the pig shaped #1076 hors d'oeuvres servers. These are indeed rare and highly collectible.

#1076 Rena Rosenthal Pig hors d'oeuvres server, Silver Green.

Fulper/Stangl Primitive #1080

Introduced: 1926
Colors: Colonial Blue, Persian Yellow, Silver Green, Tangerine

Known Pieces:

bowl, 10" oval . . . . $50 – 60	pitcher, 1 quart, hot water . . . . $65 – 75
bowl, 8" oval . . . . $35 – 45	cover, 1 qt. pitcher . . . . $15 – 20
bowl, 6" oval . . . . $25 – 30	pitcher, 1 pint, syrup . . . . $25 – 35
bowl, 10" round. . . . . $65 – 80	cover, 1 pt. pitcher . . . . $15 – 20
bowl, 8" round. . . . . $45 – 55	plate, 14" chop . . . . $65 – 80
bowl, 6" round. . . . . $30 – 40	plate, 12" chop . . . . $55 – 65
bowl, 4" round. . . . . $20 – 25	plate, 10½". $35 – 40
bowl, batter, 12½" . . . . $95 – 145	plate, 9" . . . . $30 – 35
bowl, batter, 8" . . . . $50 – 60	plate, 7" . . . . $20 – 25
cover, 8" batter bowl . . . . $25 – 35	plate, 6" . . . . $15 – 20
butter dish with cover . . . . $60 – 75	plate, 10½" grill. . . . . $35 – 45
cake plate with handle . . . . $45 – 55	platter, 14" oval. . . . . $60 – 70
coffee pot, after dinner . . . . $135 – 160	platter, 12" oval. . . . . $45 – 55
creamer . . . . $20 – 25	saucer . . . . $7 – 10
creamer, after dinner. . . . . $30 – 40	sugar . . . . $30 – 35
cup. . . . . $10 – 15	sugar, open, after dinner. . . . . $30 – 40
egg cup . . . . $20 – 25	teapot. . . . . $130 – 155
pitcher, 2 qt. waffle. . . . . $80 – 95	tea tile . . . . $25 – 30
cover, 2 qt. pitcher . . . . $15 – 20	toast cover . . . . $65 – 80
	tray, 7" x 11" . . . . $45 – 55

Primitive #1080 is characterized by concave rings around the rims of the flat pieces. The hollow ware pieces are stacked rings, reminiscent of old, hand-thrown pottery. This pattern was very popular and was in continual production from 1926 through the mid-1930s. Usually this pattern was marked with the Fulper/Stangl paper label or Fulper/Stangl die-pressed mark. The Fulper/Stangl brand name was developed in 1926 to designate Fulper Pottery Company's modernistic and primitive styled earthenware products. Items produced after 1929 were marked with the die-pressed STANGL mark. When pieces bearing the Fulper/Stangl impressed mark or paper label are found, they are generally priced slightly higher than unmarked pieces.

During the early 1930s, Primitive #1080 shapes were decorated with Tangerine glaze as special order items for R. Levin, a New York distributor. Any of the #1080 pieces glazed with Tangerine or Colonial Blue are quite rare and found more infrequently than those glazed with Persian Yellow or Silver Green.

Primitive #1080: teapot, Persian Yellow; 10" plate, Silver Green; 12" chop plate, Persian Yellow; cup & saucer, Silver Green; sugar, Silver Green; 1 quart hot water pitcher with cover, Persian Yellow.

Primitive #1080: 8" round bowl, Silver Green; 6" round bowl, Tangerine; 10" round bowl, Persian Yellow; 8" batter bowl, Silver Green; 12½" batter bowl, Tangerine.

Primitive #1080: 2 quart batter pitcher with cover, Silver Green; 1 pint syrup pitcher with cover, Silver Green; toast cover on a 9" plate, Persian Yellow.

Fulper/Stangl Square Modern #1081

Introduced: 1926
Colors: Colonial Blue, Persian Yellow, Silver Green, Tangerine
Designer: Reuben Haley

Known Pieces:

creamer	$60 – 75
cup	$25 – 30
plate, 9½" x 7½"	$60 – 70
plate, 7¼" x 6¼"	$25 – 35
plate, picnic 7¼" x 6¼"	$25 – 35
saucer	$10 – 15
sugar	$65 – 80
teapot	$155 – 175
lamp	$500 – 600

Reuben Haley, known for his Consolidated Glass and Muncie Pottery designs also developed several Art Deco shapes for Stangl. In a 1925 memo Martin Stangl states: "We have accepted nine more modern designs from R. Haley. They are five lamps, three vases, and a tea set."

Square Modern #1081 was the tea set referred to in the quoted memo. The glazed samples were available for the 1926 trade shows, and this pattern remained popular through the 1920s.

Square Modern #1080 was produced through the early 1930s. It is usually unmarked, but pieces turn up still retaining a Fulper/Stangl paper label or a die-impressed mark.

While unusual and in high demand, Square Modern, dubbed "Deco Delight" by some collectors, is not especially rare. Because of the sharp angles and edges, it is difficult to find pieces that are not nicked or chipped.

Square Modern #1081: 7¼" x 6¼" plate, Silver Green; cup & saucer, Colonial Blue; 9½" x 7½" plate, Colonial Blue; teapot, Persian Yellow.

Fulper/Stangl Round Modern #1082

Introduced: 1926
Colors: Colonial Blue, Persian Yellow, Silver Green, Tangerine

Known Pieces:

creamer	$50 – 65	saucer	$12 – 15
cup	$20 – 25	sugar	$50 – 75
plate, 7"	$35 – 45	teapot	$175 – 200

Round Modern #1082: teapot, Silver Green.

The Art Moderne styling of the Round Modern #1082 pattern is just that, round. The hollow ware pieces are globe shaped and are each encircled by a band of decorative disks. The teapot and sugar knobs are disks as well. It was produced in very limited quantities.

#1187 Levin Pitchers

Introduced: 1928
Colors: Colonial Blue, Persian Yellow, Silver Green, Tangerine, Blue of the Sky, Oxblood
Made For: R. Levin Co.

Known Pieces:

pitcher "EL," 2 quart . . . . $85 – 110	pitcher "L," 1 quart . . . . $60 – 75
cover, 2 qt. pitcher . . . . $15 – 20	pitcher "M," 1 pint . . . . $40 – 50
	pitcher "S," ½ pint . . . . $25 – 35

The #1187 series of pitchers were based on a popular "Abby Jug" shape. Several potteries, in both Europe and the United States, were producing "Abby Jugs" during the 1920s and 1930s. Stangl's #1187 pitchers were special-order products for the R. Levin Company of New York and were produced in an exceptionally small quantity. These pitchers are unusual and difficult to locate.

#1187 pitchers: ½ pint, Tangerine with green interior; ½ pint, Colonial Blue, ½ pint Silver Green.

#1212 Levin Tea Set

Introduced: 1929
Colors: Colonial Blue, Persian Yellow, Silver Green, Tangerine, Rust
Made For: R. Levin Co.

Known Pieces:

creamer . . . . $25 – 30
cup . . . . $10 – 15
lamp . . . . $130 – 160
plate, 7" . . . . $30 – 35
saucer . . . . $10 – 12
sugar . . . . $25 – 35
teapot . . . . $125 – 155

#1212 cup & saucer, Persian Yellow.

As with the #1187 pitchers, the #1212 tea set was made for Levin of New York in small quantities during the late 1920s and early 1930s. Classically styled with clean lines, the #1212 tea set was predictive of the direction dinnerware trends were to take during the 1930s.

1930s SOLID-COLOR DINNERWARE

Stangl Patterns

Beginning in 1929, Fulper Pottery's newly introduced earthenware products were marketed under the Stangl brand name. The Fulper Fayence and Fulper/Stangl lines continued to be produced bearing those trademarks until 1930 when all earthenware products were marked simply Stangl. The patterns and pattern names remained the same, only the trademarks were changed. Fulper stoneware artware continued to be produced with the Fulper Pottery glazes and logo until 1935 when the Fulper Pottery brand of artware was discontinued.

#1260 Dinnerware

Introduced: 1930
Colors: Colonial Blue, Persian Yellow, Silver Green, Tangerine, Rust
Fulper Pottery Glaze Colors: Jade Green, Venetian Blue, Cinnamon Tan, Old Ivory

Known Pieces:

Solid-Color Glazes

bowl, 10" salad	$65 – 80
bowl, 8" salad	$50 – 60
bowl, 6" salad	$30 – 40
bowl, 4" soup	$15 – 20
creamer	$30 – 40
cup	$20 – 25
pitcher, 2 quart	$80 – 95
pitcher, 1 quart	$60 – 75
pitcher, 1 pint	$40 – 50
pitcher, ½ pint	$30 – 40
plate, 12" chop	$70 – 85

plate, 10"	$35 – 45
plate, 8"	$25 – 35
plate, 6"	$20 – 25
saucer	$10 – 15
sugar	$35 – 45
teapot	$175 – 195

Fulper Pottery Glazes

pitcher, 2 quart	$120 – 155
pitcher, 1 quart	$95 – 120
pitcher, 1 pint	$65 – 80
pitcher, ½ pint	$55 – 65

This dynamic Art Deco pattern was introduced in 1930 with an aggressive advertising campaign to the home furnishings trade. The #1260 shapes are based on stacked cylinders that are further enhanced by long angular handles. Hollow ware pieces were usually marked with #1260 molded into the bottoms, while plates and cups were sometimes die-pressed with the word STANGL. This is a difficult pattern to find that was actively produced for a very short time.

Briefly during 1930 and 1931, the #1260 pitcher shapes were produced with the Fulper Pottery stoneware body and glazes. These pieces are usually marked Fulper and bear the in-mold shape number 1260.

Shape #1260: sugar, Persian Yellow, 4" soup bowl, Persian Yellow; 8" salad bowl, Silver Green.

#1260 Dinnerware *(continued)*

Shape #1260 1 quart pitcher with the Jade Green Fulper Pottery glaze.

Colonial #1388

Introduced: 1931
Colors: Colonial Blue, Persian Yellow, Silver Green, Oxblood, Tangerine, Apple Green, Turquoise, Violet, Satin Brown, Aqua Blue, Blue of the Sky, Satin White, Surf White, Lavender, Rust, Ivory, Black

Known Pieces:

ashtray, 3½"	$20 – 25
baking shell	$12 – 15
ball jug	$75 – 85
ball jug, miniature	$20 – 25
bean pot, individual	$12 – 15
bean pot, large	$65 – 80
bowl, 6" fruit	$12 – 15
bowl, 7" coupe soup	$20 – 25
bowl, 5" lug soup	$12 – 15
cover, 5" lug soup	$10 – 12
bowl, 4½" lug soup	$8 – 12
bowl, 12" oval vegetable	$60 – 75
bowl, 10" oval vegetable	$20 – 25
bowl, 14" salad	$80 – 95
bowl, 10" salad, extra deep	$45 – 55
bowl, 10" salad	$30 – 40
bowl, 8" salad	$25 – 30
bowl, 14" mixing	$95 – 125
bowl, 9" mixing	$70 – 80
bowl, 7½" mixing	$50 – 60
bowl, 5" mixing	$40 – 50
bowl, 2½" miniature	$20 – 25
bowl, 6", ice	$50 – 60
with handle & tongs	$70 – 80
butter chip	$15 – 20

cake stand, high	$25 – 35
cake stand, low	$25 – 35
candle holder, single	$10 – 12
candle holder, triple	$75 – 85
candy jar	$45 – 55
candy jar with bird knob	$85 – 115
carafe with wood handle	$65 – 75
stopper for carafe	$15 – 20
casserole, 8" covered	$50 – 65
casserole, 5" covered	$30 – 35
casserole, individual, with handle & cover	$30 – 35
cigarette box	$55 – 70
coaster/ashtray	$20 – 25
coffee pot, 8 cup	$130 – 165
coffee pot, after dinner, 6 cup	$75 – 90
compote, comport, 7"	$25 – 30
console bowl, 12" oval	$25 – 30
creamer	$12 – 15
creamer, individual	$15 – 20
cup, after dinner	$12 – 15
cup, coffee	$12 – 15
cup, tea	$10 – 12
cup, colossal, 32 oz.	$125 – 155
custard cup, 3½"	$12 – 15
egg cup	$15 – 20

gravy bowl.....................$35 − 45	plate, 11" grill ....$30 − 40
hors d'oeuvres tray,	plate, 10" grill ....$20 − 25
19"x12" large oval ....$80 − 95	plate, 9" artichoke................$35 − 45
hors d'oeuvres tray,	platter, 14" oval..................$40 − 50
12"x8" small oval ....$35 − 45	platter, 12" oval..................$25 − 35
hors d'oeuvres tray,	ramekin, 4" ....$12 − 15
12"x10" , 5 compartment.........$50 − 60	refrigerator bottle ....$85 − 110
hors d'oeuvres tray,	relish dish, single
14" square, 4 compartment ......$85 − 95	8" crescent shape ....$20 − 25
hors d'oeuvres tray,	relish, double,
9" round, 3 compartment.........$30 − 40	6½"x7" square....................$20 − 25
jelly mold, large ....$60 − 75	relish, 12" triple ....$25 − 35
jelly mold, small.................$35 − 45	salt, pepper; each ....$8 − 12
lazy susan, 15".................$80 − 90	saucer ....$5 − 6
pie baker, 11"...................$25 − 35	saucer, after dinner................$5 − 6
pitcher, 2 quart with ice lip ....$85 − 95	saucer, colossal 9"...............$25 − 30
pitcher, 2 quart waffle............$75 − 85	shirred egg......................$15 − 20
cover, 2 quart waffle............$15 − 20	sugar ....$15 − 20
pitcher, 1 quart syrup ....$35 − 45	sugar, with bird knob ....$60 − 75
cover, 1 qt. syrup ....$15 − 25	sugar, individual, open............$15 − 20
pitcher, 1½ pint..................$25 − 30	sugar, after dinner
pitcher, 1 pint ....$20 − 25	withhandles and cover ....$20 − 25
pitcher, ½ pint...................$15 − 20	teapot, 6 cup ....$75 − 95
pitcher, 6 oz.....................$15 − 20	teapot, with bird knob ....$125 − 155
pitcher, miniature................$20 − 25	teapot, individual ....$70 − 85
plate, 15" chop ....$80 − 90	tidbit, 8", with metal handle........$20 − 25
plate, 14" chop ....$60 − 70	tray, with indents
plate, 12" chop ....$40 − 50	for creamer & sugar ....$12 − 15
plate, 10".......................$20 − 25	tray, with indents for
plate, 9".........................$15 − 20	individual creamer & sugar ....$15 − 18
plate, 8".........................$12 − 15	tray, with indents
plate, 7".........................$8 − 9	for salt & pepper................$15 − 18
plate, 6".........................$6 − 7	tumbler ....$50 − 60

The Colonial dinnerware pattern was Stangl's #1388 reeded shape with solid-color glazes. The reeding on most of the larger pieces of #1388 alternated thick and thin. This was Stangl's most popular solid-color dinnerware pattern and was in continual production from 1931 through 1944. A Stangl bulletin dated April 1, 1938, stated the following:

"Since the first of this year there apparently has been a tendency to push the #2000 pattern dinnerware in preference to the #1388 pattern. We of course want business on the #2000 series but it is far more important that the #1388 pattern be made our predominating pattern with the trade.

First − It is more distinctly Stangl ware than the #2000 pattern, for the reason that there are any number of competitors putting out ware similar in pattern.

Second − The #1388 pattern is outstanding above all other patterns now being offered, and through this fact it is more recognized as Stangl ware.

Third − We believe it to be more acceptable to the housewife as it is more decorative and creates an impression not to be obtained from plainer patterns. It has a definite appeal.

Fourth — We can, to better advantage, build up the name Stangl on an outstanding pattern, than we can on one which is more or less general and in doing this we will create a general acceptance of the fact that all Stangl ware is outstanding.

To help you promote and stimulate sales on the #1388 pattern, we will make up and offer to the trade a 20 piece Starter set in this pattern, Promotion #12 with suggested retail price, $3.95 per set.

We have tried out this set with one large store and know it is good for they sold 1,000 sets in three days' time, and we feel confident that you can do an equally good job. Let us make the #1388 pattern the best known line of solid color dinnerware in the country."

From 1931 to 1933 the knobs on the Colonial teapot, candy jar, and sugar bowl lids were shaped like small pottery birds. In 1933 the bird knobs were replaced with a stylish looped handle. Naturally, pieces of Colonial with bird-shaped knobs are considerably more collectible than pieces with looped handles.

The Colonial individual and after dinner creamers are the identical shape. The individual and after dinner sugar bowls, however, are different. The after dinner sugar has handles and a cover, while the individual sugar is open and has no handles.

"With ears" is the term Stangl used to describe the lug handles applied to the round salad bowls and soup bowls in the Colonial pattern. During 1940 and 1941 the salad bowls were available without ears and marketed as "Kitchen Essentials." The mixing bowls were produced only during 1936 and 1937. They are deeper than the salad bowls and have a small rounded rim at the top. The salad bowls have no rim. The 5" soup bowl without ears is similar to the candy jar bottom, but the candy bottom is one half inch taller than the soup bowl.

The #1388 jelly mold featured the typical reeding on the exterior and an ear of corn motif on the interior bottom. This same shape was used again during the 1960s for the redware food molds sold at the Flemington Outlet.

The Colonial lazy susan was a 15" chop plate to which a metal center handle and revolving metal base were added. The lazy susan was discontinued in 1934. In 1938, Stangl began offering other metal fixtures to accessorize several of the shapes in the Colonial and Americana patterns. The metal accessories included wire racks to hold beverage sets, ramekin sets, custard sets, and individual bean pot sets. Beverage set racks were available in chrome, wire, and sprayed white finishes. The 6" ice bowl was fastened within a circular metal base and handle assembly and sold with matching ice tongs. Spring steel bail handles wrapped with rattan were also available and were designed to attach to chop plates and hors d'oeuvres trays. Chop plates with steel handles would be combined with four or eight 7" or 8" plates and sold as "Sandwich Sets." All of these metal accessory pieces were available from 1938 through the early 1940s.

During the early 1930s, dinnerware shapes glazed with Tangerine, Rust, or Oxblood glazes could be ordered with Turquoise or Silver Green interiors at extra cost. This type of two-color dinnerware glazing was discontinued by the beginning of 1937.

Shape #1388 after dinner coffee sets were produced with fired-on platinum luster over Ivory or Black glaze during 1934. These were special-order products with wholesale prices double that of Colonial with the usual solid-color glazes. Coffee sets with platinum luster were available only during 1934, and are quite uncommon.

In 1937 Stangl began promoting individually boxed "Rainbow Sets" of assorted colors. During 1937, the four colors offered in these sets were Colonial Blue, Persian Yellow, Silver Green, and Tangerine. In 1938, Rainbow Sets contained pieces with Aqua Blue glaze instead of Silver Green. Boxed dinnerware sets of premixed colors were premium priced during the late 1930s. In 1938, a twenty-five piece Rainbow luncheon set retailed for $10.98, while the same set in a single color retailed for $5.49. Stangl used the name "Rainbow" to indicate boxed sets of solid-color dinnerware only. During the 1970s, collectors began using the term "Rainbow" when describing items glazed with Stangl's Sunburst glaze, although Stangl's Sunburst glaze and Rainbow sets were unrelated.

The earliest pieces of Colonial were marked with an in-mold #1388 and STANGL die-pressed in the bottoms. Later pieces have STANGL, #1388, and sometimes USA as inmold marks on the bottoms of the pieces. Plates, when marked, were usually just die-pressed with the word STANGL.

At this time, Colonial Blue and Persian Yellow are the most popular Colonial colors, so command the higher prices. The least popular colors are Satin White and Satin Brown. Some dealers find these colors difficult to sell at any price. Glazes such as Lavender, Oxblood, Blue of the Sky, Apple Green, and Violet are extremely rare on Colonial #1388 shapes, so are particularly challenging to collect.

Colonial #1388: 9" plate, Rust; 12" oval platter, Silver Green; 10" oval platter, Colonial Blue; individual bean pot, Colonial Blue; individual creamer, individual sugar, after dinner coffee pot, Satin White; after dinner cup & saucer, Tangerine; 5" covered lug soup, Aqua Blue; coffee cup & saucer, Persian Yellow; 6" ice bowl (without metal handle and tongs), Tangerine.

Colonial #1388: single candle, Aqua Blue; butter chip, Satin White; baking shell, Satin Brown; ramekin, Silver Green; ball jug, Tangerine; ½ pint pitcher, Colonial Blue; waffle pitcher with cover, Silver Green; 6" covered casserole, Tangerine; covered casserole with handle, Tangerine; 7" plate, Persian Yellow; coaster/ashtray, Aqua Blue.

Colonial #1388: carafe, Persian Yellow; colossal cup & saucer, Colonial Blue; tea cup & saucer, Tangerine; 9" plate, Aqua Blue; triple candle holder, Satin Brown; 9" plate, Persian Yellow; candy jar with bird knob, Silver Green; cigarette box, Rust; 6" plate, Tangerine; ash tray, Silver Green.

Colonial #1388: shirred egg, Rust; gravy, Colonial Blue; triple relish tray, Persian Yellow; after dinner sugar, creamer, Silver Green; double relish tray, Tangerine; individual teapot, Satin White; 10" plate, Silver Green; creamer, sugar, Colonial Blue; tray for creamer & sugar, Satin Brown; single relish, Persian Yellow.

above: Colonial #1388: beverage set featuring 2 quart pitcher and cover, six tumblers, and original white-painted wire rack.

left: Colonial #1388: sandwich set with original spring steel handle.

below: Colonial #1388: platinum decorated after dinner cup & saucer, coffee pot, sugar, creamer.

Sunburst #1388

Designer: Martin Stangl
Introduced: 1931

Known Pieces:

bowl, 8" oval	$80 – 95
bowl, 10" salad	$90 – 110
bowl, 6" fruit	$25 – 30
bowl, 5" lug soup	$25 – 35
cover, 5" lug soup	$20 – 25
bowl, 4½" lug soup	$20 – 25
candy jar with bird knob	$150 – 175
candy jar	$85 – 110
creamer	$35 – 45
cup	$20 – 25
cup, after dinner	$20 – 25
egg cup	$25 – 30
plate, 12" chop	$90 – 135
plate, 10"	$50 – 60
plate, 9"	$45 – 55
plate, 8"	$35 – 45
plate, 7"	$25 – 35
plate, 6"	$20 – 25
platter, 12" oval	$80 – 95
saucer	$10 – 15
saucer, after dinner	$10 – 15
sugar	$45 – 55
sugar with bird knob	$80 – 95
teapot	$130 – 160
teapot with bird knob	$185 – 225

Shape #1388 was called Sunburst #1388 when decorated with Stangl's multicolored Sunburst glaze. The Sunburst glaze combined the Tangerine, Persian Yellow, Silver Green, Turquoise, and Black glazes in a drip effect. Martin Stangl was very proud of this finish, which is incorrectly referred to as "Rainbow" among collectors.

Shape #1388 was available decorated with Sunburst glaze from 1931 through 1934. Because the cost for Sunburst #1388 was twice that of Colonial #1388, this pattern was not produced in large quantities.

Sunburst #1388: sugar with bird knob, 7" plate, egg cup, tea cup & saucer, 10" plate, teapot, creamer.

#1585 – #1588 Utility Jugs

Introduced: 1932
Colors: Colonial Blue, Persian Yellow, Silver Green, Tangerine, Apple Green, Oxblood

Known Pieces:

low jug #1585 "ES"	$15 – 20	tall jug #1588 "S"	$20 – 25
low jug #1585 "S"	$25 – 30	tall jug #1588 "M"	$35 – 45
low jug #1586 "M"	$30 – 40	tall jug #1588 "L"	$50 – 65
low jug #1587 "L"	$40 – 50	sugar, open #1585	$15 – 20

Stangl originally developed these utility jugs as "Hand Made." At first these shapes were hand thrown on a potter's wheel at Factory #2 in Flemington. In 1935 when all production was shifted to the Trenton factory, most of Stangl's "Hand-Made" lines were discontinued. At that time, molds were made for the most popular shapes of this series, such the #1588 "S" and #1585 "ES" jugs and #1585 sugar. These items were then slip cast instead of hand thrown. Usually the hand-thrown jugs were not marked, but sometimes the word "Stangl" was scrawled into the bottoms of these pieces. The slip-cast pieces will bear in-mold markings and shape numbers. During 1936, 1937, and 1938, the #1585 ES low jug and #1585 open sugar were sold with a #2000 ceramic tray as a creamer and sugar set.

#1588 handmade tall jug, Tangerine; #1588 slip-cast tall jug, Apple Green; #1585 open sugar, Tangerine; #1585 "ES" slip-cast low jug, Colonial Blue; #1585 "S" handmade low jug, Silver Green; #1585 "M" handmade low jug, Tangerine; #1585 "L" handmade low jug, Persian Yellow.

Handmade Sandwich Set #1644

Introduced: 1933
Colors: Colonial Blue, Persian Yellow, Silver Green, Tangerine, Apple Green, Surf White, Matte Green

Known Pieces:

#1644 sandwich tray, 12"		#1645 plate, 8"	$25 – 35
with pottery handle	$100 – 135	#1666 pitcher, 9"	$55 – 65

The #1644 sandwich set was completely handmade. A deep swirl on the face of each piece was used as a decorative motif. The strap-shaped pottery handle on the sandwich tray is attached to each side of the 12" plate. Pieces in this pattern are either unmarked or die-pressed STANGL.

The #1666 pitcher shape was designed to coordinate with the #1644 sandwich set. Stangl also advertised this piece as "#1666 Hand Made Pitcher-Vase." All of these shapes were introduced during the time when Stangl's handmade artware lines were very popular.

Sandwich set #1644: handled sandwich tray, Apple Green; 8" plate, Tangerine; 8" plate, Surf White; #1666 pitcher, Matte Green.

#1647 Political Commemorative Beer Set

Introduced: 1933
Colors: Colonial Blue, Persian Yellow, Silver Green, Tangerine, Rust;
Underglaze Decorations

Known Pieces:

Solid-color glazes:

mug	$20 – 30
pitcher, 2 quart	$55 – 70
pretzel jar with cover	$80 – 95

Underglaze decorations:

mug	$25 – 30
pitcher, 2 quart	$65 – 90
pretzel jar with cover	$95 – 110

Commemorative motifs:

mug #1647-1 Franklin D. Roosevelt	$100 – 150
mug #1647-2 John Nance Garner	$100 – 150
mug #1647-3 Alfred Smith	$100 – 150
mug #1647-4 William Gibbs McAdoo	$100 – 150
mug #1647-5 Albert Ritchie	$100 – 150
mug #1647-6 Newton D. Baker	$100 – 150
mug #1647-7 James Farley	$100 – 150
mug #1647 "Happy Days are Here Again"	$65 – 80
pitcher #1647 Franklin D. Roosevelt	$500 – 650
pitcher #1647 "Happy Days are Here Again"	$110 – 145
mug #1647 Masonic embossed motif "Lu Lu Lodge, Trenton, NJ"	$85 – 110
pretzel jar #1647 "Happy Days are Here Again"	$110 – 145

The #1647 beer set was produced with at least three different styles of decoration. The basic mug and pitcher shapes were available with solid-color glazes or decorated with sponged or striped underglaze colors. These brilliant, deep underglaze colors were not used very often and were usually glazed with high gloss ivory- or pink-tinted glazes. The solid-color and underglaze color decorated beer sets are unusual and rarely found.

The most familiar decoration on the #1647 beer set shapes featured caricature faces of prominent members of the Democratic Party. This set was produced for Franklin Delano Roosevelt's presidential inauguration in 1933. The mugs commemorate the 1932 Chicago Democratic national convention and the party members responsible for Franklin Roosevelt's nomination as presidential candidate.

The caricature faces were molded on the pieces and left uncolored. The backgrounds were sponged with either green or brown underglaze color. At this time, pieces decorated with green are more popular than those decorated with brown.

The commemorative pieces were produced in the following three variations: a face on the front with a plain back; a face on one side and "Happy Days Are Here Again" on the other; or the "Happy Days Are Here Again" motif alone. Although more common, the commemorative versions of the #1647 beer sets are much more desirable because of the political and Masonic motifs.

#1647 beer set mugs: #1647-1 Franklin D. Roosevelt mug with brown background; #1647 mug with blue, red, green, and yellow underglaze stripes.

#1647 beer set detail of the molded "Happy Days Are Here Again" motif.

#1673 – #1682 Tony Sarg Beer Mugs — Stoby Mugs

Introduced: 1933; Reintroduced: 1967, 1974
Designer: Tony Sarg

Known Pieces:

1930s hand-painted mugs:

#1673 Yodel; Grand	$225 – 250
#1674 Smart Alec	$250 – 300
#1675 Parson	$200 – 250
#1676 Chief	$200 – 250
#1677 Depression	$200 – 250
#1678 Sport	$200 – 250
#1679 Batch	$250 – 300
#1680 Hen Peck	$200 – 250
#1681 Lord Archie; Archie	$225 – 275

1930s, 1960s, 1970s solid-colors:

#1673 Grand	$75 – 125
#1675 Parson	$75 – 125
#1676 Chief	$75 – 125
#1677 Cry Baby	$75 – 125
#1678 Sport	$75 – 125
#1679 Batch	$75 – 125
#1680 Henpeck	$75 – 125
#1681 Archie	$75 – 125

Stangl produced these novelty mugs exclusively for Tony Sarg's shop in Manhattan, New York, during 1933, 1934, and 1935. Each face was realistically hand painted with mat-finish overglaze colors. These mugs were usually marked "T.S." (Tony Sarg) or "copyright Tony Sarg" on the bottoms. Seven of the mug shapes had separate hats/lids that could be used as ash trays. The hats on #1673 Grand and #1679 Batch were not separate, but slip cast as part of the bodies of these two mugs.

In 1936, the Tony Sarg contract ended and Stangl began marketing this series as "Stangl Stoby Mugs." The Stangl versions were available with Colonial Blue, Persian Yellow, or Silver Green solid-color glazes, or brightly colored, hand-painted underglaze decorations.

Also in 1936, the name STANGL was incorporated into the molds of these mugs. The underglaze-decorated mugs were usually marked with Stangl's square underglaze stamp in addition to the in-mold trademark. During 1936 the #1674 Smart Alec shape was discontinued, the name of #1681 Lord Archie was shortened to #1681 Archie, and #1673 Yodel was changed to #1673 Grand.

The underglaze-decorated Stobies were reasonably popular during the late 1930s and early 1940s, but were discontinued by the mid-1940s. A few Stoby mugs with Terra Rose finish were produced during the 1940s but were also discontinued after a short time. At present, Stoby mugs with underglaze decorations are the most well liked type among collectors.

Beginning in 1967, Stangl reintroduced the Stoby mug shapes with Chartreuse Green, Dark Green, and Canary Yellow solid-color "fashion" glazes, and as red-bodied clear glazed pieces. Stoby mugs with the 1960s fashion color glazes were produced for one or two years and sold only at the Flemington Outlet.

In 1974, the Stoby mugs were again reintroduced. The 1974 series consisted of #1675 Parson, #1676 Chief, #1677 Cry Baby (originally #1677 Depression), #1678 Sport, #1680 Henpeck, and #1681 Archie. Not included in this reintroduction were #1673 Grand and #1679 Batch. These mugs were all glazed with Tan dinnerware glaze and detailed with Hardened Blue or Black underglaze colors. The Tan glazed Stoby mugs were individually boxed and were available through Stangl's general line catalog for 1974.

top: 1930s Stoby mugs: #1673 Yodel, mat overglaze decoration; #1673 Grand, underglaze decoration; #1674 Smart Alec (incorrect hat), mat overglaze decoration; #1675 Parson and #1676 Chief, both with underglaze decoration.

middle: 1930s Stoby mugs: #1677 Depression, #1678 Sport, #1679 Batch, #1680 Henpeck, all with underglaze color decoration; #1681 Lord Archie with mat overglaze decoration.

left: 1960s Stoby mug: #1673 Grand with Chartreuse Green fashion glaze.

#1704 Tea Set

Introduced: 1933
Colors: Colonial Blue, Persian Yellow, Silver Green, Turquoise, Tangerine, Rust
  Underglaze Decorations

Known Pieces:

Solid-color pieces:

creamer . . . . $25 – 35
cup. . . . . $10 – 15
pitcher, 1 quart . . . . $80 – 95
pitcher, 1 pint . . . . $55 – 65
plate, 12" chop . . . . $65 – 85
plate, 10" . . . . $35 – 45
plate, 9" . . . . $30 – 35
plate, 7" . . . . $25 – 30
saucer . . . . $10 – 15
sherbet. . . . . $45 – 55
sugar . . . . $40 – 50
teapot. . . . . $125 – 145

Underglaze decorated:

creamer . . . . $40 – 50
cup. . . . . $20 – 25
pitcher, 1 quart . . . . $100 – 130
pitcher, 1 pint . . . . $75 – 85
plate, 12" chop . . . . $120 – 140
plate, 10" . . . . $65 – 80
plate, 9" . . . . $55 – 65
plate, 7" . . . . $35 – 45
saucer . . . . $12 – 16
sherbet. . . . . $70 – 80
sugar . . . . $60 – 70
teapot. . . . . $175 – 195

Dinnerware shape #1704 was classically shaped and elegantly styled with graceful handles and embossed edging. This shape was produced with both solid-color glazes and a hand-painted underglaze motif. The hand-painted wreath motif of stylized chrysanthemums featured deep underglaze colors and pink-tinted glaze. This was the same underglaze colors and glaze used on the underglaze-decorated #1647 beer sets. Dinnerware shape #1704 with underglaze color decoration was a special-order product for a New York distributor. Solid-color and underglaze decorated #1704 are equally rare.

#1704 tea set: 10" plate with underglaze floral decoration;
7" plate, Tangerine.

#1747 – #1749 Cabbage

Introduced: 1933
Colors: Colonial Blue, Persian Yellow, Silver Green, Turquoise, Tangerine, Satin White

Known Pieces:
bowl, salad #1747 . . . . $60 – 75
bowl, mayonnaise #1748 . . . . $40 – 50
plate, #1749 . . . . $40 – 50

Cabbage #1749 10" plate, Tangerine glaze.

The #1747, #1748, and #1749 shapes were based on an arrangement of large, flat cabbage leaves. This scarce salad set was produced in very limited quantities during 1933 and 1934. The restyled and greatly expanded #1800 Cabbage Leaf pattern replaced the #1747, #1748, and #1749 shapes in 1934. The #1747 – #1749 Cabbage shapes were used again during the 1960s with the Antique Gold finish as part of Stangl's giftware line.

Cabbage Leaf #1800

Introduced: 1934
Designer: Martin Stangl
Colors: Persian Yellow, Silver Green, Turquoise, Maize, Ivory, Blue of the Sky, Leaf Green, Alice Blue

Known Pieces:
bowl, 10" salad . . . . $60 – 75
bowl, 9" salad . . . . $45 – 55
bowl, 6" mayonnaise . . . . $20 – 25
bowl, 4" nut . . . . $20 – 25
cakestand, 10" . . . . $25 – 35
coffee pot . . . . $95 – 120
coffee pot, after dinner . . . . $110 – 145
creamer . . . . $15 – 20
cup . . . . $10 – 15
cup, after dinner . . . . $12 – 15
plate, 20" buffet . . . . $80 – 110
plate, 14" chop . . . . $55 – 65

plate, 10" . . . . $30 – 40
plate, 9" . . . . $25 – 30
plate, 8" . . . . $20 – 25
plate, 6" . . . . $12 – 15
relish, single . . . . $15 – 25
relish, double . . . . $15 – 20
relish, triple, oblong . . . . $30 – 35
relish, triple, round . . . . $30 – 35
saucer . . . . $7 – 8
saucer, after dinner . . . . $7 – 8
sugar . . . . $25 – 30
teapot . . . . $95 – 135

Styled after European majolica wares, Stangl's Cabbage Leaf #1800 was made to resemble crinkly, Savoy-type cabbage leaves. During 1934 and early 1935, this pattern was called "Ivory Table-Ware," and at that time was produced only with the Ivory glaze. By the end of 1935, many of Stangl's other glaze colors were also applied to these shapes and Stangl began calling this pattern Cabbage Leaf.

Martin Stangl was issued a patent for the #1800 shapes and markings in December 1934. Because all of the pieces, including plates, were slip cast instead of jiggered, the name STANGL, #1800, and the size of the pieces were able to be molded into the bottom of each piece.

The #1800 Cabbage Leaf shapes were reintroduced in 1940 for Fisher, Bruce & Company with Terra Rose colors, and again during the 1960s with fashion-color glazes for the Flemington Outlet. The 1960s pieces seem to be the most prevalent while pieces with 1930s solid-color glazes are somewhat scarce. The Leaf Green glaze of the 1930s is very similar to the Dark Green glaze of the 1960s. Leaf Green, however, is a shade lighter and more transparent than Dark Green.

The #1800 double and triple relish dishes produced during the 1930s and 1940s all have twig shaped pottery handles. The fashion-color glazed relish dishes produced during the 1960s nearly always have brass-colored metal handles and are very common. Ordinarily the only #1800 relish dishes with pottery handles not from the 1930s or 1940s were those produced with brushed gold or silver finishes during the 1960s and 1970s.

Cabbage Leaf #1800: cup, Leaf Green; 6" plate, Maize; 12" chop plate, Turquoise; oblong triple relish, Ivory; 9" plate, Silver Green; sugar, Turquoise.

Daisy #1870

Introduced: 1934
Designer: Martin Stangl
Colors: Colonial Blue, Persian Yellow, Silver Green, Tangerine, Rust, Lavender, Eggplant

Known Pieces:

bowl, 10" salad, round . . . . $65 – 75	cup . . . . $12 – 15
bowl, 10" oval . . . . $45 – 55	plate, 14" chop . . . . $75 – 90
bowl, 9" salad, round . . . . $50 – 60	plate, 10" . . . . $35 – 45
bowl, 9" rim soup . . . . $20 – 25	plate, 9" . . . . $30 – 35
bowl, 6½" relish . . . . $20 – 25	plate, 8" . . . . $25 – 30
bowl, 6" fruit . . . . $15 – 20	plate, 6" . . . . $15 – 20
bowl, 5" lug soup . . . . $15 – 20	platter, 12" oval . . . . $50 – 60
bowl, 4½" nut . . . . $15 – 20	relish, double, large . . . . $25 – 30
candle holder, each . . . . $15 – 20	relish, triple, oblong . . . . $25 – 35
cake stand, 10", high . . . . $35 – 45	relish, triple, round . . . . $25 – 35
cake stand, 10", low . . . . $35 – 45	saucer . . . . $7 – 9
creamer . . . . $20 – 25	sugar . . . . $30 – 35
	teapot . . . . $135 – 160

Stangl's earliest records of this pattern indicate that Daisy #1870 was available with Lavender, Colonial Blue, Persian Yellow, and Eggplant combination glazes applied in the same manner as the #1940 Raised Fruit dinnerware pattern. The petals were glazed one color, while the centers were glazed a complementary color. By 1936, the color assortment was changed to single-color glazes of Colonial Blue, Persian Yellow, Silver Green, Tangerine, and Rust. Pieces of Daisy glazed with combination-color glazes are extremely rare.

The bold modeling of the #1870 Daisy dinnerware shapes were based on the various poses of daisy petals. This ingenious design was unfortunately discontinued at the end of 1936. Daisy #1870 pieces were marked with in-mold markings just as Cabbage Leaf #1800 pattern.

Daisy #1870: cup, Colonial Blue; 8" plate, Tangerine; 6½" relish bowl, Persian Yellow; 10" plate, Colonial Blue; low cake stand, Tangerine.

#1902 Dinnerware

Introduced: 1935
Colors: Colonial Blue, Persian Yellow, Silver Green, Aqua Blue, Blue of the Sky,
   Tangerine, Satin Brown, Satin White, Satin Green, Satin Blue, Bronze Green, Satin Aqua

Known Pieces:

bowl, 10" salad . . . . $65 – 75	pitcher, ½ pint . . . . $20 – 25
bowl, 8" salad . . . . $45 – 55	plate, 14" chop . . . . $65 – 75
bowl, 9" utility . . . . $45 – 55	plate, 12" chop . . . . $50 – 60
bowl, 2½" miniature . . . . $25 – 30	plate, 11" . . . . $35 – 45
creamer . . . . $25 – 30	plate, 10" . . . . $30 – 35
cup . . . . $12 – 15	plate, 9" . . . . $25 – 30
pitcher, 2 quart with ice lip . . . . $80 – 95	plate, 8" . . . . $15 – 20
pitcher, 2 quart . . . . $65 – 75	plate, 6" . . . . $10 – 15
pitcher, 1 quart . . . . $45 – 55	saucer . . . . $8 – 10
pitcher, 1½ pint . . . . $30 – 35	sugar . . . . $35 – 40
pitcher, 1 pint . . . . $25 – 30	teapot . . . . $120 – 145
	tumbler . . . . $20 – 25

The ringed, streamlined #1902 shape was produced only briefly as a solid-color dinnerware pattern. The simpler shapes of Colonial and Americana were more strongly promoted by Stangl sales representatives. However, #1902 pitchers, tumblers, and 9" salad bowls were offered together throughout the late 1930s and early 1940s as beverage sets. The beverage set pieces were produced with both satin and gloss solid-color glazes, while #1902 dinnerware shapes were glazed only with gloss solid-color glazes. Solid-color glazed #1902 tumblers and pitchers are rather common, but other #1902 dinnerware shapes are somewhat scarce.

During the early 1940s the #1902 shape line was expanded and decorated with hand-painted patterns for exclusive distribution by Fisher, Bruce & Co.

Dinnerware #1902: 9" utility bowl, Satin Green; 14" chop plate, Colonial Blue; tumbler, Tangerine; tumbler, Satin Aqua; ½ pint pitcher, Colonial Blue; 1 pint pitcher, Bronze Green; 1 quart pitcher, Persian Yellow.

#1902 beverage set consisting of 2 quart pitcher with ice lip and rattan-wrapped handle and six tumblers.

Raised Fruit #1940

Introduced: 1935
Colors: Colonial Blue, Persian Yellow, Silver Green, Tangerine, and the following combinations:
Blue and Yellow, Oyster White and Eggplant, Dark Green and Eggplant, Tangerine and Blue

Known Pieces:		*Single Colors:*	
Combination Colors:		bowl, 9" salad . . . . $65 – 75	
bowl, 9" salad . . . . $85 – 115		plate, 14" chop . . . . $70 – 85	
plate, 14" chop . . . . $90 – 125		plate, 9" . . . . $25 – 35	
plate, 9" . . . . $45 – 55		plate, 8" . . . . $35 – 45	

The #1940 Raised Fruit motif is a raised cluster of fruit and leaves in the center of the 14" and 9" plates and on one side of the salad bowls. The 8" plate is a cluster of fruit with no rim. This pattern was originally sold with combination two-color glazes only. In 1936, a ten-piece set of #1940 Raised Fruit combination glazes consisted of a 14" chop plate, a salad bowl, and eight 8" plates. Each set retailed for $9.95. The chop plates and salad bowls in these sets were decorated with two-color glazing, while the 8" plates were glazed with single color. By 1937, the two-color combination glazes were discontinued and #1940 Raised Fruit was produced only in single solid-color glazes.

By 1938 the solid-color #1940 Raised Fruit was no longer produced. However, during the early 1940s these shapes were re-introduced and decorated with Terra Rose colors exclusively for Frederick Lunning. During the late 1940s, the 1960s, and 1970s, the #1940 shapes were decorated with underglaze colors in natural tones and sold at the Flemington Outlet.

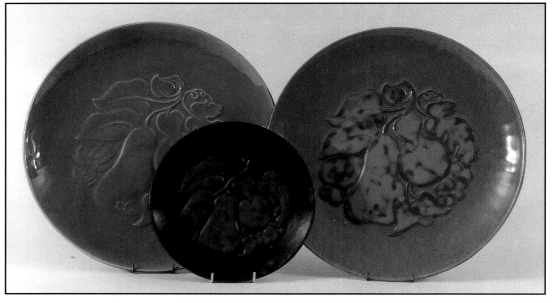

Raised Fruit #1940: 14" chop plate, Colonial Blue; 9" plate, Eggplant with Dark Green; 14" chop plate, Tangerine with Blue.

#1978 Manning Bowman Hors d'Oeuvres Tray

Introduced: 1935
Colors: Persian Yellow, Silver Green
Made For: Manning Bowman Metalworks Corp.

Known Pieces: tray, hors d'oeuvres 7" square .... $15 – 20

During the late 1930s, Stangl produced square hors d'oeuvres trays for Manning Bowman, a manufacturer of household and commercial appliances and chrome and brass giftware. Stangl wholesaled the Silver Green glazed #1978 tray to Manning Bowman at 32¢ each in 1935. Manning Bowman sold these trays with their electric appliances as gift sets. These trays have the Manning Bowman trademark and sometimes "Stangl #1978" molded on the backs.

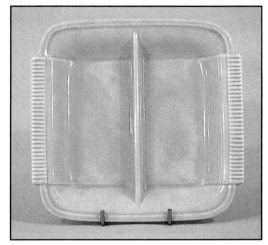

Manning Bowman tray, Silver Green.

Manning Bowman trademark.

#1997, #1998 Novelty Water Jugs

Introduced: 1935
Colors: Colonial Blue, Persian Yellow, Silver Green, Tangerine, Rust, Gray

Known Pieces:
#1997 Scallop jug .... $145 – 180   #1998 Dog jug .... $235 – 275

These peculiar water jugs were in very limited production during 1935 and 1936. Stangl referred to the #1997 swirled, football-shaped jug as "Scallop." The #1998 enigmatic animal-shaped jug was originally listed as "Dog" in Martin Stangl's notes, but salesmen's lists dated 1936 refer to this shape as "Rabbit." Both the #1997 Scallop and #1998 Dog jugs are unusual and scarce.

#1997 Scallop jug with Gray glaze.

#1997, #1998 Novelty Water Jugs (continued)

#1998 Dog jug, Persian Yellow.

Americana #2000

Introduced: 1935
Colors: Colonial Blue, Persian Yellow, Silver Green, Tangerine, Rust, Satin Brown, Maize, Blue of the Sky

Known Pieces:

ashtray, 4"	$20 – 25
ball jug	$80 – 90
bowl, 6" fruit	$10 – 12
bowl, 5" cream soup	$20 – 25
bowl, 5" lug soup	$10 – 12
cover, 5" lug soup	$10 – 15
bowl, 7½" coupe soup	$15 – 18
bowl, 10" oval vegetable	$30 – 35
bowl, 8" oval vegetable	$20 – 25
bowl, 5½" oval vegetable	$10 – 15
bowl, 12" salad, low	$60 – 75
bowl, 11½" salad	$55 – 65
bowl, 10" salad	$35 – 45
bowl, 7" salad	$20 – 25
butter chip	$15 – 20
carafe with wood handle	$65 – 80
casserole, individual, with handle & cover	$35 – 45
coffee pot, 6 cup	$95 – 120
coffee pot, 4 cup	$65 – 80
coffee pot, after dinner, 6 cup	$75 – 95
creamer	$10 – 15
creamer, after dinner	$15 – 20
creamer, individual	$15 – 20
cup, after dinner	$12 – 15
cup, coffee	$12 – 15
cup, tea	$10 – 12
gravy bowl	$25 – 35
pitcher, 2 quart with ice lip	$70 – 80
pitcher, 2 qt. waffle	$65 – 75
cover, 2 qt. waffle	$15 – 20
pitcher, 1 quart	$45 – 55
pitcher, 1½ pint	$30 – 35
pitcher, 1 pint	$25 – 30
pitcher, ½ pint	$20 – 25
pitcher, miniature	$20 – 25
plate, 14" chop	$45 – 55
plate, 12" chop	$35 – 45
plate, 10"	$20 – 25
plate, 9"	$15 – 20
plate, 8"	$12 – 15
plate, 7"	$8 – 10
plate, 6"	$6 – 8

platter, 14" oval	$40 – 45	sugar, individual	$20 – 25
platter, 12" oval	$25 – 35	sugar, open	$12 – 15
ramekin, 4"	$10 – 12	teapot, 8 cup	$95 – 135
relish, 6½" x 7"	$12 – 15	teapot, 6 cup	$60 – 75
salt, pepper; each	$10 – 12	tray, with indents	
saucer	$4 – 5	for creamer & sugar	$12 – 15
saucer, cream soup	$8 – 10	tray, with indents for	
saucer, after dinner	$4 – 5	individual creamer & sugar	$12 – 15
sugar	$15 – 20	tumbler	$20 – 25

The #2000 Americana shape was very streamlined and typical of the Moderne forms popular during the middle and late 1930s. Although Americana was produced through 1943, it is not as plentiful as Colonial. Stangl sales staff were instructed to promote the #1388 Colonial pattern over Americana. Because the Americana pattern was similar to patterns produced by several other companies, Mr. Stangl felt that Colonial was more typical of Stangl and Stangl products. Consequently, a smaller amount of Americana was produced.

Two-quart waffle and beverage pitchers vary somewhat in the #2000 shape. The waffle pitcher has a squared handle and an open top to accommodate the lid. The #2000 beverage pitcher has an ice lip and rounded handle. Sometimes this handle was wrapped with rattan when this piece was sold as part of a beverage set. The #2000 shape carafes were usually sold with cork stoppers. Shoppers at the Flemington Outlet, however, often purchased ceramic #1388 stoppers with their #2000 carafes. Consequently many #2000 Americana carafes are found with #1388 Colonial shape stoppers.

From 1938 through 1943, many of the same metal accessories sold with the #1388 Colonial shapes were also available for #2000 Americana. The ice bowl holder and tongs were not offered with Americana. A small wrought aluminum tray with a wood handle was available for the #2000 salt and pepper shakers but not for the #1388 Colonial pattern.

Americana #2000: tumbler, Tangerine; cream soup & saucer, Silver Green; 8" plate, Satin Brown; 5½" oval vegetable, Tangerine; creamer, Persian Yellow; 10" plate, Colonial Blue; teapot, Silver Green; 9" plate, Persian Yellow; tea cup & saucer, Tangerine.

Americana #2000: ramekin, Tangerine; carafe, Silver Green; after dinner cup, Colonial Blue; after dinner saucer, Silver Green; after dinner coffee pot, Persian Yellow; after dinner creamer, Silver Green; 14" oval platter, Tangerine; ash tray, Colonial Blue; salt shaker, Persian Yellow; 4 cup coffee pot, Maize; coffee cup & saucer, Tangerine.

Americana #2000: 2 quart waffle pitcher with cover, Tangerine.

#3100 Arden Farm, Mount Hope Honey Jug

Introduced: 1937
Colors: Colonial Blue, Persian Yellow, Silver Green, Tangerine, Rust
Made For: Arden Farm and Mount Hope

Known Pieces: jug, 1 pint, 9" tall. . . . . $40 – 50

These Moderne styled jugs were produced from 1937 through the early 1940s for the Arden Farm and Mount Hope honey and syrup products. The Arden Farm jugs usually have "3100" and "Arden Farm" molded in the bases while the Mount Hope pieces only bear the name "Mount Hope" with no shape number.

Mount Hope Farm of Williamstown, Massachusetts, was a privately owned experimental farm that specialized in developing new varieties of produce and livestock. From the late 1920s through the 1940s, they sold many types of produce, syrup, and honey. Stangl produced several different jars and containers for Mount Hope throughout the 1930s. The #3100 jug was the last shape produced for Mount Hope. Mount Hope Farm is currently owned by Williams College.

Arden Farm was a working dairy farm belonging to the E.H. Harriman estate in Orange County, New York. In operation before 1896 through 1972, Arden Farm produced several lines of honey and dairy products. Stangl's #3100 jug was sold to Arden Farm from 1937 through 1943.

#3100 Arden Farm, Mount Hope Honey Jugs, Silver Green and Tangerine.

#3137 Toastmaster Trays and Jars

Introduced: 1937
Colors: Colonial Blue, Persian Yellow, Silver Green, Tangerine, Rust, Satin White
Made For: McGraw Electric Co.

Known Pieces:

tray, #3137 pen 4½" x 7½" . . . . $5 – 8	jar, marmalade, covered . . . . $12 – 18
tray, hors d'oeuvres 8" square. . . . . . $10 – 15	jar, marmalade, open . . . . $12 – 18

In 1937 Stangl introduced the #3137 oblong dish as a pen tray. From 1938 through 1945, these trays were produced as "appetizer dishes" for the Toastmaster Division of McGraw Electric Company. During that time Stangl also produced great quantities of square hors d'oeuvres trays and two styles of marmalade jars for McGraw Electric. The hors d'oeuvres tray is decorated with the Toastmaster stylized logo, the back is marked "STANGL U S A." The open marmalade jar features a cross-shaped footed base and was usually glazed in Persian Yellow or Tangerine. The covered marmalade jar was always sold with the cover glazed a contrasting color to the jar. The most common color combination is a Persian Yellow jar with a Tangerine cover.

McGraw Electric offered these ceramic items with Toastmaster appliances and wood trays through-

out the early 1940s as "Hostess Sets" and "Toast & Jam Sets." These sets were very popular bridal and hostess gifts at that time. Consequently, Stangl produced tens of thousands of the Toastmaster ceramic dishes, trays, and jars. So plentiful were the #3137 trays during the early 1940s, Stangl would give a set of these trays to each bride that used Stangl's bridal registry. The covered and open marmalade jars were also used as give-away premiums to the shoppers at the Flemington Outlet.

Toastmaster products: #3137 pen trays in assorted colors, square hors d'oeuvres tray, Silver Green; open jam jar, Tangerine; covered jam jar, Persian Yellow with Tangerine cover.

#3141 Lentheric Jar

Introduced: 1937
Colors: Satin White
Made For: Lentheric

#3141 Lentheric cream jar, Satin White.

Known Pieces: jar, with cover. . . . . $65 – 75

These covered jars of Moderne styling were made for Lentheric of New York and Paris during 1937 and 1938. Lentheric, a perfumer and importer of Continental and gourmet foodstuffs, packed the jars with choice cream sauces and salad dressings. Around the rim of each jar are the words "beau pourri de Lentheric • paris • new york." The bases are marked "NET Wgt. 20 oz" and the covers feature rosebud knobs and are notched to accommodate a spoon. The end of non-essential transatlantic shipping during 1938 cut short Stangl's contract with Lentheric.

1930s and 1940s HAND-DECORATED DINNERWARE

Silk-Screen Decorated Patterns

Stangl's first mass-produced, underglaze-decorated dinnerware patterns utilized silk-screened motifs with hand-painted bands and accents. The predominant underglaze colors used on the silk-screen patterns were dark blue and dark brown with accents in light yellow or soft green. The glazes were transparent and tinted various subtle colors. There were several under-glaze logos used to mark these patterns, but usually they were not marked at all. Silk-screen decorated patterns were produced through the early 1940s.

Gazelle and Holly Leaf

Introduced: 1937
Glaze Colors: Tan, Blue, Satin Blue
Shape Style: #1388 and #2000

Known Pieces:

Gazelle:		Holly Leaf:	
plate, 8"	$65 – 75	plate, 8"	$45 – 55
plate, chop	$145 – 175	plate, chop	$120 – 150

The Gazelle motif and accents were usually decorated with dark blue or brown underglaze colors. Less common are Gazelle pieces with gray, green, or yellow decorations. Gazelle was produced as a salad set, but chop plates are exceedingly scarce.

Gazelle: #1388 8" plate, Satin Blue; #2000 8" plate, clear glaze; #2000 8" plate, Satin Blue.

The Holly Leaf pattern was decorated with blue or brown holly leaves overstroked with dark green. The "berries" were usually red, but were sometimes other colors as well. As with Gazelle, the Holly Leaf pattern was a salad set.

Holly Leaf: #2000 8" plate, Satin Blue glaze with badly flawed motif.

May Feast and Cherry

Introduced: 1937
Glaze Colors: Tan, Blue, Satin Blue, Green
Shape Style: #2000

Known Pieces:

bowl, coupe soup . . . . $15 − 18	plate, 12" chop . . . . $75 − 85
bowl, fruit . . . . $10 − 15	plate, 10" . . . . $35 − 45
bowl, 11½" salad. . . . . $70 − 85	plate, 9" . . . . $30 − 35
bowl, 10" salad . . . . $55 − 65	plate, 8" . . . . $20 − 30
bowl, 7" salad . . . . $40 − 50	plate, 7" . . . . $15 − 20
creamer . . . . $20 − 25	plate, 6" . . . . $10 − 15
cup. . . . . $10 − 12	saucer . . . . $6 − 7
plate, 14" chop . . . . $90 − 110	sugar . . . . $25 − 35
	teapot. . . . . $125 − 145

The May Feast pattern was decorated with seven different fruit motifs silk screened on the various dinnerware shapes. The motifs were apple, cherries, currants, grapes, peach, pear, and plums. The 14" chop plate was decorated with a large cluster of all of the fruits. The rim treatments used on May Feast were either single bands of color or bands with contrasting slashes.

The silk-screened Cherry pattern used the same glazes and rim treatments that were used on May Feast. However, only the cherry motif was used on the Cherry pattern. In 1938, Stangl listed these color combinations for the Cherry pattern:
#2001 – Brown band with Tan glaze and blue band for blue set.
#2002 – Blue band with Tan glaze and yellow lines for yellow set.
#2003 – Brown band with Blue glaze and green lines for green set.

These were the color combinations listed at that time, but both May Feast and Cherry were produced with several other combinations of the same colors.

May Feast: 9" plate, Green; 8" plate, Satin Blue; 12" chop plate, Tan;
7" plate, Tan; 9" plate, Blue.

Plum and Delicious Orchard

Introduced: 1937
Glaze Colors: Tan, Blue, Satin Blue, Green, Clear
Shape Style: #1388

Known Pieces:

bowl, coupe soup	$15 – 20	plate, 10"	$35 – 45
bowl, fruit	$10 – 15	plate, 9"	$30 – 40
bowl, 4½" lug soup	$10 – 15	plate, 8"	$20 – 25
bowl, 10" oval	$35 – 45	plate, 7"	$10 – 15
creamer	$20 – 25	plate, 6"	$10 – 12
cup	$10 – 12	saucer	$6 – 8
plate, 14" chop	$65 – 80	sugar	$25 – 30
plate, 12" chop	$50 – 60	teapot	$130 – 150

The Plum pattern uses the same silk-screened motif as on May Feast. Plum, however, was produced only on the #1388 shape and was decorated with brush marks around the rim, unlike the bands found on May Feast. The color combinations listed in 1938 were:
#1388 A – Green glaze with green decoration. #1388 B – Blue glaze with blue decoration. #1388 C – Tan glaze with yellow decoration.

As with May Feast and Cherry, these are not the only combinations found on Plum.

The Delicious Orchard pattern was a special-order for the Delicious Orchard Fruit Company of New York during 1937. It featured several of the May Feast fruit motifs silk-screened in vibrant blue underglaze with no banding or decoration on the rims. The pieces were glazed a bright, clear

Plum 9" plate Blue glaze; 7" plate Tan glaze.

gloss. These items usually bear the STANGL die-pressed mark. The Plum pattern is more plentiful than Delicious Orchard, with Delicious Orchard pieces selling at higher retails than Plum.

Hand-Painted Patterns

By 1938, several patterns were developed that were wholly hand painted. These used bold motifs and brighter, more attractive colors than the silk-screen designs. At first, hand-painted patterns were produced on the #1388 and #2000 shapes. By 1940, other shapes, such as #1902, had hand-painted motifs as well.

During the late 1930s, Stangl's dinnerware decorating department was very small. Only a handful of decorators were employed, and each decorator signed the back of each piece with the following: "HAND PAINTED, STANGL POTTERY, TRENTON, N.J.," the pattern number, and decorator's last name. This was done because Stangl believed that his customers should be able to differentiate between more costly hand-painted dinnerware patterns and the cheaper hand-decorated silk-screen patterns.

Some of the decorators' names found on these hand-painted patterns are Bailey, Walsh, Kennedy, O'Brien, and Ewing. Gerald Ewing was head of the decorating department until 1940. Ethel Kennedy became head of decorating in 1940 and remained in that position throughout most of the 1940s. Gerald Ewing and Ethel Kennedy each designed several of Stangl's dinnerware patterns during their respective terms of employment.

Pear #3200, Apple #3201, Cherry #3202, Plum #3203

Introduced: 1938
Designer: Gerald Ewing
Shape Style: #2000

Known Pieces:

Dark Colors, Satin Glazes:
bowl, 12" salad, low . . . . $95 − 115
bowl, 10" salad . . . . $80 − 95
plate, 14½" chop . . . . $75 − 95
plate, 10" . . . . $30 − 40
plate, 8" . . . . $20 − 30

Bright Colors, Gloss Glaze:
bowl, 12" salad, low . . . . $110 − 135
bowl, 10" salad . . . . $85 − 100
plate, 14½" chop . . . . $125 − 145
plate, 10" . . . . $50 − 65
plate, 8" . . . . $35 − 45

When first introduced, these four patterns were decorated with bright pink, blue, and yellow underglaze colors and glazed with clear gloss glaze. Shortly after introduction, the colors were changed to dark blues and browns, and the glazes used were Satin Green and Satin Blue. The brightly colored versions of these patterns are found much less frequently than those decorated with dark colors and Satin glazes.

All four of these patterns were styled after bold Italian designs popular during the late 1930s. To decorate these patterns, underglaze color was spun onto the center of each piece using a large brush to create a background. Some of the background color was then wiped away where the motif was to be placed. The motif was then stenciled on and the remaining colors were applied.

Brightly colored versions of the Plum #3203 and Pear #3200 patterns.

The Pear pattern used Satin Blue glaze with a blue swirl and a large pear outlined in brown. Apple featured a brown apple with Satin Blue glaze. The swirl on Cherry is green, while the cherries and leaves are blue and brown with Satin Green glaze. The Plum pattern featured a cluster of plums on a brown background.

Pear #3200 14½" chop plate.

Apple #3201 10" plate.

Cherry #3202 14½" chop plate, 8" plate.

Plum #3203 14½" chop plate.

Garden Pear #3300, Garden Apple #3301, Garden Cherry #3302, Garden Plum #3303

Introduced: 1939
Designer: Gerald Ewing
Glaze: Satin Blue, Satin Green
Shape Style: #2000

Known Pieces:

bowl, fruit . . . . $10 – 15	cup, coffee . . . . $12 – 15
bowl, lug soup . . . . $10 – 15	cup, tea . . . . $10 – 15
bowl, 12" salad . . . . $65 – 75	plate, 14½" chop . . . . $75 – 95
bowl, 12" salad, low . . . . $80 – 90	plate, 12½" chop . . . . $50 – 60
bowl, 10" salad . . . . $45 – 55	plate, 10" . . . . $30 – 40
bowl, 7½" salad . . . . $30 – 40	plate, 9" . . . . $25 – 35
bowl, 10" oval . . . . $35 – 45	plate, 8" . . . . $20 – 25
butter chip . . . . $15 – 20	plate, 7" . . . . $12 – 15
candle holder, #3046	plate, 6" . . . . $10 – 12
Scroll shape, each . . . . $15 – 25	platter, 12" oval . . . . $60 – 70
candle holder, #3087	salt, pepper; each . . . . $10 – 12
oblong, 2" x 3", each . . . . $15 – 25	saucer . . . . $5 – 7
carafe with handle . . . . $75 – 85	sugar . . . . $20 – 25
creamer . . . . $15 – 20	teapot . . . . $110 – 135

These patterns were decorated with the same motifs as the earlier Pear #3200, Apple #3201, Cherry #3202, and Plum #3203 patterns. The Garden Pear and Garden Cherry colors were changed to blue and brown, while Garden Apple and Garden Plum continued to be decorated with the same dark colors and Satin glazes as Apple #3201 and Plum #3203. The 6" and 7" plates in these patterns were decorated only with swirls of color, as were some of the smaller bowls and the cups.

Garden Plum 6" plate; Garden Cherry 10" plate and tea cup; Garden Apple 8" plate.

Ranger #3304

Introduced: 1939
Designer: Gerald Ewing
Glaze: Satin Yellow
Shape Style: #2000

Known Pieces:

ashtray . . . . $140 – 160	cup, coffee . . . . $60 – 70
bowl, fruit . . . . $110 – 145	cup, tea . . . . $50 – 60
bowl, lug soup . . . . $120 – 150	plate, 14½" chop . . . . $650 – 750
bowl, 12" salad . . . . $550 – 650	plate, 12½" chop . . . . $550 – 600
bowl, 12" salad, low . . . . $550 – 650	plate, 10" . . . . $275 – 325
bowl, 10" salad . . . . $450 – 550	plate, 9" . . . . $200 – 225
bowl, 7½" salad . . . . $275 – 325	plate, 8" . . . . $160 – 185
bowl, 10" oval . . . . $450 – 550	plate, 7" . . . . $100 – 130
butter chip . . . . $40 – 50	plate, 6" . . . . $75 – 90
candle holder, #3046	platter, 12" oval . . . . $500 – 600
Scroll shape, each . . . . $150 – 175	salt, pepper; each . . . . $65 – 85
candle holder, #3087	salt, pepper, #3295 /#3294
oblong, 2" x 3", each . . . . $100 – 125	Ranger Dudes; each . . . . $300 – 350
carafe with handle . . . . $650 – 750	saucer, after dinner . . . . $25 – 35
coffee pot, 6 cup . . . . $900 – 1,000	saucer . . . . $25 – 35
coffee pot, after dinner . . . . $900 – 1,000	sugar . . . . $200 – 225
creamer . . . . $100 – 125	teapot . . . . $850 – 950
cup, after dinner . . . . $85 – 110	paper price list . . . . $100 – 150

Because of its Western motif, Ranger has become one of the most sought after of Stangl's early hand-painted patterns. Ranger was decorated with Light Blue, Blue #95, Walnut Brown, and French Green under the Satin Yellow glaze. This color combination gives the motif a warm, desert-like appearance. Stangl called the #3294 Cowgirl and #3295 Cowboy salt and pepper shakers "Ranger Dudes" when decorated to match the Ranger dinnerware pattern.

Stangl's Satin Yellow glaze was prone to misfiring in the difficult to regulate beehive kilns. Ranger pieces with misfired glaze will have muddied colors lacking clarity and brilliance. Many collectors take the quality of glaze into consideration when purchasing and will pay top prices only for Ranger with bright, clear colors.

Ranger sugar, creamer, 14½" chop plate, salt & pepper, 9" plate.

Ranger Dudes salt & pepper shakers.

Field Daisy #3306

Introduced: 1939
Designer: Gerald Ewing
Shape Style: #2000

Known Pieces:

bowl, fruit	$20 – 25
bowl, lug soup	$20 – 25
bowl, 12" salad	$90 – 110
bowl, 12" salad, low	$95 – 115
bowl, 10" salad	$70 – 80
bowl, 7½" salad	$50 – 60
bowl, 10" oval	$60 – 70
butter chip	$20 – 25
candle holder, #3046	
Scroll shape, each	$15 – 25
candle holder, #3087	
oblong, 2" x 3", each	$15 – 25
carafe with handle	$85 – 110
coffee pot, 6 cup	$135 – 160
coffee pot, after dinner	$135 – 160
creamer	$20 – 25
creamer, individual	$25 – 35
cup, after dinner	$15 – 20
cup, coffee	$15 – 20
cup, tea	$10 – 15
plate, 14½" chop	$95 – 125
plate, 12½" chop	$75 – 85
plate, 10"	$40 – 50
plate, 9"	$35 – 40
plate, 8"	$25 – 30
plate, 7"	$20 – 25
plate, 6"	$10 – 15
platter, 12" oval	$85 – 100
salt, pepper; each	$12 – 15
salt, pepper, #3298	
Daisy; each	$40 – 50
saucer, after dinner	$6 – 8
saucer	$6 – 8
sugar	$25 – 30
sugar, open	$20 – 25
teapot	$125 – 145
paper price list	$40 – 50

The Field Daisy pattern was decorated with the same technique that was used for Pear #3200. The background color was swirled on, wiped away where the blossoms were to be, then the flowers were outlined and the centers applied. The original colors for this pattern were Blue #95 with the flower centers painted Yellow. Initially, Field Daisy was also produced with Satin Yellow glaze instead of clear gloss.

During the early 1940s, the Field Daisy pattern was a special-order pattern made for Carole Stupell, Limited of New York. The Field Daisy pieces produced for Carole Stupell were decorated with the original blue and yellow, as well as the following color combinations: Pink #193 background with Blue #95 flowers and Yellow centers, Light Yellow background with French Green flowers, Dark Yellow background with Blue #95 flowers, and French Green background with Dark Yellow flower centers. The pieces made for Carole Stupell were marked with both the Stangl stamp and the Carole Stupell logo on each piece. Field Daisy pieces decorated with Carole Stupell colors are usually valued a little higher than blue pieces.

The #3298 daisy-shaped salt and pepper shakers were painted light blue with the petals outlined in Blue #95, and the centers were either Blue #95 or Yellow for the Field Daisy pattern. These daisy shakers were also produced with different color combinations to coordinate with other Stangl "daisy" decorated dinnerware patterns.

Field Daisy 6" plate, Satin Yellow glaze; #2000 shape salt and pepper shakers; 10" plate, Blue #95; #3298 daisy-shape salt & pepper shakers; Carole Stupell 14½" chop plate, Pink #193 and Blue #95; Carole Stupell 8" plate, Light Yellow and French Green; teapot, creamer and sugar, Blue #95; Carole Stupell 8" plate, Pink #193.

Old Orchard #3307

Introduced: 1939
Designer: Gerald Ewing
Shape Style: #1388

Known Pieces:

bowl, fruit	$10 – 15	plate, 14½" chop	$80 – 95
bowl, 5" lug soup	$10 – 15	plate, 12½" chop	$60 – 70
cover, 5" lug soup	$8 – 12	plate, 10"	$25 – 35
bowl, 10" salad, extra deep	$75 – 85	plate, 9"	$20 – 30
bowl, 10" salad	$55 – 65	plate, 8"	$10 – 15
bowl, 8" vegetable	$40 – 50	plate, 7"	$10 – 12
bowl, 9" oval	$35 – 45	plate, 6"	$5 – 8
butter chip	$15 – 20	platter, 12" oval	$50 – 60
candle holder, each	$15 – 20	salt, pepper; each	$10 – 12
carafe with handle	$60 – 70	saucer	$5 – 6
stopper for carafe	$10 – 15	sugar	$20 – 25
creamer	$15 – 20	teapot	$85 – 110
cup	$10 – 12	paper price list	$20 – 40

Old Orchard is a bright pattern in a vibrant combination of yellow, green, and black. The motif is a cluster of French Green grapes on a Dark Yellow swirl. The smaller plates and hollow ware pieces were simply swirled with Dark Yellow and banded with French Green.

Old Orchard 8" plate, 10" plate, lug soup.

"Alium" #3314

Introduced: 1939
Glaze: Satin Blue
Shape Style: #2000

Known Pieces:

bowl, fruit . . . . $10 – 15	cup, coffee . . . . $10 – 15
bowl, lug soup. . . . . $15 – 20	cup, tea . . . . $10 – 15
bowl, 12" salad . . . . $85 – 95	plate, 14½" chop . . . . $95 – 130
bowl, 12" salad, low . . . . $95 – 125	plate, 12½" chop . . . . $85 – 95
bowl, 10" salad . . . . $60 – 70	plate, 10" . . . . $40 – 50
bowl, 7½" salad. . . . . $40 – 45	plate, 9" . . . . $30 – 40
bowl, 10" oval . . . . $50 – 60	plate, 8" . . . . $20 – 25
butter chip. . . . . $15 – 20	plate, 7" . . . . $15 – 20
candle holder, #3046	plate, 6" . . . . $12 – 15
Scroll shape, each . . . . $15 – 25	platter, 12" oval . . . . $85 – 95
candle holder, #3087	salt, pepper; each . . . . $10 – 12
oblong, 2" x 3", each. . . . . $15 – 20	saucer . . . . $6 – 7
carafe with handle . . . . $90 – 115	sugar . . . . $20 – 25
creamer . . . . $15 – 20	teapot. . . . . $95 – 125
	paper price list . . . . $50 – 60

This abstract pattern was loosely based on the ornamental onion plant, Alium Giganteum. The central motif was on the larger pieces, while the small pieces were decorated only with the hand-painted "rope" border. In limited production during 1939 and 1940, "Alium" is now an extremely rare pattern.

"Alium" 14½" chop plate.

Floral Plaid #3316

Introduced: 1939
Glaze: Satin White
Shape Style: #2000

Known Pieces:

bowl, fruit . . . . $10 – 12	cup, coffee . . . . $10 – 15
bowl, lug soup. . . . . $12 – 15	cup, tea . . . . $10 – 12
bowl, 12" salad . . . . $70 – 80	plate, 14½" chop . . . . $70 – 80
bowl, 12" salad, low . . . . $75 – 95	plate, 12½" chop . . . . $50 – 60
bowl, 10" salad . . . . $40 – 50	plate, 10" . . . . $30 – 35
bowl, 7½" salad. . . . . $35 – 45	plate, 9" . . . . $25 – 30
bowl, 10" oval . . . . $40 – 50	plate, 8" . . . . $15 – 20
butter chip. . . . . $15 – 20	plate, 7" . . . . $10 – 15
candle holder, #3046	plate, 6" . . . . $10 – 12
Scroll shape, each . . . . $10 – 15	platter, 12" oval . . . . $60 – 75
candle holder, #3087	salt, pepper; each . . . . $7 – 8
oblong, 2" x 3", each. . . . . $15 – 25	saucer . . . . $5 – 6
carafe with handle . . . . $75 – 90	saucer, after dinner . . . . $6 – 7
coffee pot, 6 cup . . . . $135 – 165	sugar . . . . $25 – 30
creamer . . . . $20 – 25	teapot. . . . . $115 – 140
cup, after dinner . . . . $15 – 20	paper price list . . . . $40 – 50

    This Moderne blue and white Floral Plaid pattern was produced from 1939 through the mid-1940s. The motif features a stylized yellow and green flower surrounded by a square blue border. The Satin White glaze on this pattern gives each piece a soft textured appearance, but sometimes obscures the brilliance of the underglaze colors. The less brilliant the motif, the less collectors are willing to pay for this pattern.

Floral Plaid #3046 Scroll candle holders, #3087 Oblong candle holders, 10" plate, tea cup & saucer.

Queen's Flower #3319

Introduced: 1939
Glaze: Satin White
Shape Style: #2000

Queen's Flower 9" plate, tea cup & saucer, 14½" chop plate, carafe.

Known Pieces:

bowl, fruit	$10 – 15
bowl, lug soup	$15 – 20
bowl, 12" salad	$55 – 65
bowl, 12" salad, low	$75 – 90
bowl, 10" salad	$45 – 55
bowl, 7½" salad	$30 – 40
bowl, 10" oval	$40 – 50
butter chip	$15 – 20
candle holder, #3046 Scroll shape, each	$10 – 15
candle holder, #3087 oblong, 2" x 3", each	$10 – 20
carafe with handle	$75 – 95
coffee pot	$125 – 150
creamer	$15 – 20
cup, after dinner	$15 – 20
cup, coffee	$10 – 15
cup, tea	$10 – 12
plate, 14½" chop	$65 – 75
plate, 12½" chop	$50 – 60
plate, 10"	$30 – 35
plate, 9"	$25 – 30
plate, 8"	$20 – 25
plate, 7"	$15 – 20
plate, 6"	$10 – 15
platter, 12" oval	$50 – 60
salt, pepper; each	$8 – 10
saucer	$5 – 6
saucer, after dinner	$6 – 7
sugar	$20 – 25
teapot	$95 – 135
paper price list	$40 – 50

The motif on the Queen's Flower pattern is a stylized blossom in pastel green and yellow. This pattern was based on a European folk-art design. The Satin White glaze on Queen's Flower gives the colors a soft, muted quality. As with most of Stangl's satin glazed dinnerware patterns of this era, unless the colors are bright and the motif is clear, many collectors will not pay high-end prices for the Queen's Flower pattern.

Valencia #3320

Introduced: 1939
Designer: Ethel Kennedy
Glaze: Satin Yellow
Shape Style: #2000

Known Pieces:

bowl, fruit	$20 – 25
bowl, lug soup	$20 – 25
bowl, 12" salad	$100 – 130
bowl, 12" salad, low	$110 – 135
bowl, 10" salad	$80 – 90
bowl, 7½" salad	$60 – 70
bowl, 10" oval	$70 – 80
butter chip	$20 – 25
candle holder, #3046 Scroll shape, each	$20 – 25
candle holder, #3087 oblong, 2" x 3", each	$20 – 25
carafe with handle	$115 – 135
creamer	$20 – 25
cup, coffee	$20 – 25
cup, tea	$20 – 25
plate, 14½" chop	$115 – 145
plate, 12½" chop	$100 – 125
plate, 10"	$55 – 65
plate, 9"	$40 – 50
plate, 8"	$25 – 35
plate, 7"	$20 – 25
plate, 6"	$15 – 20
platter, 12" oval	$100 – 125
salt, pepper; each	$10 – 15
saucer	$8 – 10
sugar	$30 – 35
teapot	$160 – 185
paper price list	$50 – 60

This pattern features an ingenuous rendering of a palm tree under a blazing sun. Both the Satin White and Satin Yellow glazes were used on the Valencia pattern. Articles glazed with Satin White are seemingly more abundant. Although many shapes were available with the Valencia motif, very little of this pattern was produced.

Valencia 10" plate, Satin White; 14½" chop plate, Satin Yellow; carafe, Satin White.

Venice #3332

Introduced: 1940
Glaze: Satin Blue
Shape Style: #2000

Known Pieces:

bowl, fruit	$10 – 12
bowl, lug soup	$12 – 15
bowl, 12" salad	$80 – 95
bowl, 12" salad, low	$90 – 110
bowl, 10" salad	$50 – 60
bowl, 7½" salad	$35 – 45
bowl, 10" oval	$40 – 50
butter chip	$10 – 15
candle holder, #3046	
Scroll shape, each	$12 – 15
candle holder, #3087	
oblong, 2" x 3", each	$12 – 15
carafe with handle	$90 – 110
creamer	$15 – 20
cup, coffee	$15 – 20
cup, tea	$10 – 15
plate, 14½" chop	$95 – 125
plate, 12½" chop	$80 – 100
plate, 10"	$35 – 45
plate, 9"	$30 – 35
plate, 8"	$25 – 30
plate, 7"	$15 – 20
plate, 6"	$10 – 15
platter, 12" oval	$75 – 85
salt, pepper; each	$7 – 8
saucer	$6 – 8
sugar	$25 – 30
teapot	$110 – 125
paper price list	$40 – 50

The Venice motif featured a stylized interpretation of a potted Streptocarpus plant. The colors were Walnut Brown flowers, Blue #95 leaves, and a Walnut Brown flower pot. The Satin Blue glaze on this pattern created a pale blue background. This is an unusual pattern that is somewhat challenging to collect.

Venice 8" plate, 10" plate.

Newport #3333

Introduced: 1940
Glaze: Satin Blue
Shape Style: #1388

Known Pieces:

ashtray	$20 – 30	plate, 14½" chop	$110 – 135
bowl, fruit	$20 – 25	plate, 12½" chop	$95 – 120
bowl, 5" lug soup	$20 – 25	plate, 10"	$50 – 60
cover, 5" lug soup	$10 – 15	plate, 9"	$45 – 55
bowl, 10" salad, extra deep	$80 – 95	plate, 8"	$30 – 35
bowl, 10" salad	$70 – 80	plate, 7"	$20 – 25
bowl, 8" vegetable	$65 – 75	plate, 6"	$15 – 20
bowl, 9" oval	$65 – 75	platter, 12" oval	$95 – 120
butter chip	$20 – 25	salt, pepper; each	$15 – 20
candle holder, each	$20 – 25	salt, pepper, #3297/#3296	
carafe with handle	$90 – 110	Jolly Tars; each	$200 – 250
stopper for carafe	$15 – 20	saucer	$8 – 10
creamer	$40 – 50	sugar	$40 – 50
cup	$20 – 25	teapot	$145 – 165
		paper price list	$60 – 75

The method that was used to apply the sailboat motif on the Newport pattern was called "rubber resist." In this technique, a thin rubber mask in the shape of the sails was placed in the center of the plate. Then the Blue #95 background color was swirled on using a wide brush, covering mask and all. The rubber mask was lifted off, revealing a sail-shaped area on the plate free of color. The wave area under the boat was sponged away by hand. All the details — boat, rigging, waves, and mast — were then hand painted with Blue #95 underglaze color.

The motifs on Newport hollow ware pieces were decorated with Light Blue and Blue #95. The pale blue background color of the hollow ware results from the use of Satin Blue glaze.

The #3296 and #3297 boy and girl sailor shakers were available decorated to match Newport dinnerware and were called Jolly Tars by Stangl.

Because the Satin Blue glaze was prone to misfires, many pieces of Newport can be found with such flaws as glaze crawling, muddied colors, and indistinct motifs. Naturally, pieces so flawed are worth considerably less than pieces with no flaws.

Newport 7" plate, 10" plate, cup & saucer, #1388 candle holders.

Jolly Tars salt & pepper shakers.

Bluebell #3334

Introduced: 1940
Designer: Ethel Kennedy
Shape Style: #1388

Known Pieces:

ashtray	$20 – 25	
bowl, fruit	$10 – 15	
bowl, 5" lug soup	$10 – 15	
bowl, 10" salad, extra deep	$75 – 90	
bowl, 10" salad	$60 – 70	
bowl, 8" vegetable	$45 – 55	
bowl, 9" oval	$45 – 55	
butter chip	$15 – 20	
candle holder, each	$15 – 20	
carafe with handle	$80 – 95	
stopper for carafe	$10 – 15	
creamer	$15 – 20	
cup	$10 – 12	
plate, 14½" chop	$95 – 115	
plate, 12½" chop	$80 – 90	
plate, 10"	$35 – 45	
plate, 9"	$30 – 35	
plate, 8"	$25 – 30	
plate, 7"	$15 – 20	
plate, 6"	$10 – 15	
platter, 12" oval	$75 – 85	
salt, pepper; each	$8 – 10	
salt, pepper, #3299 Bluebell; each	$50 – 60	
saucer	$6 – 8	
sugar	$20 – 25	
teapot	$95 – 130	

The Bluebell motif was a single Blue #95 blossom with French Green leaves and Blue #95 stem. The background swirl is bright yellow with a Blue #95 band around the rim. In this pattern, the yellow color was removed where the blossom was to be placed, but the leaves and stem were painted over the yellow background. The Bluebell shape #3299 salt and pepper shakers were decorated to complement the Bluebell dinnerware pattern.

Bluebell 10" plate, cup.

Florence #3335

Introduced: 1940
Designer: Ethel Kennedy
Shape Style: #1388

Known Pieces:

bowl, fruit	$25 – 30
bowl, 5" lug soup	$25 – 30
bowl, 10" salad, extra deep	$110 – 145
bowl, 10" salad	$110 – 145
bowl, 8" vegetable	$65 – 75
bowl, 9" oval	$65 – 75
butter chip	$20 – 25
candle holder, each	$20 – 25
carafe with handle	$125 – 150
stopper for carafe	$20 – 25
creamer	$25 – 30
cup	$15 – 20
plate, 14½" chop	$160 – 195
plate, 12½" chop	$145 – 175
plate, 10"	$70 – 85
plate, 9"	$60 – 70
plate, 8"	$40 – 50
plate, 7"	$20 – 30
plate, 6"	$20 – 25
platter, 12" oval	$130 – 145
salt, pepper; each	$10 – 15
saucer	$8 – 10
sugar	$35 – 45
teapot	$175 – 200
paper price list	$60 – 75

The central motif of the Florence pattern was a colorful house in Pink #193, Lavender, Yellow, and Blue #95 with French Green trees. The motif was surrounded by a Pink #193 swirl of color with a double band of Blue #95 on the rims.

The Pink underglaze color was somewhat volatile and often burned away if there was not enough oxygen in the kiln, a common occurrence in coal-fired beehive kilns. This is why only traces of color can be seen on the chop plate pictured. Very little of this pattern was produced.

Florence 14½" chop plate, fruit bowl.

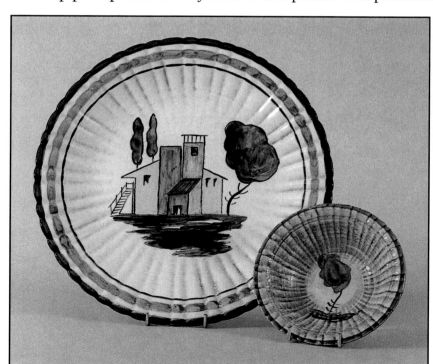

Galley #3336

Introduced: 1940
Glaze: Satin Yellow
Shape Style: #1388

Known Pieces:

bowl, fruit	$20 – 25
bowl, 5" lug soup	$20 – 25
bowl, 10" salad, extra deep	$90 – 110
bowl, 10" salad	$90 – 110
bowl, 8" vegetable	$60 – 70
bowl, 9" oval	$65 – 75
butter chip	$15 – 20
candle holder, each	$20 – 25
carafe with handle	$95 – 115
stopper for carafe	$10 – 15
creamer	$20 – 25
cup	$10 – 15
plate, 14½" chop	$90 – 110
plate, 12½" chop	$80 – 90
plate, 10"	$30 – 40
plate, 9"	$30 – 35
plate, 8"	$20 – 25
plate, 7"	$15 – 20
plate, 6"	$12 – 15
platter, 12" oval	$80 – 90
salt, pepper; each	$10 – 12
salt, pepper, #3293/#3292	
Fish; each	$50 – 65
saucer	$7 – 8
sugar	$25 – 30
teapot	$120 – 145
paper price list	$50 – 60

The Galley pattern features an ancient fishing boat with stylized fish and waves. The predominantly brown coloring of the motif coupled with the Satin Yellow glaze gives Galley a golden appearance. The #3292/#3293 Fish salt and pepper shakers were produced with solid-color glazes as well as decorated to match the Galley dinnerware motif.

Galley 10" plate, #1388 salt & pepper, cup & saucer, 14½" chop plate, 10" plate, creamer, sugar, teapot, cup & saucer.

Laurel #3337

Introduced: 1940
Glaze: Satin White
Shape Style: #2000

Known Pieces:

bowl, fruit . . . . $10 – 15	cup, coffee . . . . $12 – 15
bowl, lug soup. . . . . $12 – 15	cup, tea . . . . $10 – 15
bowl, 12" salad . . . . $60 – 75	plate, 14½" chop . . . . $80 – 95
bowl, 12" salad, low . . . . $75 – 90	plate, 12½" chop . . . . $60 – 75
bowl, 10" salad . . . . $50 – 60	plate, 10" . . . . $30 – 35
bowl, 7½" salad. . . . . $30 – 40	plate, 9" . . . . $25 – 30
bowl, 10" oval . . . . $50 – 60	plate, 8" . . . . $20 – 25
butter chip. . . . . $15 – 20	plate, 7" . . . . $10 – 15
candle holder, #3046	plate, 6" . . . . $10 – 15
Scroll shape, each . . . . $10 – 15	platter, 12" oval . . . . $70 – 80
candle holder, #3087	salt, pepper; each . . . . $8 – 10
oblong, 2" x 3", each. . . . . $10 – 15	saucer . . . . $7 – 8
carafe with handle . . . . $85 – 95	saucer, after dinner . . . . $7 – 8
coffee pot. . . . . $125 – 130	sugar . . . . $25 – 30
creamer . . . . $20 – 25	teapot. . . . . $115 – 145
cup, after dinner 12-15	paper price list . . . . $35 – 45

The Art Ware Blue brush-strokes encircling the Laurel pattern give the effect of a wreath of laurel leaves. The rim and center of Laurel are the same Art Ware Blue as the leaves. This creates a striking pattern against the bright white background. The fine brown line just inside the rim adds contrast to this orderly blue and white pattern.

Laurel 10" plate.

Tropic #3338

Introduced: 1940
Glaze: Satin White
Shape Style: #1388

Known Pieces:

bowl, fruit	$10 – 15
bowl, 5" lug soup	$10 – 15
bowl, 10" salad, extra deep	$75 – 90
bowl, 10" salad	$70 – 85
bowl, 8" vegetable	$40 – 50
bowl, 9" oval	$40 – 50
butter chip	$15 – 20
candle holder, each	$15 – 20
carafe with handle	$85 – 95
stopper for carafe	$12 – 15
creamer	$20 – 25
cup	$10 – 15
plate, 14½" chop	$85 – 110
plate, 12½" chop	$65 – 75
plate, 10"	$30 – 35
plate, 9"	$25 – 30
plate, 8"	$20 – 25
plate, 7"	$15 – 20
plate, 6"	$10 – 15
platter, 12" oval	$80 – 90
salt, pepper; each	$10 – 12
salt, pepper, #3291/#3290	
Lemon; each	$40 – 50
saucer	$5 – 7
sugar	$20 – 25
teapot	$95 – 125
paper price list	$40 – 50

The sunny Tropic pattern was actively produced from 1940 through 1945. Yellow lemons and Victoria Green leaves outlined with Blue #95 were the focal point of the Tropic motif. The #3290/3291 Lemon salt and pepper shakers were decorated to match the Tropic dinnerware pattern or simply glazed with solid-color glazes.

Tropic 8" plate, 14½" chop plate, #3290/#3291 Lemon salt & pepper.

Cosmos #3339

Introduced: 1940
Designer: Ethel Kennedy
Glaze: Pink-Tinted
Shape Style: #2000

Known Pieces:

bowl, fruit . . . . $10 – 15	cup, coffee . . . . $10 – 15
bowl, lug soup. . . . . $12 – 15	cup, tea . . . . $10 – 15
bowl, 12" salad . . . . $75 – 85	plate, 14½" chop . . . . $90 – 110
bowl, 12" salad, low . . . . $80 – 95	plate, 12½" chop . . . . $70 – 85
bowl, 10" salad . . . . $50 – 60	plate, 10" . . . . $25 – 35
bowl, 7½" salad. . . . . $35 – 45	plate, 9" . . . . $20 – 25
bowl, 10" oval . . . . $50 – 60	plate, 8" . . . . $15 – 20
butter chip. $15 – 20	plate, 7" . . . . $12 – 15
candle holder, #3046	plate, 6" . . . . $10 – 12
Scroll shape, each . . . . $15 – 20	platter, 12" oval . . . . $70 – 80
candle holder, #3087	salt, pepper; each . . . . $10 – 12
oblong, 2" x 3", each. . . . . $15 – 25	saucer . . . . $7 – 8
carafe with handle . . . . $95 – 115	saucer, after dinner . . . . $7 – 8
coffee pot, 6 cup . . . . $125 – 155	sugar . . . . $20 – 25
creamer . . . . $20 – 25	teapot. . . . . $90 – 130
cup, after dinner . . . . $12 – 18	paper price list . . . . $50 – 60

The Cosmos flowers were Light Blue, Blue #95, and Pink #160 with Yellow and Walnut Brown centers. Ethel Kennedy used the Black stem with French Green leaves device in several of her designs, including Cosmos. The bands on the rims repeated the colors Light Blue, Yellow, and Blue #95. The pink-tinted glaze creates an ivory-colored background for the floral motifs.

Cosmos fruit bowl, 10" plate, teapot, 9" plate.

Sunflower #3340

Introduced: 1940
Designer: Ethel Kennedy
Shape: #1388

Known Pieces:

bowl, fruit	$10 – 15
bowl, 5" lug soup	$15 – 20
bowl, 10" salad, extra deep	$85 – 100
bowl, 10" salad	$75 – 90
bowl, 8" vegetable	$45 – 55
bowl, 9" oval	$45 – 55
butter chip	$15 – 20
candle holder, each	$15 – 20
carafe with handle	$85 – 110
stopper for carafe	$10 – 15
creamer	$20 – 25
cup	$12 – 15
plate, 14½" chop	$95 – 120
plate, 12½" chop	$80 – 95
plate, 10"	$35 – 45
plate, 9"	$25 – 35
plate, 8"	$20 – 25
plate, 7"	$15 – 20
plate, 6"	$10 – 15
platter, 12" oval	$80 – 90
salt, pepper; each	$10 – 15
salt, pepper, #3299 Bluebell; each	$50 – 60
saucer	$7 – 8
sugar	$25 – 30
teapot	$120 – 145
paper price list	$55 – 65

The Sunflower and Bluebell motifs were identical, only the colors were reversed. The Sunflower blossom and bands were Yellow on a Blue #95 swirled background. Very little of this short-lived pattern was produced.

Sunflower 10" plate, 7" plate.

Harvest #3341

Introduced: 1940
Designer: Ethel Kennedy
Glaze: Yellow-Tinted
Shape Style: #1388

Known Pieces:

ashtray . . . . $25 – 30	plate, 14½" chop . . . . $90 – 115
bowl, fruit . . . . $15 – 20	plate, 12½" chop . . . . $80 – 95
bowl, 5" lug soup . . . . $15 – 20	plate, 10" . . . . $35 – 45
bowl, 10" salad, extra deep . . . . $85 – 110	plate, 9" . . . . $25 – 30
bowl, 10" salad . . . . $70 – 80	plate, 8" . . . . $20 – 25
bowl, 8" vegetable . . . . $40 – 50	plate, 7" . . . . $12 – 15
bowl, 9" oval . . . . $45 – 55	plate, 6" . . . . $10 – 15
butter chip . . . . $15 – 20	platter, 12" oval . . . . $85 – 110
candle holder, each . . . . $15 – 20	salt, pepper; each . . . . $10 – 12
carafe with handle . . . . $85 – 115	saucer . . . . $7 – 9
stopper for carafe . . . . $15 – 20	sugar . . . . $25 – 30
creamer . . . . $15 – 20	teapot . . . . $90 – 130
cup . . . . $12 – 15	paper price list . . . . $50 – 60

Stangl's very popular Harvest pattern was decorated with a large Pink #160 apple, a cluster of Blue #95 grapes, and Victoria Green leaves. This cheery pattern was a favorite during the 1940s, and was in active production through 1945. Harvest continues to be desired and widely collected at this time.

Harvest carafe, 10" plate, cup & saucer, sugar.

Floral #3342

Introduced: 1940
Designer: Ethel Kennedy
Shape Style: #2000

Known Pieces:

ashtray . . . . $15 – 20	creamer . . . . $15 – 20
bowl, fruit . . . . $10 – 15	cup, coffee . . . . $12 – 15
bowl, lug soup . . . . $15 – 20	cup, tea . . . . $12 – 15
bowl, 12" salad . . . . $80 – 95	plate, 14½" chop . . . . $100 – 130
bowl, 12" salad, low . . . . $90 – 110	plate, 12½" chop . . . . $85 – 95
bowl, 10" salad . . . . $50 – 60	plate, 10" . . . . $30 – 40
bowl, 7½" salad . . . . $35 – 45	plate, 9" . . . . $25 – 30
bowl, 10" oval . . . . $45 – 50	plate, 8" . . . . $20 – 25
butter chip . . . . $12 – 15	plate, 7" . . . . $15 – 20
candle holder, #3046	plate, 6" . . . . $10 – 15
Scroll shape, each . . . . $15 – 25	salt, pepper; each . . . . $8 – 10
candle holder, #3087	saucer . . . . $6 – 7
oblong, 2" x 3", each . . . . $15 – 25	sugar . . . . $25 – 30
carafe with handle . . . . $85 – 120	teapot . . . . $95 – 130
	paper price list . . . . $40 – 50

The Floral pattern features an abstract, almost Oriental floral motif. The flowers are Blue #95 accented by Yellow outlines. French Green leaves with Walnut Brown stems and twigs complete the motif. This pattern is extremely scarce, so is quite difficult to collect.

Floral lug soup, 10" plate, sugar.

American Way #3350, Ivy Leaf, Clover, Amethyst Terra Rose

Introduced: 1940
Shape Designer: Douglas Maier
Made For: the American Way Program
Shape Style: #3350, "A"-"O"

Known Pieces:

Ivy Leaf, Clover:		*Amethyst Terra Rose, Solid-Color Seconds:*	
bowl, fruit 5", "F"	$15 – 25	bowl, fruit 5", "F"	$10 – 15
bowl, 9" salad, "H"	$75 – 90	bowl, 9" salad, "H"	$45 – 55
casserole, small, "K"	$50 – 60	casserole, small, "K"	$25 – 35
casserole, large, "L"	$80 – 95	casserole, large, "L"	$50 – 60
creamer, "J"	$25 – 30	creamer, "J"	$20 – 25
cup, "D"	$12 – 18	cup, "D"	$10 – 12
pitcher, "O"	$90 – 110	pitcher, "O"	$75 – 90
plate, 14" chop, "G"	$95 – 130	plate, 14" chop, "G"	$55 – 75
plate, 9", "A"	$40 – 55	plate, 9", "A"	$30 – 40
plate, 7½", "B"	$30 – 40	plate, 7½", "B"	$20 – 25
plate, 6", "C"	$20 – 25	plate, 6", "C"	$10 – 15
relish, 15", 5 part, "M"	$85 – 110	relish, 15", 5 part, "M"	$75 – 85
saucer, "E"	$8 – 12	saucer, "E"	$5 – 7
sugar, "I"	$30 – 35	sugar, "I"	$25 – 30
tumbler, "N"	$35 – 45	tumbler, "N"	$30 – 35

One of Stangl's most notable private label accounts was for Russel Wright's American Way merchandising system. The American Way program was a sales cooperative designed to promote American-made housewares and furnishings during the early 1940s. One of the primary selling points of this program was the fact that all the products were to be handcrafted. Stangl's hand-painted dinnerware line was well suited to this program. Stangl produced three dinnerware patterns for American Way: Clover, Ivy Leaf, and Amethyst Terra Rose.

The designs for the #3350 shapes and pattern motifs were supplied by American Way. Nearly all pieces have the number 3350 and letter designation molded into the bottom. The American Way underglaze mark was stamped on most pieces as well.

The Clover pattern was designed by Petra Cabot, a prominent American artist of the Woodstock Artists' Colony during the 1930s and 1940s. The design features pink blossoms and green leaves accented with black. The handles, knobs, and rims are sponged with blue. This pattern was glazed with pink-tinted glaze.

Ivy Leaf was designed by Euphame Mallison, also of the Woodstock Artists' Colony. The large Terra Rose Green ivy leaf motif was applied only to the plates. All other pieces were decorated with a Terra Rose Green band on the rims and glazed with Silk glaze.

Amethyst Terra Rose was brushed with a violet-colored stain instead of Stangl's usual Green, Blue, or Mauve Terra Rose stains. An American Way listing describes the Amethyst Terra Rose pattern as "an unusual peasant-like group of dinnerware in a rich amethyst glaze unevenly applied."

American Way dinnerware seconds were glazed with Colonial Blue, Silver Green, and Persian Yellow instead of the hand-painted decorations described above. Solid-color glazed #3350 seconds were sold only at the Flemington Outlet.

Because the American Way program was ended in 1942, Stangl's American Way patterns are very difficult to find. There is some collector interest in these patterns due to their rarity and Russel Wright's connection with the American Way program.

American Way: Ivy Leaf 9" plate; Clover cup, small casserole, 14" chop plate; Terra Rose Amethyst tumbler; seconds treatment pitcher, Persian Yellow.

Della-Ware Patterns

Stangl Pottery produced more private label patterns for the dinnerware distributor Fisher, Bruce & Company than any other private label account. Several of the Fisher, Bruce patterns were adaptations of European designs, but most were original Stangl creations. All of the pieces made for Fisher, Bruce were marked with the Della-Ware trademark. This trademark, featuring a painter's palette and the name Della-Ware, was designed by Martin Stangl's daughter, Martha. Della-Ware pattern names were usually stamped in conjunction with the trademark, but not always.

The #1902 dinnerware shape was used for the hand-painted Della-Ware patterns to distinguish them from Stangl's other hand-painted patterns. Stangl updated the #1902 shape line by adding rings to several shapes borrowed from other lines. Items such as the salad bowls and carafe were taken from the #2000 dinnerware line, and the lug soup shape originally belonged to the Fulper Fayence #901 pattern.

Because smaller pieces of Della-Ware were not always marked with the pattern name, the colors of the bands on the rims are listed with each pattern description. The outer color of the bands is listed first and the innermost color is last.

Adrian #3360

Introduced: 1940
Designer: Ethel Kennedy
Made For: Fisher, Bruce & Company
Rim Colors: Dark Pink, Brown, Blue
Shape Style: #1902

Known Pieces:

bowl, 5" lug soup	$20 – 25	creamer	$20 – 25
cover, 5" lug soup	$8 – 10	cup, coffee	$10 – 15
bowl, rim soup	$20 – 25	cup, tea	$10 – 15
bowl, 10" salad	$80 – 90	plate, 14½" chop	$90 – 110
bowl, 7½" salad	$40 – 50	plate, 12½" chop	$60 – 75
carafe with handle	$90 – 130	plate, 10"	$30 – 40

plate, 9" . . . . $25 – 30	saucer, soup. $10 – 15
plate, 8" . . . . $20 – 25	saucer . . . . $7 – 8
plate, 6" . . . . $15 – 20	sugar . . . . $30 – 35
salt, pepper; each . . . . $10 – 12	teapot. . . . . $110 – 145

The Adrian motif features a large red apple with French Green leaves on a white, pink, brown, and blue plaid background. The apple motif was painted Pink #193 and over-brushed with darker Pink #160 creating the effect of a convincing red apple. This pattern was inspired by a similar dinnerware motif of Italian derivation.

Riviera #3361

Introduced: 1940
Made For: Fisher, Bruce & Company
Rim Colors: Dark Blue, Light Blue, Dark Blue, Light Blue
Shape Style: #1902

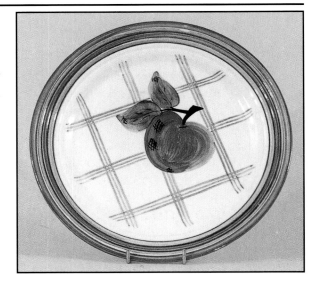

Adrian 10" plate.

Known Pieces:

bowl, 5" lug soup . . . . $25 – 30	plate, 12½" chop . . . . $80 – 95
cover, 5" lug soup. . . . . $10 – 15	plate, 10" . . . . $50 – 60
bowl, rim soup . . . . $25 – 30	plate, 9" . . . . $40 – 50
bowl, 10" salad . . . . $95 – 110	plate, 8" . . . . $20 – 30
bowl, 7½" salad. . . . . $60 – 70	plate, 6" . . . . $20 – 25
carafe with handle . . . . $130 – 155	salt, pepper; each . . . . $12 – 15
creamer . . . . $20 – 25	saucer, soup. $12 – 18
cup, coffee. $12 – 15	saucer . . . . $8 – 10
cup, tea . . . . $12 – 15	sugar . . . . $30 – 40
plate, 14½" chop . . . . $120 – 145	teapot. . . . . $145 – 165

The Riviera pattern featured a sleek sailboat in Light Blue and Blue #95 on a bright white background. This spirited pattern with simple, uncluttered lines was actively produced for only a short time.

Riviera 8" plate, 10" plate, cup.

Granada #3362

Introduced: 1940
Made For: Fisher, Bruce & Company
Rim Colors: French Green, Blue
Shape Style: #1902

Known Pieces:

bowl, 5" lug soup . . . . $15 – 20	plate, 12½" chop . . . . $70 – 80
cover, 5" lug soup. . . . . $10 – 12	plate, 10" . . . . $30 – 40
bowl, rim soup . . . . $20 – 25	plate, 9" . . . . $25 – 30
bowl, 10" salad . . . . $75 – 90	plate, 8" . . . . $20 – 25
bowl, 7½" salad. . . . . $50 – 60	plate, 6" . . . . $15 – 20
carafe with handle . . . . $95 – 135	salt, pepper; each . . . . $10 – 12
creamer . . . . $20 – 25	saucer, soup. . . . . $10 – 15
cup, coffee. $10 – 15	saucer . . . . $7 – 8
cup, tea . . . . $10 – 15	sugar . . . . $30 – 35
plate, 14½" chop . . . . $80 – 110	teapot. . . . . $110 – 140

The bold Granada pattern was decorated with stylized foliage resembling the Mexican Agave plant. The warm pink and yellow leaves are in sharp contrast to the cool blue and green bands encircling the rim. Granada is one of the more difficult Della-Ware patterns to locate.

Granada #3362 12½" chop plate.

Bonita #3363

Introduced: 1940
Designer: Ethel Kennedy
Made For: Fisher, Bruce & Company
Glaze: Yellow-Tinted
Rim Colors: Blue, Yellow, Pink
Shape Style: #1902

Known Pieces:

bowl, 5" lug soup	$20 – 25	plate, 12½" chop	$70 – 80
cover, 5" lug soup	$10 – 12	plate, 10"	$30 – 40
bowl, rim soup	$20 – 25	plate, 9"	$25 – 30
bowl, 10" salad	$80 – 95	plate, 8"	$20 – 25
bowl, 7½" salad	$45 – 55	plate, 6"	$12 – 15
carafe with handle	$90 – 125	salt, pepper; each	$10 – 12
creamer	$20 – 25	saucer, soup	$10 – 15
cup, coffee	$10 – 15	saucer	$7 – 8
cup, tea	$10 – 15	sugar	$30 – 35
plate, 14½" chop	$80 – 100	teapot	$110 – 135

Bonita is very similar to Cosmos #3339 in design and color. The two blossoms on the Bonita pattern are Light Blue, Blue #95, and Pink #160. Both flowers have yellow centers. As with Cosmos #3339, the leaves are French Green and stems are Black. Bonita is a bright, colorful pattern that is still quite popular.

Bonita teapot, 9" plate, carafe.

Norma #3364

Introduced: 1940
Designer: Ethel Kennedy
Made For: Fisher, Bruce & Company
Glaze: Pink-Tinted
Rim Colors: Pink, Yellow, Blue, Pink
Shape Style: #1902

Known Pieces:

bowl, 5" lug soup	$15 – 20	plate, 12½" chop	$75 – 85
cover, 5" lug soup	$10 – 12	plate, 10"	$35 – 40
bowl, rim soup	$20 – 25	plate, 9"	$25 – 30
bowl, 10" salad	$80 – 95	plate, 8"	$20 – 25
bowl, 7½" salad	$60 – 70	plate, 6"	$15 – 20
carafe with handle	$95 – 135	salt, pepper; each	$10 – 15
creamer	$20 – 25	saucer, soup	$10 – 15
cup, coffee	$10 – 15	saucer	$8 – 10
cup, tea	$10 – 15	sugar	$30 – 35
plate, 14½" chop	$85 – 115	teapot	$120 – 145

The distinctive Norma pattern featured stylized Pink #193 and Yellow pears with Light Blue and French Green blossoms. The two-toned Victoria Green and Pennsylvania Dutch Green leaves are an interesting complement to the bi-colored fruit.

Norma 10" plate.

Tulip #3365

Introduced: 1940
Made For: Fisher, Bruce & Company
Glaze: Pink-Tinted
Rim Colors: Pink, Green, Yellow
Shape Style: #1902

Known Pieces:

bowl, 5" lug soup	$15 – 20	plate, 12½" chop	$70 – 85
cover, 5" lug soup	$10 – 12	plate, 10"	$30 – 40
bowl, rim soup	$20 – 25	plate, 9"	$25 – 30
bowl, 10" salad	$80 – 90	plate, 8"	$20 – 25
bowl, 7½" salad	$50 – 60	plate, 6"	$15 – 20
carafe with handle	$95 – 135	salt, pepper; each	$10 – 12
creamer	$20 – 25	saucer, soup	$10 – 15
cup, coffee	$10 – 15	saucer	$7 – 8
cup, tea	$10 – 15	sugar	$30 – 35
plate, 14½" chop	$80 – 100	teapot	$110 – 140

The Tulip #3365 motif is a group of tulip blossoms with Victoria Green leaves and stems. Each blossom was over-brushed with a darker color to give the illusion of depth. The Pink #193 blossom was over-brushed with the darker Pink #160, the Lavender with Lavender again, and the Yellow with Walnut Brown.

Tulip 9" plate.

Rialto #3366

Introduced: 1940
Designer: Ethel Kennedy
Made For: Fisher, Bruce & Company
Rim Colors: Yellow, Blue, Yellow
Shape Style: #1902

Known Pieces:

bowl, 5" lug soup . . . . $15 – 20	plate, 12½" chop . . . . $70 – 85
cover, 5" lug soup. . . . . $8 – 10	plate, 10" . . . . $30 – 40
bowl, rim soup . . . . $20 – 25	plate, 9" . . . . $20 – 30
bowl, 10" salad . . . . $75 – 85	plate, 8" . . . . $20 – 25
bowl, 7½" salad. . . . . $45 – 55	plate, 6" . . . . $15 – 20
carafe with handle . . . . $95 – 135	salt, pepper; each . . . . $10 – 12
creamer . . . . $20 – 25	saucer, soup. . . . . $10 – 15
cup, coffee. . . . . $10 – 15	saucer . . . . $7 – 8
cup, tea . . . . $10 – 15	sugar . . . . $30 – 35
plate, 14½" chop . . . . $80 – 100	teapot. . . . . $115 – 145

The Rialto pattern was decorated with the same rubber resist technique that was used to decorate Newport. After the Blue #95 background was applied, the yellow blossom and other colors were added. The two-toned Victoria Green and French Green leaves are very similar to the leaves on the Norma pattern.

Rialto creamer, salt shaker, 10" plate, lug soup.

Sandra #3367

Introduced: 1940
Made For: Fisher, Bruce & Company
Glaze: Silk Glaze
Rim Colors: Dark Blue, Green
Shape Style: #1902

Known Pieces:

bowl, 5" lug soup . . . . $15 – 20	plate, 12½" chop . . . . $65 – 75
cover, 5" lug soup . . . . $8 – 10	plate, 10" . . . . $30 – 40
bowl, rim soup . . . . $20 – 25	plate, 9" . . . . $25 – 30
bowl, 10" salad . . . . $75 – 85	plate, 8" . . . . $20 – 25
bowl, 7½" salad . . . . $45 – 55	plate, 6" . . . . $15 – 20
carafe with handle . . . . $90 – 130	salt, pepper; each . . . . $10 – 12
creamer . . . . $20 – 25	saucer, soup . . . . $10 – 15
cup, coffee . . . . $10 – 15	saucer . . . . $7 – 8
cup, tea . . . . $10 – 15	sugar . . . . $30 – 35
plate, 14½" chop . . . . $75 – 95	teapot . . . . $100 – 135

The Sandra pattern features a cluster of green cherries with Art Ware Blue outlines. The same green and Art Ware blue colors are on the raised portions of the Sandra pieces. This pattern was glazed with Silk glaze, which created a hazy, pink effect.

Sandra 10" plate, 6" plate.

"Wood Hyacinth"

Introduced: 1940
Made For: Fisher, Bruce & Company
Rim Colors: French Green, Blue
Shape Style: #1902

Known Pieces:

bowl, 5" lug soup	$20 – 25	plate, 12½" chop	$75 – 85
cover, 5" lug soup	$10 – 12	plate, 10"	$30 – 40
bowl, rim soup	$20 – 25	plate, 9"	$25 – 30
bowl, 10" salad	$80 – 95	plate, 8"	$20 – 25
bowl, 7½" salad	$45 – 55	plate, 6"	$15 – 20
carafe with handle	$90 – 130	salt, pepper; each	$10 – 12
creamer	$20 – 25	saucer, soup	$10 – 12
cup, coffee	$10 – 15	saucer	$7 – 8
cup, tea	$10 – 15	sugar	$30 – 35
plate, 14½" chop	$95 – 115	teapot	$110 – 145

The "Wood Hyacinth" dinnerware pattern features a stylized, willowy, floral motif decorated with Blue #95 and Pennsylvania Dutch Green. The rim colors are French Green with Blue #95. This pattern is not listed in Martin Stangl's personal records, so apparently it was produced for a very brief period of time.

"Wood Hyacinth" 12½" chop plate.

Terra Rose Patterns

In 1940, Stangl introduced the novel Terra Rose glaze effect. This finish was applied to several dinnerware patterns and artware lines at that time. Terra Rose dinnerware patterns were produced throughout the 1940s and into the 1950s. Terra Rose artware was very popular and remained in continual production from 1940 through the early 1960s.

Originally, Terra Rose items were white bodied. They would be lightly and irregularly sprayed with red iron oxide, then decorated with metallic stains in green, blue, or mauve. The stains were applied in bold bands and patterns and then glazed with Silk glaze. Zirconium in the Silk glaze reacted with the metallic stains to soften the color and slightly blur the designs. The presence of the sprayed red iron oxide on the surface created a tawny-pink background color. Wherever there was no red iron oxide, the Silk glaze would have a yellowish-green cast. Pieces of Green Terra Rose often have a black metallic sheen. This was caused by a heavy application of the green copper-based metallic stain reacting with glaze.

During 1943 Stangl converted all Terra Rose dinnerware production to red-colored clay. From then on it was no longer necessary to individually spray each piece of Terra Rose with red iron oxide. The red iron oxide in the red-colored clay created the same end result on the Terra Rose patterns.

Dinnerware swirled with Terra Rose Green was used as a seconds treatment during the 1950s. In 1962, this same application of Terra Rose Green was used on the coupe shape and introduced as the Fathom Green dinnerware pattern.

Fruit #3434, Terra Rose, Floral #3504, Wreath #3505

Introduced: 1940, 1941
Glaze: Terra Rose Finish, Blue, Green, Mauve
Shape Style: #3434 Rim

Known Pieces:

bowl, covered soup	$40 – 50	plate, 11" plain	$20 – 30
bowl, relish	$30 – 35	plate, 11" decorated	$30 – 40
bowl, 11" salad	$75 – 90	plate, 10" plain	$20 – 25
candle holder, each	$20 – 25	plate, 10" decorated	$25 – 30
casserole, 8½" skillet shape	$30 – 35	plate, 8" plain	$10 – 15
casserole, 6" skillet shape	$20 – 25	plate, 8" decorated	$15 – 20
creamer	$15 – 20	plate, 6"	$10 – 12
cup	$12 – 15	relish, crescent shape	$12 – 15
mug	$35 – 45	saucer	$8 – 10
plate, 16" plain	$60 – 75	shell dish	$55 – 70
plate, 16", decorated	$85 – 115	sherbet	$30 – 35
plate, 14½" plain	$40 – 50	sugar	$15 – 25
plate, 14½" decorated	$80 – 95	warmer, square #3412	$10 – 15

The war in Europe and America's attraction to peasant-styled ceramics prompted Stangl to develop the rustic handmade #3434 dinnerware line. The primitive styling and bold decoration proved quite popular, consequently this pattern was produced throughout the 1940s.

Beginning in 1940, the #3434 rim shape was decorated with two distinctive motifs. One was the Fruit #3434 motif, the other a bold swirl of color. The fruit motif was applied only to the 16", 14½", 11", and 10" plates. All of the other pieces in this pattern were decorated simply with swirled color. In January 1941 the Floral #3504 and Wreath #3505 motifs were added. At that time, all size plates except 6" were available with all three motifs. The #3434 was used for both the Terra Rose Fruit motif and the rimmed dinnerware shape. Several of the #3434 Terra Rose shapes, particularly the covered soup bowl, were distributed by Sak's Fifth Avenue. These items were marked with Sak's Fifth Avenue underglaze marks.

Green and Mauve are the colors most often found on these Terra Rose dinnerware patterns. Terra Rose Blue seems to have been used the least. Blue decorated Terra Rose dinnerware shapes (especially plates) are somewhat rare. The #3434 mug, 16" chop plate, and relish bowl shapes were discontinued before 1941, so are also quite difficult to come by.

The #3412 warmer was available in all three Terra Rose colors and was intended to be used with any of the Terra Rose dinnerware patterns. The #3412 warmer shape was produced from 1940 until Stangl's close in 1978. Consequently, this warmer can be found in all sorts of glaze treatments, all valued approximately the same.

Terra Rose patterns: Mug, Mauve; Fruit #3434 10" plate, Green; 10" plate, Blue; 14½" chop plate, Mauve; sherbet, Green; 11" salad bowl, Mauve, covered soup bowl, Blue.

Terra Rose patterns: Wreath #3505 10" plate; Floral #3504 11" plate.

Sak's Fifth Avenue Terra Rose Serve Ware

Introduced: 1940, 1942
Made For: Sak's Fifth Avenue
Glaze: Terra Rose Finish, Blue, Green, Mauve
Shapes: #3460 – #3487
Shapes: #3640 – #3660

Known Pieces:

1940 Introductions:

#3460 bowl, 4" square . . . . $20 – 25
#3461 bowl, 6" heart . . . . $20 – 25
#3462 bowl, double 10" x 8"
    with ribbon handles . . . . $35 – 45
#3464 tray, 2 part 8½" . . . . $30 – 35
#3465 tray, 2 part 10½" . . . . $35 – 40
#3466 plate, 8" . . . . $40 – 50
#3472 relish, 3 part 16½" x 9 ¾" . . . . $45 – 55
#3473 bowl, double 10" x 9"
    with ribbon handles . . . . $40 – 50
#3476 tray, high handle
    2 part, 10½" x 6½" . . . . $45 – 55
#3477 tray, high handle
    2 part, 15½" x 7½" . . . . $60 – 75
#3478 tray, side handle
    2 part, 11" x 7" . . . . $45 – 55
#3479 tray, side handle
    2 part, 13" x 8" . . . . $50 – 60
#3480 platter, 15" x 9" . . . . $60 – 70
#3481, dish, 15" x 6" & centerpiece . . $75 – 90
#3482, cocktail dish . . . . $35 – 40
#3483, shell dish . . . . $20 – 25
#3484, vegetable dish 15" x 7½" . . . . . $35 – 45
#3485 bread basket 11½" x 7½" . . . . . $45 – 55
#3486 double shell . . . . $40 – 45
#3487 shell 10" x 10" . . . . $35 – 40

1942 Introductions:

#3640 serving dish with
    3 handles, 16" x 10" x 5" . . . . $75 – 85
#3641 hors d'oeuvres
    4 part, 4½" x 3" . . . . $30 – 40
#3642 oval pear, 11" x 9" . . . . $30 – 35
#3643 double vegetable 10" x 5½" . . . $35 – 40
#3644 ovoid cup . . . . $25 – 30
#3645 shrimp cup . . . . $40 – 50
#3646 saucer for shrimp cup . . . . $12 – 15
#3647 pitcher . . . . $70 – 85
#3648 bowl, salad 10½" x 3" . . . . $60 – 75
#3649 casserole, pie crust
    8" with cover . . . . $80 – 90
#3650 hors d'oeuvres boat,
    12" with attached celery vase . . . . $95 – 110
#3651 mug . . . . $35 – 45
#3652 hors d'oeuvres 4 part plate . . . $50 – 65
#3653 mayonnaise bowl
    for hors d'oeuvres plate . . . . $25 – 30
#3654 ladle for mayonnaise bowl . . . $30 – 35
#3655 cover for 4 part plate . . . . $25 – 30
#3656 casserole, 9½" open, fluted . . . $35 – 45
#3657 casserole, 8" open, fluted . . . . . $30 – 40
#3658 casserole, 6¼" open, fluted . . . $25 – 30
#3659 punch bowl, 14" x 7¾" . . . . . $110 – 150
#3660 ladle, punch bowl . . . . $45 – 60

    The exclusive Sak's Fifth Avenue serve ware line was introduced as two groups during 1940 and 1942. This line was completely handmade with many of the shapes featuring hand-formed flowers or handles. Because this was a specialty line and the Sak's Fifth Avenue department store maintained limited distribution, very few of these Sak's Fifth Avenue pieces were produced. These pieces were usually marked "SAKS 5TH AVE," with the shape number either scratched into, or painted on the bottom. Sometimes the Stangl Terra Rose rubber-stamp mark accompanied the Sak's Fifth Avenue markings.

above: Sak's Fifth Avenue #3462 double bowl;
#3466 8" plate; #3460 square bowl.

left: Sak's Fifth Avenue #3645 shrimp cup.

below: Sak's Fifth Avenue #3650 hors d'oeuvres boat
with attached celery vase.

Pie Crust #3506, Terra Rose

Introduced: 1941
Made For: Carole Stupell Ltd.
Glaze: Terra Rose Finish: Blue, Green, Mauve
Bright Colors: Blue, Pink, Green, Yellow
Shape Style: #3506 Pie Crust

Known Pieces:

bowl, 5" fruit	$15 – 20
bowl, 5½" soup plain	$20 – 25
with berry & leaf	$25 – 30
with loop handle	$20 – 25
bowl, 10" salad	$60 – 75
bowl, 9" salad	$50 – 60
bowl, 8" salad	$35 – 45
casserole, handled, 8" open	$30 – 40
casserole, handle 5" open	$20 – 25
creamer	$20 – 25
cup	$10 – 15
cup, pedestal	$20 – 25
mug	$40 – 50
plate, 14" chop	$70 – 85
plate, 12" chop	$60 – 75
plate, 11"	$30 – 40
plate, 10"	$25 – 30
plate, 8"	$20 – 25
plate, 6"	$15 – 20
relish	$25 – 30
saucer	$7 – 9
sherbet	$35 – 40
sugar, open	$20 – 25

During the early 1940s, quaint handcrafted styles were very much in vogue. Capitalizing on this, Stangl introduced the handmade #3506 Pie Crust dinnerware line. These shapes were all hand thrown, but more refined than the #3434 shapes. During the early 1940s, #3506 Pie Crust dinnerware was exclusively distributed by Carole Stupell Ltd.

By 1946, molds were made for the #3506 Pie Crust shapes, enabling these items to be slip cast. The slip-cast pieces are heavier than the hand-thrown pieces and have the number 3506 molded into the bases of the hollow ware. The hand-thrown pieces are marked with the Terra Rose or Carole Stupell rubber-stamp marks.

The 5½" soup bowl was produced plain and with two different hand-applied decorations. One was a loop handle; the other a hand-formed berry and leaf, with the berry usually glazed in Persian Yellow. The large and small casseroles were the same bowls as the 8" salad and 5" fruit but with applied handles.

The #3506 Pie Crust dinnerware shapes were produced in the three Terra Rose colors until the late 1940s. During 1941 and 1942, these shapes were decorated with swirls of bright underglaze colors for Carole Stupell. The underglaze colors used were French Green, Blue #95, Yellow, and Pink #193. The brightly colored Pie Crust was distributed on a limited basis and is exceptionally uncommon.

Terra Rose Pie Crust #3506 5" open casserole, 8" plate, soup bowl, 11" plate, sherbet, cup & saucer, 8" plate, 6" plate, creamer.

Olivia, Orlando, Paoli #3507

Introduced: 1941
Made For: Fisher, Bruce & Company
Glaze: Terra Rose Finish, Blue, Green, Mauve
Shape Style: #1902

Known Pieces:

bowl, 5" lug soup . . . . $15 – 20	plate, 12½" chop . . . . $75 – 85
cover, 5" lug soup. . . . . $10 – 12	plate, 10" . . . . $30 – 35
bowl, rim soup . . . . $20 – 25	plate, 9" . . . . $25 – 30
bowl, 10" salad . . . . $50 – 65	plate, 8" . . . . $20 – 25
bowl, 7½" salad. . . . . $35 – 45	plate, 6" . . . . $10 – 15
creamer . . . . $20 – 25	salt, pepper; each . . . . $10 – 12
cup, coffee. $10 – 15	saucer, soup. $10 – 15
cup, tea . . . . $10 – 15	saucer . . . . $7 – 8
plate, 14½" chop . . . . $80 – 95	sugar . . . . $25 – 30
	teapot. . . . . $95 – 135

Olivia, Orlando, and Paoli all use the same motif, each with a different Terra Rose color. Olivia is decorated with Terra Rose Green, Orlando, Terra Rose Mauve, and Paoli with Terra Rose Blue. The motif consists of two boldly painted plums with leaves, surrounded by several dots of color and a wide colored rim. The bands, handles, and knobs on some of the smaller pieces were painted with yellow underglaze color on Olivia and green underglaze color on Paoli.

These patterns were made until the mid-1940s, and can be found on both white and red bodies. All three are rather uncommon but Paoli is the most difficult to find.

Olivia 10" plate, Orlando 12½" chop plate, Olivia covered soup,
Paoli 10" plate, Olivia 6" plate.

Ross Ware Dinnerware #3508

Introduced: 1941
Glaze: Terra Rose Finish, Blue,
  Green, Mauve
Shape Style: #3508

Ross Ware salt & pepper shakers, Terra Rose Green.

Known Pieces:
salt, pepper; each . . . . $20 – 25

According to Martin Stangl's records, this pattern was a complete dinnerware set, but no specific pieces are listed. At present there have been no other records found pertaining to the Ross Ware line. The salt and pepper shakers turn up occasionally and are nearly always clearly marked with the in-mold words "ROSS WARE."

Arbor, #1940

Introduced: 1941
Made For: Frederik Lunning, Inc.
Glaze: Terra Rose Finish, Green, Mauve, Blue
Shape Style: #1940 Raised Fruit

Known Pieces:

bowl, 9" salad . . . . $65 – 80	plate, 14" chop . . . . $70 – 90
	plate, 9" . . . . $20 – 30

The Arbor pattern was a re-introduction of the #1940 Raised Fruit shapes decorated with Terra Rose colors. The raised motifs were usually painted with bold strokes of color under the Silk glaze. The jobber Frederik Lunning Inc. was the exclusive distributor for this Terra Rose pattern. A 1943 Lunning flyer described this pattern as "softly muted mauve earthenware decorated with a striking, raised fruit design. Also available with the design in blue on a blue-gray background."

During the late 1940s, the Arbor pattern was produced with white engobe over the red body and the motifs outlined with carving. A small amount of color was applied to the motifs and the pieces glazed with clear glaze. Pieces of Arbor with carved decoration are less common than earlier pieces with the bold Terra Rose colors under Silk glaze.

Arbor 9" plate, Terra Rose Mauve; 9" plate with carved decoration; 9" salad bowl, Terra Rose Mauve.

Blue Mist #1388, Green Mist #1388, Mauve Mist #1388

Introduced: 1941
Made For: Frederik Lunning, Inc.
Glaze: Terra Rose Finish, Blue, Green, Mauve
Shape Style: #1388

Known Pieces:

bowl, 5" lug soup	$15 – 20	plate, 10"	$25 – 35
cover, 5" lug soup	$12 – 15	plate, 9"	$20 – 25
cover, with rose knob	$15 – 20	plate, 8"	$15 – 20
bowl, 10", salad, extra deep	$80 – 110	plate, 6"	$12 – 15
bowl, 10", salad	$70 – 80	salt, pepper; each	$10 – 15
bowl, 8" vegetable	$40 – 50	saucer	$5 – 7
creamer	$15 – 20	sugar	$20 – 25
cup	$10 – 15	sugar with rose knob	$30 – 35
plate, 14" chop	$70 – 85	teapot	$80 – 110
plate, 12" chop	$50 – 60	teapot with rose knob	$110 – 135

In 1941, a small portion of the extensive #1388 line was re-introduced with the Terra Rose colors Blue, Green, and Mauve for Frederik Lunning. These patterns were named Blue Mist, Green Mist, and Mauve Mist respectively. When the Terra Rose Mist pattern was first produced, the handles on the sugar and lug soup covers were hand-formed rosebuds with leaves. These were gradually made smaller until they were eventually replaced with a molded stem and leaf handle similar to that used on the #3434 covered soup. Although not common, #1388 shaped Blue Mist, Green Mist, and Mauve Mist patterns were produced throughout the 1940s.

Green Mist and Blue Mist 10" plate, cup & saucer, covered soup, salt & pepper, 6" plate.

Lunning Fruit

*Lunning Fruit
14½" chop plate.*

Introduced: 1941
Made For: Frederik Lunning, Inc.
Glaze: Satin White
Shape Style: #2000

Known Pieces:

bowl, fruit	$10 – 15
bowl, lug soup	$12 – 15
bowl, 12" salad	$70 – 80
bowl, 10" salad	$50 – 60
bowl, 7½" salad	$30 – 40
bowl, 10" oval	$35 – 45
cup	$12 – 15
plate, 14½" chop	$80 – 95
plate, 12½" chop	$60 – 75
plate, 10"	$25 – 35
plate, 9"	$20 – 25
plate, 8"	$15 – 20
plate, 6"	$12 – 15
saucer	$6 – 7
teapot	$110 – 135

This simple blue and white pattern was produced for Lunning in very limited quantities. The motif is the same as #3434 Fruit but is on the #2000 coupe shape instead of the #3434 rim shape. The Art Ware Blue motif complements the white coupe shape of these pieces.

Cabbage Leaf #1800, Terra Rose

Introduced: 1941
Made For: Fisher, Bruce & Company
Glaze: Terra Rose Finish, Green, Mauve, Blue
Shape Style: #1800

Known Pieces:

*Terra Rose Cabbage Leaf double relish,
10" plate, creamer.*

bowl, 10" salad	$60 – 75
bowl, 9" salad	$40 – 50
bowl, 6"	$20 – 25
cake stand, 10"	$25 – 35
creamer	$15 – 20
cup	$10 – 15
plate, 14" chop	$65 – 80
plate, 10"	$25 – 30
plate, 9"	$20 – 25
plate, 8"	$15 – 20
plate, 6"	$10 – 12
relish, single	$15 – 20
relish, double	$15 – 20
relish, triple, round	$25 – 35
saucer	$6 – 7
sugar	$20 – 25
teapot	$95 – 135

The #1800 Cabbage Leaf shape was produced with Terra Rose colors throughout the 1940s. The double and triple relish dishes seem to be the pieces most often found with the Terra Rose finish. Made for Fisher, Bruce, this pattern was usually marked with the Della-Ware backstamp.

Pennsylvania Traditional Dower Chest, Dowry Chest

Introduced: 1941
Designer: Lee Ehrlich Below
Made For: Fisher, Bruce & Company
Rim Colors: Dark Blue, Light Blue, Brown, Green
Shape Style: #1902

Known Pieces:

bowl, 5" lug soup . . . . $20 – 25	plate, 12½" chop . . . . $85 – 100
cover, 5" lug soup . . . . $12 – 15	plate, 10" . . . . $30 – 40
bowl, rim soup . . . . $25 – 30	plate, 9" . . . . $25 – 35
bowl, 10" salad . . . . $85 – 110	plate, 8" . . . . $20 – 25
bowl, 7½" salad . . . . $50 – 60	plate, 6" . . . . $15 – 20
creamer . . . . $20 – 25	salt, pepper; each . . . . $10 – 15
cup, coffee . . . . $12 – 15	saucer, soup . . . . $10 – 15
cup, tea . . . . $12 – 15	saucer . . . . $8 – 10
plate, 14½" chop . . . . $110 – 135	sugar . . . . $30 – 35
	teapot . . . . $125 – 155

Lee Below adapted this Pennsylvania Traditional pattern from an Early American Pennsylvania Dutch design. The stylized motif features a blue heart with blue tulips, green stems, and brown tendrils. The only other Stangl dinnerware pattern to bear the Pennsylvania Traditional designation was Quaint Tree, also designed by Lee Below.

This pattern can be found marked either Dowry Chest or Dower Chest. Pieces with the Dower Chest mark seem to be the most plentiful. Very little of this charming pattern was produced.

Dower Chest sugar, 9" plate, tea cup & saucer.

Pennsylvania Traditional Quaint Tree

Introduced: 1941
Designer: Lee Ehrlich Below
Made For: Fisher, Bruce & Company
Rim Colors: Light Blue, Green, Yellow
Shape Style: #1902

Known Pieces:

bowl, 5" lug soup . . . . $25 – 30	plate, 12½" chop . . . . $90 – 110
cover, 5" lug soup. . . . . $12 – 15	plate, 10" . . . . $40 – 50
bowl, rim soup . . . . $25 – 35	plate, 9" . . . . $35 – 40
bowl, 10" salad . . . . $80 – 115	plate, 8" . . . . $25 – 30
bowl, 7½" salad. . . . . $60 – 75	plate, 6" . . . . $20 – 25
creamer . . . . $25 – 30	salt, pepper; each . . . . $12 – 15
cup, coffee. $12 – 18	saucer, soup. $12 – 18
cup, tea . . . . $12 – 18	saucer . . . . $10 – 12
plate, 14½" chop . . . . $110 – 135	sugar . . . . $35 – 45
	teapot. . . . . $135 – 165

The two Pennsylvania Traditional patterns, Dower Chest and Quaint Tree represent Stangl's first use of the Pennsylvania Dutch style of decoration for dinnerware patterns. Both patterns were developed by freelance designer Lee Ehrlich Below. Lee Below was married to Henry Below, Stangl's manager from 1929 through 1949 and founder of Pennsbury Pottery Company in 1950.

The bird motif on the Quaint Tree pattern is typical of Early American Pennsylvania Dutch stylized decorations. The Yellow and Pink #160 bird is perched in a potted Pennsylvania Dutch Green tree.

Quaint Tree saucer, tea cup, 10" plate.

Terra Rose Serve Ware Shapes #3543 – #3587

Introduced: 1941
Glaze: Terra Rose Finish, Green, Mauve, Blue

Known Pieces:

#3543 tray, apple 16½" x 16" . . . . $60 – 70	#3550 bowl, apple double 12" . . . . . . $30 – 35
#3544 tray, pear 18" x 13" . . . . $60 – 75	#3551 bowl, pear double 11" . . . . $30 – 35
#3545 tray, fish 18" x 13½" . . . . $95 – 135	#3552 bowl, apple single 6½" . . . . $15 – 20
#3546 tray, small apple 12½" x 12" . . $40 – 50	#3553 bowl, pear single 8" . . . . $15 – 20
#3547 tray, small pear 14" x 10½" . . . $45 – 55	#3564 plate, apple 8" . . . . $20 – 30
#3548 tray, small fish 14" x 11¼" . . . . $80 – 95	#3565 bowl, apple 9" . . . . $60 – 75
	#3587 relish, apple triple . . . . $40 – 50

This group of Terra Rose serving pieces possessed a rough-cast appearance and featured hand-formed details such as leaf and fruit shaped handles. The quaint and primitive styling of this line was intended to complement the #3434 Terra Rose dinnerware line. The apple shaped #3543 tray and #3565 salad bowl were sold with six #3564 8" plates as an "apple shaped" salad set.

Terra Rose Serve Ware #3546 small apple tray, #3543 large apple tray, #3587 apple triple relish.

Della-Ware Terra Rose Serve Ware Shapes #3570 – #3579

Introduced: 1941
Made For: Fisher, Bruce & Company
Glaze: Terra Rose Finish, Green, Mauve, Blue

Known Pieces:

#3570 relish, leaf 4 part 12¾" x 9¼" . . . . $45 – 55
#3571 relish, leaf 3 part 12" x 12" . . . . $35 – 45
#3573 relish, shell 3 part 11¼" . . . . $40 – 50
#3574 tray, 2 handles 13½" x 8" . . . . $50 – 60
#3575 tray, round 12" with applied pear . . . . . . $40 – 50
#3576 bowl, scalloped 14" x 2½" . . . . $55 – 65
#3577 bowl, scalloped 12" x 2½" . . . . $50 – 60
#3578 relish, with apple 11½" x 6½" . . . . $40 – 50
#3579 relish, with pear 13½" x 11" . . . . $50 – 60

Della-Ware Serve Ware #3579 relish w/pear.

These Della-Ware Terra Rose serving pieces are sleek in appearance, with classically styled fluting and scallops. Several of the pieces have applied apple or pear ornaments. The ornaments were slip cast, as opposed to the hand-formed ornaments found on other Terra Rose serve ware lines.

Verna #3600

Introduced: 1941
Designer: Kay Hackett
Made For: Fisher, Bruce & Company
Shape Style: #3600 Fluted

Known Pieces:

bowl, cereal	$20 – 25	plate, 14" chop	$110 – 145
bowl, fruit	$20 – 25	plate, 12" chop	$90 – 110
bowl, lug soup	$25 – 30	plate, 10"	$40 – 50
bowl, 11" salad	$85 – 110	plate, 9"	$35 – 45
bowl, 10" salad	$80 – 90	plate, 8"	$20 – 30
bowl, 8" vegetable	$50 – 60	plate, 6"	$15 – 20
creamer	$25 – 30	salt, pepper; each	$12 – 15
cup	$15 – 20	saucer	$10 – 12
egg cup	$20 – 25	sugar	$30 – 35
		teapot	$145 – 170

The number "3600" was used to designate the Verna dinnerware pattern as well as the newly-designed fluted dinnerware shape. Kay Hackett designed the Verna motif as a spray of stylized calendulas or "pot marigolds." The blossoms are bright Orange and Tan with Pennsylvania Dutch Green leaves. This engaging pattern was produced in very limited quantities and is very difficult to collect. Because shape #3600 had no salt and pepper shakers, shape #2000 shakers were decorated with Orange and Tan bands to match the Verna motif.

Verna fruit bowl, lug soup, 12" chop plate, 8" plate.

Kay Hackett's Marigold

Introduced: 1941
Designer: Kay Hackett
Shape Style: #2000

Known Pieces:

bowl, fruit	$45 – 55
bowl, lug soup	$45 – 55
bowl, 11" salad	$160 – 185
bowl, 10" salad	$125 – 150
bowl, 8" vegetable	$100 – 125
carafe	$200 – 250
creamer	$60 – 75
cup	$45 – 55
plate, 14" chop	$250 – 300
plate, 12" chop	$250 – 300
plate, 10"	$100 – 125
plate, 8"	$80 – 100
plate, 6"	$60 – 75
platter, 14" oval	$250 – 300
platter, 12" oval	$200 – 250
salt, pepper; each	$35 – 50
saucer	$20 – 25
sugar	$60 – 75
teapot	$300 – 350

Kay Hackett adapted her marigold motif to the #2000 shape as a dinner set for her mother. She accomplished this by paying Stangl 50% off and 50% off again retail for the materials and firing and by doing all the decorating on her own time. The Verna and Marigold patterns differ in that Marigold is a larger motif and the leaves are French Green instead of the Pennsylvania Dutch Green used on Verna. Kay Hackett signed the back of each piece of Marigold with her stylized "kay" signature within a circle. Due to the popularity of Kay Hackett herself, her Marigold pieces are in high demand.

Kay Hackett's Marigold 10" plate, salt & pepper, 12" oval platter.

1940s HAND-CARVED, HAND-PAINTED DINNERWARE

In 1942, Stangl introduced the now-famous "Hand-Carved, Hand-Painted" line of dinnerware. This Pennsylvania Dutch styled dinnerware was originally only a small portion of Stangl's overall dinnerware output. By the late 1940s, "Hand-Carved, Hand-Painted" had become the only type of dinnerware produced by Stangl Pottery.

During the early 1940s, Stangl's red-bodied, hand-carved patterns were molded with a rough texture on the faces of the plates and bowls. The white covering of engobe was brushed on very thinly, allowing much of the red body to show through. This gave the effect of antique, hand-made earthenware, similar to the original Pennsylvania Dutch redware. Dinnerware of this type was marked Terra Rose and, when finished correctly, was very artistic.

Many Stangl customers did not appreciate the thinly brushed Terra Rose engobe. They claimed that the dishes looked dirty. Therefore, by the mid-1940s, all the pieces were made smooth and engobe was brushed on more heavily so less of the red clay body was evident. The background color of the pieces with heavier engobe is a brighter white, but the characteristic swirl is still evident.

Single Bird #3632, Yellow Canary

Introduced: 1942
Designer: Kay Hackett
Made For: Frederik Lunning, Inc.
Shape Style: #3434 Rim

Single Bird 8" plate, salt shaker, 10" plate, egg cup.

Known Pieces:

bowl, fruit	$15 – 20
bowl, rim soup	$25 – 30
bowl, lug soup	$20 – 25
bowl, 12" salad #3608	$110 – 145
bowl, 10" salad	$70 – 80
bowl, 8" vegetable	$35 – 40
casserole, 8" covered	$80 – 90
casserole, 6" covered	$25 – 30
cigarette box	$100 – 125
coaster/ashtray	$45 – 55
creamer	$20 – 25
cup	$12 – 15
cup, mother or father	$35 – 45
egg cup	$15 – 20
pitcher, 2 quart	$85 – 110
pitcher, 1 quart	$60 – 75
pitcher, 1 pint	$30 – 40
pitcher, ½ pint	$25 – 30
plate, 14½" chop	$95 – 115
plate, 12½" chop	$65 – 75
plate, 11"	$35 – 45

plate, 10"	$25 – 35
plate, 9"	$20 – 25
plate, 8"	$15 – 20
plate, 6"	$10 – 15
relish dish	$25 – 35
salt, pepper; each	$10 – 15
saucer	$10 – 12
saucer, mother or father	$15 – 20
sherbet	$45 – 55
sugar	$20 – 25
teapot	$95 – 120

The jobber Frederik Lunning, Inc., was the exclusive distributor for Stangl's Single Bird dinnerware pattern. Lunning called this pattern "Yellow Canary," while Stangl always referred to it as "Single Bird." A Lunning advertising flyer from 1943 states "Yellow Canary, colorful peasant-type earthenware bordered in deep green and decorated with a cheerful Pennsylvania Dutch design in green and yellow on a soft, café-au-lait background."

Single Bird was Stangl's first hand-carved dinnerware pattern. The motif was based on a Pennsylvania Dutch design that featured a Walnut Brown and Orange bird on a branch with a wide Pennsylvania Dutch Green rim. Single Bird was widely distributed, and was in active production until the mid-1950s. Single Bird pieces made after Lunning's contract ended in 1953 were marked Stangl instead of Lunning. Some of these Stangl Single Bird pieces were on the #3774 Coupe shape instead of the original #3434 rim shape.

As per Lunning's contract, Lunning seconds were to have the Lunning trademark obliterated in some way. Usually, Stangl would cover the Lunning mark with black glaze and fire those pieces again. Sometimes, however, the Lunning mark was simply over-stamped with the Stangl "second" underglaze mark before clear glaze was applied.

During the 1940s, the #3608 12" salad bowl was exclusive to Lunning patterns. Stangl-brand dinnerware patterns on the #3434 rim shape were supplied with a newly designed #3434 11" salad bowl.

Double Bird #3633, Distlefink

Introduced: 1942
Designer: Kay Hackett
Made For: Frederik Lunning, Inc.
Shape Style: #3434 Rim

Known Pieces:

bowl, 12" salad #3608	$130 – 165
bowl, 10" salad	$85 – 110
cigarette box	$115 – 145
coaster/ashtray	$55 – 65
creamer	$25 – 30
cup	$15 – 20
plate, 14½" chop	$125 – 145
plate, 12½" chop	$95 – 130
plate, 10"	$55 – 65
plate, 8"	$25 – 35
plate, 6"	$20 – 25
saucer	$10 – 12
sherbet	$60 – 75
sugar	$30 – 35
teapot	$140 – 165

Named "Distlefink" by Lunning, the Double Bird pattern features a very traditional Pennsylvania Dutch motif of two stylized birds flanking a heart and tulip. The colors were Pink #160, Pennsylvania Dutch Green, Victoria Green, and Walnut Brown. Both the Single Bird and Double Bird motifs were originally developed as cigarette sets, but were quickly expanded to dinnerware shapes. Double Bird, however, was produced in fairly limited quantities, making this a very difficult pattern to find.

Double Bird teapot with heavily brushed engobe of the mid-1940s, 14½" chop plate showing the original rough texture and thinly brushed engobe of Stangl's early hand-carved dinnerware, 8" plate.

Yellow Tulip #3637

Introduced: 1942
Designer: Kay Hackett
Shape Style: #3434 Rim

Known Pieces:

bean pot/cookie jar . . . . $45 – 50	gravy underplate. . . . . $10 – 12
bowl, cereal. . . . . $20 – 25	mug, 2 cup. . . . . $30 – 35
bowl, fruit . . . . $12 – 15	pitcher, 2 quart . . . . $80 – 90
bowl, coupe soup . . . . $20 – 25	pitcher, 1 quart . . . . $65 – 75
bowl, lug soup. . . . . $15 – 20	pitcher, 1 pint . . . . $30 – 40
bowl, 11" salad . . . . $70 – 80	pitcher, ½ pint. . . . . $20 – 25
bowl, 10" salad . . . . $50 – 60	pitcher, 6 ounce . . . . $25 – 30
bowl, 8" vegetable. . . . . $30 – 35	plate, 14½" chop . . . . $75 – 85
bowl, 10" divided round. . . . . $50 – 65	plate, 12½" chop . . . . $65 – 75
bowl, oval divided vegetable . . . . . . $35 – 45	plate, 11" . . . . $25 – 30
butter dish. . . . . $35 – 40	plate, 10" . . . . $20 – 25
casserole, 8" covered. . . . . $75 – 85	plate, 9" . . . . $20 – 25
casserole, 6" covered. . . . . $20 – 25	plate, 8" . . . . $10 – 15
casserole, 8" skillet shape. . . . . $30 – 35	plate, 6" . . . . $8 – 10
casserole, 6" skillet shape. . . . . $20 – 25	platter, 13¾" casual. . . . . $70 – 80
cigarette box . . . . $50 – 60	relish dish . . . . $20 – 25
coaster/ashtray . . . . $15 – 20	salt, pepper; each . . . . $6 – 8
coffee pot, 8 cup . . . . $80 – 110	saucer . . . . $6 – 7
coffee pot, individual . . . . $70 – 80	saucer, mother or father . . . . $12 – 15
creamer . . . . $15 – 20	sherbet. . . . . $30 – 35
creamer, individual. . . . . $20 – 25	sugar . . . . $20 – 25
cup. . . . . $10 – 12	sugar, individual. . . . . $20 – 25
cup, Mother or Father. . . . . $30 – 40	teapot. . . . . $85 – 95
egg cup . . . . $15 – 20	tidbit, 10". . . . . $10 – 15
gravy boat . . . . $20 – 25	paper price list . . . . $15 – 20

The stylized blossoms of the Tulip motif were painted Orange and Yellow on the Yellow Tulip pattern and Blue #95 on Blue Tulip. The leaves and accents were Victoria Green and Grass Green on both patterns. Whether blue or yellow, Stangl usually referred to both patterns as "Tulip #3637." Some 1960s price sheets list Blue Tulip and Yellow Tulip as separate patterns. The names Blue Tulip and Yellow Tulip are in common usage at this time.

In advertising and price lists from the early 1940s, Yellow Tulip was referred to as "Stangl Early Pennsylvania Pottery Dinnerware." This was one of Stangl's most popular Pennsylvania Dutch styled dinnerware patterns during the 1940s. The Yellow Tulip pattern continued to sell well even after it became inactive in 1949. Consequently, it was re-introduced and produced periodically throughout the 1950s and 1960s. Newer shapes that had not been originally produced with the Yellow Tulip motif were added during the later production runs. For this reason, shapes introduced during the 1950s, such as the coffee pot, oval divided vegetable, and gravy boat are rather uncommon.

Yellow Tulip produced during the early 1960s was sometimes marked "Made exclusively for Bloomingdale's by Stangl Pottery" or "Made exclusively for Marshall Field by Stangl Pottery." These marks may add a few dollars to the value for interest's sake as they are somewhat uncommon.

Yellow Tulip 10" plate, gravy & underplate, 12½" chop plate, sugar, creamer, 9" plate, coaster/ashtray,

Blue Tulip #3637

Introduced: 1942
Designer: Kay Hackett
Made For: Marshall Field & Company
Shape Style: #3434 Rim

Known Pieces:

bean pot/cookie jar	$55 – 65
bowl, cereal	$20 – 25
bowl, fruit	$15 – 20
bowl, coupe soup	$30 – 35
bowl, lug soup	$20 – 25
bowl, 11" salad	$90 – 125
bowl, 10" salad	$60 – 75
bowl, 8" vegetable	$40 – 50
bowl, 10" divided round	$65 – 75
bowl, oval divided vegetable	$35 – 45
butter dish	$40 – 50
casserole, 8" covered	$80 – 95
casserole, 6" covered	$30 – 35
casserole, 8" skillet shape	$30 – 40
casserole, 6" skillet shape	$25 – 30
cigarette box	$85 – 110
coaster/ashtray	$25 – 35
coffee pot, 8 cup	$115 – 135
coffee pot, individual	$95 – 110
creamer	$20 – 25
creamer, individual	$25 – 30
cup	$12 – 15
cup, Mother or Father	$50 – 60
egg cup	$20 – 25
gravy boat	$25 – 30
gravy underplate	$15 – 20
mug, 2 cup	$40 – 50
pitcher, 2 quart	$95 – 110
pitcher, 1 quart	$75 – 85
pitcher, 1 pint	$45 – 55
pitcher, ½ pint	$25 – 35
pitcher, 6 ounce	$30 – 35
plate, 14½" chop	$85 – 110
plate, 12½" chop	$75 – 85
plate, 11"	$35 – 40
plate, 10"	$25 – 30
plate, 9"	$20 – 25
plate, 8"	$15 – 20
plate, 6"	$10 – 15
platter, 13¾" casual	$80 – 100
relish dish	$25 – 35
salt, pepper; each	$12 – 15
saucer	$8 – 10
saucer, mother or father	$15 – 18
sherbet	$45 – 50
sugar	$20 – 25
sugar, individual	$25 – 30
teapot	$95 – 115
tidbit, 10"	$12 – 15

During the 1940s, the Blue Tulip pattern was sold exclusively through Marshall Field's department store in Chicago, whereas Yellow Tulip was sold through hundreds of retail stores across the country. Consequently, considerably less Blue Tulip was produced. Blue Tulip was also sold at the Flemington Outlet, but not in quantities near that of Yellow Tulip. Stangl's Blue Tulip pattern is more avidly collected at this time than Yellow Tulip.

During the early 1960s, Blue Tulip was "made exclusively" for both Bloomingdale's in New York and Marshall Field in Chicago. Such pieces are usually marked with one of the "Made exclusively for…" underglaze stamps and are somewhat desirable.

Blue Tulip 8 cup coffee pot, 12½" chop plate, cup & saucer, 10" plate, individual coffee pot.

Cosmos #3667, Dogwood #3668, Tulip #3669, Morning Glory #3670

Introduced: 1942
Designer: August Jacob
Made For: Fisher, Bruce & Company

Known Pieces:

Dogwood:		Cosmos, Tulip, Morning Glory:	
bowl, 10" salad	$75 – 85	bowl, 10" salad	$85 – 110
creamer	$20 – 25	creamer	$25 – 30
cup	$12 – 15	cup	$15 – 18
plate, 14" chop	$85 – 95	plate, 14" chop	$110 – 145
plate, 10"	$25 – 30	plate, 10"	$35 – 45
plate, 8"	$20 – 25	plate, 8"	$25 – 30
plate, 6"	$10 – 15	plate, 6"	$15 – 20
saucer	$7 – 8	saucer	$10 – 12
sugar	$20 – 25	sugar	$30 – 35

August Jacob, designer of Stangl's popular bird figurines, also created several dinnerware shapes during the early 1940s. The shapes were scalloped and featured raised floral decoration on the rims of the pieces. Four of these raised patterns were produced for Fisher, Bruce & Company during the 1940s.

On these patterns, the raised motifs were outlined with carving and decorated in natural colors. Dogwood #3668 was produced the longest and is easiest to find. Morning Glory is a bit more difficult to acquire, but it is nearly impossible to locate the Cosmos #3667 and Tulip #3669 patterns.

During the 1960s, several patterns with raised dogwood and cosmos motifs were introduced using the same molds that had been used for the Della-Ware raised patterns. The 1960s raised patterns were not carved; the decoration was simply painted over the molded design.

Morning Glory #3670 8" plate, 14½" chop plate; Dogwood #3668 creamer, cup & saucer, 10" plate.

Festival #3677, Laurita #3678, El Rosa #3679

Introduced: 1942
Designer: Kay Hackett
Made For: Fisher, Bruce & Company
Shape Style: #3434 Rim

Known Pieces:

bowl, fruit . . . . $10 – 15	pitcher, #3722 1 pint . . . . $30 – 40
bowl, lug soup . . . . $15 – 20	pitcher, #3722 ½ pint . . . . $20 – 25
bowl, fluted 14" #3576 . . . . $125 – 150	plate, 14½" chop . . . . $85 – 95
bowl, fluted 12" #3577 . . . . $85 – 110	plate, 12½" chop . . . . $65 – 75
bowl, 11" salad . . . . $75 – 85	plate, 11" . . . . $30 – 35
bowl, 10" salad . . . . $50 – 60	plate, 10" . . . . $20 – 30
bowl, 8" vegetable . . . . $30 – 40	plate, 9" . . . . $20 – 25
candy dish . . . . $45 – 55	plate, 8" . . . . $15 – 20
creamer . . . . $20 – 25	plate, 6" . . . . $8 – 12
cup . . . . $10 – 12	salt, pepper; each . . . . $8 – 12
cup, mother or father . . . . $35 – 45	saucer . . . . $8 – 10
egg cup . . . . $20 – 25	saucer, mother or father . . . . $10 – 15
pitcher, #3722 4 quart . . . . $120 – 145	sherbet . . . . $30 – 40
pitcher, #3722 2 quart . . . . $85 – 100	sugar . . . . $20 – 25
pitcher, #3722 1 quart . . . . $50 – 65	teapot . . . . $85 – 110
	tray, 12" round #3575 . . . . $110 – 135

These three patterns were adapted from European designs by Kay Hackett for Fisher, Bruce & Company.

The #3575 round tray and the #3576 and #3577 fluted bowls were available with the El Rosa, Festival, and Laurita motifs only during 1942, so are quite rare. They were listed in Stangl catalogs as "Fisher, Bruce Fancy Pieces." The distinctive Della-Ware pitcher shape was introduced in 1943 as shape #3722. The four-quart size was too large for the average person to handle, so was eliminated before the end of 1943. The large-sized mother and father cup and saucer shapes were decorated with Della-Ware and Lunning patterns throughout the 1940s. During the mid-1950s, the mother and father cup shapes were decorated with several Stangl brand dinnerware patterns as well.

Festival plates and serving bowls were decorated with wreaths of naturally colored fruit around the centers. The hollow ware pieces featured a cherry and pear motif. All pieces have a wide Orange and narrow Pennsylvania Dutch Green band on the rims.

above:
Festival teapot, #3575 round tray,
½ pint pitcher, 8" plate, sherbet.

left:
Festival #3576 14" fluted bowl.

The Laurita pattern was decorated with a balanced arrangement of three Pink #160, Orange, and Blue #95 blossoms. Pennsylvania Dutch Green and Walnut Brown were used on the stems and leaves. Laurita was decorated with the same rim colors as Festival.

Laurita 1 pint pitcher, ½ pint pitcher, 10" plate, cup & saucer, candy dish.

The El Rosa motif was a large, stylized Pink #193 rose within a cluster of Lavender buds and Green and Yellow leaves. A wide Pennsylvania Dutch Green band with a narrow Orange stripe is on the rims of El Rosa pieces.

El Rosa creamer, 10" plate, cup & saucer, 14½" chop plate, father cup.

Of these three patterns, Festival and Laurita are the most popular. Although El Rosa is not as desirable, it is more difficult to find. Laurita and Festival were produced until 1954. In 1960, the Festival motif was modified slightly and re-introduced on the #3774 Coupe shape as Festival #5072.

Quimper, Brittany #3680

Introduced: 1942
Designer: Kay Hackett
Made For: Fisher, Bruce & Company
Shape Style: #3600, Fluted

Known Pieces:

bowl, cereal	$35 – 45
bowl, fruit	$30 – 40
bowl, lug soup	$35 – 45
bowl, 11" salad	$150 – 175
bowl, 10" salad	$125 – 150
bowl, 8" vegetable	$90 – 110
creamer	$40 – 50
cup	$20 – 30
egg cup	$35 – 45
plate, 14" chop	$300 – 350
plate, 12" chop	$225 – 275
plate, 10"	$135 – 165
plate, 9"	$135 – 165
plate, 8"	$85 – 120
plate, 6"	$45 – 55
salt, pepper; each	$20 – 25
saucer	$15 – 20
sugar	$50 – 65
teapot	$225 – 250

Stangl's Della-Ware Quimper/Brittany pattern was decorated with very finely detailed motifs of a man and woman in peasant dress. The woman was on the 14", 10", 8" plates and salad bowls while the 12", 9", 6" plates and fruit bowls were decorated with the man. A ring of Pink #160 and Blue #95 flowers and Blue #95 bands encircle the rims. The cups, saucers, and lug soups all sport a coordinating floral motif.

The name of this pattern was changed from Quimper to Brittany due to legal implications with French Quimper manufacturers. Collectors use either name equally when referring to this Della-Ware pattern.

The Quimper/Brittany pattern was produced in very limited quantities for about one year. Because of all the small lines and details in this pattern, a great deal of time and accuracy was required to decorate each piece. According to Kay Hackett, "Too many pieces were coming out with fat legged women with crossed eyes." Since the quality of decoration on this pattern became so costly, it was discontinued. Stangl's Quimper and Brittany patterns are now very rare and have recently gained a great deal of interest among collectors.

Quimper/Brittany 6" plate, 9" plate, cup & saucer, teapot, 10" plate, lug soup, fruit bowl.

Andalusia

Introduced: 1942
Made For: Fisher, Bruce & Company
Shape Style: #3600 Fluted or #3670 Plain Scallop

Known Pieces:

bowl, fruit	$20 – 25
bowl, lug soup	$25 – 30
bowl, 11" salad	$125 – 165
bowl, 10" salad	$100 – 145
bowl, 8" vegetable	$65 – 80
creamer	$30 – 35
cup	$15 – 20
egg cup	$25 – 35
plate, 14" chop	$200 – 250
plate, 12" chop	$200 – 250
plate, 10"	$75 – 95
plate, 8"	$50 – 60
plate, 6"	$25 – 30

Andalusia 10" plate, #3670 Plain Scallop.

salt, pepper; each	$15 – 20
saucer	$10 – 15
sugar	$35 – 45
teapot	$200 – 250

The Andalusia pattern depicts a dancing girl in traditional Spanish dress with pink roses painted around the rim. This pattern was produced on both the #3600 Fluted and #3670 Plain Scallop shapes. The #3670 Plain Scallop is the same basic shape as #3670 Morning Glory but without the raised decoration on the rims. Andalusia is an extremely scarce pattern; very little has been found.

Fruit #3697

Introduced: 1942
Designer: Kay Hackett
Shape Style: #3434 Rim

Known Pieces:

ashtray, 5" fluted*	$12 – 15
bean pot/cookie jar*	$110 – 125
bowl, cereal	$20 – 25
bowl, cereal‡	$8 – 12
bowl, fruit	$15 – 20
bowl, coupe soup	$25 – 30
bowl, lug soup	$15 – 20
bowl, 12" #3608*	$95 – 125
bowl, 11" salad	$70 – 80
bowl, 10" salad	$55 – 65
bowl, 10" salad‡	$15 – 25

bowl, 8" vegetable	$35 – 45
bowl, 8" vegetable‡	$15 – 20
bowl, 10" divided round	$60 – 75
bowl, oval divided vegetable	$35 – 45
bowl, 9" mixing*	$75 – 95
bowl, 7" mixing*	$60 – 70
bowl, 5½ mixing*	$50 – 60
bowl, 4" mixing*	$40 – 50
bowl, 8" covered vegetable	$140 – 160
bread tray	$60 – 75
butter dish	$55 – 65

cache pot/planter, square 7½" x 7½"*	$70 – 85	plate, 11"	$30 – 35
cake stand	$20 – 25	plate, 10"	$25 – 30
candy dish, covered*	$95 – 125	plate, 10⅝"✦	$10 – 15
casserole, 8" covered	$85 – 100	plate, 9"	$20 – 25
casserole, 6" covered	$50 – 60	plate, 8"	$15 – 20
casserole, 8" skillet shape	$25 – 35	plate, 8¼"✦	$8 – 12
casserole, 6" skillet shape	$20 – 25	plate, 7"	$20 – 25
casserole, individual,		plate, 6"	$10 – 12
with handle & cover	$50 – 60	plate, 6"✦	$4 – 6
clock	$45 – 55	plate, grill*	$50 – 60
coaster/ashtray*	$15 – 20	plate, 10" picnic*	$10 – 12
coffee pot, 8 cup	$90 – 120	plate, 8" picnic*	$10 – 12
coffee pot, 4 cup	$100 – 130	platter, 14¾" oval	$95 – 125
coffee pot, individual	$80 – 95	platter, 14⅜" oval✦	$50 – 60
coffee server, casual	$175 – 200	platter, 11½" oval	$110 – 140
creamer	$20 – 25	platter, 13¾" casual	$75 – 95
creamer, casual	$50 – 65	pickle dish	$25 – 30
creamer, individual	$20 – 30	relish dish	$30 – 40
creamer, #5129 Tiara✦	$8 – 12	salt, pepper; each	$8 – 12
cruet with stopper	$40 – 50	salt, pepper; each✦	$4 – 6
cup	$8 – 12	salt shaker, wood top	$65 – 80
cup, #4024✦	$6 – 8	pepper mill, wood top	$65 – 80
cup, mother or father	$65 – 75	sauce boat	$50 – 60
egg cup	$20 – 25	saucer	$8 – 10
gravy boat	$30 – 40	saucer✦	$4 – 6
gravy underplate	$20 – 25	saucer, mother or father	$15 – 25
lamp #637 jug shape	$175 – 200	saucer, 2 cup mug, 7"	$15 – 20
lamp #3837 or #835		sherbet	$30 – 40
5-tier coffee warmer	$200 – 250	sugar	$20 – 25
lamp, cylinder	$175 – 200	sugar, casual	$50 – 65
lamp, coffee pot*	$100 – 125	sugar, individual	$20 – 30
lazy susan*	$125 – 150	sugar, open	$45 – 55
lazy susan, divided*	$125 – 150	sugar, #5129 Tiara✦	$10 – 15
mug, coffee	$30 – 35	teapot	$85 – 95
mug, 2 cup	$40 – 50	teapot #3774 Coupe✦	$60 – 70
pitcher, 2 quart	$90 – 115	teapot #5129 Tiara✦	$25 – 35
pitcher, 1 quart	$65 – 75	tidbit, 10"	$10 – 15
pitcher, 1 pint	$40 – 50	tidbit, 2 tier	$25 – 30
pitcher, ½ pint	$25 – 30	tile, 6"*	$20 – 25
pitcher, 6 ounce	$25 – 30	tray, 7½" square*	$40 – 50
pitcher, 1½ pint✦	$20 – 25	tray, square #5154*	$40 – 50
pitcher & bowl set*	$250 – 300	tray for cruets	$35 – 40
plate, 14½" chop	$80 – 110	warmer	$35 – 40
plate, 14½" 4-sided	$150 – 175	paper napkin, each	$1 – 2
plate, 12½" chop	$60 – 75	paper placemat, each	$6 – 7
plate, 12½" chop✦	$30 – 40	paper price list	$15 – 20

✦These items were produced on the white body used after 1974.

*These items are usually found without carving and marked only with the brown "second" mark and no pattern name. Such pieces were sold only in Flemington. Occasionally these items were produced with carved decoration and marked with the pattern name. Carved pieces are considered scarce and worth 50 – 75% more than non-carved pieces.

The Fruit motif incorporated several brightly colored fruits realistically decorated. Many of the shapes in this pattern also included a band of French Green with a narrow Orange stripe on the rims. The leaves on the Fruit pattern were always French Green. Unmarked "Fruit" pieces with leaves decorated any other shade of green usually belong to the Festival pattern.

Fruit with brushed engobe usually bore the "Terra Rose" designation. Fruit marked with this name continued to be produced through the late 1940s before the designation was dropped from hand-carved, hand-decorated dinnerware patterns. There is a collector following for both hand-brushed "Terra Rose" fruit and fruit with smooth, white backgrounds.

Fruit, Terra Rose 10" round divided vegetable bowl, cup & saucer, 14½" chop plate, 6" plate, 8" plate.

The Fruit pattern was first introduced as a salad set in 1942. The pieces offered were a 14½" chop plate, 10" salad bowl, and six 8" plates. Each of the 8" salad plates featured a different fruit motif. The fruits used were apple, pear, grapes, plum, peach, and cherries. As the Fruit salad set became increasingly popular, more shapes were added. The first additions, made in 1945, were the 12½" chop plate, 10" plate, 11" salad bowl, cup, and saucer. By 1948, each of the #3434 shapes produced by Stangl at that time were available decorated with the Fruit motifs.

Fruit 14½" chop plate, creamer, sugar, cup & saucer, 10" plate, butter dish, egg cup.

Stangl continued to produce Fruit 8" plates with the six different fruit motifs until the mid-1960s. During the late 1960s, 8" plates were decorated only with cherries or pears. By 1970, Fruit 8" plates were produced with the cherry motif only.

Fruit 14½" four-sided chop plate.

The unusual four-sided chop plate shape was decorated with the Fruit motif in 1947. Engobe was brushed only on the centers of these plates. The rims were left natural brown, giving these pieces a distinctive appearance. Similarly unconventional chop plate shapes were produced with the Kumquat and Lime patterns during this time as well.

The casual coffee server was produced with the Fruit motif only during 1954. The open sugar shape is larger than the individual sugar and was decorated with an apple. Stangl's open sugar shape was introduced in 1957 when the individual sugar and creamer shapes were discontinued.

From 1945 through 1952, Fruit cups were decorated with a leaf motif. The cup decoration was changed to a peach motif in 1952. In 1957, the shape of the cup was changed to the re-styled #4024 coupe shape cup. The peach motif remained the same. The #4024 cup was also the cup shape used after the conversion to white-bodied production. The cups with the peach motif are most popular with collectors.

Fruit salt and pepper shakers also went through several changes over the years. The original #3434 shakers were flat-topped cylinders. This shape was replaced by round-topped coupe shakers in 1950 because of the

Fruit casual coffee server, 12½" chop plate, individual covered casserole with handle, vinegar cruet, open sugar.

difficulty encountered in spraying engobe evenly on the flat-topped shakers. The #3434 flat-top shaker shape was re-introduced in 1975 when all production was changed to white body. White-bodied #3434 flat-top shakers were decorated with French Green and Orange bands only.

Fruit #4024 cup & saucer, 14¾" oval platter, sauce boat, mug.

The rim edge-treatment of the Fruit pattern was modified as production methods changed. On early pieces with brushed engobe, the engobe covered the edge of each piece and was painted the same color as the rim. When the spraying of engobe was begun in 1950, engobe was trimmed from the rim of most patterns, leaving a brown edge. Fruit, Garden Flower, and Tulip, however, continued to have engobe applied to the edges of the rims. This enabled the edges to be painted the same color as the rims. This was a costly practice and the engobe on the edges was very prone to chipping. Con-

sequently, by 1957 engobe was trimmed from the edges of all patterns. Fruit produced after that date was finished with a brown edge.

Because of the continued popularity of this pattern, during the 1960s several coordinating pieces were decorated with the Fruit motif for the Flemington Outlet. These pieces, usually called "Flemington items" or "Flemington Exclusives" were inexpensively decorated with popular dinnerware motifs and sold en masse at the Flemington Outlet. Many novel and sometimes

Fruit, Flemington items; coaster/ashtray, ashtray, divided lazy susan, lazy susan, covered candy, 8" picnic plate with cherry, 8" picnic plate with peach, #4024 shape cup.

rare Flemington shapes can be found decorated with the Fruit motif. The square tray #5154 was designed as a wall decoration and a serving piece as well. Stangl's #3434 coaster/ashtray shape was not decorated with a Fruit motif until the late 1950s, and these were made primarily for the Flemington Outlet. Stangl was decorating lamp bases with the Fruit motif as early as the 1950s, but most Fruit lamps were produced during the 1960s and 1970s.

Fruit bean pot/cookie jar, square tray #5154.

The Fruit pattern was in active production from 1942 until the closing of Stangl in 1978. In 1975 when red-bodied patterns were discontinued, Fruit was adapted to the white body and remained in production. Several of the dinnerware shapes were modified at this time. The white-bodied Fruit teapot was

right: Fruit jug lamp #637.

Fruit, Flemington bowls; #3608 12" salad bowl, 4" mixing bowl, 9" mixing bowl, 7" mixing bowl, 5½" mixing bowl.

Fruit cylinder lamp.

Fruit, white body 10⅝" plate, 8¼" plate, #3774 Coupe teapot.

produced on the #3774 Coupe shape and the #5129 Tiara shape. The white-bodied creamer, sugar, and 1½ pint pitcher were all the #5129 Tiara shape. Several of the white-bodied shapes were decorated only with French Green and Yellow bands instead of the usual Fruit motifs. The pieces often found with this simplified decoration are the shakers, creamers, sugars, #5129 Tiara teapots, and 1½ pint pitchers.

One of the reasons for the popularity of Stangl's Fruit pattern was that it was decorated with a bright, proportional arrangement of colors. Because the Fruit motif employed the primary colors red, blue, and yellow, it was easily coordinated with nearly any home color scheme. The Fruit pattern continues as Stangl's most widely collected dinnerware pattern.

Garden Flower #3700

Introduced: 1942
Designer: Kay Hackett
Shape Style: #3434 Rim

Known Pieces:

bowl, cereal . . . . $20 – 25	bowl, 10" salad . . . . $55 – 65
bowl, fruit . . . . $12 – 15	bowl, 8" vegetable . . . . $35 – 45
bowl, lug soup . . . . $15 – 20	bowl, 10" divided round . . . . $50 – 60
bowl, 11" salad . . . . $80 – 95	candy dish . . . . $65 – 75
	casserole, 8" covered . . . . $75 – 85

casserole, 6" covered	$25 – 30	pitcher, #3722 1 quart	$85 – 95
casserole, 8" skillet shape	$25 – 35	plate, 14½" chop	$80 – 95
casserole, 6" skillet shape	$20 – 25	plate, 12½" chop	$55 – 65
cigarette box	$50 – 60	plate, 11"	$40 – 50
coaster/ashtray	$15 – 20	plate, 10"	$20 – 25
coffee pot	$225 – 250	plate, 9"	$15 – 20
coffee pot, individual	$90 – 110	plate, 8"	$15 – 20
creamer	$20 – 25	plate, 6"	$10 – 12
creamer, individual	$20 – 25	salt, pepper; each	$8 – 10
cup	$8 – 12	saucer	$5 – 6
egg cup	$20 – 25	sherbet	$30 – 35
pitcher, 2 quart	$90 – 110	sugar	$20 – 25
pitcher, 1 quart	$65 – 75	sugar, individual	$20 – 25
pitcher, 1 pint	$40 – 50	teapot	$85 – 95
pitcher, ½ pint	$25 – 30	paper price list	$10 – 20

The Fruit and Garden Flower patterns were designed to mix and match, so were decorated with the same coloration and rim treatments. The Garden Flower pattern was very popular throughout the 1940s. It continued to sell well during the early 1950s but became inactive by 1957. Salt and pepper shakers made after 1950 are the rounded #3774 Coupe shape instead of the original #3434 flat-topped cylinder shape.

The #3434 coffee pot shape was introduced during 1946. This shape was derived from the #3434 teapot shape. The sheer size of this coffee pot shape caused it to be quite ungainly, so very few were made. The #3434 coffee pot shape was produced only with the Garden Flower Canterbury Bells motif.

Cigarette box and coaster/ashtray sets were produced bearing several dinnerware motifs but marketed separately from the dinnerware. These cigarette sets were numbered with different numbers than those of the dinnerware patterns. Some of the dinnerware and cigarette set patterns numbered separately were Garden Flower, Tulip, Mountain Laurel, and Thistle. The Garden Flower cigarette set was numbered 3698 while the dinnerware pattern bore the number 3700.

Garden Flower coffee pot, individual coffee pot, 12½" chop plate, teapot.

The charm of the Garden Flower pattern was the ten different flower motifs appearing on each of the dinnerware shapes. The flowers and the pieces they decorate are listed below.

Balloon Flower — 11" salad bowl, 10" divided vegetable, 8" and 6" covered casseroles, 6" skillet casserole, 1 quart pitcher, 6" plate, individual coffee pot, candy dish.
Bleeding Heart — 8" plate, individual sugar.
Canterbury Bells — 10" salad bowl, egg cup, ½ pint pitcher, coffee pot.
Flax — salt and pepper, sherbet.
Marigold — fruit bowl, one side of sugar and creamer.
Morning Glory — cereal bowl, lug soup, other side of sugar and creamer.
Phlox — 8" vegetable bowl.
Single Rose — cigarette box, coaster/ashtray, individual creamer, cup, 1 pint pitcher, #3722 1 quart pitcher, 10" plate.
Sunflower — 2 quart pitcher, 11" plate, teapot.
Tiger Lily — 8" skillet casserole, 9" plate.

The 12½" chop plate was decorated with an arrangement of the Single Rose, Tiger Lily, and Balloon Flower motifs. The 14½" chop plate featured Sunflowers and Morning Glories.

The #3434 candy dish was originally called "olive dish" by Stangl. This shape was primarily decorated with the Della-Ware Festival, Laurita, El Rosa, and Red Cherry patterns. It is extremely rare decorated with any of Stangl's other dinnerware patterns.

above: Garden Flower 8" plate, salt & pepper, 11" plate, creamer, sugar, sherbet, 10" plate, individual creamer, individual sugar, coaster/ashtray.

left: Garden Flower candy/olive dish.

Blue Crocus #3343, Pink Crocus #3344

Introduced: 1943
Designer: Kay Hackett
Glaze: Yellow-Tinted
Shape Style: #1388

Crocus 9" plate, pink; 7" plate, blue.

Known Pieces:

bowl, fruit	$20 – 25
bowl, 5" lug soup	$20 – 25
bowl, 10" salad	$90 – 125
bowl, 8" vegetable	$60 – 75
bowl, 9" oval	$60 – 70
butter chip	$20 – 25
candle holder	$20 – 25
carafe with handle	$95 – 135
stopper for carafe	$10 – 15
creamer	$25 – 30
cup	$15 – 20
plate, 14½" chop	$100 – 145
plate, 12½" chop	$90 – 130
plate, 10"	$40 – 50
plate, 9"	$35 – 45
plate, 8"	$25 – 35
plate, 7"	$20 – 25
plate, 6"	$15 – 20
platter, 12" oval	$80 – 110
platter, 10" oval	$70 – 95
salt, pepper; each	$10 – 15
saucer	$8 – 10
sugar	$30 – 35
teapot	$145 – 165

Since most of Stangl's pattern numbers were assigned chronologically, the numbers on the #3343 to #3344 Crocus and #3345 to #3347 Daisy patterns are somewhat misleading. Numbers were assigned as each new pattern or shape was introduced, so nearly all Stangl patterns follow in chronological/numerical order. In 1940, however, the block of numbers 3332 to 3347 was set aside to be used exclusively for dinnerware patterns. These numbers continued to be assigned through 1943, causing several of the patterns introduced during that year to appear out of sequence when compared to the numbers issued to other patterns during the early 1940s.

The blue and pink Crocus patterns were identical except for the color of the motifs. On these patterns, the leaves and stripe were French Green, the stems Walnut Brown, and the inner band on the rim Victoria Green. The blossoms were either Blue #95 or Pink #193.

Brown-Eyed Daisy #3345, Blue Mountain Daisy #3346, Pink Mountain Daisy #3347

Introduced: 1943
Designer: Kay Hackett
Made For: Black, Star & Gorm, Boston
Shape Style: #2000

Known Pieces:

bowl, fruit	$20 – 25
bowl, lug soup	$20 – 25
bowl, 12" salad	$90 – 125
bowl, 12" salad, low	$95 – 130

bowl, 10" salad	$80 – 90	plate, 8"	$25 – 35
bowl, 7½" salad	$50 – 60	plate, 7"	$20 – 25
bowl, 10" oval	$55 – 65	plate, 6"	$15 – 20
carafe with handle	$95 – 130	platter, 12" oval	$80 – 110
creamer	$20 – 25	platter, 10" oval	$70 – 90
cup, tea	$12 – 15	salt, pepper; each	$10 – 15
plate, 14½" chop	$100 – 145	salt, pepper, #3298 Daisy; each	$45 – 60
plate, 12½" chop	$85 – 125	saucer	$8 – 10
plate, 10"	$40 – 50	sugar	$30 – 35
plate, 9"	$35 – 45	teapot	$145 – 165

As with the Crocus patterns, these three Daisy motifs were the same, only the flower and rim colors were different. On these patterns, the stems and flower centers were Walnut Brown and the leaves are French Green. The Brown-Eyed Daisy blossoms were Orange, Blue Mountain Daisy was Blue #95, and Pink Mountain Daisy used Pink #193. The smaller pieces were simply decorated with coordinating bands of color or a single blossom.

The #3298 daisy-shaped salt and pepper shakers were decorated to match these daisy patterns as well as the Field Daisy pattern. The Field Daisy shakers have either blue or yellow centers, whereas the shakers in these patterns were decorated with blue or brown centers.

Blue Mountain Daisy 9" plate, 12½" chop plate; Brown-Eyed Daisy 7" plate; Pink Mountain Daisy 8" plate, salt, fruit bowl.

Five-Petal Flower

Introduced: 1943
Designer: Kay Hackett
Made For: Jordan Marsh, Boston
Glaze: Yellow-Tinted
Shape Style: #1388
Flower and Band Colors: Pink, Blue, Yellow, Green

Known Pieces:

bowl, fruit	$20 – 25	butter chip	$20 – 25
bowl, 5" lug soup	$20 – 25	candle holder	$20 – 25
bowl, 10" salad	$85 – 95	carafe with handle	$90 – 120
bowl, 8" vegetable	$50 – 60	stopper for carafe	$10 – 15
bowl, 9" oval	$50 – 60	creamer	$20 – 25

cup . . . . $12 – 15	plate, 6" . . . . $15 – 20
plate, 14½" chop . . . . $85 – 115	platter, 12" oval . . . . $80 – 90
plate, 12½" chop . . . . $80 – 95	platter, 10" oval . . . . $65 – 75
plate, 10" . . . . $40 – 45	salt, pepper; each . . . . $10 – 12
plate, 9" . . . . $35 – 40	saucer . . . . $8 – 10
plate, 8" . . . . $25 – 30	sugar . . . . $30 – 35
plate, 7" . . . . $20 – 25	teapot . . . . $145 – 165

The Five-Petal Flower motif was produced in Pink #160, Victoria Green, Blue #95, and Light Yellow. This was an inexpensive pattern that was decorated on the wheel. Each decorator would paint a particular color or portion of the motif then pass it to the next decorator to add the next part. By using this assembly-line decorating procedure and not back stamping each piece, Stangl was able to offer Five-Petal Flower to Jordan Marsh at a very low cost.

Five-Petal Flower 10" plate, 9" plate, cup.

Jonquil #3744

Introduced: 1944
Designer: Betty Stangl
Adapted By: Cleo Salerno
Made For: Frederik Lunning, Inc.
Shape Style: #3434 Rim

Known Pieces:

bowl, cereal . . . . $20 – 25	pitcher, 2 quart . . . . $95 – 125
bowl, fruit . . . . $20 – 25	pitcher, 1 quart . . . . $80 – 90
bowl, lug soup . . . . $20 – 25	pitcher, 1 pint . . . . $40 – 50
bowl, rim soup . . . . $30 – 35	pitcher, ½ pint . . . . $25 – 35
bowl, 12" salad #3608 . . . . $110 – 135	plate, 14½" chop . . . . $95 – 120
bowl, 11" salad . . . . $80 – 90	plate, 12½" chop . . . . $70 – 85
bowl, 10" salad . . . . $60 – 70	plate, 11" . . . . $35 – 40
bowl, 8" vegetable . . . . $40 – 50	plate, 10" . . . . $25 – 35
bowl, 10" divided round . . . . $65 – 75	plate, 9" . . . . $20 – 25
casserole, 8" covered . . . . $90 – 115	plate, 8" . . . . $15 – 20
casserole, 6" covered . . . . $30 – 40	plate, 6" . . . . $10 – 15
coffee pot, individual . . . . $125 – 150	salt, pepper; each . . . . $12 – 15
creamer . . . . $20 – 25	saucer . . . . $8 – 10
cup . . . . $12 – 15	saucer, mother or father . . . . $10 – 15
cup, mother or father . . . . $40 – 50	sherbet . . . . $40 – 50
egg cup . . . . $20 – 25	sugar . . . . $25 – 30
	teapot . . . . $110 – 135

The pastoral Jonquil pattern incorporated two Yellow and Orange daffodils with a wide border of Orange and French Green. Martin Stangl's daughter Betty designed the Jonquil motif while attending Alfred University during the early 1940s. In 1944, Cleo Salerno, Stangl designer and classmate of Betty, adapted this motif to the #3434 dinnerware shape. The Jonquil pattern was produced for Frederik Lunning on the #3434 rim shape until the early 1950s. In 1954, Jonquil was re-introduced on the #3774 Coupe shape and marked with the Stangl trademark.

Jonquil 6" plate, 10" plate, egg cup, cup & saucer.

Mountain Laurel #3745

Introduced: 1944
Designer: Cleo Salerno
Shape Style: #3434 Rim

Mountain Laurel 1 pint pitcher, 8" plate, cup & saucer, 12½" chop plate, teapot, 10" plate, creamer.

Known Pieces:

bowl, cereal	$20 – 25
bowl, fruit	$20 – 25
bowl, lug soup	$20 – 25
bowl, 11" salad	$90 – 110
bowl, 10" salad	$65 – 75
bowl, 8" vegetable	$40 – 50
bowl, 10" divided round	$65 – 75
casserole, 8" covered	$95 – 120
casserole, 6" covered	$30 – 40
casserole, 8" skillet shape	$35 – 45
casserole, 6" skillet shape	$25 – 35
cigarette box	$50 – 60
coaster/ashtray	$20 – 25
coffee pot, individual	$100 – 125
creamer	$20 – 25
creamer, individual	$25 – 30
cup	$12 – 15
egg cup	$20 – 25
pitcher, 2 quart	$95 – 125
pitcher, 1 quart	$80 – 90
pitcher, 1 pint	$40 – 50
pitcher, ½ pint	$25 – 35
plate, 14½" chop	$95 – 120
plate, 12½" chop	$80 – 90
plate, 11"	$40 – 45
plate, 10"	$30 – 35
plate, 9"	$25 – 30
plate, 8"	$20 – 25
plate, 6"	$10 – 15
salt, pepper; each	$10 – 15
saucer	$8 – 10
sherbet	$40 – 50
sugar	$25 – 30
sugar, individual	$25 – 30
teapot	$110 – 135
paper price list	$20 – 25

When Cleo Salerno designed this floral pattern, she wanted to call it "Azalea." Mr. Stangl, however, renamed it Mountain Laurel after the native American shrub. Mr. Stangl felt that the name "Azalea" might seem too Oriental, especially when the United States was still at war with Japan. The bright pink and yellow coloring of this design continues to charm collectors of this pleasing and popular pattern.

American Garden #3763

Introduced: 1946
Designer: Martin Stangl
Made For: Frederik Lunning, Inc.
Shape Style: #3434 Rim

American Garden sherbet, 10" plate, sugar, creamer, 6" plate.

Known Pieces:

bowl, cereal . . . . $20 – 25	
bowl, fruit . . . . $20 – 25	
bowl, lug soup . . . . $25 – 30	
bowl, rim soup . . . . $30 – 35	
bowl, 11" salad . . . . $110 – 125	
bowl, 10" salad . . . . $90 – 100	
bowl, 8" vegetable . . . . $55 – 65	plate, 11" . . . . $50 – 65
casserole, 8" covered . . . . $95 – 125	plate, 10" . . . . $35 – 45
casserole, 6" covered . . . . $50 – 60	plate, 9" . . . . $25 – 35
cigarette box . . . . $85 – 110	plate, 8" . . . . $20 – 25
coaster/ashtray . . . . $25 – 35	plate, 6" . . . . $15 – 20
egg cup . . . . $25 – 30	salt, pepper; each . . . . $12 – 15
creamer . . . . $25 – 30	saucer . . . . $10 – 12
cup . . . . $15 – 20	sherbet . . . . $45 – 55
plate, 14½" chop . . . . $135 – 150	sugar . . . . $35 – 40
plate, 12½" chop . . . . $100 – 130	teapot . . . . $150 – 175

American Garden was designed with a patriotic red, white, and blue color scheme in an attempt to benefit from the patriotic fervor following World War II. American Garden is a well-proportioned design with a balanced color arrangement of Pink #160, Blue #95, and Yellow. There were several features unique to this pattern, outstanding of which was the wide Delphinium Blue rim with five tightly-spaced rings on the shoulder. The added details caused the production costs of this pattern to be higher than most Stangl dinnerware patterns. Frederik Lunning, however, was always willing to pay more to be able to offer distinctive, quality dinnerware patterns.

American Garden was a short-lived pattern that is now difficult to find. Because of the clever use of color in the design and the quality of the decorating, this pattern is becoming increasingly popular at this time.

Bower Salad Set

Introduced: 1946
Made For: Flemington Outlet
Shape Style: #3434 Rim

Known Pieces:

bowl, 10" salad . . . . $70 – 85	plate, 14½" chop . . . . $100 – 135
	plate, 8" . . . . $30 – 40

The Bower pattern was produced in modest quantities for a short time during 1946. This pattern was tried as a market test salad set at the Flemington Outlet in three color variations. The motif consisted of an intertwining vine of French Green leaves with blossoms on the rims and a ring of color in the centers of each piece. Version "A" featured Yellow blossoms with Blue #95 centers, a Yellow rim and Pink #160 ring. Version "B" was decorated with a Blue #95 rim and blossoms with Yellow centers and a Yellow ring. The "C" version featured a French Green rim and central ring, Victoria Green leaves, and Pink #193 blossoms with Yellow centers. Apparently there was not enough interest in any of the Bower motifs to warrant further production beyond the initial short run.

Bower, version "B" 10" bowl.

Waterlily

Introduced: 1946
Designer: Cleo Salerno
Shape Style: #3434 Rim

Known Pieces:		
bowl, cereal	$20 – 25	cup . . . $15 – 18
bowl, fruit	$20 – 25	plate, 14½" chop . . . $115 – 140
bowl, lug soup	$25 – 30	plate, 12½" chop . . . $95 – 115
bowl, 11" salad	$90 – 115	plate, 10" . . . $45 – 55
bowl, 10" salad	$70 – 80	plate, 8" . . . $25 – 35
bowl, 8" vegetable	$60 – 70	plate, 6" . . . $15 – 20
casserole, 8" covered	$95 – 125	salt, pepper; each . . . $12 – 15
casserole, 6" covered	$50 – 60	saucer . . . $8 – 12
creamer	$25 – 30	sugar . . . $25 – 35
		teapot . . . $145 – 165

The red clay body of this pattern was used as a background for the white, slip-trailed engobe flowers and bands. Black and Pennsylvania Dutch Green stripes encircle each piece. The leaves were colored with Art Ware Green to represent a watery appearance. Very little of this unusual pattern was produced. According to Cleo Salerno, the slip-trail motif was too difficult for the decorators to apply correctly at that time. Mr. Stangl felt that the pattern would not be popular enough to warrant training the decorators in slip-trail production. As a result, Cleo Salerno's Waterlily pattern is very scarce.

Waterlily 8" plate.

Bountiful Salad Set

*Beautiful 14"
chop plate.*

Introduced: 1946
Adapted By: Cleo Salerno
Made For: Flemington Outlet
Shape Style: #1940 Raised Fruit

Known Pieces:
bowl, 9" salad . . . . $80 – 110
plate, 14" chop . . . . $125 – 160
plate, 9" . . . . $50 – 60

Bountiful was another decorative adaptation of the #1940 Raised Fruit shapes. This pattern featured a white brushed engobe background with the cluster of fruits painted in bright natural colors. The raised fruits and leaves were all further defined with carved outlines and details. Production of the Bountiful pattern was very short-lived, lasting less than one year.

Mr. Stangl's Farm Life

Produced: 1946
Designer: Kurt Weise
Adapted By: Cleo Salerno
Shape Style: #3434 Rim

Known Pieces, with motif description:
bowl, cereal — lamb . . . . $200 – 250
bowl, fruit — colt . . . . $200 – 250
bowl, 11" salad — sitting hen . . . . . $450 – 500
bowl, 10" salad — pig at fence . . . $450 – 500
bowl, 8" vegetable — tied calf . . . . $350 – 400
covered casserole, 8" — pony, calf . $600 – 700
covered casserole, 6" —
   rooster, hen, eggs . . . . $250 – 300
creamer — pouncing cat . . . . $300 – 350
creamer — hen . . . . $200 – 250

cup — standing hen . . . . $125 – 150
pitcher, 2 quart — sitting hen . . . . $500 – 550
pitcher, ½ pint — kid goat . . . . $400 – 450
plate, 11" — farmer . . . . $600 – 650
plate, 10" — farmer's wife . . . . $550 – 600
plate, 10" — rooster . . . . $550 – 600
plate, 9" — horse . . . . $550 – 600
plate, 8" — grazing cow . . . . $450 – 500
plate, 6" — crowing rooster . . . . . . $175 – 225
salt, pepper — duckling or
   chick with eggshells; each . . . . . . $125 – 175
saucer — nest of eggs . . . . $125 – 150
sherbet — turkey . . . . $400 – 450
sugar — trotting dog . . . . $300 – 350
sugar — rooster . . . . $200 – 250

Kurt Weise, a well known children's book author and illustrator, had been a very close friend of Martin Stangl. Throughout the 1940s, Kurt Weise occasionally visited Stangl's factory in Trenton. During some of these visits, Mr. Weise tried his hand at designing dinnerware patterns and would have Cleo Salerno adapt his designs to dinnerware shapes.

Martin Stangl apparently liked Weise's samples depicting farm scenes. Mr. Stangl had Cleo Salerno create a dinner service for 12 for use at his farm near Stockton, New Jersey. The Walnut Brown, French Green, and Victoria Green banding on this pattern was one of Cleo Salerno's favorite color combinations. She used this same device on several of her own pattern designs.

In addition to Mr. Stangl's dinner set, a number of Farm Life seconds were also produced. The motifs on the seconds were either completely French Green or French Green with a few other colors.

In 1950, Martin Stangl had Kay Hackett make several Farm Life replacement pieces for those which had become damaged or broken. The original pieces done by Cleo Salerno have brushed engobe, the oval Terra Rose stamp, and no decorator's mark. Kay Hackett's replacement pieces have sprayed engobe and are marked with the plain, oval Stangl-Trenton mark. Kay Hackett's lower case "k" initial is on most, but not all, of the replacement pieces she had done.

During 1952, Martin Stangl decided he no longer needed the Farm Life set, so he sold most of it at the Flemington Outlet at a discounted price to one of his employees. The remainder of the set was dispersed and lost.

Farm Life sherbet, sugar, creamer, 9" plate, cereal bowl.

Farm Life 6" plate.

Jersey Shore Series

Introduced: 1947
Designer: Kurt Weise
Adapted By: Cleo Salerno
Shape Style: #3434 Rim

Known Motifs:

Angel Fish	$450 – 550	Marlin & fishing boat	$400 – 500
Barnegat lighthouse	$650 – 750	Sailboat	$400 – 500
Crown Conch	$350 – 450	Sea Gull on piling	$400 – 500
Flounder	$350 – 450	Shells & Starfish	$350 – 450

This series of 11" plates was based on Kurt Weise's sketches of the Island Beach area of New Jersey. Each of these subjects can be found along the New Jersey coastline. Flounder are indigenous to the area, as are starfish, moon snails, channel whelks, and crown conch. Marlin and angel fish are native to tropical regions, but frequently will travel the Gulf Stream along the East Coast. Sailboats, fishing trawlers, and all manner of sea gulls can still be seen along New Jersey's shoreline.

The Jersey Shore plates were produced only for the Flemington Outlet. These plates were customarily stamped with the oval Terra Rose backstamp, but not all were marked. Although Cleo Salerno decorated the majority of these plates, other decorators were involved in their production as well.

Jersey Shore Flounder and Sea Gull 11" plates.

Jersey Shore Marlin and Sailboat 11" plates.

Cleo Salerno's original adaptation of the Jersey Shore series was decorated with a Dark Turquoise and Blue #95 wave device on the rims. Later versions were decorated with a simplified Blue #95 wave on the rims.

Stangl's Jersey Shore plates were produced in such small quantities, they are now extremely rare. The realistically rendered nautical subjects have generated considerable interest among collectors.

Jersey Shore Shells & Starfish and Crown Conch 11" plates.

Jersey Shore Barnegat lighthouse 11" plate with original rim treatment, Barnegat lighthouse 11" plate with simplified Blue #95 rim.

Vineyard #3767

Introduced: 1947
Designer: Cleo Salerno
Shape Style: #3434 Rim

Vineyard 8" plate.

Known Pieces:

bowl, cereal	$20 – 25
bowl, fruit	$20 – 25
bowl, lug soup	$20 – 25
bowl, 11" salad	$90 – 110
bowl, 10" salad	$75 – 85
bowl, 8" vegetable	$55 – 65
bowl, 10" divided round	$75 – 85
casserole, 8" covered	$95 – 125
casserole, 6" covered	$45 – 55
casserole, 8" skillet shape	$50 – 60
casserole, 6" skillet shape	$30 – 40
coffee pot, individual	$120 – 145
creamer	$20 – 25
creamer, individual	$25 – 30
cup	$12 – 18
egg cup	$20 – 25
pitcher, 2 quart	$100 – 130
pitcher, 1 quart	$85 – 95
pitcher, 1 pint	$65 – 75
pitcher, ½ pint	$45 – 55
plate, 14½" chop	$110 – 135
plate, 12½" chop	$90 – 110
plate, 11"	$50 – 60
plate, 10"	$40 – 50
plate, 9"	$30 – 40
plate, 8"	$20 – 25
plate, 6"	$15 – 20
salt, pepper; each	$12 – 15
saucer	$8 – 9
sherbet	$45 – 55
sugar	$25 – 30
sugar, individual	$25 – 30
teapot	$125 – 145

The Vineyard pattern features Victoria Green grapes with Pennsylvania Dutch Green leaves and rims. The band on the shoulders of the plates is Walnut Brown. Although this is a very scarce pattern, pieces are occasionally found.

Vineyard exhibits a pleasing balance and color contrast but lacks the brightness found in other Stangl patterns of that period. Cleo Salerno was told by Stangl's sales manager, Ed Hawley, "If it's not pink and blue or yellow, it won't sell." Martin Stangl liked this pattern and put it into production regardless of the sales manager's opinion.

Flora #3768

Introduced: 1947
Designer: Martin Stangl
Shape Style: #3434 Rim

Flora 6" plate, individual coffee pot, 10" plate, sherbet.

Known Pieces:

bowl, cereal	$12 – 18
bowl, fruit	$10 – 15

bowl, lug soup	$15 – 20	pitcher, 1 pint	$35 – 45
bowl, 11" salad	$75 – 85	pitcher, ½ pint	$20 – 25
bowl, 10" salad	$60 – 70	plate, 14½" chop	$75 – 85
bowl, 8" vegetable	$30 – 40	plate, 12½" chop	$50 – 60
bowl, 10" divided round	$50 – 60	plate, 11"	$25 – 30
casserole, 8" covered	$60 – 70	plate, 10"	$20 – 25
casserole, 6" covered	$20 – 25	plate, 9"	$15 – 20
casserole, 8" skillet shape	$25 – 30	plate, 8"	$10 – 15
casserole, 6" skillet shape	$15 – 20	plate, 6"	$6 – 8
coffee pot, individual	$85 – 95	salt, pepper; each	$6 – 8
creamer	$15 – 20	saucer	$5 – 6
creamer, individual	$20 – 25	sherbet	$30 – 35
cup	$10 – 12	sugar	$20 – 25
egg cup	$15 – 20	sugar, individual	$20 – 25
pitcher, 2 quart	$80 – 90	teapot	$90 – 100
pitcher, 1 quart	$50 – 60	paper price list	$15 – 20

The Flora motif was similar in design to Martin Stangl's American Garden pattern. Flora was much simpler, with a vibrant French Green, Pink #160, and Orange color scheme. This was a very popular pattern during the late 1940s and early 1950s. Today, the Flora pattern is relatively easy to find.

Prelude #3769

Introduced: 1947
Shape Style: #3774 Coupe

Prelude 6" plate, 4" covered casserole, 14½" chop plate, cup & saucer, coffee pot.

Known Pieces:

bowl, fruit	$10 – 15		
bowl, lug soup	$10 – 15		
bowl, 12" salad	$65 – 75		
bowl, 10" salad	$45 – 55		
bowl, 8" vegetable	$25 – 35		
casserole, 4" individual	$20 – 25		
coaster/ashtray	$15 – 20		
coffee pot	$65 – 80		
creamer	$15 – 20	plate, 9"	$15 – 20
cup	$10 – 12	plate, 8"	$10 – 15
egg cup	$12 – 15	plate, 6"	$6 – 8
plate, 14½" chop	$60 – 75	salt, pepper; each	$5 – 7
plate, 12½" chop	$35 – 45	saucer	$5 – 6
plate, 11"	$25 – 30	sugar	$15 – 20
plate, 10"	$20 – 25	paper price list	$15 – 20

The Prelude motif featured an oversized pink flower and bud with bi-colored leaves. This is a bold pattern reminiscent of the tropical floral decoration that was used extensively on wallpaper, drapes, and upholstery during the late 1940s.

Prelude was Stangl's first pattern introduced on the modern #3774 Coupe shape. This shape line included a 4" individual casserole, low-profile 10" and 12" salad bowls, and an easy-to-handle coffee pot. During the 1950s the #3774 coffee pot was Stangl's standard coffee pot shape until the #5129 Tiara coffee pot shape was introduced in 1963.

Blueberry #3770

Introduced: 1947
Designer: Kay Hackett
Shape Style: #3774 Coupe

Known Pieces:

ashtray, leaf*	$30 – 40
ashtray, rectangular	$30 – 35
bowl, cereal	$20 – 25
bowl, fruit	$15 – 20
bowl, coupe soup	$25 – 30
bowl, lug soup	$20 – 25
bowl, 12" salad	$85 – 100
bowl, 10" salad	$75 – 85
bowl, 8" vegetable	$45 – 55
bowl, oval divided vegetable	$40 – 50
bowl, 9" mixing*	$100 – 135
bowl, 7" mixing*	$85 – 100
bowl, 5½" mixing*	$65 – 80
bowl, 4" mixing*	$60 – 70
bowl, 8" covered vegetable	$85 – 100
bread tray	$50 – 60
butter dish	$60 – 75
cake stand	$20 – 25
casserole, 8" covered	$85 – 100
casserole, 6" covered	$35 – 45
casserole, 8" skillet shape	$30 – 40
casserole, 6" skillet shape	$25 – 30
casserole, 4" individual	$25 – 30
casserole, individual, with handle & cover	$60 – 70
cigarette box	$80 – 95
clock	$35 – 45
coaster/ashtray	$20 – 25
coffee pot, 8 cup	$90 – 120
coffee pot, 4 cup	$100 – 130
coffee pot, individual	$100 – 130
coffee server, casual	$175 – 200
creamer	$20 – 25
creamer, individual	$25 – 30
cruet with stopper	$40 – 50
cup	$8 – 12
cup, mother or father	$55 – 65
egg cup	$20 – 25
gravy boat	$25 – 35
gravy underplate	$15 – 20
lazy susan*	$125 – 150
lazy susan, divided*	$125 – 150
mug, coffee	$30 – 35
mug, 2 cup	$40 – 50
pitcher, 2 quart	$90 – 115
pitcher, 1 quart	$65 – 75
pitcher, 1 pint	$45 – 55
pitcher, ½ pint	$25 – 30
pitcher, 6 ounce	$25 – 30
plate, 14½" chop	$85 – 105
plate, 12½" chop	$65 – 80
plate, 11"	$30 – 35
plate, 10"	$25 – 30
plate, 9"	$20 – 25
plate, 8"	$15 – 20
plate, 6"	$8 – 10
plate, grill*	$60 – 75
plate, 10" picnic*	$10 – 12
plate, 8" picnic*	$8 – 10
platter, 14¾" oval	$110 – 120
platter, 11½" oval	$115 – 130
platter, 13¾" casual	$95 – 110
pickle dish	$25 – 30
relish dish	$25 – 30
salt, pepper; each	$8 – 12
salt shaker, wood top	$60 – 75
pepper mill, wood top	$60 – 75
sauce boat	$45 – 55
saucer	$7 – 8
saucer, mother or father	$15 – 20
sugar	$20 – 25

sugar, individual	$25 – 30	tray for cruets	$35 – 45
sugar, open	$35 – 45	warmer	$40 – 50
teapot	$90 – 110	paper napkin, each	$1 – 2
tidbit, 10"	$10 – 15	paper place mat, each	$5 – 6
tile, 6"*	$25 – 30	paper price list	$15 – 20

*These items are usually found without carving and marked only with the brown "second" mark and no pattern name. Such pieces were sold only in Flemington. Occasionally these items were produced with carved decoration and marked with the pattern name. Carved pieces are considered scarce and are worth 50 – 75% more than non-carved pieces.

Blueberry is a cheerful pattern that features a twig of naturally colored blueberries and leaves surrounded by a very wide bright Yellow border. Due to the bright coloring, Blueberry was very popular during its production and is still a favorite pattern with collectors today.

Until the early 1950s, Blueberry seconds were usually painted Blue #95, but other single colors, such as French Green or Walnut Brown were used as well. At this time, the Blue #95 seconds are the most popular and are valued equally to Blueberry pieces decorated with natural colors.

top left: Blueberry cruet, 10" plate, individual covered casserole.

top right: Blueberry grill plate made for the Flemington Outlet.

left: Blueberry 6" plate and 10" plate with the Blue #95 seconds treatment.

Red Cherry #3771

Introduced: 1947
Made For: Fisher, Bruce & Company
Shape Style: #3434 Rim

Red Cherry 1 quart pitcher, 10" plate, salt shaker.

Known Pieces:

bowl, cereal	$12 – 18
bowl, fruit	$10 – 15
bowl, lug soup	$15 – 20
bowl, 11" salad	$80 – 90
bowl, 10" salad	$65 – 75
bowl, 8" vegetable	$35 – 45
candy dish	$45 – 55
casserole, 8" skillet shape	$30 – 35
casserole, 6" skillet shape	$20 – 25
creamer	$20 – 25
cup	$10 – 12
cup, mother or father	$35 – 45
egg cup	$15 – 20
pitcher, #3722 2 quart	$85 – 95
pitcher, #3722 1 quart	$50 – 60
pitcher, #3722 1 pint	$30 – 40
pitcher, #3722 ½ pint	$20 – 25
plate, 14½" chop	$90 – 110
plate, 12½" chop	$65 – 75
plate, 11"	$25 – 30
plate, 10"	$20 – 30
plate, 9"	$20 – 25
plate, 8"	$15 – 20
plate, 6"	$8 – 12
salt, pepper; each	$10 – 12
saucer	$6 – 7
saucer, mother or father	$12 – 15
sherbet	$35 – 40
sugar	$20 – 25
teapot	$90 – 110

The Red Cherry motif was a cluster of bold Pink #160 cherries with French Green leaves, Gold accents, and a wide Gold rim. The Gold underglaze color is rather unusual and was used very briefly during the 1940s and on very few Stangl patterns. A similar color called Old Gold was featured on several dinnerware patterns introduced during the early 1960s.

Flemington Swirl Seconds

Introduced: Late 1940s
Made For: Flemington Outlet
Shape Style: #3434 Rim, #3774 Coupe

Known Pieces:

bowl, cereal	$8 – 10
bowl, fruit	$6 – 8
bowl, lug soup	$8 – 10
bowl, 11" salad	$45 – 60
bowl, 10" salad	$30 – 45
bowl, 8" vegetable	$15 – 25
bowl, 10" divided round	$30 – 45
casserole, 8" covered	$45 – 60
casserole, 6" covered	$15 – 20
casserole, 8" skillet shape	$15 – 20
casserole, 6" skillet shape	$10 – 15
cigarette box	$25 – 35
coaster/ashtray	$8 – 12
coffee pot	$50 – 65
coffee pot, individual #3434 teapot shape	$50 – 65

coffee pot, individual
    #3774 coffee pot shape . . . . $60 – 75
creamer . . . . $15 – 20
creamer, individual. . . . . $15 – 20
cup. . . . . $6 – 8
egg cup . . . . $10 – 12
pitcher, 2 quart . . . . $40 – 50
pitcher, 1 quart . . . . $20 – 30
pitcher, 1 pint . . . . $15 – 20
pitcher, ½ pint. . . . . $10 – 15
plate, 14½" chop . . . . $40 – 50
plate, 12½" chop . . . . $30 – 35
plate, 11" . . . . $12 – 18
plate, 10" . . . . $10 – 15
plate, 9" . . . . $10 – 12
plate, 8" . . . . $8 – 10
plate, 6" . . . . $5 – 6
salt, pepper; each . . . . $4 – 6
saucer . . . . $5 – 6
sherbet. . . . . $20 – 25
sugar . . . . $15 – 20
sugar, individual. . . . . $15 – 20
teapot. . . . . $50 – 60

Flemington Swirl Seconds: 9" plate, French Green; cup & saucer, Orange; 12½" chop plate, French Green; 8" plate, Orange.

1940s Seconds Treatments: Kumquat 8" plate, French Green; Blueberry 10" plate, Blue #95; Tulip 8" plate, no color.

This treatment was not so much a pattern as it was an inexpensive way to transform badly flawed seconds into saleable items. The colors most often used were French Green or Orange, but Pennsylvania Dutch Green, Gold, and Walnut Brown were used as well. Swirled seconds were produced through the late 1940s. By the early 1950s, Martin Stangl decided there was more profit in decorating seconds with popular patterns than with dull swirls that few people wanted.

During the 1940s and early 1950s, seconds motifs were sometimes decorated with a single color or glazed with no color at all. Pieces with single-color motifs are usually valued in the same range as swirled seconds.

Lime #3775, Kumquat #3776

Introduced: 1948
Designer: Kay Hackett
Shape Style: #3774 Coupe

Known Pieces:
Kumquat:
bowl, 11" salad, oval. . . . . $100 – 135
bowl, 12" salad, round . . . . $70 – 80

bowl, 10" salad, round . . . . $50 – 60
cup. . . . . $10 – 12
lamp, teapot shape . . . . $175 – 200
plate, 14" chop, five-sided . . . . $110 – 135

plate, 14½" chop, round . . . . $80 – 95	bowl, 10" salad, round . . . . $45 – 55
plate, 12½" chop, square. . . . . $110 – 135	cup . . . . $8 – 10
plate, 12½" chop, round . . . . $60 – 70	lamp, teapot shape . . . . $175 – 200
plate, 10" . . . . $25 – 30	plate, 14" chop, five-sided . . . . $110 – 135
plate, 9" . . . . $20 – 25	plate, 14½" chop, round . . . . $70 – 85
plate, 8" . . . . $15 – 20	plate, 12½" chop, square. . . . . $110 – 135
saucer . . . . $7 – 8	plate, 12½" chop, round . . . . $50 – 60
teapot. . . . . $110 – 135	plate, 10" . . . . $20 – 25
	plate, 9" . . . . $15 – 20
Lime:	plate, 8" . . . . $15 – 20
bowl, 11" salad, oval. . . . . $100 – 125	saucer . . . . $6 – 7
bowl, 12" salad, round . . . . $70 – 80	teapot. . . . . $110 – 125

The Kumquat motif was a cluster of Orange fruits with Pink #160 over-strokes and a French Green band around the rim. The Lime pattern featured a Victoria Green lime, Willow Green leaves, and a bright Yellow border. Both patterns were produced until 1953, but less Kumquat was manufactured than Lime.

An interesting aspect of the Kumquat and Lime patterns is that they were used to introduce the square and five-sided chop plate and oval salad bowl shapes. These novel pieces were produced for a very short time. There was not enough profit in these pieces to warrant continued production. Round chop plates and salad bowls are the type most easily found. The teapot shape used for these patterns was the #3434 shape with a modified lid. During 1949, lamps based on the #3434 teapot shape with Kumquat and Lime motifs were made for the Mutual Sunset Lamp Co. Kumquat and Lime teapots and lamps were produced in very limited quantities and are extremely rare.

*Kumquat 14½" round chop plate,
8" plate, cup & saucer,
14" five-sided chop plate.*

*Lime oval salad bowl,
12½" round chop plate,
12½" square chop plate,
cup & saucer, 8" plate.*

Olive #3777, Fig #3778, Gooseberry, Cranberry, Strawberry Salad Sets

Introduced: 1948
Designer: Kay Hackett
Shape Style: #3774 Coupe

Known Pieces:

Olive, Fig:

bowl, 10" salad . . . . $80 – 95

plate, 12½" chop . . . . $85 – 110

plate, 8" . . . . $20 – 25

Gooseberry, Cranberry, Strawberry:

bowl, 10" salad . . . . $115 – 145

plate, 12½" chop . . . . $130 – 165

plate, 8" . . . . $40 – 50

These salad set patterns are similar in design, so could be used alone or mixed and matched. All of them have a wide, colored band surrounding a cluster of fruit and leaves. Blueberry, Kumquat, and Lime were originally designed as elements of this salad set series but were developed as full dinner sets.

The Gooseberry, Cranberry, and Strawberry patterns were produced in very small amounts for market tests at the Flemington Outlet. Interest was lacking in these three patterns so plans for them were abandoned before they were put into actual production.

Fig — A Saddle Brown band surrounds two Brown and Yellow figs with Victoria Green leaves.

Gooseberry — Victoria Green gooseberries and Pennsylvania Dutch Green leaves are surrounded by a wide Pennsylvania Dutch Green band.

Olive — An Olive Green band encircles a cluster of Black olives with Pennsylvania Dutch Green leaves.

Strawberry — A very wide band of Yellow surrounds a group of Pink #160 berries.

Cranberry — A sprig of cranberries is enclosed by a wide Yellow band.

above: Fig 8" plate; Olive 8" plate.

right: Gooseberry 10" salad bowl.

Terra Rose Serve Ware Shapes #3779 – #3790, #3855 – #3860

Introduced: 1948, 1951
Glaze: Terra Rose Finish Green, Mauve, Blue, Yellow

Known Pieces:

1948 Introductions:

#3779 tray, leaf 13"	$40 – 45
#3780 tray, oval 12"	$25 – 35
#3781 relish, 12" triple shell	$35 – 45
#3782 dish, double pear	$20 – 25
#3783 dish, single pear	$15 – 20
#3784 dish, double apple	$20 – 25
#3785 dish, 6" single apple	$15 – 20
#3786 bowl, 4½" square	$15 – 20
#3787 dish, heart 6"	$15 – 20
#3788 dish, heart 8"	$20 – 25
#3789 clam shell 10½"	$25 – 35
#3790 leaf 19" x 12"	$35 – 45

1951 Introductions:

#3855 dish, leaf 9" x 5"	$20 – 25
#3856 dish, apple 7" x 8"	$20 – 25
#3857 dish, clover 20-25	$25 – 30
#3858 footed compote 8"	$20 – 30
#3859 dish, leaf 8" x 4"	$20 – 25
#3860 relish dish	$25 – 30

The first group of these smooth, streamlined serving pieces became very popular during the late 1940s and early 1950s. So much so, that six more items were added to the line in 1951. All of these shapes were produced throughout the 1950s and well into the 1960s. Occasionally these shapes are found with gray, green, or white engobe and clear glaze. During the late 1960s and early 1970s, these shapes were produced with Stangl's Mediterranean, Caribbean, and brushed gold finishes. These shapes, regardless of decoration, are valued about the same as those decorated with Terra Rose colors.

Terra Rose Serve Ware #3787 6" heart, green; #3855 leaf, yellow; #3860 relish dish, blue; #3857 clover, green.

Willow #3806

Introduced: 1949
Designer: Kay Hackett
Shape Style: #3774 Coupe

Known Pieces:

bowl, fruit	$10 – 15
bowl, lug soup	$10 – 15
bowl, 12" salad	$60 – 70
bowl, 10" salad	$40 – 50
bowl, 8" vegetable	$25 – 35
casserole, 4" individual	$20 – 25
coaster/ashtray	$20 – 25
coffee pot	$90 – 110
creamer	$20 – 25
cup	$8 – 10
egg cup	$10 – 15
lamp #3838 ovoid, 11"	$150 – 175
plate, 14½" chop	$75 – 90
plate, 12½" chop	$55 – 65
plate, 11"	$30 – 35

plate, 10"	$25 – 30	salt, pepper; each	$6 – 8
plate, 9"	$20 – 25	saucer	$6 – 7
plate, 8"	$15 – 20	sugar	$20 – 25
plate, 6"	$8 – 10	paper price list	$20 – 25

Kay Hackett originally designed the Willow motif in 1941 for white-bodied production. The pattern was shelved until 1949 when it was adapted to the red-bodied #3774 Coupe shapes brushed with white engobe. The heavily sculpted swirl of brushed engobe dramatically emphasizes the simple bough motif with an illusion of depth and airiness. Willow was one of Stangl's earliest red-bodied patterns that did not rely on carving as an integral part of the design.

Willow was the first pattern to use the underglaze color Willow Green. This color was far more opaque than Pennsylvania Dutch Green, and became Stangl's predominant Dark Green used throughout the 1950s.

Willow 9" plate, sugar, creamer, 14½" chop plate, cup & saucer.

Water Lily #3808

Introduced: 1949
Designer: Kay Hackett
Shape Style: #3434 Rim

Known Pieces:

bowl, cereal	$20 – 25	pitcher, 2 quart	$100 – 120
bowl, fruit	$15 – 20	pitcher, 1 quart	$85 – 95
bowl, lug soup	$20 – 25	pitcher, 1 pint	$55 – 65
bowl, 11" salad	$90 – 110	pitcher, ½ pint	$30 – 40
bowl, 10" salad	$75 – 85	plate, 14½" chop	$110 – 135
bowl, 8" vegetable	$50 – 60	plate, 12½" chop	$80 – 90
bowl, 10" divided round	$75 – 85	plate, 11"	$50 – 60
casserole, 8" covered	$95 – 125	plate, 10"	$40 – 45
casserole, 6" covered	$40 – 50	plate, 9"	$30 – 35
casserole, 8" skillet shape	$50 – 60	plate, 8"	$15 – 25
casserole, 6" skillet shape	$30 – 40	plate, 6"	$10 – 15
coffee pot, individual	$110 – 125	salt, pepper; each	$10 – 15
creamer	$20 – 25	saucer	$8 – 9
creamer, individual	$25 – 30	sugar	$25 – 30
cup	$12 – 15	sugar, individual	$25 – 30
egg cup	$15 – 20	teapot	$125 – 145
		paper price list	$20 – 30

The Water Lily motif was decorated with Grass Green leaves and bands, and Yellow and Orange blossoms. Dark Turquoise strokes were used to represent water.

Kay Hackett had some difficulty in developing this pattern. It seems that everyone, from Martin Stangl to the sales-men, had some sort of "suggestion" concerning the Water Lily design. Because of this, a large number of sample plates and trial pieces were created before this pattern was finally put into production.

Water Lily cup & saucer, 10" plate, sugar.

Chicory #3809

Introduced: 1949
Designer: Kay Hackett
Shape Style: #3774 Coupe

Known Pieces:

bowl, cereal	$20 – 25
bowl, fruit	$15 – 20
bowl, coupe soup	$20 – 25
bowl, lug soup	$15 – 20
bowl, 12" salad	$80 – 95
bowl, 10" salad	$70 – 80
bowl, 8" vegetable	$35 – 45
bowl, oval divided vegetable	$35 – 45
bread tray	$50 – 60
butter dish	$60 – 75
casserole, 8" covered	$85 – 100
casserole, 6" covered	$30 – 40
casserole, 8" skillet shape	$35 – 45
casserole, 6" skillet shape	$25 – 30
casserole, 4" individual	$25 – 35
casserole, individual, with handle & cover	$50 – 60
cigarette box	$80 – 95
coaster/ashtray	$25 – 30
coffee pot, 8 cup	$90 – 120
coffee pot, individual	$100 – 130
creamer	$20 – 25
creamer, individual	$25 – 30
cruet with stopper	$40 – 50
cup	$10 – 15
egg cup	$15 – 20
gravy boat	$30 – 35
gravy underplate	$15 – 20
mug, coffee	$25 – 30
mug, 2 cup	$45 – 55
pitcher, 2 quart	$90 – 115
pitcher, 1 quart	$65 – 75
pitcher, 1 pint	$45 – 55
pitcher, ½ pint	$25 – 30
pitcher, 6 oz.	$25 – 30
plate, 14½" chop	$85 – 105
plate, 12½" chop	$65 – 80
plate, 11"	$30 – 35
plate, 10"	$25 – 30
plate, 9"	$20 – 25
plate, 8"	$15 – 20
plate, 6"	$8 – 10
platter, 13¾" casual	$95 – 110
pickle dish	$20 – 25
relish dish	$20 – 25
salt, pepper; each	$8 – 10
saucer	$6 – 7
sugar	$20 – 25
sugar, individual	$25 – 30
teapot	$95 – 115
tidbit, 10"	$10 – 15
warmer	$50 – 60
paper price list	$15 – 20

Although Chicory is an uncomplicated pattern, it was designed with such depth that the motifs seem three-dimensional. The Chicory pattern was produced on the original #3774 Coupe shape with brushed engobe for nearly two years before being discontinued in 1951. The Chicory motif was re-introduced in 1960 as Chicory #5046 with the re-styled #4024 coupe shape sugar, creamer, and cup. Also at that time, the Chicory color was changed from Blue #95 to the Dark Blue underglaze color.

Because of these two periods of production, the Chicory pattern can be found with either brushed or sprayed engobe, and with two styles of sugar, creamer, and cup. The only price difference is that pieces with brushed engobe are sometimes slightly less than pieces with sprayed engobe. Chicory is a popular pattern that always seems to be in short supply.

Chicory 6" plate with sprayed engobe, #4024 cup & saucer, 10" plate with brushed engobe, #3774 cup.

1950s HAND-CARVED, HAND-PAINTED DINNERWARE

Thistle #3847

Introduced: 1950
Designer: Kay Hackett
Shape Style: #3774 Coupe

Known Pieces:

ashtray, 7" fluted . . . . $30 – 40	bread tray . . . . $45 – 55
ashtray, leaf* . . . . $30 – 40	butter dish . . . . $50 – 60
ashtray, rectangular. . . . . $25 – 30	cake stand . . . . $15 – 25
bowl, cereal . . . . $20 – 25	casserole, 8" covered. . . . . $80 – 90
bowl, fruit . . . . $10 – 15	casserole, 6" covered. . . . . $35 – 45
bowl, coupe soup . . . . $20 – 25	casserole, 8" skillet shape. . . . . $30 – 35
bowl, lug soup. . . . . $12 – 15	casserole, 6" skillet shape. . . . . $20 – 25
bowl, 12" salad . . . . $85 – 110	casserole, 4" individual . . . . $20 – 25
bowl, 10" salad . . . . $60 – 75	casserole, individual,
bowl, 8" vegetable. . . . . $40 – 50	with handle & cover. . . . . $50 – 60
bowl, 8" covered vegetable . . . . $75 – 85	cigarette box . . . . $35 – 45
bowl, oval divided vegetable . . . . $35 – 40	coaster/ashtray . . . . $15 – 20
bowl, 9" mixing* . . . . $85 – 110	coffee pot, 8 cup . . . . $85 – 95
bowl, 7" mixing* . . . . $75 – 90	coffee pot, 4 cup . . . . $95 – 120
bowl, 5½ mixing* . . . . $60 – 70	coffee pot, individual . . . . $95 – 125
bowl, 4" mixing* . . . . $50 – 60	coffee pot with filter, 4 cup . . . . . . $135 – 150
	coffee server, casual . . . . $125 – 145

creamer	$15 – 20	plate, 10" picnic*	$5 – 8
creamer, casual	$35 – 45	plate, 8" picnic*	$4 – 6
creamer, individual	$20 – 25	platter, 14¾" oval	$90 – 110
cruet with stopper	$30 – 40	platter, 13¾" casual	$85 – 95
cup	$8 – 10	pickle dish	$15 – 20
cup, mother or father	$50 – 60	relish dish	$20 – 25
egg cup	$10 – 15	salt, pepper; each	$8 – 10
gravy boat	$20 – 25	salt shaker, wood top	$55 – 65
gravy underplate	$10 – 15	pepper mill, wood top	$55 – 65
lazy susan*	$85 – 115	sauce boat	$45 – 55
lazy susan, divided*	$85 – 115	saucer	$5 – 7
mug, coffee	$20 – 25	saucer, mother or father	$10 – 15
mug, 2 cup	$40 – 45	server, #3787 heart 7"	$30 – 40
pitcher, 2 quart	$85 – 110	server, #3788 heart 9"	$40 – 50
pitcher, 1 quart	$55 – 65	server, #3855 leaf 11"	$60 – 70
pitcher, 1 pint	$30 – 40	sugar	$15 – 20
pitcher, ½ pint	$20 – 25	sugar, casual	$35 – 45
pitcher, 6 ounce	$20 – 25	sugar, individual	$20 – 25
plate, 14½" chop	$60 – 75	sugar, open	$25 – 30
plate, 12½" chop	$45 – 55	teapot	$85 – 95
plate, 11"	$30 – 35	tidbit, 10"	$12 – 15
plate, 10"	$20 – 25	tray for cruets	$30 – 35
plate, 9"	$15 – 20	tumbler, 12 ounce	$65 – 75
plate, 8"	$10 – 15	warmer	$40 – 50
plate, 6"	$6 – 8	paper napkin, each	$1 – 2
plate, grill, 11"*	$50 – 60	paper place mat, each	$3 – 5
plate, grill, 9"*	$45 – 55	paper price list	$15 – 20

*These items are usually found without carving and marked only with the brown "second" mark and no pattern name. Such pieces were sold only at the Flemington Outlet. Occasionally these items were produced with carved decoration and marked with the pattern name. Carved pieces are considered scarce and are worth 50 – 75% more than non-carved pieces.

Kay Hackett originally designed the Thistle motif as a cigarette set. Ed Hawley, sales manager at that time, asked her to adapt this motif to dinnerware shapes, which she did. Martin Stangl, however, disapproved of Thistle dinnerware. To him, thistles were weeds; and he felt that no one would purchase dishes with "weeds" on them. He was known to have claimed: "Only cows like thistles!"

In spite of Mr. Stangl's opinion, Thistle became extremely popular and was actively produced until 1967. During the early 1950s, Thistle was one of Stangl's bestselling patterns. At that time it was not unusual to find ten decorators cumulatively producing over five hundred Thistle plates per day just to fill outstanding orders.

Stangl's lazy susan shapes were introduced in 1959. They were first produced with carved decoration for department store distribution. During the 1960s, however, the lazy susan shapes were decorated with uncarved motifs and sold only at the Flemington Outlet.

Throughout the 1960s, the small leaf-shaped ashtrays were decorated at the Flemington Outlet during decorating demonstrations. These items were then fired in a small electric kiln in the Flemington workshop and sold as souvenirs at the outlet showroom.

*Thistle individual coffee pot, cup &
saucer, 10" plate, father cup &
saucer, 12½" chop plate, teapot.*

*Thistle lazy susan with carved motif;
Flemington items without carving:
leaf ash tray, 4" mixing bowl,
9" grill plate.*

New Yorker Cartoon Pieces

Introduced: 1950
Shape Style: #3774 Coupe

*New Yorker
cartoon
beer mug,
"Teacher, I'm
all ears."*

Known Pieces:

mug, beer . . . . $95 – 125
pitcher, 2 quart . . . . $150 – 200
plate, 12½" chop . . . . $200 – 300
plate, 10" . . . . $125 – 150
teapot bank, "A Penny Saved
   is a Penny Earned" . . . . $300 – 400
tile . . . . $125 – 150

During 1950, approximately one hundred different items were produced with motifs based on cartoons and James Thurber drawings that had appeared in the *New Yorker* magazine. Most of these items had brushed engobe and a wide band of color on the rims. Many of the cartoon motifs were somewhat risqué. Cartoons depicting partial nudity and sexual innuendo were typical decorations.

The New Yorker cartoon pieces were to have been marketed in conjunction with the *New Yorker* magazine. But because Stangl held no legal rights to these drawings the project was dropped and all the cartoon pieces were sold through the Flemington Outlet.

New Yorker 12½" chop plate with Herbert Hoover caricature.

Fruit and Butterflies #3854

Introduced: 1951
Designer: Kay Hackett
Made For: Frederik Lunning, Inc.
Shape Style: #3774 Coupe

Known Pieces:

bowl, fruit	$20 – 25	plate, 12½" chop	$80 – 95
bowl, lug soup	$25 – 30	plate, 11"	$50 – 60
bowl, 12" salad	$95 – 125	plate, 10"	$40 – 50
bowl, 10" salad	$80 – 90	plate, 9"	$35 – 40
bowl, 8" vegetable	$45 – 55	plate, 8"	$25 – 30
casserole, 4" individual	$30 – 40	plate, 6"	$15 – 20
coffee pot	$150 – 175	relish dish	$25 – 35
creamer	$30 – 35	salt, pepper; each	$15 – 20
cup	$10 – 15	saucer	$10 – 12
egg cup	$20 – 25	sugar	$30 – 35
plate, 14½" chop	$110 – 135	teapot	$150 – 175

During the 1940s and 1950s, there was resistance in the ceramics trade to dinnerware with insect motifs. When Martin Stangl asked Kay Hackett to adapt this pattern from a French design, she retained the insects for interest. Apparently, the insects were innocuous enough to cause the Fruit and Butterflies pattern to become one of Lunning's most popular patterns during the early 1950s.

Because of the small, detailed motifs and engobe and decorations on the interiors and exteriors of the bowls, Lunning's Fruit and Butterflies pattern was expensive to produce. But Frederik Lunning, Inc. was always willing to pay extra for more distinctive patterns. The Fruit and Butterflies pattern was actively produced for nearly three years. It was discontinued during 1953. Because this pattern was produced during the fledgling years of sprayed engobe, Fruit and Butterflies pieces can be found with the engobe either brushed or sprayed. Seconds usually have the Lunning mark blackened out.

Fruit and Butterflies lug soup, fruit bowl, 9" plate, creamer, sugar, teapot.

Fruit and Butterflies coffee pot, 8" plate, cup & saucer, 10" plate, salt & pepper, 6" plate.

Star Flower #3864

Introduced: 1952
Designer: Kay Hackett
Shape Style: #3774 Coupe

Known Pieces:

ashtray, rectangular	$20 – 25
bowl, cereal	$10 – 15
bowl, fruit	$10 – 12
bowl, lug soup	$10 – 15
bowl, 12" salad	$50 – 60
bowl, 10" salad	$40 – 50
bowl, 8" vegetable	$25 – 35
bowl, oval divided vegetable	$25 – 35
bowl, 8" covered vegetable	$55 – 65
bread tray	$25 – 35
butter dish	$30 – 40
casserole, 4" individual	$20 – 25
cigarette box	$35 – 45
coaster/ashtray	$10 – 15
coffee pot, 8 cup	$50 – 60
coffee pot, individual	$70 – 80
creamer	$10 – 15
creamer, individual	$20 – 25
cup	$8 – 10
egg cup	$10 – 15
gravy boat	$20 – 25
gravy underplate	$10 – 15
mug, coffee	$25 – 30
plate, 14½" chop	$50 – 60
plate, 12½" chop	$40 – 45
plate, 11"	$30 – 35
plate, 10"	$20 – 25
plate, 9"	$15 – 20
plate, 8"	$10 – 15
plate, 6"	$6 – 8
pickle dish	$15 – 20
relish dish	$20 – 25
salt, pepper; each	$8 – 10
saucer	$5 – 6
sugar	$15 – 20
sugar, individual	$20 – 25
sugar, open	$25 – 30
teapot	$55 – 75
tidbit, 10"	$10 – 12
warmer	$20 – 25
paper napkin, each	$1 – 2
paper place mat, each	$3 – 4
paper price list	$10 – 15

Star Flower 8" covered vegetable, 4" individual casserole, 14½" chop plate, coffee mug, oval divided vegetable bowl.

By 1952 the spraying of engobe had been perfected to the point that colored engobes were possible. Star Flower was the first dinnerware pattern Stangl produced on colored engobe. Martin Stangl originally named this pattern "Christmas Rose," but renamed it Star Flower so that it could be marketed year round. He did not want this pattern to become holiday pattern with limited retail opportunities.

The hellebore blossoms that adorn the Star Flower pattern were decorated with White #10. This was a heavy color that was not used in the same manner as other underglaze colors. To apply White #10, a decorator would have to drizzle or "skate" the color onto the piece, completely covering the desired areas. If applied too thinly, there would be dark brush-marks or shadows showing in the white.

Often Star Flower seconds were produced without the White #10 blossoms. The pieces were carved and the leaves painted Willow Green, but the flower portion only shows the background engobe. These seconds are valued about half that of fully decorated Star Flower pieces.

Grape #3865

Introduced: 1952
Designer: Kay Hackett
Shape Style: #3774 Coupe

Grape 9" plate.

Known Pieces:

bowl, fruit	$10 – 15
bowl, lug soup	$15 – 20
bowl, 12" salad	$65 – 75
bowl, 10" salad	$45 – 55
bowl, 8" vegetable	$35 – 40
casserole, 4" individual	$25 – 30
coffee pot	$85 – 95
creamer	$20 – 25
cup	$10 – 15
egg cup	$12 – 15
plate, 14½" chop	$85 – 110
plate, 12½" chop	$60 – 70
plate, 10"	$35 – 40
plate, 9"	$25 – 30
plate, 8"	$20 – 25
plate, 6"	$10 – 15
relish dish	$25 – 35
salt, pepper; each	$10 – 15
saucer	$7 – 8
sugar	$20 – 25
teapot	$85 – 95

Kay Hackett's naturalistic Grape pattern, decorated with Willow Green, Victoria Green, and Walnut Brown, was produced for an extremely short time and is nearly impossible to find. This same motif, however, was decorated with Art Ware Green underglaze color and Satin White glaze in 1957 and introduced as the Vintage salad set pattern.

Mr. Stangl's Breakfast Set

Introduced: 1952
Designer: Kay Hackett
Shape Style: #3774 Coupe

Mr. Stangl's Breakfast Set 9" plate, cup and saucer.

Known Pieces:

bowl, 10" salad	$150 – 175
cup	$20 – 25
plate, 12½" chop	$200 – 250
plate, 9"	$75 – 95
plate, 8"	$50 – 65
plate, 6"	$35 – 45
saucer	$15 – 20

The stylized engobe leaves in the center of this pattern were brushed with Yellow underglaze color to create the Yellow hue. The wide band on each piece was brushed with a very heavy application of Art Ware Green. The cups were Art Ware Green on the outside with bright Yellow interiors.

Because of the difficulty the decorators would have had applying Art Ware Green correctly in a mass-production atmosphere, this pattern was not produced for retail sales. However, Mr. Stangl personally liked it, so he had Kay Hackett decorate a small set for his own use. Nearly all of the pieces were marked with Kay Hackett's lower case "k" initial.

Holly #3869

Introduced: 1952
Designer: Kay Hackett
Shape Style: #3774 Coupe

Known Pieces:

ashtray, 5" fluted	$25 – 35	mug, coffee	$25 – 35
ashtray, rectangular	$35 – 40	mug, 2 cup	$45 – 55
ashtray, 8" wind-proof	$50 – 60	pitcher, 2 quart	$90 – 115
bowl, cereal	$20 – 30	pitcher, 1 quart	$70 – 80
bowl, coupe soup	$30 – 40	pitcher, 1 pint	$45 – 55
bowl, fruit	$20 – 25	pitcher, ½ pint	$30 – 35
bowl, 12", #3608	$125 – 150	pitcher, 6 ounce	$25 – 30
bowl, 12" salad	$115 – 135	plate, 14½" chop	$100 – 125
bowl, 10" salad	$70 – 80	plate, 12½" chop	$75 – 95
bowl, 8" vegetable	$40 – 50	plate, 10"	$35 – 45
cake stand	$30 – 40	plate, 8"	$20 – 30
cigarette box	$125 – 150	plate, 6"	$15 – 20
coaster/ashtray	$30 – 35	saucer	$10 – 12
creamer	$20 – 30	sugar	$30 – 40
cup	$20 – 25	teapot	$150 – 175
cup, punch	$50 – 60	tidbit	$15 – 20
		paper price list	$20 – 25

Holly 6" plate, 12½" chop plate, ½ pint pitcher, quart pitcher, 10" plate, #4024 cup & saucer.

Stangl's Holly is a very simple, yet striking, pattern. The white engobe and Pink #160 berries ideally complement the dark Willow Green band and leaves. This pattern was originally offered as a salad set that retailed for $11.75 in 1952. Various dinnerware pieces were added to the Holly assortment throughout the 1950s.

The #3608 12" bowl was produced with the Holly motif during 1959. This piece was intended to be used as either a salad bowl or punch bowl. Originally the cups offered with the punch bowl were the coffee mug shape. The punch cup shape was added during 1962.

Holly was made in relatively small quantities throughout the 1950s, but was hardly produced during the early 1960s. In 1967, however, this pattern was re-introduced as Holly #5189. The Holly #5189 pattern featured the re-styled #4024 cup, sugar, and creamer shapes. All Holly was completely discontinued during 1969.

Magnolia #3870

Introduced: 1952
Designer: Kay Hackett
Shape Style: #3774 Coupe

Known Pieces:

ashtray, rectangular	$20 – 25
bowl, cereal	$10 – 15
bowl, fruit	$10 – 12
bowl, coupe soup	$15 – 20
bowl, lug soup	$10 – 15
bowl, 12" salad	$45 – 55
bowl, 10" salad	$35 – 45
bowl, 8" vegetable	$20 – 25
bowl, oval divided vegetable	$20 – 30
bowl, 8" covered vegetable	$60 – 75
bread tray	$25 – 30
butter dish	$30 – 35
casserole, 8" covered	$60 – 75
casserole, 6" covered	$20 – 25
casserole, 8" skillet shape	$30 – 35
casserole, 6" skillet shape	$20 – 25
casserole, 4" individual	$15 – 20
casserole, individual, with handle & cover	$25 – 30
cigarette box	$35 – 45
coaster/ashtray	$12 – 15
coffee carafe, shape #2000	$115 – 145
coffee pot, 8 cup	$50 – 60
coffee pot, 4 cup	$75 – 85
coffee pot, individual	$75 – 85
coffee server, casual	$85 – 110
creamer	$10 – 15
creamer, individual	$20 – 25
cruet with stopper	$20 – 30
cup	$6 – 9
egg cup	$8 – 12
gravy boat	$10 – 15
gravy underplate	$8 – 12
mug, coffee	$20 – 25
mug, 2 cup	$30 – 35
pitcher, 2 quart	$65 – 75
pitcher, 1 quart	$50 – 60
pitcher, 1 pint	$30 – 35
pitcher, ½ pint	$25 – 30
pitcher, 6 ounce	$20 – 25
plate, 14½" chop	$45 – 55
plate, 12½" chop	$35 – 45
plate, 11"	$20 – 25
plate, 10"	$12 – 15
plate, 9"	$10 – 12

plate, 8" . . . . $8 – 12
plate, 6" . . . . $5 – 7
platter, 13¾" casual. . . . . $50 – 60
pickle dish. . . . . $15 – 20
relish dish . . . . $15 – 20
salt, pepper; each . . . . $8 – 10
saucer . . . . $5 – 6
sugar . . . . $15 – 20

sugar, individual. . . . . $20 – 25
sugar, open . . . . $25 – 30
teapot. . . . . $55 – 65
tidbit, 10". . . . . $10 – 12
tray for cruets . . . . $15 – 25
tumbler, 12 ounce . . . . $60 – 75
warmer . . . . $15 – 20
paper price list . . . . $10 – 15

The Magnolia pattern was on green engobe with blossoms decorated Pink #160 and White #10. Magnolia chop plates, cups, saucers, and bowls were all encircled with a wide Pink #160 band. When on the green engobe background, the Pink #160 underglaze color creates a maroon/red effect.

In 1954 the old #2000 carafe shape was tried as a coffee server with the Magnolia motif. This shape, however, was dropped in favor of the sleek, modern, casual coffee server. The #2000 coffee carafes with Magnolia decoration are extremely rare pieces.

Magnolia 4" individual casserole, 10" plate, teapot, 12½" chop plate, sugar, creamer.

Golden Harvest #3887

Introduced: 1953
Designer: Kay Hackett
Shape Style: #3774 Coupe

Known Pieces:

ashtray, rectangular. . . . . $15 – 20
bowl, cereal. . . . . $10 – 12
bowl, fruit . . . . $8 – 12
bowl, coupe soup . . . . $15 – 20
bowl, lug soup. . . . . $10 – 12
bowl, 12" salad . . . . $40 – 50
bowl, 10" salad . . . . $30 – 40
bowl, 8" vegetable. . . . . $20 – 25
bowl, oval divided vegetable . . . . $20 – 25
bowl, 8" covered veg. . . . . $50 – 60
bread tray . . . . $20 – 25
butter dish. . . . . $30 – 35
casserole, individual,
 with handle & cover. . . . . $25 – 30
casserole, 8" covered. . . . . $60 – 75
casserole, 6" covered. . . . . $20 – 25
casserole, 8" skillet shape. . . . . $20 – 30
casserole, 6" skillet shape. . . . . $15 – 20

casserole, 4" individual . . . . $15 – 20
cigarette box . . . . $30 – 40
coaster/ashtray . . . . $15 – 20
coffee pot, 8 cup . . . . $40 – 50
coffee pot, 4 cup . . . . $65 – 75
coffee pot, individual . . . . $70 – 80
coffee server, casual . . . . $75 – 95
creamer . . . . $10 – 15
creamer, casual . . . . $20 – 25
creamer, individual. . . . . $20 – 25
cruet with stopper. . . . . $25 – 35
cup. . . . . $6 – 8
egg cup . . . . $10 – 15
gravy boat . . . . $10 – 15
gravy underplate. . . . . $8 – 12
mug, coffee . . . . $20 – 25
mug, 2 cup. . . . . $30 – 40
pitcher, 2 quart . . . . $60 – 70
pitcher, 1 quart . . . . $45 – 55

pitcher, 1 pint	$25 – 30		pepper mill, wood top	$45 – 55
pitcher, ½ pint	$20 – 25		sauce boat	$25 – 30
pitcher, 6 ounce	$20 – 25		saucer	$5 – 6
plate, 14½" chop	$45 – 55		sugar	$10 – 15
plate, 12½" chop	$35 – 45		sugar, casual	$20 – 25
plate, 11"	$20 – 25		sugar, individual	$20 – 25
plate, 10"	$15 – 20		sugar, open	$25 – 30
plate, 9"	$10 – 15		teapot	$45 – 55
plate, 8"	$8 – 12		tidbit, 10"	$10 – 12
plate, 6"	$5 – 7		tray for cruets	$20 – 25
platter, 13¾" casual	$45 – 55		tumbler, 12 ounce	$60 – 75
pickle dish	$15 – 20		warmer	$10 – 15
relish dish	$15 – 20		paper napkin, each	$1 – 2
salt, pepper; each	$8 – 10		paper place mat, each	$3 – 4
salt shaker, wood top	$45 – 55		paper price list	$10 – 15

Beginning in 1953, Stangl Pottery began following *House & Garden* magazine's color recommendations. If a housewares manufacturer created a product using the *House & Garden* "fashion" colors for that year, *House & Garden* would showcase that product in a feature article, and the manufacturer could advertise at a reduced rate in the back of the magazine. This was a relatively inexpensive way for manufacturers to gain national advertising.

To take advantage of this advertising promotion, Stangl began to incorporate the featured fashion colors in some of their new dinnerware designs during the 1950s. Since the colors for 1953 were gray and brown, a gray engobe was developed and used as the background for the informal Golden Harvest pattern. To get an opaque yellow for the blossoms, White #10 was mixed with Yellow underglaze color. This color was referred to as Golden Harvest Yellow.

Because Golden Harvest was featured in *House & Garden*, it was also highly promoted by Stangl's sales representatives. As a result of this, Golden Harvest was very popular throughout the 1950s and 1960s. Because of its long production span, many items were added to the Golden Harvest shape assortment over the years.

The tumbler shape was tried only during 1954. Like the Magnolia #2000 coffee carafe, this piece is quite rare.

Golden Harvest casual coffee server, tumbler, 12½" chop plate, individual creamer, individual sugar, individual coffee pot, 4 cup coffee pot, 8 cup coffee pot, 10" plate.

Pink Lily #3888

Pink Lily 10" plate.

Introduced: 1953
Designer: Kay Hackett
Shape Style: #3774 Coupe

Known Pieces:

ashtray, rectangular	$20 – 25
bowl, cereal	$15 – 20
bowl, fruit	$10 – 15
bowl, lug soup	$10 – 15
bowl, 12" salad	$60 – 75
bowl, 10" salad	$45 – 55
bowl, 8" vegetable	$25 – 30
bowl, oval divided vegetable	$20 – 25
bowl, 8" covered vegetable	$65 – 75
bread tray	$45 – 55
butter dish	$25 – 30
casserole, 4" individual	$20 – 25
cigarette box	$55 – 65
coaster/ashtray	$20 – 25
coffee pot, 8 cup	$80 – 90
coffee pot, individual	$85 – 110
creamer	$15 – 20
creamer, individual	$20 – 25
cup	$8 – 10
egg cup	$12 – 15
gravy boat	$10 – 15
gravy underplate	$8 – 10
mug, coffee	$20 – 25
plate, 14½" chop	$60 – 75
plate, 12½" chop	$50 – 60
plate, 11"	$20 – 25
plate, 10"	$20 – 25
plate, 9"	$15 – 20
plate, 8"	$15 – 20
plate, 6"	$7 – 8
pickle dish	$15 – 20
relish dish	$15 – 20
salt, pepper; each	$8 – 10
saucer	$6 – 7
sugar	$15 – 20
sugar, individual	$20 – 25
sugar, open	$20 – 25
teapot	$70 – 85
tidbit, 10"	$10 – 15
warmer	$20 – 25
paper price list	$15 – 20

The Pink Lily pattern was decorated with the same stencils and gray engobe as Golden Harvest, but the motif colors were Willow Green, Pink, and White #10. In the same manner as Golden Harvest, an opaque pink for the blossoms was created by mixing White #10 and Pink #193.

The Pink Lily pattern did not use the 1953 "fashion" colors, so it was not well promoted. Because it was not pushed by the sales department, interest in this pattern lagged so it became inactive on January 1, 1955. During Pink Lily's two years of active production, very little of this pattern was produced.

Marine #3890 Salad Set

Introduced: 1953
Designer: Kay Hackett
Shape Style: #3774 Coupe

Known Pieces:

bowl, 10" salad . . . . $125 – 150

plate, 12½" chop . . . . $125 – 150

plate, 8" . . . . $40 – 50

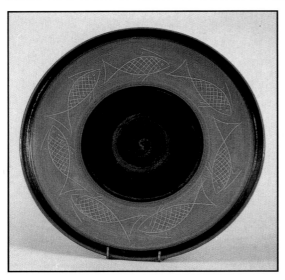

Marine 8" plate.

The Marine motif is very simple, yet striking. This pattern utilizes the red body of Stangl ware with no engobe. The motif is a band of fish carved around the rims of the pieces with Dark Turquoise brushed over the fish. The color would deposit in the carvings, causing the fish to be outlined with Dark Turquoise.

Art Ware Green was brushed on the centers and rims of Marine. When a very heavy application of Art Ware Green is put on the red body under a clear glaze, as it is with Marine, it becomes very dark, verging on black. The effect of this pattern was of a dark green, watery pool surrounded by a subtle ring of blue fish.

Marine was also tried with Yellow instead of Dark Turquoise on the fish. Samples were made and occasionally can be found, but very little Yellow Marine, if any, was produced.

Blossom Time #3891 Salad Set

Introduced: 1953
Designer: Kay Hackett
Shape Style: #3774 Coupe

Blossom Time 8" plate.

Known Pieces:

bowl, 10" salad . . . . $85 – 110

cigarette box . . . . $60 – 70

coaster/ashtray . . . . $20 – 25

plate, 12½" chop . . . . $90 – 120

plate, 8" . . . . $25 – 35

The Blossom Time motif was a Black tree covered with small White #10 flowers and Victoria Green leaves. Blossom Time dinnerware was on green engobe with a wide Tan band. This tree motif did not gain favor as a dinnerware decoration. It was much more popular as a cigarette set and was produced as such well into the late 1950s. The cigarette sets were banded with Willow Green instead of the Tan color used on the dinnerware shapes.

Song Bird #3892 Salad Set

Introduced: 1953
Designer: Kay Hackett
Shape Style: #3774 Coupe

Known Pieces:

bowl, 10" salad . . . . $185 − 225	plate, 12½" chop . . . . $225 − 250
	plate, 8" . . . . $85 − 125

The Song Bird 8" plate and salad bowl feature a rufous-sided towhee on a Black branch with Willow Green leaves. Two Towhees occupy the branch on the Song Bird chop plate. All of the pieces have a wide Black band around the rim. An eight-piece set of this pattern retailed for $18.00 in 1953. Song Bird is a striking and attractive pattern, and is quite collectable.

Song Bird 8" plate, 12½" chop plate.

Wind Fall #3893 Salad Set

Introduced: 1953
Designer: Kay Hackett
Shape Style: #3774 Coupe

Known Pieces:

bowl, 10" salad . . . . $110 − 135	plate, 12½" chop . . . . $125 − 150
	plate, 8" . . . . $50 − 60

The Wind Fall motif was an arrangement of life-size maple leaves and seeds in autumn colors. Wind Fall was inspired by the trend during the early 1950s of using actual pressed leaves in home decoration. There were several major designers using this type of adornment on their lines of home furnishings.

The intricacy of the Wind Fall pattern forced the decorators to spend too much time on each piece, increasing production costs and lowering profitability. Consequently, Wind Fall was discontinued before the end of 1953.

Because the concept of using leaf decoration was still popular after Wind Fall was discontinued, a simplified variation of this pattern was introduced in 1955. The newer version had smaller, easily painted leaves in pink and brown. The name was also changed slightly. The maple leaf Wind Fall #3893 was spelled as two words, whereas Windfall #3930 was spelled as one word.

Wind Fall 10" salad bowl, 12½" chop plate, 8" plate.

Brown Tulip #3894 Salad Set

Introduced: 1953
Designer: Kay Hackett
Shape Style: #3774 Coupe

Known Pieces:	plate, 12½" chop . . . . $100 – 125
bowl, 10" salad . . . . $90 – 110	plate, 8" . . . . $45 – 55

The Pennsylvania Dutch Brown Tulip pattern was quite striking in its contrasts of light and dark, but was not popular during 1953. However, in 1957 this same motif was used again for the red and yellow Provincial pattern, and sold well throughout the 1960s. This tulip motif was also produced as a brightly colored pattern made for the Flemington Outlet during 1957.

Brown Tulip 8" plate.

Banquet #3895 Salad Set

Introduced: 1953
Designer: Kay Hackett
Shape Style: #3774 Coupe

Known Pieces:	plate, 12½" chop . . . . $125 – 150
bowl, 10" salad . . . . $100 – 125	plate, 8" . . . . $50 – 60

The bright fruit and floral motif of the Banquet pattern featured oranges, grapes, and cherries with tiny White #10 flowers on green engobe. The chop plates each have a wide Black band on the rims. The salad bowls had engobe and bands on both the inside and outside surfaces, which added labor and cost to this pattern. The festive motif, coupled with the Black and Green borders, make Banquet a visually rich dinnerware pattern.

Banquet 8" plate 10" salad bowl.

Rose Salad Set

Introduced: 1953
Made For: Flemington Outlet

Known Pieces:

bowl, 9" salad	$45 – 55	plate, 8"	$20 – 25

These novelty salad set shapes were produced throughout the 1950s and were sold only at the Flemington Outlet. The shape for the salad bowl was based on the #3410 console set, but the plates were newly designed. The center of each piece was painted with a pastel underglaze color while the surrounding petals remained white.

Rose 8" plate, Pink #160; 8" plate, Blue #95; 8" plate, Lavender; 9" salad bowl, Victoria Green.

Lyric #3896

Introduced: 1954
Designer: Kay Hackett
Shape Style: #3774 Coupe

Known Pieces:

bowl, lug soup	$20 – 25	creamer, casual	$35 – 45
bowl, 10" salad	$75 – 95	cup	$15 – 20
bowl, 8" vegetable	$50 – 60	mug, coffee	$35 – 45
bowl, oval divided vegetable	$45 – 55	plate, 12½" chop	$110 – 140
casserole, individual, with handle & cover	$55 – 65	plate, 10"	$45 – 55
casserole, 4" individual	$40 – 50	plate, 8"	$25 – 30
cigarette box	$120 – 135	plate, 6"	$15 – 20
coaster/ashtray	$35 – 45	saucer	$10 – 12
coffee server, casual	$125 – 150	sugar, casual	$35 – 45
		tidbit	$25 – 35
		paper price list	$20 – 25

During the late 1940s and early 1950s, flowing, free-form patterns were becoming increasingly popular as decorative motifs. Lyric was Stangl's contribution to this style of decoration. Kay Hackett's inspiration for this pattern was an art-class project her children had been doing at the time.

Lyric was the first pattern to use the #3896 Casual sugar, creamer, coffee server, and coffee mug shapes. These four shapes were designed by Ed Pettingil, who also designed for Blenko Glass Company during the 1950s.

Handled tidbits with the Lyric motif and colored stripes on the rims were produced for the Flemington Outlet during the late 1950s. These pieces were decorated with either a single color or a combination of colors. They are usually priced about the same as black and white Lyric tidbits.

Lyric coaster/ashtray, 10" plate, casual coffee server, casual creamer, casual sugar.

Amber-Glo #3899

Amber-Glo lazy susan.

Introduced: 1954
Designer: Kay Hackett
Shape Style: #3774 Coupe

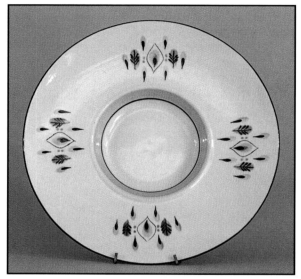

Known Pieces:

ashtray, square, #3914	$40 – 50
ashtray, rectangular	$20 – 25
bowl, cereal	$10 – 15
bowl, fruit	$8 – 10
bowl, coupe soup	$15 – 20
bowl, lug soup	$10 – 12
bowl, 12" salad	$50 – 60
bowl, 10" salad	$35 – 45
bowl, 8" vegetable	$20 – 25
bowl, oval divided vegetable	$20 – 25
bowl, 8" covered vegetable	$50 – 65
bread tray	$25 – 30
butter dish	$35 – 45
casserole, 8" covered	$50 – 65
casserole, 6" covered	$20 – 25
casserole, 8" skillet shape	$20 – 25
casserole, 6" skillet shape	$15 – 20
casserole, 4" individual	$20 – 30
casserole, individual, with handle & cover	$25 – 35
cigarette box	$60 – 70
coaster/ashtray	$15 – 20
coffee pot, 8 cup	$50 – 65
coffee pot, 4 cup	$70 – 85
coffee pot, individual	$80 – 95
coffee server, casual	$75 – 90
creamer	$15 – 20
creamer, casual	$20 – 25
creamer, individual	$20 – 25
cruet with stopper	$20 – 25
cup	$6 – 8
egg cup	$10 – 12
gravy boat	$10 – 15
gravy underplate	$8 – 12
lazy susan	$70 – 85
mug, coffee	$15 – 20
mug, 2 cup	$25 – 35
pitcher, 2 quart	$50 – 60
pitcher, 1 quart	$40 – 50
pitcher, 1 pint	$25 – 30
pitcher, ½ pint	$20 – 25
pitcher, 6 oz.	$15 – 20
plate, 14½" chop	$45 – 55
plate, 12½" chop	$35 – 45
plate, 11"	$20 – 25
plate, 10"	$15 – 20
plate, 9"	$10 – 15

plate, 8"	$8 – 12	sugar, open	$20 – 25
plate, 6"	$5 – 6	teapot	$50 – 65
platter, 13¾" casual	$40 – 50	tidbit, 10"	$8 – 12
pickle dish	$10 – 15	tray for cruets	$20 – 25
relish dish	$15 – 20	vase #3952, 10"	$50 – 60
salt, pepper; each	$6 – 8	vase #3952, 8"	$40 – 50
saucer	$5 – 6	vase #3952, 6"	$30 – 35
sugar	$15 – 20	vase #3952, 4"	$25 – 30
sugar, casual	$20 – 25	warmer	$15 – 20
sugar, individual	$20 – 25	paper price list	$10 – 15

The modern Amber-Glo pattern was based on the Scandinavian styles that were popular during the mid-1950s. Kay Hackett was once asked if she had studied design in Europe because of the authentic Scandinavian appearance of Amber-Glo. Originally designed using Dark Turquoise with Lavender overstrokes, the colors for this pattern were changed to gray and brown to follow *House & Garden's* preferred colors for 1954. The use of these colors enabled Amber-Glo to be advertised as a "mix-n-match" with the popular Golden Harvest pattern. Amber-Glo was very popular during the 1950s and remained in active production until 1960.

The #3952 vases and the #3914 ashtray were not part of the Amber-Glo dinnerware line, but were available through Stangl's giftware catalogs during 1957. The #3914 ashtrays were produced with coral engobe, gray engobe, or white engobe, all with Dark Turquoise decoration. The design on the #3952 vases is varied slightly from the Amber-Glo dinnerware motif.

Amber-Glo 8" plate, 14½" chop plate, salt, pepper, cruets on tray, #3952 10" vase.

Carnival #3900

Introduced: 1954
Designer: Kay Hackett
Shape Style: #3774 Coupe

Carnival coaster/ashtray, 10" plate, teapot, 12½" chop plate, egg cup, 6" plate.

Known Pieces:

ashtray, rectangular	$20 – 25
bowl, cereal	$10 – 12
bowl, fruit	$6 – 8
bowl, coupe soup	$15 – 20
bowl, lug soup	$8 – 10
bowl, 12" salad	$40 – 50
bowl, 10" salad	$30 – 40
bowl, 8" vegetable	$20 – 25
bowl, oval divided vegetable	$20 – 30
bowl, 8" covered vegetable	$45 – 55
bread tray	$25 – 30
butter dish	$30 – 35
casserole, 8" covered	$45 – 55
casserole, 6" covered	$20 – 25
casserole, 8" skillet shape	$20 – 25
casserole, 6" skillet shape	$15 – 20
casserole, 4" individual	$15 – 20
casserole, individual, with handle & cover	$25 – 30
cigarette box	$30 – 40
coaster/ashtray	$10 – 15
coffee pot, 8 cup	$60 – 70
coffee pot, 4 cup	$75 – 85
coffee pot, individual	$80 – 95
coffee server, casual	$75 – 85
creamer	$10 – 12
creamer, casual	$20 – 25
creamer, individual	$20 – 25
cruet with stopper	$20 – 25
cup	$6 – 8
egg cup	$10 – 12
gravy boat	$15 – 20
gravy underplate	$8 – 10
mug, coffee	$15 – 20
pitcher, 2 quart	$55 – 65
pitcher, 1 quart	$35 – 45
pitcher, 1 pint	$25 – 30
pitcher, ½ pint	$20 – 25
pitcher, 6 ounce	$20 – 25
plate, 14½" chop	$50 – 60
plate, 12½" chop	$35 – 45
plate, 11"	$20 – 25
plate, 10"	$12 – 15
plate, 9"	$10 – 12
plate, 8"	$8 – 10
plate, 6"	$6 – 7
platter, 13¾" casual	$35 – 45
pickle dish	$10 – 15
relish dish	$20 – 25
salt, pepper; each	$6 – 8
saucer	$5 – 6
sugar	$15 – 20
sugar, casual	$20 – 25
sugar, individual	$20 – 25
sugar, open	$20 – 25
teapot	$50 – 60
tidbit, 10"	$10 – 12
tray for cruets	$20 – 25
warmer	$15 – 20
paper price list	$10 – 12

This lively pattern was designed with New Year's Eve entertaining in mind. The festive pink and black starbursts with green streamers caused Carnival to be a popular pattern throughout the 1950s. The underglaze color Carnival Green was developed specifically for this pattern. It was made by combining the Victoria Green and Olive Green underglaze colors.

Carnival was an ideal pattern for beginning decorators learn hand-painting techniques. Mistakes were not as obvious on Carnival's free-flowing motifs as they would be on Stangl's more exacting patterns.

Plain Color, Red Edge Dinnerware #3901

Introduced: 1954
Shape Style: #3774 Coupe

Known Pieces:

bowl, fruit . . . . $4 – 6	plate, 12½" chop . . . . $15 – 20
bowl, 10" salad . . . . $20 – 25	plate, 10" . . . . $8 – 12
bowl, 8" vegetable . . . . $10 – 15	plate, 9" . . . . $5 – 7
casserole, individual,	plate, 8" . . . . $4 – 6
with handle & cover . . . . $15 – 20	plate, 6" . . . . $3 – 4
coffee pot . . . . $45 – 55	relish dish . . . . $10 – 12
creamer . . . . $8 – 10	salt, pepper; each . . . . $3 – 5
cup . . . . $4 – 6	saucer . . . . $3 – 4
egg cup . . . . $6 – 8	sugar . . . . $10 – 15
plate, 14½" chop . . . . $20 – 30	teapot . . . . $35 – 45

Stangl's Plain Color, Red Edge dinnerware consisted of plain shapes simply sprayed with white, gray, or green engobe. A razor-knife was used to trim the edge, creating the distinctive, wide red edge.

This pattern was Stangl's answer to the widely distributed solid-color plastic dinnerware of the time. Although retailed to be competitively priced, Red Edge dinnerware turned out to be less than popular, so became a Flemington item for a short time during the 1950s.

Plain color, Red Edge 6" plate, white; cup & saucer, green; 10" plate, gray.

Jonquil

Re-introduced: 1954
Shape Style: #3774 Coupe

Known Pieces:

bowl, cereal . . . . $20 – 25	pitcher, 1 pint . . . . $40 – 50
bowl, fruit . . . . $15 – 20	pitcher, ½ pint . . . . $25 – 35
bowl, coupe soup . . . . $25 – 30	pitcher, 6 ounce . . . . $20 – 25
bowl, lug soup . . . . $20 – 25	plate, 14½" chop . . . . $95 – 120
bowl, 12" salad . . . . $90 – 110	plate, 12½" chop . . . . $65 – 75
bowl, 10" salad . . . . $65 – 75	plate, 10" . . . . $25 – 35
bowl, 8" vegetable . . . . $40 – 50	plate, 9" . . . . $20 – 25
coffee pot, 8 cup . . . . $110 – 130	plate, 8" . . . . $15 – 20
creamer . . . . $20 – 25	plate, 6" . . . . $10 – 15
cup . . . . $12 – 15	relish dish . . . . $25 – 35
egg cup . . . . $15 – 20	salt, pepper; each . . . . $10 – 12
pitcher, 2 quart . . . . $95 – 125	saucer . . . . $7 – 8
pitcher, 1 quart . . . . $80 – 90	sugar . . . . $20 – 25
	teapot . . . . $95 – 125

During the 1940s, Cleo Salerno's original #3744 Jonquil pattern was produced for Frederik Lunning on the #3434 rim shape. When Stangl's contract with Lunning ended, Jonquil was re-introduced on the #3774 coupe shape and backstamped with the Stangl trademark. The French Green and Orange motif was identical on both versions of this pattern.

Jonquil cup & saucer, 10" plate, 6" plate.

Veiled Dinnerware

Introduced: 1954
Developed By: Dave Thomas

Known Pieces:

ashtray, 8" wind-proof	$55 – 65	pitcher, 1 pint	$30 – 40
bowl, fruit	$15 – 20	pitcher, ½ pint	$20 – 30
bowl, lug soup	$15 – 20	pitcher, 6 ounce	$20 – 25
bowl, 12" salad	$65 – 75	plate, 14½" chop	$90 – 115
bowl, 10" salad	$50 – 60	plate, 12½" chop	$60 – 70
bowl, 8" vegetable	$35 – 45	plate, 11"	$45 – 50
coffee pot	$100 – 125	plate, 10"	$40 – 50
creamer	$20 – 25	plate, 9"	$30 – 35
cup	$10 – 15	plate, 8"	$25 – 30
egg cup	$12 – 15	plate, 6"	$15 – 20
gravy boat	$20 – 25	relish dish	$25 – 30
gravy underplate	$10 – 15	salt, pepper; each	$8 – 10
mug	$40 – 50	saucer	$7 – 8
pitcher, 2 quart	$85 – 95	sugar	$15 – 25
pitcher, 1 quart	$50 – 60	teapot	$100 – 125

The best account of the development of this pattern comes from the person responsible for its production. In addition to being Martin Stangl's son-in-law, Dave Thomas was Stangl's plant manager and in charge of all production during Martin Stangl's absences. Following is Dave Thomas's account of the production of Veiled Dinnerware.

"The PEMCO company of Baltimore, Maryland, developed a spray gun which put out a single continuous stream of glaze (or color) rather than an atomized spray as is normally done in spray glazing. They had to develop an additive for the color or glaze so that the single, fine line of material would hold together and not break up or become separated. This spray gun, with paint, was used to veil wastebaskets, toys, etc. as a design motif. Their salesman brought the gun and some material to the Stangl factory in Trenton and we sprayed a few plates. It went fast and certainly was different!

"About that time, Mr. Stangl took another of his trips to Europe and was gone for a month or so. During this time we had need of some 'fill' for the kilns. So I took a thousand or so plates, cups, and saucers, etc., from the bisque storage and we 'veiled' them. This was done on a weekend as I recall.

"When they came out of the kiln, we packed them in ware boxes and hustled them off to Flemington — very few of the employees knew what was going on. Well, when Merrill [Merrill Bacheler, manager of the Flemington Outlet, and a son-in-law of Mr. Stangl] saw them he stated flatly that they would not sell; but he did put them on display. He was right — no sale! He sent them back to Trenton. It seems that at that time we had a program going on whereby we were replacing some of the wood planking floors with six inches of cement. With Mr. Stangl due back any day, I wanted this horrible nightmare out of sight before he got in. So we dug a bit deeper in the floor area and dumped several hundred plates etc. and smashed them down for fill. On goes the concrete and the mess is gone — out of sight forever!"

Obviously some pieces of this pattern were sold out of Flemington, but so few that the remaining Veiled pieces are very scarce.

Veiled Dinnerware 8" wind-proof ashtray, 10" plate, gravy boat, 2 quart pitcher, 10" plate.

American Bone China

Introduced: 1955
Developed By: Martin Stangl

Known Pieces:		
coffee pot	$80 – 95	
creamer	$20 – 30	
cup	$10 – 15	
plate	$40 – 50	
saucer	$10 – 15	
sauce tureen, covered	$90 – 110	
sauce underplate	$15 – 20	
sauce ladle	$25 – 35	
sugar	$25 – 35	
teapot	$95 – 120	
vase	$60 – 95	

Stangl's American Bone China was developed to take advantage of the popularity of gold-decorated ceramics during the 1950s. American Bone China was a translucent porcelain product, which, contrary to its name, contained no calcium phosphate — the technical name for "bone." The principle component of American Bone China was nepheline syenite, a composition of pre-fired material that was used to produce creamy colored china products at the same relatively low firing temperatures used for Stangl's earthenware lines.

The most common items produced in the American Bone China line were coffee pot, creamer, and sugar sets based on #3434 shapes. These pieces were decorated with various stylized gold luster motifs or hand-painted florals done in underglaze or fired-on overglaze colors.

The American Bone China teapot, creamer, and sugar sets utilized an experimental shape originally designed in 1942. This shape was brought out again in 1955 specifically for the American Bone China line. Since the #3636 small cigarette box with yellow flowers had been discontinued by this time, Martin Stangl reassigned the #3636 to these teapot, creamer, sugar, plate, cup, and saucer shapes. The gold luster decorations applied to the #3636 pieces were usually artistically rendered floral motifs. Very little American Bone China was produced on the #3636 shape so these pieces are quite rare.

Other shapes resurrected for the American Bone China line were #1800 Cabbage teapot, creamer, and sugar shapes and about one dozen different medium-sized vase shapes. Nearly all of these shapes were decorated with simple gold bands or pin striping.

Because of production difficulties, American Bone China was a very short-lived product. The leading problem encountered was maintaining the clean environment necessary for china production. This was nearly impossible in the red iron oxide atmosphere of Stangl's earthenware production facility. By the end of 1955, American Bone China was dropped. Stangl then put more emphasis on developing earthenware dinnerware patterns decorated with gold luster.

left: American Bone China coffee pot, creamer, and sugar with overglaze floral decoration.

right: American Bone China sauce tureen with underplate and ladle (cover missing), creamer, sugar, coffee pot.

Wild Rose #3929

Introduced: 1955
Designer: Kay Hackett
Shape Style: #3774 Coupe

Known Pieces:

bowl, cereal	$15 – 20	cake stand	$20 – 25
bowl, fruit	$10 – 15	casserole, 8" covered	$75 – 85
bowl, coupe soup	$20 – 25	casserole, 6" covered	$25 – 30
bowl, lug soup	$12 – 15	casserole, 8" skillet shape	$30 – 35
bowl, 12" salad	$70 – 80	casserole, 6" skillet shape	$20 – 25
bowl, 10" salad	$45 – 55	casserole, individual,	
bowl, 8" vegetable	$35 – 45	with handle & cover	$30 – 40
bowl, oval divided vegetable	$30 – 34	cigarette box	$60 – 75
bowl, 8" covered vegetable	$75 – 85	coaster/ashtray	$20 – 25
bread tray	$35 – 45	coaster/ashtray, 150th anniversary	$45 – 55
butter dish	$35 – 45	coffee pot, 8 cup	$85 – 95

coffee pot, 4 cup . . . . $95 – 120	plate, 9" . . . . $15 – 20
creamer . . . . $15 – 20	plate, 8" . . . . $10 – 15
cruet with stopper. . . . . $30 – 40	plate, 6" . . . . $6 – 8
cup. . . . . $8 – 10	platter, 13¾" casual. . . . . $80 – 90
egg cup . . . . $10 – 15	pickle dish. . . . . $15 – 20
gravy boat . . . . $15 – 25	relish dish . . . . $25 – 30
gravy underplate. . . . . $8 – 12	salt, pepper; each . . . . $8 – 10
mug, coffee . . . . $20 – 25	salt shaker, wood top . . . . $55 – 65
mug, 2 cup. . . . . $40 – 45	pepper mill, wood top . . . . $55 – 65
pitcher, 2 quart . . . . $75 – 85	saucer . . . . $6 – 7
pitcher, 1 quart . . . . $55 – 65	sugar . . . . $15 – 20
pitcher, 1 pint . . . . $30 – 40	sugar, open . . . . $20 – 25
pitcher, ½ pint. . . . . $20 – 25	teapot. . . . . $85 – 95
pitcher, 6 ounce . . . . $20 – 25	tidbit, 10". . . . . $10 – 15
plate, 14½" chop. . . . . $60 – 75	tray for cruets . . . . $25 – 35
plate, 12½" chop. . . . . $45 – 55	warmer . . . . $20 – 25
plate, 11". . . . . $30 – 35	paper napkin, each . . . . $1 – 2
plate, 10". . . . . $20 – 25	paper price list . . . . $10 – 15

Kay Hackett styled the Wild Rose pattern after the popular old-fashioned climbing rose American Pillar. The Wild Rose motif is composed of Pink #193 single-rose blossoms with Willow and Victoria Green leaves. This pattern was quite popular during the late 1950s and early 1960s. By 1967, however, pink was no longer a fashionable color, so Wild Rose became inactive. Currently, many collectors still enjoy this colorful pattern.

Wild Rose 10" plate, individual casserole with handle, 12½" chop plate, 4 cup coffee pot.

Windfall #3930

Introduced: 1955
Designer: Kay Hackett
Shape Style: #3774 Coupe

Known Pieces:

bowl, cereal. . . . . $10 – 12	butter dish. . . . . $25 – 30
bowl, fruit . . . . $6 – 8	casserole, 8" covered. . . . . $40 – 50
bowl, coupe soup . . . . $15 – 20	casserole, 6" covered. . . . . $20 – 25
bowl, lug soup. $8 – 10	casserole, 8" skillet shape. . . . . $15 – 20
bowl, 12" salad . . . . $40 – 50	casserole, 6" skillet shape. . . . . $10 – 15
bowl, 10" salad . . . . $30 – 40	casserole, individual,
bowl, 8" vegetable. . . . . $20 – 25	with handle & cover. . . . . $25 – 30
bowl, oval divided vegetable . . . . $20 – 25	cigarette box . . . . $60 – 75
bowl, 8" covered vegetable. . . . . $40 – 50	coaster/ashtray . . . . $15 – 20
bread tray . . . . $20 – 25	coaster/ashtray,
	150th anniversary mark. . . . . $25 – 35

coffee pot, 8 cup . . . . $55 – 65	plate, 8" . . . . $8 – 12
coffee pot, 4 cup . . . . $75 – 85	plate, 6" . . . . $6 – 7
creamer . . . . $12 – 15	platter, 13¾" casual. . . . . $35 – 45
cruet with stopper. . . . . $20 – 25	pickle dish. . . . . $10 – 15
cup. . . . . $6 – 8	relish dish . . . . $15 – 20
egg cup . . . . $8 – 10	salt, pepper; each . . . . $6 – 8
gravy boat . . . . $10 – 15	saucer . . . . $5 – 6
gravy underplate. . . . . $8 – 10	sugar . . . . $15 – 20
mug, coffee . . . . $15 – 20	sugar, open . . . . $20 – 25
pitcher, 2 quart . . . . $50 – 60	teapot. . . . . $55 – 65
pitcher, 1 quart . . . . $35 – 45	tidbit, 10". . . . . $10 – 12
pitcher, 1 pint . . . . $25 – 30	tray for cruets . . . . $15 – 20
pitcher, ½ pint. . . . . $20 – 25	vase #3952, 10" . . . . $50 – 60
pitcher, 6 ounce . . . . $15 – 20	vase #3952, 8" . . . . $40 – 50
plate, 14½" chop . . . . $50 – 60	vase #3952, 6" . . . . $30 – 35
plate, 12½" chop . . . . $35 – 45	vase #3952, 4" . . . . $25 – 30
plate, 10" . . . . $15 – 20	warmer . . . . $10 – 15
plate, 9" . . . . $10 – 15	paper price list . . . . $10 – 12

The Windfall #3930 motif was a modern, orderly arrangement of small leaves. Stangl's price list stated "...the crisp, clear-cut design of Stangl's Windfall brings refreshing sophistication to every meal!" This brisk pattern was decorated with Orange, Pink #193, and Walnut Brown.

During 1955 Stangl celebrated the 150th anniversary of the establishment of the company, based on the erroneous founding date of 1805. For this occasion, coaster/ashtrays with the Wild Rose and Windfall motifs were produced with a backstamp commemorating this anniversary. These coaster/ashtrays were used in sales promotions and sold at the Flemington Outlet. Since Windfall #3930 was introduced toward the end of the craze for foliar motifs, a relatively small amount of this pattern was produced before it became inactive in 1957.

Kay Hackett designed the #3952 cylinder vases with a stylized Windfall motif in 1956. These vases were not part of the Windfall dinnerware line, but were sold through Stangl's giftware catalogs during fall 1956 and all of 1957.

Windfall sugar, 10" plate, coffee mug, coaster/ashtray.

Country Garden #3943

Introduced: 1956
Designer: Kay Hackett
Shape Style: #3774 Coupe

Known Pieces:

ashtray, 5" fluted*. . . . . $10 – 15
ashtray, leaf*. . . . . $25 – 35
bowl, cereal . . . . $15 – 20
bowl, cereal✢ . . . . $8 – 10
bowl, fruit. . . . . $12 – 15
bowl, coupe soup . . . . $20 – 25
bowl, lug soup . . . . $15 – 20

bowl, 6¼" porridge‡	$20 – 25	pitcher, 6 ounce	$20 – 25
bowl, 12" salad	$80 – 90	plate, 14½" chop	$70 – 80
bowl, 10" salad	$65 – 75	plate, 12½" chop	$50 – 60
bowl, 10" salad‡	$30 – 35	plate, 12½" chop‡	$30 – 40
bowl, 8" vegetable	$35 – 40	plate, 11"	$30 – 40
bowl, 8" vegetable‡	$20 – 25	plate, 10"	$20 – 25
bowl, oval divided vegetable	$30 – 35	plate, 10⅝"‡	$10 – 15
bread tray	$40 – 50	plate, 9"	$30 – 35
butter dish	$45 – 55	plate, 8"	$10 – 12
cake stand	$25 – 30	plate, 8¼"‡	$6 – 8
casserole, 8" covered	$95 – 110	plate, 6"	$6 – 7
casserole, 8" skillet shape	$30 – 40	plate, 6" ‡	$3 – 4
casserole, 6" skillet shape	$20 – 30	plate, grill, 11"*	$40 – 50
casserole, individual,		plate, grill, 9"*	$40 – 50
with handle & cover	$35 – 45	plate, 10" picnic*	$5 – 8
cigarette box	$80 – 95	plate, 8" picnic*	$4 – 6
clock, round	$35 – 45	platter, 14¾" oval	$95 – 115
clock, scalloped edge	$60 – 75	platter, 14⅜" oval‡	$40 – 50
coaster/ashtray*	$10 – 15	platter, 13¾" casual	$85 – 95
coffee pot, 8 cup	$90 – 110	pickle dish	$20 – 25
coffee pot, 4 cup	$95 – 120	relish dish	$20 – 30
coffee pot with filter	$110 – 140	salt, pepper; each	$8 – 10
creamer	$15 – 20	salt shaker, wood top	$60 – 70
cruet with stopper	$30 – 40	pepper mill, wood top	$60 – 70
cup	$10 – 12	sauce boat	$35 – 45
egg cup	$12 – 15	saucer	$5 – 6
gravy boat	$20 – 25	sugar	$15 – 20
gravy underplate	$10 – 15	sugar, open	$30 – 40
mug, coffee	$20 – 25	teapot	$85 – 95
mug, 2 cup	$35 – 45	tidbit, 10"	$10 – 15
mug, stack	$35 – 45	tidbit, 2 tier	$25 – 35
pitcher, 2 quart	$85 – 95	tile*	$15 – 20
pitcher, 1 quart	$60 – 70	tray for cruets	$30 – 35
pitcher, 1½ pint‡	$35 – 45	warmer	$25 – 30
pitcher, 1 pint	$35 – 45	paper napkin, each	$1 – 2
pitcher, ½ pint	$25 – 30	paper price list	$10 – 12

‡These items were produced on the white body used after 1974.
*These items are usually found without carving and marked only with the brown "second" mark and no pattern name. Such pieces were sold only at the Flemington Outlet. Occasionally these items were produced with carved decoration and marked with the pattern name. Carved pieces are considered scarce and are worth 50 – 75% more than non-carved pieces.

Stangl's Country Garden motif featured an array of colorful, stylized garden flowers. The primary colors red, blue, and yellow were used throughout this pattern to achieve a balanced color arrangement in the table setting. Some of the flowers on this pattern were styled after hibiscus, daffodils, flax, primrose, marigold, iris, tiger lily, sunflower, campanula, and tulips. On the rims of most pieces are narrow bands of Willow Green and Dark Turquoise. Kay Hackett originally designed this pattern with narrow Walnut Brown and Dark Turquoise bands on the rims. The contrasting brown and turquoise bands added dimension to the central motifs, but Mr. Stangl felt that Willow Green would be a better color for the inner band.

Because Country Garden was not designed with fashion colors (which tend to be fashionable for only short periods of time), this pattern remained popular and in continual production through 1977. Country Garden is still a relatively popular pattern enjoyed by many collectors.

Country Garden had been in production for two years when the shape of the cup was changed from the #3774 coupe shape to the #4024 shape in 1958. At first the #4024 cups were sold only with boxed sets of Country Garden, while the older #3774 coupe shape cups were available as replacement pieces ordered from Trenton and at the Flemington Outlet. By 1970 only #4024 shape cups were available with this pattern.

The salt shaker and pepper mill with the wood tops were introduced in 1959 as department store items. This type of salt and pepper were produced in several patterns during that year and are rather uncommon.

The filter coffee pot shape was tried during the early 1960s. The pot shape itself was based on the #3434 teapot shape. This pot and filter set was not a well-received item. They are found infrequently and were tried with only a few patterns.

Stangl began producing dinnerware pattern clocks during the late 1960s. Some were made exclusively for the clock company Verichron, but most of the clocks were put together at the Flemington Outlet. This was done as a means to stretch a few more dollars out of flawed 10" plates. The round clocks assembled in Flemington were made from drilled 10" plates with inexpensive clock movements and self-stick numerals. The Country Garden clocks on the scalloped #5226 Queen Anne plates were made specifically for Verichron, and usually have fired-on decal numerals and the Verichron name.

Country Garden was produced on the newer white bodied shapes from 1975 through 1977. Most of these white-bodied dinnerware pieces are less desirable, so are usually priced lower than the hand-carved, red-bodied pieces.

above right: Country Garden 6" plate, cup & saucer, 10" plate, filter coffee pot with filter & lid, 9" plate, sauce boat, round tile.

above: Country Garden Verichron clock, wood top salt shaker & pepper mill.

right: Country Garden cigarette box.

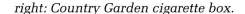

Country Life #3946

Introduced: 1956
Designer: Kurt Weise
Adapted By: Kay Hackett
Shape Style: #3434 Rim

Known Pieces:

bowl, coupe soup, one duck	$50 – 65
bowl, coupe soup, two ducks	$100 – 125
bowl, fruit, colt	$50 – 65
bowl, fruit, rooster	$30 – 40
bowl, 10" salad, pig	$150 – 175
bowl, 8" vegetable, calf	$150 – 175
bowl, 8" vegetable, one duck	$75 – 85
bowl, 8" divided, duck and ducklings	$200 – 225
bread tray, hen and chicks	$260 – 290
coaster, duckling	$40 – 45
creamer, hen	$30 – 40
cup hen	$20 – 25
egg cup chick	$40 – 50
plate, 14½" chop, barn	$225 – 250
plate, 14½" chop, barn and farm name	$600 – 700
plate, 12½" chop, house and garden	$375 – 425
plate, 12½" chop, with house and lane	$225 – 250
plate, 11", farmer	$85 – 110
plate, 10", rooster	$50 – 60
plate, 10", farmer's wife	$100 – 125
plate, 8", cow	$80 – 90
plate, 8", pig	$60 – 75
plate, 6", rooster	$20 – 30
platter, 13¾" casual with hen and ducklings	$250 – 275
salt, pepper, ducklings, each	$20 – 25
salt shaker, wood top	$75 – 85
pepper mill, wood top	$75 – 85
saucer, with nest of eggs	$15 – 20
sugar, rooster	$45 – 55
paper price list	$40 – 50

In 1955 Martin Stangl asked Kay Hackett to develop a commercially feasible dinnerware pattern from the original samples for his Farm Life set. She accomplished this by brightening the original French Green, Victoria Green, and Walnut Brown color scheme with reds and yellows, and by reducing the number of strokes needed to carve and paint each piece. After numerous samples and sketches were created during the first six months of 1956, the Country Life pattern was finally approved and put into production on July 11, 1956.

Because of the elaborate, detailed motifs, Country Life required much more precise decorating than many simpler patterns. As a result of the extra attention required in its production, Country Life was more expensive than similar Stangl patterns. For this reason, several of the Country Life motifs were modified in 1958 to help streamline production and reduce the cost: the dunking duck was eliminated from the 8" coupe soup; the house and garden motif on the 12½" chop plate was changed to a house and lane; the fruit bowl motif was changed from a colt to a rooster; the cow on the 8" plate was replaced with a pig and the calf on the 8" vegetable bowl was replaced with the same duck used on the coupe soup.

All of the revised motifs used fewer, bolder brush strokes that cut down on the time required to produce each piece. Also, boxed sets included only the easily-decorated rooster 10" plates instead of the more costly farmer's wife 10" plates. The farmer's wife plates were still produced, but only through special order.

For a short time, Country Life 14½" chop plates with the barn motif could be ordered from Trenton with "your own" farm name painted around the rim. These personalized chop plates were produced in small quantities and are extremely rare.

In spite of the effort to reduce costs, Country Life remained expensive, so became inactive before 1960. The charm of the Country Life design and its scarcity make its value considerably higher than most other Stangl dinnerware patterns.

Country Life fruit bowl, 12½" chop plate with house and garden motif, salt shaker, coupe soup with original ducks, 14½" chop plate, cup & saucer, coupe soup with revised duck, 12½" chop plate with revised house, creamer, sugar.

Country Life 8" vegetable bowl, 10" plate with rooster, wood top salt shaker & pepper mill, 8" plate with original cow motif, 11" plate with farmer, 8" plate with revised pig motif, egg cup, 10" plate with farmer's wife, coaster/ashtray.

Christmas Tree #3957, Jewelled Holiday, Jewelled Christmas Tree

Introduced: 1956
Designer: Kay Hackett
Shape Style: #3774 Coupe

Known Pieces:

bowl, 12" salad #3608	$160 – 185
bowl, 12" salad #5150	$200 – 225
bowl, 9" salad	$70 – 85
cigarette box	$110 – 135
coaster/ashtray	$30 – 40
creamer	$30 – 35
cup	$20 – 25
cup, punch	$50 – 65
mug, coffee	$45 – 55
pitcher, 2 quart	$100 – 125
pitcher, 1 quart	$70 – 85
pitcher, 1 pint	$50 – 65
pitcher, ½ pint	$35 – 45
pitcher, 6 ounce	$30 – 40
plate, 14½" chop	$115 – 145
plate, 12½" chop	$90 – 115
plate, 10"	$40 – 50
plate, 8"	$25 – 30
plate, 6"	$20 – 25
saucer	$8 – 12
sugar	$30 – 35
teapot	$150 – 175
tidbit 10"	$20 – 30
tidbit, 2 tier	$35 – 45
paper price list	$12 – 15

Stangl's Christmas Tree was a very simple, yet rich pattern. This richness was achieved by the green on green color scheme with platinum and 22-karat gold decorations. The circular "ornaments" were carved using a Dremel Moto-Tool with carbide cutting bits purchased from a dental supply company.

Christmas Tree was the name used for this pattern from 1956 through 1969. This pattern was actively produced through 1960 for holiday sales promotions. Throughout the 1960s the Christmas Tree pattern was technically inactive, available as special order only. In 1970, this pattern was re-introduced and renamed Jewelled Christmas Tree. Also at that time, the tree motif was enlarged on the plates; and the cup, sugar, and creamer were changed from the #3774 coupe shape to the restyled #4024 shapes. For a very short time during 1970 the words "Merry Christmas" were stamped on the fronts of all the pieces in this pattern.

On May 7, 1956, Kay Hackett carved the first samples for the Chrismas Tree pattern. The development of this pattern took place during May and June of 1956, and was fully approved and in production by the second week of July.

During the early 1970s, the specialty shop Carole Stupell Ltd. carried the Jewelled Christmas Tree pattern. This pattern was not exclusive to Carole Stupell, but the Carole Stupell trademark was stamped in gold on the backs of the pieces sold at that shop. Pieces bearing the Carole Stupell Ltd. backstamp are usually valued about 50% higher than typical Jewelled Christmas Tree items.

Between 1972 and 1974, certain items with the Christmas tree motif were produced with platinum luster only and no gold. These items were marked Jewelled Holiday and marketed as a separate pattern from Jewelled Christmas Tree. Items marked Jewelled Holiday are quite rare and desirable.

Two different salad/punch bowl shapes were produced with a Christmas Tree motif. The #3608 12" salad bowl was introduced in 1956 and available until 1960. The 12" #5150 salad bowl was decorated with the Jewelled Christmas Tree motif only during 1974.

Cigarette boxes were decorated either with a single tree or with a tree and a band of "jewels" on either side of the tree.

Jewelled Christmas Tree 6" plate; Jewelled Holiday punch cup; Christmas Tree 14½" chop plate, coaster/ashtray, 1 pint pitcher, 10" plate, Jewelled Christmas Tree creamer.

Jewelled Christmas Tree 10" plate with "Merry Christmas" stamped on front.

Red Ivy #3961, Wildwood #3962

Introduced: 1957
Designer: Kay Hackett
Shape Style: #3434 Rim

Known Pieces:

bowl, rim soup	$25 – 30
bowl, 12" #3608 salad	$90 – 120
cigarette box	$90 – 110
coaster/ashtray	$30 – 35
coffee pot	$100 – 135
creamer	$20 – 25
cup	$10 – 15
pitcher, 1 pint	$45 – 55
pitcher, ½ pint	$30 – 40
pitcher, 6 ounce	$25 – 30
plate, 14½" chop	$85 – 95
plate, 12½" chop	$60 – 70
plate, 11"	$30 – 35
plate, 10"	$25 – 30
plate, 8"	$15 – 20
plate, 6"	$10 – 12
saucer	$5 – 6
sugar	$8 – 10
teapot	$100 – 135
tidbit	$10 – 15
paper price list	$15 – 20

The striking Red Ivy motif features an arrangement of Pink #160 leaves with 22-karat gold dots. The bands are Pink #160 and Orange with a 22-karat gold band on the rim. The Red Ivy motif was originally designed on green engobe, but was produced on white engobe only.

Wildwood was decorated with stylized blossoms in the pastel colors Pink #193, Yellow, Dark Turquoise, Orange, and Victoria Green. Platinum and 22-karat gold were used for the dots and centers of the flowers. This adds a sparkle that would otherwise be lacking from this floral pattern.

In 1957, Stangl's gold decorated dinnerware retailed for about twice that of typical Stangl patterns. A Red Ivy 11" plate retailed for $6.00, while a Provincial 11" plate was $3.00 retail. The Wildwood pattern was even more costly with 11" plates retailing for $8.00 each. Red Ivy

and Wildwood boxed three-piece cigarette sets and pitcher sets retailed at $10.00 and $8.00 respectively. These two patterns were produced for less than two years. They are uncommon and somewhat difficult to find.

Wildwood cigarette box, 11" plate, sugar; Red Ivy 11" plate, cup & saucer, 8" plate.

Frosted Fruit #3963, Concord #3964

Introduced: 1957
Designer: Kay Hackett
Shape Style: #3434 Rim

Known Pieces:

bowl, rim soup	$25 – 30	pitcher, 6 ounce	$20 – 25
bowl, 12" #3608 salad	$90 – 120	plate, 14½" chop	$75 – 85
bowl, 8" vegetable	$35 – 45	plate, 12½" chop	$50 – 60
cigarette box	$80 – 100	plate, 11"	$25 – 35
coaster/ashtray	$20 – 25	plate, 10"	$20 – 30
coffee pot	$85 – 115	plate, 8"	$15 – 20
creamer	$15 – 20	plate, 6"	$10 – 12
cup	$10 – 12	saucer	$5 – 6
pitcher, 2 quart	$80 – 90	sugar	$20 – 25
pitcher, 1 quart	$55 – 65	teapot	$90 – 120
pitcher, 1 pint	$35 – 45	tidbit	$10 – 15
pitcher, ½ pint	$25 – 30	paper price list	$15 – 20

Both the Frosted Fruit and Concord patterns were decorated with Satin White glaze and 22-karat gold trim. The Satin White glaze gives these patterns a soft, misty appearance that, coupled with the gold decoration, was quite distinctive. These patterns retailed for the same prices as the Red Ivy pattern. In spite of the higher retail, Frosted Fruit and Concord were reasonably popular during the late 1950s and early 1960s. Because of increased labor costs, Frosted Fruit and Concord became inactive in 1966, and were completely discontinued on July 10, 1968.

Frosted Fruit plates and bowls were covered with a swirl of Frosted Fruit Green, with the fruit motifs well defined with gold luster. The Frosted Fruit hollow ware pieces were glazed Satin White, only the fruits and bands were Frosted Fruit Green. The motif on Concord was decorated with Blue #95 on a white background. The 22-karat gold decoration adds depth and character to this blue and white pattern.

Concord 11" plate, sugar, creamer; Frosted Fruit 8" plate, cigarette box, 10" plate, coffee pot.

Tiger Lily #3965

Introduced: 1957
Designer: Kay Hackett
Shape Style: #3774 Coupe

Known Pieces:

bowl, cereal	$20 – 25	mug, coffee	$25 – 30
bowl, fruit	$12 – 15	pitcher, 2 quart	$85 – 95
bowl, coupe soup	$20 – 25	pitcher, 1 quart	$55 – 65
bowl, lug soup	$15 – 20	pitcher, 1 pint	$35 – 45
bowl, 12" salad	$95 – 110	pitcher, ½ pint	$25 – 30
bowl, 10" salad	$60 – 70	pitcher, 6 ounce	$20 – 25
bowl, 8" vegetable	$35 – 45	plate, 14½" chop	$90 – 110
bowl, oval divided vegetable	$30 – 40	plate, 12½" chop	$65 – 75
bread tray	$40 – 50	plate, 11"	$40 – 50
butter dish	$55 – 65	plate, 10"	$25 – 30
casserole, 8" covered	$80 – 90	plate, 9"	$20 – 25
casserole, 8" skillet shape	$25 – 30	plate, 8"	$15 – 20
casserole, 6" skillet shape	$15 – 25	plate, 6"	$10 – 12
casserole, individual, with handle & cover	$50 – 60	platter, 13¾" casual	$65 – 75
cigarette box	$95 – 110	pickle dish	$15 – 20
coaster/ashtray	$25 – 30	relish dish	$20 – 30
coffee pot, 8 cup	$90 – 120	salt, pepper; each	$10 – 12
coffee pot, 4 cup	$100 – 130	saucer	$8 – 10
creamer	$20 – 25	sugar	$20 – 25
cruet with stopper	$45 – 55	sugar, open	$25 – 30
cup	$12 – 15	teapot	$90 – 120
egg cup	$20 – 25	tidbit, 10"	$10 – 15
gravy boat	$25 – 35	tray for cruets	$20 – 25
gravy underplate	$15 – 20	warmer	$30 – 40
		paper price list	$15 – 20

Kay Hackett based the graceful Tiger Lily pattern on the Turk's Cap lilies that grew wild in rural New Jersey. This pattern was decorated with Orange and Pink #160 blossoms with Victoria

Green and Willow Green leaves. Willow Green was also used for the wide bands on the bowls and chop plates. The Tiger Lily pattern became inactive in 1962, so is not very plentiful.

Tiger Lily oil cruet, 10" plate, sugar, cup & saucer, 6" plate.

Provincial #3966

Introduced: 1957
Designer: Kay Hackett
Shape Style: #3434 Rim

Provincial teapot, 10" plate, open sugar, warmer, 8" picnic plate, cup & saucer, egg cup.

Known Pieces:

bowl, cereal . . . . $10 – 15
bowl, fruit . . . . $8 – 12
bowl, coupe soup . . . . $20 – 25
bowl, lug soup. . . . . $10 – 15
bowl, 11" salad . . . . $50 – 60
bowl, 10" salad . . . . $40 – 50
bowl, 8" vegetable . . . . $25 – 30
bowl, oval divided vegetable . . . . . . $20 – 25
bread tray . . . . $20 – 30
butter dish. $25 – 35
casserole, 8" covered. . . . . $60 – 75
casserole, 8" skillet shape. . . . . $20 – 25
casserole, 6" skillet shape. . . . . $15 – 20
casserole, individual,
 with handle & cover. . . . . $20 – 25
cigarette box . . . . $60 – 75
coaster/ashtray . . . . $20 – 25
coffee pot, 8 cup . . . . $60 – 70
coffee pot, 4 cup . . . . $85 – 95
creamer . . . . $10 – 15
cruet with stopper. . . . . $20 – 30
cup. . . . . $8 – 10
egg cup . . . . $10 – 12
gravy boat . . . . $10 – 15
gravy underplate. . . . . $8 – 10
mug, coffee . . . . $20 – 25
mug, 2 cup. $35 – 45

pitcher, 2 quart . . . . $60 – 70
pitcher, 1 quart . . . . $40 – 50
pitcher, 1 pint . . . . $25 – 30
pitcher, ½ pint. . . . . $20 – 25
pitcher, 6 ounce . . . . $20 – 25
plate, 14½" chop . . . . $55 – 65
plate, 12½" chop . . . . $40 – 45
plate, 11" . . . . $20 – 25
plate, 10" . . . . $15 – 20
plate, 9" . . . . $12 – 18
plate, 8" . . . . $10 – 15
plate, 6" . . . . $6 – 7
plate, picnic, 8". . . . . $10 – 15
platter, 13¾" casual. . . . . $40 – 50
pickle dish. $12 – 15
relish dish . . . . $20 – 25
salt, pepper; each . . . . $8 – 10
saucer . . . . $4 – 6
sherbet. . . . . $30 – 35
sugar . . . . $15 – 20
sugar, open . . . . $20 – 25
teapot. . . . . $75 – 85
tidbit, 10". . . . . $8 – 12
tray for cruets . . . . $20 – 25
warmer . . . . $20 – 25
paper price list . . . . $10 – 15

Kay Hackett adapted the Provincial motif from her earlier Brown Tulip pattern. The colors were simplified to Orange, Yellow, and Walnut Brown with a Pink #160 blossom for this pattern. She had originally intended Provincial to be on the coupe shape with a wide yellow rim, similar to Blueberry. Because of the popularity of the Fruit pattern, it was decided that the Fruit rim treatment should be used instead. The Provincial pattern was actively produced only until 1962. This is one of the few patterns in which the 8" picnic plate was produced with carved decoration.

Haarlem

Haarlem 10" plate, 6 ounce pitcher.

Introduced: 1957
Designer: Kay Hackett
Made For: Flemington Outlet
Shape Style: #3434 Rim

Known Pieces:

bowl, cereal	$20 – 25
bowl, fruit	$12 – 15
bowl, coupe soup	$25 – 30
bowl, lug soup	$20 – 25
bowl, 11" salad	$85 – 110
bowl, 10" salad	$65 – 75
bowl, 8" vegetable	$40 – 50
bowl, oval divided vegetable	$35 – 45
bread tray	$45 – 55
coffee pot, 8 cup	$100 – 135
creamer	$25 – 30
cup	$10 – 15
egg cup	$20 – 25
mug, coffee	$30 – 40
pitcher, 2 quart	$90 – 125
pitcher, 1 quart	$70 – 80
pitcher, 1 pint	$40 – 50
pitcher, ½ pint	$30 – 35
pitcher, 6 ounce	$25 – 30
plate, 14½" chop	$100 – 125
plate, 12½" chop	$70 – 80
plate, 10"	$30 – 40
plate, 8"	$20 – 25
plate, 6"	$15 – 20
pickle dish	$20 – 25
relish dish	$30 – 35
salt, pepper; each	$10 – 15
saucer	$8 – 12
sugar	$25 – 30
teapot	$100 – 135
tidbit, 10"	$15 – 20
warmer	$30 – 40

Haarlem was the tentative name used for this brightly-colored variation of the Provincial pattern. This pattern was tried at the Flemington Outlet for a short time during 1957. Because *House & Garden* was advocating reds and yellows in their fashion color recommendations for 1957, Provincial was favored over the more colorful Haarlem pattern.

Woodmere #3967, Wakefield #3968

Introduced: 1957
Designer: Kay Hackett
Shape Style: #3434 Rim

Known Pieces:

bowl, rim soup	$20 – 25	plate, 12½" chop	$60 – 70
bowl, 12" #3608 salad	$90 – 120	plate, 11"	$30 – 40
cigarette box	$85 – 95	plate, 10"	$25 – 35
coaster/ashtray	$30 – 35	plate, 8"	$20 – 25
creamer	$20 – 25	plate, 6"	$10 – 15
cup	$12 – 15	saucer	$8 – 10
pitcher, 1 pint	$50 – 60	sugar	$20 – 25
pitcher, ½ pint	$30 – 40	teapot	$130 – 150
pitcher, 6 ounce	$25 – 30	tidbit	$10 – 15
plate, 14½" chop	$85 – 95	paper price list	$15 – 20

Both of these patterns used gray engobe as background for the motifs. The Woodmere pattern was decorated with stylized brown and yellow flowers with gold accents. The edge of each plate had a 22-karat gold band.

The Wakefield motif was based on the Chinese Lantern plant. The colors were turquoise and white with platinum and 22-karat gold accents. Both Woodmere and Wakefield are exceedingly hard to come by.

Wakefield 11" tidbit with handle removed; Woodmere 1 pint pitcher.

C. D. Peacock Plates

C. D. Peacock 11" plate.

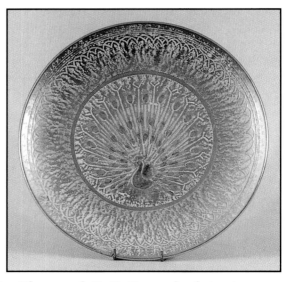

Introduced: 1957
Designer: Kay Hackett
Made For: C. D. Peacock
Shape Style: #3774 Coupe

Known Pieces:

plate, 14½" chop	$130 – 150
plate, 11"	$90 – 125

In 1957 the Chicago jeweler, C. D. Peacock, contracted Stangl to supply a distinctive plate featuring a peacock motif for holiday promotions. C. D. Peacock ordered a quantity of these plates for the holiday season each year throughout the late 1950s and early 1960s. The usual C. D. Peacock plate size was 11", although 14½" chop plates were produced in limited quantities. Although the majority of these pieces were shipped to Chicago, seconds, of course, were sold through the Flemington Outlet.

C. D. Peacock plate back showing the hand-painted "C. D. Peacock" name.

Vintage Salad Set

Introduced: 1957
Designer: Kay Hackett
Made For: Flemington Outlet
Shape Style: #3774 Coupe

Known Pieces:	
bowl, 10" salad . . . . $60 – 75	plate, 12½" chop . . . . $80 – 110
	plate, 8" . . . . $30 – 40

The Vintage pattern used the same motif that decorated Kay Hackett's earlier green Grape #3865 pattern. Vintage, however, was decorated with Frosted Fruit Green underglaze color and Satin White glaze. The vintage motif was arranged in such a way that there is no distinct top and bottom to the pattern. Kay Hackett designed this pattern to be set on the table in any direction and always look "up-side right." This pattern was tried at the Flemington Outlet for a short time, then was dropped before 1958.

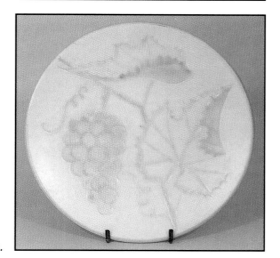

Vintage 8" plate.

Antique Gold #1902

Introduced: 1957
Developed By: Martin Stangl
Shape Style: #1902

Known Pieces:	
bowl, lug soup. . . . . $15 – 20	plate, 12½" chop . . . . $40 – 50
bowl, rim soup . . . . $25 – 30	plate, 11" . . . . $25 – 30
bowl, 10" salad . . . . $50 – 60	plate, 10" . . . . $25 – 30
bowl, 9" vegetable. . . . . $30 – 40	plate, 8" . . . . $15 – 20
creamer . . . . $20 – 25	plate, 6" . . .·. $10 – 15
cup. . . . . $6 – 8	saucer . . . . $8 – 10
pitcher, 1 pint . . . . $50 – 60	sugar . . . . $25 – 30
pitcher, ½ pint. . . . . $30 – 35	teapot. . . . . $115 – 135
plate, 14½" chop . . . . $60 – 75	tidbit . . . . $10 – 12
	paper price list . . . . $15 – 20

The Satin White glaze was brushed instead of sprayed on the Antique Gold #1902 dinnerware pattern. The brushing created red/brown swirls and streaks that showed through the white glaze. Twenty-two-karat gold luster was then applied using the "dry-brush" technique. Dry-brushing the gold allowed the white and brown background to show.

Where the gold luster was very thin, the luster fired to a purple stain. The purple stain on each piece gives this pattern a lavender cast. Antique Gold #1902 tidbits are often more blue than purple. These pieces were usually decorated with Frosted Fruit Green underglaze color under the Satin White glaze. Antique Gold #1902 dinnerware was produced only briefly during 1957.

Antique Gold #1902 teapot, 10" tidbit, cup & saucer, 8" plate, creamer, sugar.

Fruit and Flowers #4030

Introduced: 1958
Designer: Kay Hackett
Shape Style: #3774 Coupe

Known Pieces:

ashtray, 5" fluted*	$15 – 20
ashtray, leaf*	$30 – 35
bowl, cereal	$20 – 25
bowl, fruit	$12 – 15
bowl, coupe soup	$25 – 30
bowl, lug soup	$20 – 25
bowl, 12" salad	$90 – 110
bowl, 10" salad	$70 – 80
bowl, 8" vegetable	$30 – 40
bowl, oval divided vegetable	$40 – 50
bread tray	$35 – 45
butter dish	$60 – 75
cake stand	$25 – 30
casserole, 8" covered	$80 – 90
casserole, 8" skillet shape	$30 – 35
casserole, 6" skillet shape	$20 – 25
casserole, individual, with handle & cover	$60 – 75
cigarette box	$100 – 125
coaster/ashtray	$25 – 30
coffee pot, 8 cup	$95 – 120
coffee pot, 4 cup	$100 – 130
creamer	$20 – 25
cruet with stopper	$30 – 40
cup	$10 – 12
egg cup	$20 – 25
gravy boat	$20 – 25
gravy underplate	$10 – 15
mug, coffee	$25 – 35
mug, 2 cup	$40 – 50
mug, soup, 14 ounce	$65 – 80
pitcher, 2 quart	$90 – 115
pitcher, 1 quart	$65 – 75
pitcher, 1 pint	$45 – 55
pitcher, ½ pint	$25 – 30
pitcher, 6 ounce	$20 – 25
plate, 14½" chop	$85 – 100
plate, 12½" chop	$65 – 80
plate, 11"	$30 – 35
plate, 10"	$25 – 30
plate, 9"	$25 – 30
plate, 8"	$15 – 20
plate, 7"	$20 – 25
plate, 6"	$8 – 10
plate, grill, 11"*	$50 – 60
plate, grill, 9"*	$45 – 55
plate, 10" picnic*	$7 – 9

plate, 8" picnic*	$5 – 8	sugar	$20 – 25
platter, 13¾" casual	$80 – 90	sugar, open	$35 – 45
platter, 14¾" oval	$95 – 110	teapot	$90 – 110
platter, 11½" oval	$95 – 110	tidbit, 10"	$10 – 15
pickle dish	$20 – 25	tidbit, 2 tier	$25 – 35
relish dish	$30 – 35	tile*	$15 – 20
salt, pepper; each	$10 – 12	tray for cruets	$30 – 40
sauce boat	$40 – 50	warmer	$30 – 40
saucer	$5 – 7	paper napkin, each	$1 – 2
saucer, mug, 7"	$10 – 12	paper price list	$10 – 15

*These items are usually found without carving and marked only with the brown "second" mark and no pattern name. Such pieces were sold only in Flemington. Occasionally these items were produced with carved decoration and marked with the pattern name. Carved pieces are considered scarce and are worth 50 – 75% more than non-carved pieces.

Fruit and Flowers, with its many bright colors, was designed to harmonize with any style of home decor. This pattern was originally planned for a 1957 introduction. It was held back and introduced in 1958 with the re-styled #4024 creamer, sugar, and cup shapes. The Fruit and Flowers pattern has always been a favorite with collectors and was in continual production throughout the 1960s, and into the 1970s. This pattern became inactive in 1975. Fruit and Flowers pieces produced after 1974 were made of the white-colored clay in use at that time.

The 7" plate was produced with only a few patterns for a very short time during the first few months of 1965. For this reason, the 7" plate is extremely rare in any red-bodied pattern. The soup mug shape was tried with the Fruit and Flowers motif during the early 1960s. The soup mugs are quite rare as well.

Fruit and Flowers teapot, 12" chop plate, cup & saucer, 10" plate, 4 cup coffee pot.

Fruit and Flowers 14 ounce soup mug.

Florentine, Heritage #4031

Introduced: 1958
Designer: Kay Hackett
Shape Style: #3774 Coupe

Florentine 6" plate, cup, 10" plate, sherbet.

Known Pieces:

bowl, coupe soup	$20 – 25	plate, 8"	$15 – 20
bowl, 12" #3608 salad	$85 – 95	plate, 6"	$10 – 12
bowl, 8" vegetable	$30 – 35	saucer	$8 – 10
cigarette box	$75 – 90	sherbet	$30 – 35
coaster/ashtray	$25 – 30	sugar	$20 – 25
coffee pot	$85 – 95	teapot	$85 – 100
creamer	$20 – 25	tidbit	$10 – 15
cup	$8 – 10	paper price list	$10 – 15
pitcher, 1 pint	$40 – 50		
pitcher, ½ pint	$25 – 35		
pitcher, 6 ounce	$20 – 25		
plate, 14½" chop	$70 – 80		
plate, 12½" chop	$50 – 60		
plate, 11"	$25 – 30		
plate, 10"	$20 – 25		

When first introduced, Stangl named this pattern Heritage. Shortly after introduction, however, the name was changed to Florentine. Pieces of this pattern can be found marked with either name.

The motif consists of a carved border and central medallion that are lightly brushed with Frosted Fruit Green. Gold luster was dry-brushed over the carved areas. The Florentine sherbet was added in 1959 and bears the number 4063. The Florentine pattern became inactive in 1966, and was discontinued in July 1967, became inactive again during fall 1967 and was discontinued a final time on January 1, 1969.

Turquoise Band Kitchenware

Introduced: 1958
Shape Style: #3774 Coupe

Known Pieces:

bowl, 9" footed mixing	$80 – 95	cup	$8 – 10
bowl, 7" footed mixing	$65 – 75	plate, 12½" chop	$60 – 75
bowl, 5½" footed mixing	$50 – 60	plate, 10"	$20 – 25
bowl, 4½" footed mixing	$40 – 50	plate, 8"	$15 – 20
bowl, 10" salad	$40 – 50	plate, 6"	$10 – 15
bowl, 8" vegetable	$30 – 35	saucer	$8 – 10
creamer	$15 – 20	sugar	$20 – 25

This utilitarian pattern was made for less than a year and was sold only at the Flemington Outlet. The footed mixing bowl shapes seem to have been decorated with the Turquoise Band decoration only. The 6" plates are the easiest pieces to come by. All of the other pieces are rather difficult to find.

Turquoise Band Kitchenware 6" plate, cup & saucer, 10" plate, 5½" mixing bowl.

Fluted #3600

Introduced: 1958
Made For: Flemington Outlet

Known Pieces:		
ashtray, 5"	$15 – 20	egg cup .... $15 – 20
bowl, fruit	$8 – 12	plate, 14" chop .... $50 – 60
bowl, lug soup	$10 – 15	plate, 12" chop .... $35 – 45
bowl, 11" salad	$60 – 75	plate, 10" .... $15 – 20
bowl, 10" salad	$40 – 50	plate, 8" .... $10 – 15
bowl, 8" vegetable	$20 – 25	plate, 6" .... $8 – 10
cigarette box	$40 – 50	saucer .... $7 – 8
creamer	$15 – 20	sugar .... $20 – 25
cup	$10 – 12	teapot .... $80 – 90
		tidbit, 10" .... $10 – 12

This plain white, fluted dinnerware was made from the same molds as the Verna and Quimper patterns during the early 1940s. Stangl called this plain white version "Fluted" and sold it only at the Flemington Outlet. The white Fluted dinnerware was produced on a limited basis from 1958 through 1960.

Fluted cup & saucer, 10" plate, lug soup, sugar, creamer, 6" plate.

"Narrow Flute"

Introduced: 1958
Made For: Flemington Outlet

Known Pieces:

bowl, fruit	$8 – 10	plate, 12" chop	$35 – 45
bowl, lug soup	$10 – 12	plate, 10"	$15 – 20
bowl, 11" salad	$45 – 55	plate, 8"	$10 – 15
bowl, 10" salad	$30 – 40	plate, 6"	$6 – 8
bowl, 8" vegetable	$20 – 25	saucer	$4 – 5
creamer	$15 – 20	sugar	$15 – 20
cup	$8 – 10	teapot	$80 – 95
plate, 14" chop	$50 – 60	tidbit, 10"	$10 – 12

"Narrow Flute" dinnerware, with sharp, narrow fluting, was originally tried in 1958 with Satin White glaze and Antique Gold on the rims. The Antique Gold versions lasted a very short time. The "Narrow Flute" shapes were more often produced with plain, clear gloss glaze for the Flemington Outlet during the late 1950s and early 1960s. This pattern is much more difficult to find than Fluted #3600. Pieces of "Narrow Flute" with Satin White glaze and Antique Gold usually retail about double the value of those that are plain white.

"Narrow Flute" 10" plate with Satin White glaze and Antique Gold rim; cup & saucer, gloss white.

Garland #4067

Introduced: 1959
Designer: Kay Hackett
Shape Style: #3774 Coupe

Known Pieces:

bowl, cereal	$20 – 25	cake stand	$20 – 25
bowl, fruit	$12 – 15	casserole, 8" covered	$85 – 95
bowl, coupe soup	$25 – 30	casserole, 8" skillet shape	$25 – 35
bowl, lug soup	$15 – 20	casserole, 6" skillet shape	$20 – 25
bowl, 12" salad	$80 – 95	casserole, individual,	
bowl, 10" salad	$60 – 70	with handle & cover	$50 – 60
bowl, 8" vegetable	$35 – 45	cigarette box	$85 – 110
bowl, oval divided vegetable	$35 – 45	coaster/ashtray	$25 – 30
bread tray	$40 – 50	coffee pot, 8 cup	$90 – 120
butter dish	$55 – 65	creamer	$15 – 20

cruet with stopper	$35 – 45	plate, 8"	$15 – 20
cup	$10 – 12	plate, 6"	$10 – 12
egg cup	$20 – 25	platter, 13¾" casual	$65 – 75
gravy boat	$20 – 25	pickle dish	$20 – 25
gravy underplate	$10 – 15	relish dish	$25 – 30
mug, coffee	$25 – 30	salt, pepper; each	$10 – 12
mug, 2 cup	$40 – 45	salt shaker, wood top	$50 – 60
pitcher, 2 quart	$85 – 95	pepper mill, wood top	$50 – 60
pitcher, 1 quart	$55 – 65	saucer	$8 – 10
pitcher, 1 pint	$35 – 45	sugar	$15 – 20
pitcher, ½ pint	$25 – 30	sugar, open	$30 – 35
pitcher, 6 ounce	$20 – 25	teapot	$90 – 115
plate, 14½" chop	$85 – 100	tidbit, 10"	$10 – 15
plate, 12½" chop	$60 – 70	tidbit, 2 tier	$20 – 25
plate, 11"	$25 – 30	tray for cruets	$30 – 35
plate, 10"	$25 – 30	warmer	$30 – 40
plate, 9"	$20 – 25	paper price list	$15 – 20

This dainty floral pattern was inspired by busy transfer type decorations. Stangl's newly developed light gray engobe was a perfect foil for Garland's Pink #160 blossoms and Willow Green leaves.

The Garland pattern has recently been gaining in popularity, although it is somewhat challenging to collect. Garland was an active pattern until January 1, 1963, and was discontinued on January 1, 1971.

Garland casual platter, individual covered casserole with handle, 14½" chop plate, gravy with underplate, 8" plate.

Fairlawn, Caprice #4068

Introduced: 1959
Designer: Kay Hackett
Shape Style: #3774 Coupe

Known Pieces:

bowl, cereal	$20 – 25	casserole, 8" covered	$80 – 90
bowl, fruit	$10 – 15	casserole, 8" skillet shape	$20 – 25
bowl, coupe soup	$20 – 25	casserole, 6" skillet shape	$10 – 15
bowl, lug soup	$15 – 20	casserole, individual,	
bowl, 12" salad	$80 – 90	with handle & cover	$45 – 55
bowl, 10" salad	$45 – 55	cigarette box	$80 – 95
bowl, 8" vegetable	$30 – 40	coaster/ashtray	$30 – 35
bowl, oval divided vegetable	$30 – 35	coffee pot, 8 cup	$85 – 95
bread tray	$40 – 50	creamer	$20 – 25
butter dish	$40 – 50	cruet with stopper	$30 – 40
		cup	$10 – 12

egg cup . . . . $10 – 15	plate, 6" . . . . $8 – 10
gravy boat . . . . $20 – 25	platter, 13¾" casual . . . . $50 – 60
gravy underplate . . . . $10 – 15	pickle dish . . . . $10 – 15
mug, coffee . . . . $20 – 25	relish dish . . . . $15 – 20
mug, 2 cup . . . . $35 – 40	salt, pepper; each . . . . $6 – 8
pitcher, 2 quart . . . . $85 – 95	salt shaker, wood top . . . . $45 – 55
pitcher, 1 quart . . . . $55 – 65	pepper mill, wood top . . . . $45 – 55
pitcher, 1 pint . . . . $30 – 40	saucer . . . . $8 – 10
pitcher, ½ pint . . . . $25 – 30	sugar . . . . $20 – 25
pitcher, 6 ounce . . . . $20 – 25	sugar, open . . . . $20 – 25
plate, 14½" chop . . . . $80 – 90	teapot . . . . $80 – 90
plate, 12½" chop . . . . $45 – 55	tidbit, 10" . . . . $10 – 15
plate, 11" . . . . $25 – 30	tidbit, 2 tier . . . . $15 – 25
plate, 10" . . . . $20 – 25	tray for cruets . . . . $25 – 30
plate, 9" . . . . $15 – 20	warmer . . . . $20 – 25
plate, 8" . . . . $12 – 15	paper price list . . . . $10 – 15

The Fairlawn motif, like Garland, was based on the transfer-ware style of decoration. The design consists of a stylized floral motif repeating around a central medallion. The strength of this pattern relies on the strong blue and yellow color contrast. The under-glaze colors used were Blue #95, Light Blue, and Orange. Shortly after introduction Stangl changed the name of this pattern from Caprice to Fairlawn. The Fairlawn pattern was in active production for only two years, from 1959 to January 1961.

Fairlawn sugar, 10" plate, butter dish.

Doily #5001

Doily 10" tidbit, #3774 coupe shape.

Introduced: 1959
Shape Style: #3434 Rim

Known Pieces:

bowl, cereal . . . . $8 – 12
bowl, fruit . . . . $8 – 12
bowl, coupe soup . . . . $15 – 20
bowl, 10" salad . . . . $35 – 45
bowl, 8" vegetable . . . . $25 – 35
creamer . . . . $20 – 25
cup . . . . $8 – 12
plate, 14½" chop . . . . $60 – 70

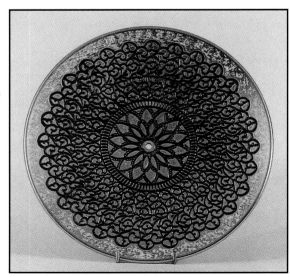

plate, 12½" chop	$40 – 50	saucer	$5 – 6
plate, 10"	$20 – 25	sugar	$20 – 25
plate, 8"	$15 – 20	teapot	$85 – 110
plate, 6"	$10 – 15	tidbit, 10"	$10 – 15

The Antique Gold decorated Doily pattern was produced for a very brief time during 1959. The motif was a doily design molded in the center of each piece. Stangl's Antique Gold finish enhanced the deep modeling of the motif. Doily dinnerware was produced on the #3434 rim shape, but 10" tidbits were available on both #3434 rim and #3774 coupe shaped plates. Doily was very short-lived and was discontinued before 1960.

Blue Mill, Pomona, Poppy

Introduced: 1959
Made For: Carbone, Inc.
Adapted By: Irene Sarnecki

Known Pieces:

Blue Mill:

bowl, 10" salad	$85 – 110	sugar	$20 – 25
plate, 12½" chop	$90 – 125	teapot	$95 – 125
plate, 8"	$35 – 45		

Poppy:

bowl, 10" salad	$75 – 85	*Pomona:*	
creamer	$20 – 25	bowl, 10" salad	$40 – 50
cup	$10 – 12	creamer	$15 – 20
plate, 14" chop	$80 – 90	cup	$10 – 12
plate, 10"	$25 – 30	plate, 14½" chop	$75 – 85
plate, 8"	$20 – 25	plate, 12½" chop	$50 – 60
plate, 6"	$10 – 15	plate, 10"	$20 – 25
platter, 14" oval, #1388 shape	$70 – 85	plate, 8"	$15 – 20
saucer	$8 – 10	plate, 6"	$10 – 12
		saucer	$7 – 8
		sugar	$15 – 20
		teapot	$80 – 95

The designs for these three patterns were supplied by Carbone and adapted to the Stangl shapes by Irene Sarnecki. Each pattern used a different dinnerware shape and style of decoration.

The Blue Mill pattern is the most elaborate, most popular, and most difficult to find of the three. It uses the #3434 rim shape with the central mill motif surrounded by a flowering vine device on the rim. The colors used on Blue Mill were Yellow, Blue #95, Dark Blue, and Pomona Green.

Pomona was the forerunner of Stangl's muted brown and green patterns that became very popular during the 1960s. A bold fruit motif dominates the #3774 coupe

Blue Mill 8" plate.

shapes used for this pattern. The Pomona Green and Pomona Brown underglaze colors used on Pomona were actually Carnival Green and Willow Green mixed with Walnut Brown. Pomona Brown was used for the stems with Lyric Black and Pink #160 accents.

Pomona 12½" chop plate, cup & saucer, 8" plate.

Poppy creamer, 8" plate, cup & saucer.

The Poppy pattern features a detailed poppy motif on the #3600 fluted shape. The blossoms are Pink #193 and Amber Gray with Victoria Green and Pomona Green leaves. Orange is in the centers of the blossoms; Lyric Black accents were used throughout the stems and foliage. The #1388 oval platter shape was used with the Poppy pattern, as there was no oval platter with the #3600 fluted shape.

Spring Tide

Introduced: Late 1950s
Made For: Flemington Outlet

Known Pieces:

bowl, fruit	$10 – 12	plate, 12½" chop	$80 – 95
bowl, lug soup	$10 – 15	plate, 10"	$25 – 30
bowl, 12" salad	$75 – 85	plate, 8"	$20 – 25
bowl, 10" salad	$50 – 60	plate, 6"	$10 – 15
bowl, 8" vegetable	$30 – 40	saucer	$7 – 8
creamer	$20 – 25	sugar	$20 – 25
cup	$8 – 12	teapot	$90 – 115
		tidbit, 10"	$10 – 15

Spring Tide creamer, 10" plate.

The diminutive motif of this pattern was produced on both gray and green engobes. Willow Green bands and leaves complement the tiny White #10 and Orange blossoms. The Spring Tide pattern was tried for a very short time, then was discontinued. It is exceptionally uncommon at this time.

1960s HAND-CARVED, HAND-PAINTED DINNERWARE

Bella Rosa #5047

Introduced: 1960
Designer: Kay Hackett
Shape Style: #3774 Coupe

Known Pieces:

bowl, cereal	$15 – 20	mug, coffee	$20 – 25
bowl, fruit	$12 – 15	mug, 2 cup	$40 – 45
bowl, coupe soup	$20 – 25	pitcher, 2 quart	$80 – 90
bowl, lug soup	$12 – 15	pitcher, 1 quart	$55 – 65
bowl, 12" salad	$75 – 85	pitcher, 1 pint	$35 – 45
bowl, 10" salad	$55 – 65	pitcher, ½ pint	$25 – 30
bowl, 8" vegetable	$30 – 40	pitcher, 6 oz.	$20 – 25
bowl, oval divided vegetable	$35 – 45	plate, 14½" chop	$85 – 105
bread tray	$30 – 35	plate, 12½" chop	$60 – 70
butter dish	$30 – 40	plate, 11"	$25 – 30
casserole, 8" covered	$75 – 85	plate, 10"	$20 – 25
casserole, 8" skillet shape	$20 – 30	plate, 9"	$15 – 20
casserole, 6" skillet shape	$15 – 25	plate, 8"	$12 – 15
casserole, individual, with handle & cover	$20 – 30	plate, 6"	$8 – 10
cigarette box	$75 – 85	platter, 13¾" casual	$55 – 65
coaster/ashtray	$20 – 25	pickle dish	$15 – 20
coffee pot, 8 cup	$80 – 90	relish dish	$20 – 25
creamer	$15 – 20	saucer	$5 – 6
cruet with stopper	$25 – 35	salt, pepper; each	$8 – 10
cup	$10 – 12	sugar	$15 – 20
egg cup	$15 – 20	teapot	$80 – 90
gravy boat	$15 – 20	tidbit, 10"	$10 – 15
gravy underplate	$10 – 15	warmer	$20 – 30
		paper price list	$10 – 15

The Bella Rosa pattern featured a large, realistic rose surrounded by foliage and sprays of lily-of-the-valley. This pattern was on the same light gray engobe that was also applied to the Garland pattern. The carved details and the raised White #10 areas give Bella Rosa a three-dimensional appearance. Because Bella Rosa was in active production only from 1960 to January 1, 1961, it is a challenging pattern to collect.

Bella Rosa 10" plate, 8" plate, salt & pepper.

Cookrite Bakeware, French Maid Bakeware

Introduced: 1960

Known Pieces:

baker, oval 16"	$15 – 20
baker, oval 13½"	$15 – 20
baker, oval 11"	$10 – 15
baker, oval 10"	$8 – 12
baker, oval 8"	$7 – 10
baker, oval 6"	$5 – 7
casserole, 8" covered	$20 – 25
casserole, 7" covered	$15 – 20
custard cup	$3 – 5
pitcher, 6 oz.	$8 – 12
soufflé, round 10"	$15 – 20
soufflé, round 8"	$10 – 15
soufflé, round 7"	$8 – 12
soufflé, round 6"	$6 – 8
soufflé, round 5"	$5 – 6
soufflé, round 4"	$3 – 5
soufflé underplate/cover	$10 – 15
sugar, coupe shape	$10 – 15
warmer	$8 – 10
paper price list	$10 – 15

Cookrite was Stangl's attempt to produce a line of bakeware suitable for gourmet cooking. It was advertised as "a convenient and attractive line of baking dishes in all white" and "guaranteed oven proof."

During 1960 and 1961, Cookrite was available in gloss white, 22-karat gold luster, and a shaded burnt-orange. Pieces with the gold luster or burnt-orange finish are quite rare, but usually are priced only slightly higher than pieces in white.

Cookrite bakeware was very popular during the early 1960s but interest waned later in the decade. In 1974, the line was brought back with several additions, including the 10" soufflé and the soufflé underplate/cover. In certain areas of the country, the Cookrite line was marketed as "French Maid Bake-Ware"; these items are very scarce.

During the 1970s, Cookrite was distributed in great quantities across the country. In 1978, several Cookrite shapes were glazed with the Maize-ware glazes, Pioneer-Brown, Summer-Green, Harvest-Yellow, and Winter-Tan.

Although Cookrite bakeware is oven proof and perfectly usable for baking, proper care should be taken in its use. If Cookrite or any Stangl dinnerware is subjected to rapid change in temperature, crazing of the glaze or breaking of the vessel may occur. Many pieces of Cookrite can be found with such damage.

Cookrite, burnt-orange 4" soufflé, 6" soufflé, 6" oval baker, 8" round soufflé, sugar, 6 ounce pitcher, burnt-orange.

Pheasant #3774 Salad Set

Introduced: 1960
Adapted By: Irene Sarnecki
Shape Style: #3774 Coupe

Known Pieces:

bowl, 10" salad	$110 – 140
cup	$20 – 25
plate, 14½" chop	$80 – 110
plate, 11"	$40 – 50
plate, 8"	$50 – 60
saucer	$10 – 15

Because of the popularity of Stangl's Sportsman line of smokers' items, a Sportsman dinnerware was tried. Designer Irene Sarnecki adapted Kay Hackett's original Sportsman pheasant motif to the #3774 dinnerware shapes. This motif is a naturally-colored pheasant, with stalks of wheat on gray engobe.

Because the 11" and 14½" plates were produced as part of the Sportsman series from 1955 through 1972, these are the pieces most often found. The 8" plates, cups, saucers, and salad bowls were added in 1960 and were produced for less than a year.

Pheasant 8" plate, cup & saucer.

Hearts & Flowers

Introduced: 1960
Made For: Flemington Outlet
Developed By: Martin Stangl
Shape Style: #3774 Coupe

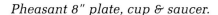

Known Pieces:

bowl, fruit	$15 – 20	plate, 8"	$15 – 20
creamer	$25 – 30	plate, 6"	$10 – 12
cup	$10 – 15	saucer	$8 – 10
plate, 14" chop	$70 – 80	sugar	$25 – 30
plate, 12" chop	$55 – 65	teapot	$90 – 100
plate, 10"	$25 – 30	tidbit, 10"	$10 – 12

This novelty pattern with molded decoration and clear gloss glaze was never produced in large quantities. In 1965, however, 10" tidbits and two-tier servers with the Hearts & Flowers motif were produced with the Caribbean and Antique Gold finishes. Stangl did not class these servers as dinnerware, but offered them as part of the 1965 and 1966 giftware assortments.

Hearts & Flowers 8" plate, 12½" chop plate, creamer, sugar.

Festival #5072

Introduced: 1961
Adapted By: Irene Sarnecki
Shape Style: #3774 Coupe

Festival #5092 2 cup mug, 10" plate, egg cup, 6" plate.

Known Pieces:

bowl, cereal	$20 – 25
bowl, fruit	$15 – 20
bowl, coupe soup	$25 – 30
bowl, lug soup	$15 – 20
bowl, 12" salad	$80 – 95
bowl, 10" salad	$60 – 70
bowl, 8" vegetable	$35 – 45
bowl, oval divided vegetable	$25 – 35
bread tray	$50 – 60
butter dish	$50 – 60
cake stand	$20 – 25
casserole, 8" covered	$85 – 110
casserole, 8" skillet shape	$20 – 30
casserole, 6" skillet shape	$15 – 20
casserole, individual, w/handle & cover	$50 – 60
cigarette box	$100 – 125
coaster/ashtray	$30 – 35
coffee pot, 8 cup	$90 – 120
creamer	$20 – 25
cruet with stopper	$35 – 45
cup	$10 – 15
egg cup	$20 – 25
gravy boat	$25 – 30
gravy underplate	$15 – 20
mug, 2 cup	$40 – 50
pitcher, 2 quart	$90 – 115
pitcher, 1 quart	$65 – 75
pitcher, 1 pint	$40 – 50

pitcher, ½ pint	$25 – 30
pitcher, 6 oz.	$20 – 30
plate, 14½" chop	$90 – 115
plate, 12½" chop	$85 – 95
plate, 11"	$35 – 45
plate, 10"	$25 – 30
plate, 9"	$25 – 30
plate, 8"	$20 – 25
plate, 6"	$10 – 15
platter, 13¾" casual	$75 – 85
pickle dish	$20 – 25
relish dish	$20 – 30
salt, pepper; each	$10 – 15
saucer	$8 – 10
sugar	$20 – 25
sugar, open	$25 – 30
teapot	$90 – 115
tidbit, 10"	$10 – 15
tray for cruets	$30 – 40
warmer	$35 – 45
paper price list	$15 – 20

Stangl's Festival #5072 pattern was a re-introduction of the Festival #3677 pattern produced for Fisher, Bruce & Company during the 1940s. The newer Festival #5072 was produced on the #3774 coupe shape and the motifs on the smaller plates and the serving bowls were simplified to clusters of large fruit, as opposed to the rings of small fruit motifs that decorated the 1940s Della-Ware pattern. The Festival #5072 dinnerware pattern was actively produced from 1961 until January 1, 1964.

The #5092 two cup mug shape was introduced in 1961 and replaced the coffee mug shape used throughout the 1950s. The #5092 mug shape was used for most dinnerware patterns until 1968.

Sometimes the occasional piece of unmarked Festival is mistaken for a piece belonging to the Fruit pattern. A primary difference between the two patterns is the leaves. Festival leaves are Willow Green, while Fruit leaves will always be French Green.

Florette #5073

Introduced: 1961
Designer: Betty Powell
Shape Style: #3434 Rim

Known Pieces:

bowl, cereal . . . . $10 – 15
bowl, fruit . . . . $8 – 12
bowl, coupe soup . . . . $20 – 25
bowl, lug soup . . . . $8 – 12
bowl, 11" salad . . . . $50 – 60
bowl, 10" salad . . . . $35 – 45
bowl, 8" vegetable . . . . $25 – 35
bowl, oval divided vegetable . . . . $25 – 35
bread tray . . . . $30 – 40
butter dish . . . . $30 – 40
casserole, 8" covered . . . . $65 – 75
casserole, 8" skillet shape . . . . $20 – 25
casserole, 6" skillet shape . . . . $15 – 20
casserole, individual, w/handle & cover. $35 – 45
coaster/ashtray . . . . $30 – 35
coffee pot, 8 cup . . . . $70 – 85
creamer . . . . $15 – 20
cruet with stopper . . . . $20 – 25
cup . . . . $8 – 10
egg cup . . . . $15 – 20
gravy boat . . . . $15 – 20
gravy underplate . . . . $10 – 12
mug, 2 cup . . . . $35 – 45
pitcher, 2 quart . . . . $55 – 65
pitcher, 1 quart . . . . $35 – 45
pitcher, 1 pint . . . . $25 – 30
pitcher, ½ pint . . . . $20 – 25

Florette relish dish, coaster/ashtray, 12½" chop plate,

pitcher, 6 oz. . . . . $20 – 25
plate, 14½" chop . . . . $55 – 65
plate, 12½" chop . . . . $35 – 45
plate, 11" . . . . $20 – 25
plate, 10" . . . . $15 – 20
plate, 9" . . . . $10 – 15
plate, 8" . . . . $8 – 12
plate, 6" . . . . $6 – 7
platter, 13¾" casual . . . . $35 – 45
pickle dish . . . . $10 – 15
relish dish . . . . $20 – 25
saucer . . . . $4 – 5
salt, pepper; each . . . . $8 – 10
sugar . . . . $15 – 20
teapot . . . . $65 – 75
tidbit, 10" . . . . $10 – 15
tidbit, 2 tier . . . . $15 – 20
tray for cruets . . . . $20 – 25
warmer . . . . $20 – 25
paper price list . . . . $10 – 15

The colorful Florette pattern features a classically-styled urn and floral arrangement. The rim is a wide band of Green #1431 with narrow bands of Willow Green and Pink #160. This pattern was not in regular production very long. During 1962 Florette had become inactive, so there is not a great abundance of this pattern available.

Orchard Song #5110

Introduced: 1962
Designer: Irene Sarnecki
Shape Style: #3774 Coupe

Orchard Song square tile, sugar,
divided lazy susan, creamer, 10" plate,
6 ounce pitcher, ½ pint pitcher.

Known Pieces:

ashtray, 5" fluted	$8 – 12	mug, 2 cup	$30 – 35
ashtray, leaf*	$10 – 15	mug, stack	$30 – 35
bowl, cereal	$10 – 15	lamp #637 jug shape	$85 – 135
bowl, fruit	$10 – 12	lamp #3837 or #835	
bowl, coupe soup	$15 – 20	5-tier coffee warmer	$85 – 135
bowl, lug soup	$12 – 15	lamp, coffee pot*	$75 – 90
bowl, 12" mixing #5150	$50 – 60	lazy susan*	$65 – 75
bowl, 10" mixing #5150	$40 – 50	lazy susan, divided*	$65 – 75
bowl, 8" mixing #5150	$30 – 40	pitcher, 2 quart	$55 – 65
bowl, 12" salad	$45 – 55	pitcher, 1 quart	$35 – 45
bowl, 12" salad #3608	$65 – 75	pitcher, 1 pint	$25 – 30
bowl, 11" salad #3434	$50 – 60	pitcher, ½ pint	$20 – 25
bowl, 10" salad	$35 – 45	pitcher, 6 oz.	$20 – 25
bowl, 8" vegetable	$25 – 30	plate, 14½" chop	$55 – 65
bowl, 8" covered vegetable	$55 – 65	plate, 12½" chop	$35 – 45
bowl, oval divided vegetable	$25 – 35	plate, 11"	$20 – 25
bread tray	$30 – 35	plate, 10"	$15 – 20
butter dish	$30 – 35	plate, 8"	$8 – 12
cake stand	$10 – 15	plate, 6"	$5 – 6
canister, concave L*	$40 – 50	plate, 10" picnic*	$5 – 6
canister, concave M*	$30 – 40	plate, 8" picnic*	$4 – 5
canister, concave S*	$25 – 30	platter, 13¾" casual	$35 – 45
casserole, 8" covered	$55 – 65	platter, 14¾" oval	$40 – 50
casserole, 8" skillet shape	$20 – 25	pickle dish	$12 – 15
casserole, 6" skillet shape	$15 – 20	relish dish	$20 – 25
casserole, individual,		salt, pepper; each	$8 – 10
with handle & cover	$20 – 25	sauce boat	$25 – 30
coaster/ashtray	$4 – 8	saucer	$5 – 6
coffee pot, 8 cup	$55 – 65	sugar	$15 – 20
coffee pot, 4 cup	$70 – 85	teapot	$55 – 65
coffee filter	$20 – 25	tidbit, 10"	$10 – 12
creamer	$10 – 15	tidbit, 2 tier	$20 – 25
cruet with stopper	$20 – 30	tile*	$10 – 15
cup	$8 – 10	tray, 7" square #5154*	$20 – 25
egg cup	$8 – 12	warmer	$15 – 20
gravy boat	$15 – 20	paper napkin, each	$1 – 2
gravy underplate	$8 – 10	paper price list	$10 – 15

* These items were usually sold only at the Flemington Outlet.

Orchard Song was styled after Carbone's Pomona pattern. The Orchard Song motif featured Tan and Pomona Green fruit with Pomona Brown Dark stems and tendrils. This color scheme was recommended by the *House and Garden* fashion color program for 1962. Orchard Song was immensely popular during the 1960s. By 1974, this pattern was no longer advertised in Stangl catalogs, but was available as an inactive pattern for two more years. Consequently, Orchard Song is a reasonably easy pattern to collect.

Several Orchard Song items, such as the stack mugs and #5150 mixing bowls, were produced during the late 1970s, so these pieces are usually on the white body. Orchard Song lamps were produced on the #637 jug and #835 teapot-stand shapes. A third type of lamp was made for the Flemington Outlet from coffee pots that were drilled and fitted with sockets.

Bittersweet #5111

Introduced: 1962
Designer: Irene Sarnecki
Shape Style: #3774 Coupe

Known Pieces:

ashtray, 5" fluted	$6 – 10	mug, stack	$25 – 35
bowl, cereal	$12 – 15	pitcher, 2 quart	$50 – 60
bowl, fruit	$8 – 12	pitcher, 1 quart	$30 – 40
bowl, coupe soup	$12 – 20	pitcher, 1 pint	$25 – 30
bowl, lug soup	$10 – 12	pitcher, ½ pint	$20 – 25
bowl, 12" salad	$40 – 50	pitcher, 6 oz.	$15 – 20
bowl, 10" salad	$30 – 40	plate, 14½" chop	$50 – 60
bowl, 8" vegetable	$25 – 35	plate, 12½" chop	$30 – 40
bowl, oval divided vegetable	$20 – 30	plate, 10"	$15 – 20
bread tray	$30 – 35	plate, 8"	$8 – 12
butter dish	$30 – 40	plate, 6"	$6 – 7
cake stand	$20 – 25	plate, 10" picnic*	$5 – 8
casserole, 8" covered	$55 – 65	plate, 8" picnic*	$4 – 6
casserole, 8" skillet shape	$25 – 35	platter, 13¾" casual	$35 – 45
casserole, 6" skillet shape	$20 – 25	platter, 14¾" oval	$35 – 45
casserole, individual, with handle & cover	$20 – 30	pickle dish	$12 – 15
coaster/ashtray*	$8 – 12	relish dish	$15 – 20
coffee pot, 8 cup	$70 – 80	salt, pepper; each	$8 – 10
coffee pot with filter	$90 – 110	sauce boat	$25 – 30
creamer	$10 – 15	saucer	$5 – 6
cruet with stopper	$25 – 30	sugar	$15 – 20
cup	$8 – 10	teapot	$55 – 65
egg cup	$12 – 15	tidbit, 10"	$8 – 12
gravy boat	$15 – 20	tidbit, 2 tier	$15 – 25
gravy underplate	$10 – 12	warmer	$20 – 25
mug, 2 cup	$30 – 35	paper napkin, each	$1 – 2
		paper price list	$10 – 12

* These items were usually sold only at the Flemington Outlet.

The Bittersweet colors were based on *House and Garden's* 1962 color recommendations. This bright orange and green motif was decorated with Tan and Carnival Green with a small amount of Walnut Brown. This was a popular pattern that remained in active production until January 1, 1969, and was available inactively until 1978.

In 1968, the #5092 two-cup mug, which had been cast in one piece, was replaced with the #5206 mug shape. The #5206 mug was jiggered instead of cast, and the handle was applied separately. Many patterns were produced with both #5092 and #5206 mug shapes, and at this time there is no price difference between the two. The Bittersweet filter coffee pot is the same shape as the Country Garden filter coffee pot.

Bittersweet coaster/ashtray, salt & pepper, 10" plate, #5206 jiggered 2 cup mug.

Sunrise #5122

Sunrise 10" plate.

Introduced: 1962
Shape Style: #3434 Rim

Known Pieces:

bowl, cereal	$10 – 15
bowl, fruit	$8 – 10
bowl, coupe soup	$10 – 15
bowl, 10" salad	$40 – 50
bowl, 8" vegetable	$20 – 30
coffee pot, 8 cup	$60 – 70
creamer	$10 – 15
cup	$6 – 8
mug, 2 cup	$25 – 35
plate, 12½" chop	$40 – 50
plate, 10"	$20 – 25
plate, 8"	$10 – 15
plate, 6"	$8 – 10
salt, pepper; each	$7 – 8
saucer	$7 – 8
sugar	$15 – 20
teapot	$50 – 60
tidbit, 10"	$8 – 10

The Sunrise pattern was first brushed entirely with yellow, then decorated with concentric rings of red and two shades of green. This pattern was made for a very short time and is particularly scarce. Sunrise was apparently made for a private account as the pattern name was rarely applied to these pieces.

Brandy #5124, Crescent Blue #5125

Introduced: 1962
Made For: Jordan Marsh and Bloomingdale's
Shape Style: #3774 Coupe

Known Pieces:

bowl, cereal	$8 – 10
bowl, fruit	$6 – 8
bowl, coupe soup	$10 – 15

bowl, 10" salad	$40 – 50		pitcher, 6 oz.	$10 – 15
bowl, 8" vegetable	$30 – 40		plate, 14½" chop	$40 – 50
bowl, oval divided vegetable	$20 – 25		plate, 12½" chop	$30 – 35
bread tray	$25 – 30		plate, 10"	$20 – 25
butter dish	$20 – 25		plate, 8"	$10 – 15
casserole, 8" covered	$45 – 55		plate, 6"	$6 – 10
coffee pot, 8 cup	$60 – 65		pickle dish	$10 – 12
creamer	$10 – 15		relish dish	$12 – 15
cup	$6 – 8		saucer	$4 – 5
pitcher, 2 quart	$40 – 50		salt, pepper; each	$5 – 6
pitcher, 1 quart	$30 – 40		sugar	$10 – 15
pitcher, 1 pint	$25 – 30		teapot	$55 – 65
pitcher, ½ pint	$15 – 20		tidbit, 10"	$10 – 12

Brandy and Crescent Blue were both special order patterns for Jordan Marsh and Bloomingdale's. These patterns can be found marked either "Made For Bloomingdale's by Stangl Pottery" or "Made For Jordan Marsh by Stangl Pottery." Brandy and Crescent Blue were both meager sellers. Consequently very little of these patterns were produced so now they are especially scarce.

Both patterns were decorated directly on the red dinnerware body with no application of engobe. The Brandy pattern was swirled with Yellow underglaze color and had a narrow band of Art Ware Blue on the edge. Crescent Blue pieces were decorated with a swirl of Willow Green and a wide Art Ware Blue band. Even the backs of these patterns were decorated with swirls of color.

Crescent Blue 10" tidbit, cereal bowl; Brandy coffee pot, 10" plate.

Fathom Green #5127

Introduced: 1962
Made For: Jordan Marsh
Shape Style: #3774 Coupe

Known Pieces:

bowl, cereal	$10 – 15		bowl, oval divided vegetable	$25 – 30
bowl, fruit	$8 – 12		bread tray	$20 – 25
bowl, coupe soup	$12 – 18		butter dish	$25 – 35
bowl, lug soup	$10 – 12		casserole, 8" covered	$60 – 70
bowl, 12" salad	$50 – 60		casserole, 8" skillet shape	$20 – 25
bowl, 10" salad	$35 – 45		casserole, 6" skillet shape	$15 – 20
bowl, 8" vegetable	$20 – 30		casserole, individual, with handle & cover	$20 – 25

coaster/ashtray	$20 – 25	plate, 12½" chop	$40 – 50
coffee pot, 8 cup	$70 – 80	plate, 10"	$25 – 30
creamer	$15 – 20	plate, 9"	$20 – 25
cruet with stopper	$20 – 25	plate, 8"	$15 – 20
cup	$8 – 10	plate, 6"	$10 – 12
egg cup	$10 – 15	platter, 13¾" casual	$35 – 45
gravy boat	$15 – 20	pickle dish	$12 – 15
gravy underplate	$10 – 15	relish dish	$15 – 20
mug, 2 cup	$30 – 40	saucer	$7 – 8
pitcher, 2 quart	$50 – 60	salt, pepper; each	$8 – 10
pitcher, 1 quart	$40 – 50	sugar	$20 – 25
pitcher, 1 pint	$30 – 35	teapot	$60 – 70
pitcher, ½ pint	$25 – 30	tidbit, 10"	$10 – 12
pitcher, 6 oz.	$20 – 25	warmer, round	$15 – 20
plate, 14½" chop	$55 – 65	warmer, square #3412	$10 – 15

The Fathom Green pattern was produced during the early 1960s for Jordan Marsh. This dinnerware pattern was decorated with the same process that was used for the Terra Rose finish. Art Ware Green was swirled under the Silk glaze to achieve the misty green effect. Stangl used this same Terra Rose-Fathom Green finish on dinnerware seconds throughout the 1950s and into the 1960s. Prices for Fathom Green dinnerware and seconds decorated with Terra Rose Green are roughly the same. However, pieces marked Fathom Green usually sell for a little more.

Fathom Green cup & saucer, 8" plate.

"Red Flower"

Introduced: 1962
Made For: Bloomingdale's
Shape Style: #3774 Coupe

"Red Flower"
6" plate.

Known Pieces:

bowl, cereal	$10 – 15
bowl, fruit	$8 – 10
bowl, coupe soup	$15 – 20
bowl, 10" salad	$50 – 60
bowl, 8" vegetable	$30 – 40
coffee pot, 8 cup	$75 – 85
creamer	$15 – 20
cup	$8 – 12
plate, 12½" chop	$65 – 80

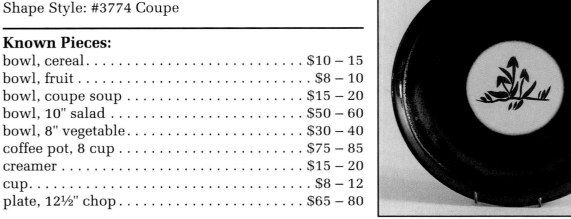

plate, 10" . . . . $30 – 40	saucer . . . . $8 – 10
plate, 8" . . . . $15 – 20	sugar . . . . $20 – 25
plate, 6" . . . . $10 – 15	teapot. . . . . $70 – 80
salt, pepper; each . . . . $6 – 8	tidbit, 10". . . . . $10 – 15

This unusual pattern was decorated with a group of stylized flowers within a wide band of heavy Art Ware Green. Willow Green was applied to the edges and backs of these pieces. Very little of the "Red Flower" pattern has surfaced, and nearly all of the pieces have been marked: "Made For Bloomingdale's by Stangl Pottery, Trenton, N.J."

Antique Gold Cabbage Salad Set

Introduced: Early 1960s
Made For: Flemington Outlet
Shape Style: #1747 Cabbage

Known Pieces:
bowl, salad #1747. . . . . $60 – 75
bowl, mayonnaise #1748 . . . . $30 – 40
plate, #1749. . . . . $30 – 40

Antique Gold Cabbage plate.

During the early 1960s, Stangl re-introduced the 1930s #1747 Cabbage shapes with the Antique Gold finish for the Flemington Outlet. Although Stangl's Antique Gold artware was at the height of popularity and the dry-brushed gold luster accentuated the texture of these shapes, very little Antique Gold Cabbage was produced.

Golden Grape #5129

Introduced: 1963
Designer: Irene Sarnecki
Shape Style: #5129 Tiara

Known Pieces:
ashtray, 5" fluted . . . . $6 – 10	casserole, 8" covered. . . . . $50 – 60
bowl, cereal. . . . . $8 – 10	casserole, 8" skillet shape. . . . . $20 – 25
bowl, fruit . . . . $8 – 10	casserole, 6" skillet shape. . . . . $15 – 20
bowl, coupe soup . . . . $10 – 15	casserole, individual,
bowl, lug soup. . . . . $8 – 10	with handle & cover. . . . . $15 – 25
bowl, 11" salad . . . . $35 – 45	coaster/ashtray . . . . $8 – 12
bowl, 10" salad . . . . $25 – 35	coffee pot, 8 cup . . . . $50 – 60
bowl, 8" vegetable. . . . . $20 – 25	coffee pot, 6 cup . . . . $40 – 50
bowl, oval divided vegetable . . . . $20 – 25	coffee filter . . . . $15 – 20
bread tray . . . . $20 – 25	creamer . . . . $10 – 12
butter dish. . . . . $30 – 35	cruet with stopper. . . . . $20 – 30
cake stand . . . . $10 – 15	cup. . . . . $8 – 10

egg cup	$8 – 10	plate, 8" picnic*	$5 – 6
gravy boat	$10 – 15	platter, 13¾" casual	$30 – 40
gravy underplate	$8 – 10	platter, 14¾" oval	$35 – 45
mug, 2 cup	$25 – 35	pickle dish	$12 – 15
pitcher, 2 quart	$40 – 50	relish dish	$15 – 20
pitcher, 1 quart	$30 – 35	salt, pepper; each	$6 – 8
pitcher, 1 pint	$25 – 30	sauce boat	$20 – 30
pitcher, ½ pint	$20 – 25	saucer	$4 – 5
pitcher, 6 oz.	$15 – 20	saucer, mug, 7"	$8 – 10
plate, 14½" chop	$40 – 50	sugar	$10 – 15
plate, 12½" chop	$25 – 35	teapot	$35 – 45
plate, 10"	$12 – 18	tidbit, 10"	$8 – 12
plate, 8"	$10 – 12	tidbit, 2 tier	$20 – 25
plate, 7"	$10 – 12	warmer	$15 – 20
plate, 6"	$4 – 6	paper napkin, each	$1 – 2
plate, 10" picnic*	$6 – 7	paper price list	$10 – 12

* These items were usually sold only at the Flemington Outlet.

Golden Grape was Stangl's first pattern to use the new #5129 Tiara shape. Plates in the Tiara shape were fashioned with a narrow rim, and the hollow ware pieces were a tapered, conical shape. The number 5129 was used for both this new dinnerware shape and the Golden Grape pattern.

Stangl advertising stated that the Golden Grape pattern "offers the latest *House & Garden* colors of Gold and Green on an entirely new shape. This delightful hand-painted design is a real winner." The Golden Grape colors were Old Gold with Walnut Brown overstrokes for the large grapes, and Carnival Green and Pomona Green on the leaves and smaller motifs. Golden Grape was a popular pattern throughout the 1960s. It became inactive in 1968 and was discontinued in 1974.

Golden Grape ½ pint pitcher, 10" plate, 6 cup coffee pot, 12½" chop plate, 8 cup coffee pot, coffee filter.

Paisley #5130

Introduced: 1963
Designer: Irene Sarnecki
Shape Style: #3774 Coupe

Known Pieces:

ashtray, 5" fluted	$8 – 10	bowl, lug soup	$6 – 10
bowl, cereal	$10 – 15	bowl, 12" salad	$50 – 60
bowl, fruit	$8 – 10	bowl, 10" salad	$35 – 45
bowl, coupe soup	$15 – 20	bowl, 8" vegetable	$20 – 25

bowl, oval divided vegetable . . . . $20 – 25	pitcher, ½ pint. . . . . $20 – 25
bread tray . . . . $25 – 30	pitcher, 6 oz. $15 – 20
butter dish. . . . . $30 – 35	plate, 14½" chop . . . . $50 – 60
cake stand . . . . $10 – 15	plate, 12½" chop . . . . $30 – 35
casserole, 8" covered. . . . . $50 – 60	plate, 11" . . . . $20 – 25
casserole, 8" skillet shape. . . . . $20 – 25	plate, 10" . . . . $15 – 20
casserole, 6" skillet shape. . . . . $15 – 20	plate, 8" . . . . $10 – 15
casserole, individual,	plate, 6" . . . . $5 – 7
with handle & cover. . . . . $30 – 35	platter, 13¾" casual. . . . . $30 – 40
coaster/ashtray . . . . $15 – 20	platter, 14¾" oval . . . . $40 – 50
coffee pot, 8 cup . . . . $55 – 65	pickle dish. . . . . $12 – 15
creamer . . . . $10 – 15	relish dish . . . . $15 – 20
cruet with stopper. . . . . $25 – 30	salt, pepper; each . . . . $6 – 8
cup. . . . . $6 – 8	sauce boat . . . . $25 – 30
egg cup . . . . $8 – 12	saucer . . . . $5 – 6
gravy boat . . . . $15 – 20	sugar . . . . $10 – 15
gravy underplate. . . . . $8 – 12	teapot. . . . . $50 – 60
mug, 2 cup. . . . . $25 – 35	tidbit, 10". . . . . $10 – 15
pitcher, 2 quart . . . . $45 – 55	warmer . . . . $10 – 15
pitcher, 1 quart . . . . $30 – 40	paper napkin, each . . . . $1 – 2
pitcher, 1 pint . . . . $25 – 30	paper price list . . . . $10 – 12

Paisley was decorated with an allover pattern of stylized warm brown blossoms. This monochromatic color scheme was recommended by the *House & Garden* 1963 color chart. The Old Gold and Walnut Brown underglaze colors were further enhanced by a speckled background. The Paisley pattern was quite fashionable during 1963 and 1964, but became inactive on January 1, 1965.

Paisley, teapot, 12½" chop plate, 10" plate.

Blue Daisy #5131

Introduced: 1963
Designer: Irene Sarnecki
Shape Style: #5129 Tiara

Known Pieces:

ashtray, 5" fluted. . . . . $10 – 12	bowl, oval divided vegetable . . . . $25 – 30
bowl, cereal. $10 – 15	bread tray . . . . $25 – 30
bowl, fruit . . . . $10 – 12	butter dish. . . . . $30 – 35
bowl, coupe soup . . . . $15 – 20	casserole, 8" covered. . . . . $55 – 65
bowl, lug soup. . . . . $10 – 15	casserole, 8" skillet shape. . . . . $20 – 25
bowl, 11" salad . . . . $50 – 60	casserole, 6" skillet shape. . . . . $15 – 20
bowl, 10" salad . . . . $35 – 45	casserole, individual,
bowl, 8" vegetable. . . . . $20 – 30	with handle & cover. . . . . $30 – 35
	coaster/ashtray . . . . $15 – 20

coffee pot, 8 cup	$50 – 65	plate, 6"	$5 – 7
coffee pot, 6 cup	$45 – 55	plate, 10" picnic*	$5 – 6
coffee pot, 3 cup	$40 – 50	plate, 8" picnic*	$3 – 5
creamer	$10 – 15	platter, 13¾" casual	$40 – 50
cruet with stopper	$25 – 35	platter, 14¾" oval	$45 – 55
cup	$8 – 10	pickle dish	$15 – 20
egg cup	$10 – 12	relish dish	$15 – 20
gravy boat	$12 – 15	sauce boat	$20 – 25
gravy underplate	$10 – 12	saucer	$4 – 5
mug, 2 cup	$30 – 35	saucer, mug, 7"	$7 – 9
pitcher, 2 quart	$45 – 55	salt, pepper; each	$8 – 10
pitcher, 1 quart	$30 – 40	salt, pepper, #3298 Daisy; each*	$50 – 60
pitcher, 1 pint	$25 – 30	sugar	$10 – 15
pitcher, ½ pint	$20 – 25	teapot	$35 – 45
pitcher, 6 oz.	$15 – 20	tidbit, 10"	$10 – 12
plate, 14½" chop	$45 – 55	tidbit, 2 tier	$15 – 25
plate, 12½" chop	$30 – 40	tile*	$10 – 15
plate, 10"	$12 – 18	warmer	$15 – 20
plate, 8"	$10 – 12	paper napkin, each	$1 – 2
plate, 7"	$15 – 20	paper price list	$10 – 12

*These items were usually sold only at the Flemington Outlet.

The Blue Daisy pattern, with its Dark Turquoise blossoms, speckled background and Satin White glaze, was immediately popular. After the 1965 fire, however, Blue Daisy was unavailable due to the loss of the kiln necessary for the firing of Satin White glaze. A "confidential" interoffice memo dated December 1965 states "it is impossible to match the Blue Daisy colors and

glaze with the remaining kiln, so Blue Daisy will be replaced with Bachelor's Button." This memo goes on to state that "consumers will doubtless accept the Bachelor's Button pattern as readily as they did Blue Daisy."

The Bachelor's Button pattern was identical to Blue Daisy in colors and motif, but lacked the speckles, Satin White glaze, and carved scrolling on the border. Bachelor's Button was apparently no substitute for Blue Daisy, for it became inactive on January 1, 1968. Production of Blue Daisy was resumed in 1966, but as an inactive pattern only. In January 1970,

Blue Daisy #5092 2 cup mug, pickle dish, sauce boat, 10" plate, cup & saucer.

Blue Daisy was re-introduced "by popular demand" and remained in active production until discontinued in 1975. The Blue Daisy pattern is still relatively popular, although not as avidly sought after as some of Stangl's more colorful hand-carved patterns.

For a very short time during early 1965, the #3298 Daisy shape salt and pepper shakers were decorated with Blue Daisy colors and Satin White glaze for the Flemington Outlet. These shakers very scarce and much desired by Blue Daisy collectors.

Scandinavia

Introduced: 1964
Shape Style: #5129 Tiara

Known Pieces:

ashtray, 5" fluted	$10 – 15	gravy boat	$12 – 15
ashtray #5097 apple shape	$10 – 15	gravy underplate	$8 – 10
bowl, cereal	$10 – 15	mug, 2 cup	$30 – 35
bowl, fruit	$8 – 10	pitcher, 2 quart	$40 – 50
bowl, coupe soup	$12 – 15	pitcher, 1 quart	$30 – 35
bowl, lug soup	$8 – 10	pitcher, 1 pint	$25 – 30
bowl, 11" salad	$40 – 50	pitcher, ½ pint	$20 – 25
bowl, 10" salad	$35 – 45	pitcher, 6 oz.	$15 – 20
bowl, 8" vegetable	$20 – 25	plate, 14½" chop	$45 – 55
bowl, oval divided vegetable	$20 – 25	plate, 12½" chop	$30 – 40
bread tray	$15 – 25	plate, 10"	$20 – 25
butter dish	$20 – 25	plate, 8"	$15 – 20
cigarette box	$80 – 95	plate, 6"	$10 – 15
casserole, 8" covered	$45 – 60	platter, 13¾" casual	$35 – 45
coaster/ashtray	$20 – 25	pickle dish	$10 – 15
coffee pot, 8 cup	$55 – 65	relish dish	$12 – 18
creamer	$10 – 15	saucer	$5 – 6
cruet with stopper	$20 – 25	salt, pepper; each	$6 – 8
cup	$8 – 10	sugar	$10 – 15
egg cup	$8 – 10	teapot	$50 – 60
		tidbit, 10"	$10 – 15

The Scandinavia pattern was simply Black underglaze color sponged around the rims of plain, red-clay shapes with no engobe. Scandinavia cups were produced on both the #5129 Tiara shape and the #4024 coupe shape. This was an interesting, but short-lived pattern.

Silver Haze #5140

Introduced: 1964
Designer: Martin Stangl
Shape Style: #5129 Tiara, #1388

Known Pieces:

ashtray, 5" fluted	$10 – 15	creamer, #5140	$25 – 30
bowl, fruit	$8 – 12	cup, after dinner	$10 – 15
bowl, coupe soup	$15 – 20	cup, tea	$10 – 15
bowl, 3½" porringer	$20 – 25	plate, 12½" chop	$45 – 55
bowl, 5" porringer	$30 – 35	plate, 10"	$20 – 25
bowl, 10" salad	$45 – 55	plate, 8"	$10 – 15
bowl, 8" vegetable	$25 – 35	plate, 6"	$8 – 10
cigarette box, fluted	$65 – 80	saucer, after dinner	$5 – 6
coffee pot, #5140	$90 – 120	saucer, tea	$5 – 6
creamer, #1388	$20 – 25	sugar, #1388	$20 – 25

sugar, #5140 . . . . $25 – 30		tidbit, 10" . . . . $10 – 15	
tankard mug, 12 oz. . . . . $30 – 40		vase, 5¾" bud #5093 . . . . $30 – 35	
teapot, #1388 . . . . $80 – 95		paper price list . . . . $15 – 20	

Silver Haze 10" #5129 Tiara plate,
#5140 creamer & sugar.

Silver Haze was a novelty pattern produced for a very short time during 1964. Each piece was plain gray with platinum luster applied to rims and handles of most pieces. The bud vase and after dinner cup shapes were covered entirely with platinum. The Silver Haze pattern was used to introduce the #5140 shape line. The #5140 creamer, sugar, and coffee pot shapes were tried with other dinnerware motifs, but the fire in August 1965 curtailed any further research with these shapes. However, the #5140 after dinner cup and saucer shapes were decorated with the Antique Rose motif for the Flemington Outlet and the #5140 tankard mug was used again during the late 1960s with several other dinnerware patterns. Because Silver Haze was a novelty pattern, various unrelated dinnerware shapes, such as #1388, will unexpectedly turn up with the Silver Haze finish.

Caughley #5150

Introduced: 1964
Made For: Tiffany & Co.

Known Pieces:	Blue	Yellow Pink, Green	Brown Dark Green
ashtray, 5" fluted	$20 – 25	$15 – 20	$10 – 15
baking dish, 12" x 9½"	$85 – 95	$50 – 65	$40 – 50
baking dish, 9" x 6½"	$65 – 80	$45 – 55	$25 – 35
bowl, cereal	$20 – 25	$15 – 20	$10 – 12
bowl, coupe soup	$30 – 35	$20 – 25	$10 – 15
bowl, rim soup	$30 – 35	$25 – 30	$10 – 15
bowl, 12" salad	$95 – 135	$70 – 80	$35 – 45
bowl, 10" salad	$70 – 80	$40 – 50	$20 – 30
bowl, 9" salad	$70 – 80	$30 – 40	$20 – 30
bowl, 8" vegetable	$40 – 50	$25 – 35	$15 – 25
butter dish, covered	$60 – 75	$30 – 35	$20 – 25
cache pot, 5½" square	$60 – 75	$35 – 45	$35 – 45
candlestick #5299, 7½" tall; each	$45 – 55	$30 – 40	$20 – 30
casserole, 3 qt. round	$125 – 150	$60 – 75	$50 – 60
casserole, 2 qt. round	$80 – 95	$45 – 55	$30 – 40
casserole, 4½ pint, oval	$75 – 90	$40 – 50	$30 – 40

	Blue	Yellow Pink, Green	Brown Dark Green
casserole, 2½ pint, oval	$55 – 65	$35 – 45	$25 – 35
casserole, 1½ pint, oval	$45 – 55	$25 – 35	$20 – 30
coffee pot, 8 cup	$100 – 135	$75 – 85	$30 – 40
coffee pot, 6 cup	$85 – 95	$70 – 80	$25 – 35
creamer	$20 – 25	$15 – 20	$8 – 10
cup	$15 – 20	$8 – 12	$6 – 8
desert mold, fluted 6"	$45 – 55	$30 – 40	$20 – 25
dog bowl #5200	$95 – 125	$50 – 60	$40 – 50
flowerpot, 7"	$60 – 75	$35 – 45	$25 – 35
flowerpot, 6"	$40 – 50	$30 – 40	$20 – 30
flowerpot, 5"	$35 – 45	$25 – 35	$15 – 25
flowerpot, 4"	$30 – 40	$20 – 30	$10 – 20
flowerpot, 3"	$20 – 30	$10 – 20	$8 – 12
ginger jar	$100 – 135	$65 – 85	$45 – 55
gravy boat	$40 – 50	$30 – 40	$20 – 25
gravy underplate	$25 – 35	$15 – 20	$10 – 15
hurricane lamp	$25 – 35	$20 – 25	$10 – 15
lamp, rectangular	$200 – 250	$100 – 150	$75 – 100
mug, baby	$80 – 95	$70 – 85	$55 – 65
mug, 2 cup coffee	$45 – 55	$35 – 45	$25 – 30
mug, 13oz. coffee	$45 – 55	$35 – 45	$25 – 30
napkin ring, each	$25 – 35	$20 – 30	$10 – 15
pie plate, 11"	$60 – 75	$35 – 45	$25 – 30
pitcher, 2 quart	$95 – 115	$70 – 80	$50 – 60
pitcher, 1 quart	$60 – 70	$50 – 60	$40 – 50
pitcher, 1 pint	$45 – 55	$35 – 45	$25 – 35
pitcher, ½ pint	$35 – 40	$25 – 35	$20 – 25
pitcher, 6 oz.	$30 – 35	$20 – 25	$15 – 20
plate, 12½" cheese	$85 – 110	$60 – 70	$35 – 45
plate, 12½" chop	$75 – 95	$60 – 70	$35 – 45
plate, 10" or 10⅝"	$30 – 40	$25 – 30	$15 – 20
plate, 8" or 8¼"	$20 – 25	$15 – 20	$10 – 15
plate, 6"	$15 – 20	$10 – 15	$8 – 10
platter, 14⅜" oval	$65 – 75	$55 – 65	$35 – 45
platter, 11½" oval	$45 – 55	$35 – 45	$25 – 35
relish dish, single 8" crescent shape	$30 – 40	$20 – 25	$15 – 20
saucer	$7 – 10	$3 – 5	$2 – 3
salt, pepper; each	$10 – 15	$8 – 12	$7 – 8
soup tureen, covered	$185 – 225	$165 – 200	$80 – 100
ladle for tureen	$50 – 75	$40 – 50	$25 – 35
sugar	$25 – 30	$20 – 25	$10 – 15
sugar, 2¾" open	$20 – 25	$15 – 20	$10 – 12
sugar, #4024 open, handled	$35 – 45	$25 – 30	$20 – 25
teapot, 6 cup	$85 – 110	$75 – 85	$55 – 65
teapot, 4 cup	$80 – 90	$65 – 75	$45 – 55
tray, 8¼" oval	$25 – 35	$15 – 25	$10 – 15

	Blue	Yellow Pink, Green	Brown Dark Green
tray, 7½" square	$30 – 40	$20 – 25	$15 – 20
tidbit, 10"	$20 – 30	$15 – 20	$8 – 12
tidbit, 2 tier	$30 – 40	$25 – 25	$15 – 20
tile	$25 – 35	$20 – 25	$15 – 20
vase, triple cylinder	$50 – 60	$30 – 40	$20 – 30
dealer sign	$250 – 350	$100 – 150	$100 – 150
paper price list	$20 – 25		

The Caughley pattern was special-ordered by Tiffany & Company, and was produced according to their specifications. The front, back, and edge of each piece was covered with white engobe; Tiffany wanted none of Stangl's distinctive red body to show. The decoration involved a two-step sponging process. The first color was sponged on lightly; a second, darker color was sponged over the first color. Both the front and back were entirely sponged with color. The finished piece of Caughley was to have as little white background showing as possible.

The colors used for Blue Caughley were Blue #95 and Art Ware Blue; Dark Green Caughley was Victoria Green and Pomona Green; Green Caughley was Victoria Green and Green #1431; Yellow Caughley used Yellow and Orange. Pink Caughley and Brown Caughley each used a light, then heavy application of a single color. Pink Caughley was decorated with Pink #193, Brown Caughley with Walnut Brown.

When first introduced, Caughley was available only in blue with a very limited number of shapes. By 1967, Pink Caughley and Dark Green Caughley were added, and the shape line was greatly expanded. In 1969 Pink Caughley was discontinued because it tended to fade in the kiln, and Dark Green Caughley was replaced with Green Caughley. Also in 1969, Yellow Caughley and Brown Caughley were introduced. Brown Caughley, however, was never in demand and lasted less than a year.

The Caughley pattern was very popular, and was continually produced from 1964 until Stangl's close in 1978. Because Tiffany distributed Caughley in several major cities, and Stangl was allowed to sell Tiffany patterns in areas where there were no Tiffany stores, Caughley was well promoted across the nation.

Caughley consisted of an unusual combination of dinnerware shapes. The plates, salt, pepper, rim soup, cereal bowl, and 8" vegetable bowl were the #3434 rim shape. The cup and saucer were shape #4024, while the creamer, sugar, pitchers, tea and coffee pots were the #5129 Tiara shape. Some of the Caughley shapes were shared with the Town & Country pattern, such as the gravy, butter dish, baking dishes, and salad bowls. Many of the remaining shapes were designed specifically for the Caughley pattern. The last shapes added to the Caughley line were the ginger jar and hurricane lamp in 1977.

Caughley 6" plate, Pink; 10" plate, Dark Green; mug, Green; cup & saucer, Yellow; 10⅝" plate, Green; relish dish, Blue; 10" plate, Yellow; open sugar, Yellow; square tray, Green; cup & saucer, Pink.

Caughley 3 quart casserole, Blue.

Golden Blossom #5155

Introduced: 1964
Designer: Irene Sarnecki
Shape Style: #5129 Tiara

Known Pieces:

ashtray, 5" fluted . . . . $8 – 10	pitcher, 1 quart . . . . $30 – 35
bowl, cereal . . . . $10 – 12	pitcher, 1 pint . . . . $25 – 30
bowl, fruit . . . . $8 – 10	pitcher, ½ pint . . . . $20 – 25
bowl, coupe soup . . . . $12 – 15	pitcher, 6 oz. . . . . $15 – 20
bowl, lug soup . . . . $10 – 12	plate, 14½" chop . . . . $40 – 50
bowl, 11" salad . . . . $35 – 45	plate, 12½" chop . . . . $25 – 35
bowl, 10" salad . . . . $25 – 35	plate, 10" . . . . $12 – 15
bowl, 8" vegetable . . . . $20 – 30	plate, 8" . . . . $8 – 10
bowl, oval divided vegetable . . . . $20 – 25	plate, 7" . . . . $10 – 12
bread tray . . . . $20 – 25	plate, 6" . . . . $4 – 6
butter dish . . . . $30 – 40	plate, 10" picnic* . . . . $5 – 8
candle holder, #4064, 4"* . . . . $20 – 25	plate, 8" picnic* . . . . $5 – 8
casserole, 8" covered . . . . $50 – 60	platter, 13¾" casual . . . . $30 – 40
casserole, 8" skillet shape . . . . $20 – 25	platter, 14¾" oval . . . . $35 – 45
casserole, 6" skillet shape . . . . $15 – 20	pickle dish . . . . $12 – 18
casserole, individual, with handle & cover . . . . $20 – 25	relish dish . . . . $15 – 20
coaster/ashtray . . . . $10 – 15	salt, pepper; each . . . . $6 – 8
coffee pot, 8 cup . . . . $50 – 60	sauce boat . . . . $20 – 30
coffee pot, 6 cup . . . . $45 – 55	saucer . . . . $4 – 5
creamer . . . . $10 – 12	saucer, mug, 7" . . . . $8 – 10
cruet with stopper . . . . $25 – 30	sugar . . . . $10 – 15
cup . . . . $8 – 10	teapot . . . . $35 – 45
deviled egg plate #5199 . . . . $30 – 40	tidbit, 10" . . . . $8 – 12
egg cup . . . . $8 – 10	tidbit, 2 tier . . . . $20 – 25
gravy boat . . . . $15 – 20	tile* . . . . $12 – 15
gravy underplate . . . . $8 – 12	tray, 7½" square* . . . . $20 – 25
mug, 2 cup . . . . $25 – 30	warmer . . . . $15 – 20
pitcher, 2 quart . . . . $40 – 50	paper napkin, each . . . . $1 – 2
	paper price list . . . . $10 – 12

* These items were usually sold only at the Flemington Outlet.

Golden Blossom is a capricious pattern featuring stalks of stylized lupine blossoms in Old Gold and Dark Yellow with soft green leaves. The carved scroll border on the rims and speckled glaze add to the charm of this sunny pattern.

Golden Blossom octagonal tile, creamer, sugar, 12½" chop plate, #4064 candle holders, 8" plate.

The #5199 deviled egg plate with the Golden Blossom motif was added in October 1967. The #5199 deviled egg plate shape was offered in Stangl's 1968 giftware catalog and was sold at the Flemington Outlet as well. Deviled egg plates were produced with both plain and speckled glaze and were sometimes drilled for a handle.

The Golden Blossom pattern was also produced on the white-bodied shapes of the late 1970s. Although Golden Blossom is not as popular as some of Stangl's other gold and green patterns, it is still moderately collected.

Antique Rose

Introduced: 1964
Shape Style: #3434
  Rim with #5129 Tiara

Antique Rose 10" plate with rose motif, salt and pepper shakers with daisy motif, "Rose" punch cup.

Known Pieces:

bowl, fruit	$20 – 25
bowl, coupe soup	$30 – 40
bowl, 10" salad	$90 – 110
bowl, 8" vegetable	$50 – 60
creamer	$20 – 30
coffee pot	$95 – 120
cup	$10 – 15
plate, 14½" chop	$90 – 110
plate, 12½" chop	$60 – 70
plate, 10"	$30 – 40
plate, 8"	$20 – 25
plate, 6"	$10 – 15
salt, pepper; each	$10 – 15
saucer	$8 – 10
sugar	$20 – 30
teapot	$90 – 110
tidbit	$15 – 20
"Rose" punch cup & saucer	$30 – 35

The Antique Rose pattern shared the diminutive rose motif with Stangl's "Antique" pitcher and bowl sets, also introduced in 1964. The Pink #193 flowers (both rose and daisy motifs were used on the dinnerware) were surrounded by a delicate sponging of Blue #95. Antique Rose dinnerware was a special promotional pattern, offered only to a few of Stangl's better distributors, with seconds, of course, being sold at the Flemington Outlet. Antique Rose was in very limited production during 1964 and 1965. This pattern was not manufactured after the fire of August 1965, which explains its rarity today.

Similar to Antique Rose dinnerware were the "Rose" punch cup and saucer sets. These cups and saucers utilized the #5140 after dinner cup and saucer shapes. Although these cups and the Antique Rose dinnerware pattern shared the same rose motif, the punch cups and saucers were decorated with a green band instead of the sponged Blue #95 border and were produced only for the Flemington Outlet. They were designed to coordinate with the #5157/#5158 "Antique" pitcher and bowl sets, with the bowls serving as punch bowls.

Apple Delight #5161

Introduced: 1965
Designer: Kay Hackett
Shape Style: #5129 Tiara

Known Pieces:

ashtray, 5" fluted	$10 – 12	pitcher, 1 quart	$45 – 55
bowl, cereal	$12 – 15	pitcher, 1 pint	$30 – 40
bowl, fruit	$8 – 12	pitcher, ½ pint	$25 – 30
bowl, coupe soup	$20 – 25	pitcher, 6 oz.	$20 – 25
bowl, lug soup	$10 – 15	plate, 14½" chop	$60 – 70
bowl, 11" salad	$60 – 70	plate, 12½" chop	$35 – 40
bowl, 10" salad	$40 – 50	plate, 10"	$20 – 25
bowl, 8" vegetable	$30 – 35	plate, 8"	$10 – 15
bowl, oval divided vegetable	$25 – 30	plate, 7"	$10 – 15
bread tray	$25 – 30	plate, 6"	$7 – 8
butter dish	$30 – 40	plate, 10" picnic*	$5 – 8
casserole, 8" covered	$60 – 70	plate, 8" picnic*	$3 – 5
casserole, 8" skillet shape	$25 – 35	platter, 13¾" casual	$50 – 60
casserole, 6" skillet shape	$15 – 25	platter, 14¾" oval	$60 – 70
casserole, individual, with handle & cover	$30 – 35	pickle dish	$15 – 20
coaster/ashtray	$15 – 20	relish dish	$20 – 25
coffee pot, 8 cup	$75 – 85	salt, pepper; #5129 Tiara shape, each	$8 – 10
coffee pot, 6 cup	$65 – 75	salt, pepper; apple shape, each	$40 – 50
coffee pot, #5140	$165 – 190	sauce boat	$30 – 35
creamer	$10 – 15	saucer	$5 – 6
creamer, #5140	$45 – 65	saucer, mug, 7"	$8 – 9
cruet with stopper	$25 – 35	sugar	$12 – 15
cup	$8 – 12	sugar, #5140	$45 – 65
egg cup	$12 – 15	teapot	$45 – 55
gravy boat	$20 – 25	tidbit, 10"	$10 – 15
gravy underplate	$10 – 15	tidbit, 2 tier	$15 – 25
mug, 2 cup	$40 – 50	tile*	$15 – 20
mug, stack	$40 – 50	warmer	$20 – 25
pitcher, 2 quart	$60 – 75	paper napkin, each	$1 – 2
		paper price list	$10 – 15

* These items were usually sold only at the Flemington Outlet.

Apple Delight is a bright pattern that was relatively popular throughout the 1960s and into the 1970s. Very collectable are the apple-shape salt and pepper shakers. These were usually hand painted with Pink #160 and a Yellow stripe, or Yellow with various spots and splotches of Pink #160 or Victoria Green. The least common finish used on the apple shakers was a sprayed-on version of Stangl's earlier Oxblood glaze. The Apple Delight apple shakers were produced from January 1965 until the fire in August 1965. When production of Apple Delight was resumed after the fire, the apple-shape shakers were no longer part of the line. The #5129 Tiara shakers were decorated with the Apple Delight motif and used with the pattern instead.

The #5140 coffee pot, creamer, and sugar shapes were tried with the Apple Delight motif just prior to the 1965 fire. Very few of these shapes were produced with this motif, these shapes are most commonly found with the Silver Haze gray engobe and platinum luster decoration.

Apple Delight 6" plate, apple salt & pepper, #5129 Tiara salt & pepper, 14¾" oval platter, teapot.

Rustic #5164, Spun Gold #5165, Maple Whirl #5166

Introduced: 1965
Designer: Kay Hackett
Shape Style: #3434 Rim with #5129 Tiara

Known Pieces:

bean pot/cookie jar	$40 – 50
bowl, cereal	$8 – 10
bowl, fruit	$6 – 8
bowl, coupe soup	$10 – 15
bowl, 10" salad	$40 – 50
bowl, 8" vegetable	$20 – 25
creamer	$10 – 12
cup	$6 – 8
mug, 2 cup	$25 – 35

Rustic 8" plate; Spun Gold 10" plate; Maple Whirl 6" plate, sugar, creamer.

pitcher, 1 pint	$25 – 35
plate, 12½" chop	$40 – 50
plate, 10"	$12 – 18
plate, 8"	$8 – 12
plate, 6"	$6 – 8
saucer	$5 – 6
sugar	$10 – 15
teapot	$35 – 45
tidbit, 10"	$8 – 10
paper price list	$10 – 15

Maple Whirl, Spun Gold, and Rustic were introduced as Stangl's "Casual Dinnerware." These patterns were initiated as a result of innumerable requests to Stangl salesmen by their customers for earthtone dinnerware of this type.

Maple Whirl was decorated with a swirl of Saddle Brown surrounded by a Pomona Green rim. Spun Gold used Pomona Green on the rim with an Old Gold swirl in the center. Both of these patterns were glazed with gloss glaze. The Rustic pattern was glazed with Silk glaze. This pattern featured a Walnut Brown swirl and carried a Yellow band on the rims.

In spite of the fact that these patterns were based on supposedly popular colors, there was very little demand for Maple Whirl, Spun Gold, or Rustic during 1965. After the fire in August of that year, the Casual Dinnerware patterns became inactive due to lack of sales. Stangl management, however, used the fire as the reason these three patterns were no longer produced.

At most, Maple Whirl, Spun Gold, and Rustic were in active production for less than eight months. Despite the scarcity of these patterns, there is very little interest in them at this time.

White Dogwood #5167, Dogwood

Introduced: 1965
Developed By: Martin Stangl, Kay Hackett
Shape Style: #3668 Dogwood

Known Pieces:

bowl, cereal	$15 – 20	plate, 6"	$7 – 9
bowl, lug soup	$10 – 15	plate, 10" picnic*	$4 – 6
bowl, 10" salad	$50 – 60	plate, 8" picnic*	$3 – 4
bowl, 8" vegetable	$30 – 35	platter, 14¾" oval	$50 – 60
creamer	$15 – 20	saucer	$5 – 6
cup	$10 – 12	salt, pepper; plain, each	$6 – 8
mug, 2 cup, plain	$20 – 25	salt, pepper; floral, each	$10 – 12
mug, 13oz. floral motif	$40 – 45	sugar	$15 – 20
pitcher, 1 pint, plain	$25 – 30	teapot, 4 cup, plain	$30 – 35
pitcher, 1½ pint, floral motif	$50 – 60	tidbit, 10"	$8 – 12
plate, 14½" chop	$50 – 60	tidbit, 2 tier	$20 – 25
plate, 12½" chop	$35 – 45	tile*	$15 – 20
plate, 10"	$15 – 20	paper napkin, each	$1 – 2
plate, 8"	$10 – 12	paper price list	$10 – 12

* These items were usually sold only at the Flemington Outlet.

The 1965 White Dogwood pattern utilized the same molds as the Dogwood #3668 pattern, originally introduced in 1942. The pattern was updated with a new soft green engobe; a complementary background for the White #10 blossoms and Pomona Green leaves.

When first introduced in 1965, this pattern was called Dogwood. After the fire in August 1965, the pattern was renamed White Dogwood, and was consistently addressed as such until 1975. During 1975, Stangl listed this pattern both as Dogwood and White Dogwood. The name was simply Dogwood during 1976, but became White Dogwood again during 1977 and 1978.

White Dogwood, and subsequent patterns with similar raised decoration, were advertised as "Prestige Dinnerware." During 1965, White Dogwood was considerably more expensive than Stangl's hand-carved, hand-decorated patterns. By 1966 retail prices for this pattern were more in line with Stangl's other dinnerware patterns.

White Dogwood cups and saucers utilized the original #3668 Dogwood cup shape until 1967 when the cup was changed to the #4024 shape. So that customers with White Dogwood sets made prior to 1967 would be able to match replacement cups, #3668 Dogwood shape cups could be ordered from Trenton or Flemington.

A teapot shape was never developed for the #3668 Dogwood shape line. The White Dogwood teapot is the #5129 Tiara 4 cup teapot shape with green engobe and Walnut Brown striping. The original White Dogwood salt and pepper shakers were #3774 coupe shape shakers with green engobe and a Walnut Brown stripe. In 1977, salt and pepper shakers, a 13 ounce mug shape and a 1½ pint pitcher shape with raised White Dogwood motif were introduced. Produced for only a year, these shapes are somewhat desirable.

Since the White Dogwood pattern has no carving, it adapted very well to Stangl's total conversion to white body production in 1975. This pattern continued to sell well until Stangl closed in 1978.

White Dogwood 8" picnic plate, #4024 cup, #3668 cup & saucer, 12½" chop plate, plain salt shaker, decorated salt shaker, teapot, 10" plate, square tile.

Gray Dogwood

Introduced: 1965
Developed By: Martin Stangl
Made For: Flemington Outlet
Shape Style: #3668 Dogwood

Known Pieces:		
bowl, lug soup	$20 – 25	plate, 14½" chop . . . . . . $80 – 95
bowl, 10" salad	$80 – 95	plate, 10" . . . . . . $30 – 40
bowl, 8" vegetable	$35 – 45	plate, 8" . . . . . . $20 – 30
creamer	$25 – 30	plate, 6" . . . . . . $10 – 15
cup	$10 – 15	saucer . . . . . . $8 – 10
		sugar . . . . . . $25 – 30

The Gray Dogwood pattern was never as popular as any of Stangl's other Dogwood patterns, and was made for a few months at most. Martin Stangl, however, insisted on its production. Being color blind, Martin Stangl found the sharp light and dark contrast of Gray Dogwood very appealing.

Gray Dogwood cup & saucer, 8" plate, creamer, sugar.

Filter Coffee Makers #5129

Introduced: 1965
Shape Style: #5129 Tiara
Glaze Colors: Chartreuse Green, Dark Green, Canary Yellow, White, Satin White, Peach,
  Clear glaze, Manganese Brown

Known Pieces:

coffee pot, 8 cup	$35 – 45	filter top, 3 cup	$8 – 15
coffee pot, 6 cup	$25 – 35	warmer, double	$20 – 25
coffee pot, 3 cup	$15 – 25	warmer, single	$10 – 15
coffee pot, individual #3434 teapot shape	$50 – 75	Stangl filter papers, package of 50	$20 – 25
filter top, 6 or 8 cup	$8 – 15	paper price list	$8 – 12

By 1965, Stangl had stopped producing filter coffee pots with dinnerware decorations. Instead, this assortment of filter coffee makers was introduced with solid-color glazes designed to coordinate with the dinnerware patterns popular at that time. These modern, solid-color glazes Canary Yellow, Chartreuse Green, Dark Green, Peach, and Manganese Brown were also used on various other items produced for the Flemington Outlet. The filter coffee makers were also available in plain white with Old Gold bands.

Stangl furnished each coffee maker with a supply of filter papers. If needed, replacement coffee maker parts and filter papers could be ordered from the Trenton factory. This series of coffee pots was produced through the 1960s and well into the 1970s.

Filter Coffee Makers #5129 3 cup filter top, 6–8 cup filter top, 3 cup coffee pot, 8 cup coffee pot, 6 cup coffee pot, warmer.

Bachelor's Button #5177

Introduced: 1965
Designer: Irene Sarnecki
Shape Style: #5129 Tiara

Known Pieces:

ashtray, 5" fluted	$6 – 8	bread tray	$20 – 25
bowl, cereal	$10 – 12	butter dish	$30 – 35
bowl, fruit	$8 – 10	casserole, 8" covered	$40 – 50
bowl, coupe soup	$12 – 15	casserole, 8" skillet shape	$15 – 20
bowl, lug soup	$8 – 12	casserole, 6" skillet shape	$10 – 15
bowl, 11" salad	$40 – 50	coaster/ashtray	$10 – 15
bowl, 10" salad	$25 – 35	coffee pot, 8 cup	$45 – 55
bowl, 8" vegetable	$20 – 30	coffee pot, 6 cup	$25 – 35
bowl, oval divided vegetable	$20 – 25	creamer	$10 – 12
		cruet with stopper	$20 – 25

cup	$8 – 10	plate, 10" picnic*	$5 – 8
egg cup	$10 – 12	plate, 8" picnic*	$3 – 4
gravy boat	$10 – 15	platter, 13¾" casual	$30 – 40
gravy underplate	S7 – 10	platter, 14¾" oval	$35 – 45
mug, 2 cup	$25 – 30	pickle dish	$10 – 15
pitcher, 2 quart	$40 – 45	relish dish	$15 – 20
pitcher, 1 quart	$30 – 35	saucer	$4 – 5
pitcher, 1 pint	$20 – 25	salt, pepper; each	$6 – 8
pitcher, ½ pint	$15 – 20	sugar	$10 – 12
pitcher, 6 oz.	$10 – 15	teapot	$35 – 45
plate, 14½" chop	$35 – 40	tidbit, 10"	$10 – 12
plate, 12½" chop	$25 – 30	tidbit, 2 tier	$20 – 25
plate, 10"	$10 – 15	tile*	$10 – 15
plate, 8"	$8 – 10	warmer	$12 – 15
plate, 6"	$4 – 6	paper price list	$10 – 12

* These items were usually sold only at the Flemington Outlet.

The Bachelor's Button pattern was intended to replace Blue Daisy after the 1965 fire at the Trenton plant. Bachelor's Button, however, did not have the scrolled rim, speckle background, or Satin White glaze of Blue Daisy, so was no substitute. Because of this, the Bachelor's Button pattern was very poorly received. It became even less acceptable once Blue Daisy was again manufactured in 1966. Therefore, the Bachelor's Button pattern became inactive on January 1, 1968, and was discontinued during 1973.

Bachelor's Button sugar, creamer, 10" plate, ½ pint pitcher.

Cosmos #5178, Pink Cosmos

Introduced: 1966
Developed By: Martin Stangl, Irene Sarnecki
Shape Style: #3667 Cosmos

Known Pieces:

bowl, lug soup	$10 – 12	plate, 12½" chop	$40 – 50
bowl, 10" salad	$40 – 50	plate, 10"	$20 – 25
bowl, 8" vegetable	$20 – 30	plate, 8"	$10 – 15
cake stand	$20 – 30	plate, 6"	$8 – 10
creamer	$15 – 20	platter, 14¾" oval	$50 – 65
cup	$8 – 12	saucer	$5 – 6
		salt, pepper; each	$8 – 10

sugar . . . . $15 – 20	paper napkin, each . . . . $1 – 2
tidbit, 10". . . . . $10 – 15	paper price list . . . . $10 – 15

The Cosmos #5178 pattern was an updated version of August Jacob's Cosmos #3667 design originally introduced in 1942. Irene Sarnecki worked out the attractive Pink #193 and Pomona Green color combination.

From 1965 until 1967 this pattern was called Cosmos and was produced using the original #3667 Cosmos molds. In 1967 the pattern was reworked and the name changed to Pink Cosmos.

At that time the cup shape was changed from the #3667 shape to the #4024 coupe shape, and the motif on the plate rims was modified from a complete ring of blossoms to three evenly spaced sprays of flowers. In 1970 Pink Cosmos became an inactive pattern and was re-named Cosmos. Therefore, plates with either motif can be found marked Cosmos or Pink Cosmos.

Pink Cosmos 6" plate, 12½" chop plate;
Cosmos cup & saucer, 10" plate.

Sculptured Fruit #5179

Introduced: 1966
Shape Style: #5179 Raised Fruit

Known Pieces:

bowl, cereal . . . . $12 – 15	plate, 12½" chop . . . . $45 – 55
bowl, fruit . . . . $8 – 12	plate, 10" . . . . $15 – 20
bowl, coupe soup . . . . $12 – 20	plate, 8" . . . . $10 – 15
bowl, lug soup. . . . . $8 – 12	plate, 6" . . . . $6 – 8
bowl, 10" salad . . . . $40 – 50	plate, 10" picnic* . . . . $4 – 6
bowl, 8" vegetable . . . . $25 – 35	plate, 8" picnic* . . . . $3 – 5
butter dish. . . . . $30 – 35	platter, 14¾" oval . . . . $45 – 55
cake stand, 10" . . . . $10 – 20	saucer . . . . $5 – 6
candy dish, covered* . . . . $70 – 85	salt, pepper; each . . . . $8 – 10
compote, 6" . . . . $10 – 15	sugar . . . . $15 – 20
creamer . . . . $15 – 20	teapot, 4 cup, plain . . . . $25 – 30
cup. . . . . $8 – 10	tidbit, 10". . . . . $10 – 15
mug, stack* plain . . . . $20 – 25	tidbit, 2 tier . . . . $20 – 30
mug, 13oz. fruit motif. . . . . $25 – 35	tile* . . . . $12 – 15
pitcher, 1½ pint, fruit motif . . . . $40 – 50	paper napkin, each . . . . $1 – 2
pitcher, 1 pint, plain. . . . . $20 – 25	paper price list . . . . $8 – 15

* These items were usually sold only at the Flemington Outlet.

The #5179 Raised Fruit shape was newly designed in 1965 and was loosely based on the motifs of the #1940 Raised Fruit salad set pattern. Colors for the Sculptured Fruit motif were selected by customers at the Flemington Outlet. Fourteen different #5179 raised fruit samples were sent to Flemington so that outlet customers could vote on their favorites. Ten of the samples were decorated with the fruits in assorted natural colors. The remaining four samples were painted with diverse gold, green, and brown combinations recommended by *House & Garden*.

Of these fourteen samples, the four decorated with monotone colors received more votes than the ten with natural-colored fruit. The sample receiving the most votes was decorated with Old Gold fruit and Pomona Green leaves. This was then put into production as Sculptured Fruit. This method of having Flemington Outlet patrons vote on patterns considered for introduction was used extensively during the late 1960s and 1970s.

During 1968 and 1969, Sculptured Fruit was heavily advertised in print and on the television game shows Concentration and Eye Guess. This created an overwhelming demand for the Sculptured Fruit pattern, sales for which surpassed all other Stangl patterns of that period. By the mid 1970s, however, the Sculptured Fruit craze had ended. Sculptured Fruit is still fairly popular, but the great quantities of this pattern yet available keep prices for most pieces at moderate levels.

There were no teapot or coffee pot shapes designed with the #5179 Raised Fruit line. The Sculptured Fruit teapot is the #5129 Tiara teapot shape with Old Gold and Pomona Green bands. The typical Sculptured Fruit mug has only the raised pear and leaves painted. In 1973 the #5179 Raised Fruit mug shape was used as part of a promotional assortment, but was decorated with an Old Gold band in addition to the decorated pear and leaves.

Sculptured Fruit octagonal tile, salt & pepper, 12½" chop plate, covered candy dish, 10" plate, mug.

Two of the sample plates decorated in monotone colors used to determine the coloration of the Sculptured Fruit pattern.

Mediterranean #5186

Introduced: 1966
Designer: Irene Sarnecki
Shape Style: #3434 Rim with #5129 Tiara

Known Pieces:

ashtray, 5" fluted	$20 – 25	bowl, fruit ... $10 – 15
bowl, cereal	$20 – 25	bowl, coupe soup ... $25 – 30

bowl, lug soup. . . . . $15 – 20	pitcher, 1 pint . . . . $35 – 45
bowl, 11" salad . . . . $70 – 80	pitcher, ½ pint. . . . . $25 – 30
bowl, 10" salad . . . . $45 – 55	pitcher, 6 ounce . . . . $20 – 25
bowl, 8" vegetable. . . . . $35 – 45	plate, 12½" chop . . . . $60 – 70
bowl, oval divided vegetable . . . . . . $45 – 45	plate, 10" . . . . $25 – 30
butter dish. . . . . $40 – 45	plate, 8" . . . . $15 – 20
casserole, 8" covered. . . . . $75 – 90	plate, 6" . . . . $8 – 12
cigarette box . . . . $75 – 95	platter, 13¾" casual. . . . . $55 – 65
coaster/ashtray . . . . $20 – 25	platter, 14¾" oval . . . . $60 – 70
coffee pot, 8 cup . . . . $85 – 95	relish dish . . . . $25 – 30
creamer . . . . $15 – 20	saucer . . . . $6 – 8
cruet with stopper. . . . . $30 – 40	salt, pepper; each . . . . $8 – 10
cup. . . . . $12 – 15	sugar . . . . $15 – 20
egg cup . . . . $15 – 20	teapot. . . . . $65 – 75
gravy boat . . . . $20 – 25	tidbit, 10". . . . . $12 – 15
gravy underplate. . . . . $12 – 15	tidbit, 2 tier . . . . $25 – 35
mug, 2 cup. . . . . $40 – 50	tile* . . . . $20 – 25
pitcher, 2 quart . . . . $85 – 95	paper napkin, each . . . . $1 – 2
pitcher, 1 quart . . . . $45 – 55	paper price list . . . . $5 – 10

The Mediterranean pattern was advertised as "a sublime blend of rich blues and greens truly reflecting the brilliant colors of the ageless Mediterranean." This watery effect was achieved by using Art Ware Green and Art Ware Blue sponged together under clear gloss glaze.

Until 1967, the backs of Mediterranean plates were decorated with Artware Green and Artware Blue, identical to the fronts. But beginning in 1967, Mediterranean was simplified to cut production costs and the plate backs were simply sponged with Art Ware Blue.

The unique Mediterranean finish was very popular during the late 1960s. Consequently, Stangl introduced a whole line of Mediterranean artware products. This line was composed of such shapes as vases, ashtrays, servers, and console sets.

Mediterranean 6" plate, cereal bowl, 10" plate, cup, mug.

White Grape #5187

Introduced: Spring 1967
Designer: Rose Herbeck

White Grape 8" plate, cup, 11" plate.

Known Pieces:

cake plate, 11" footed	$35 – 45
candy dish, covered	$55 – 65
cigarette box	$80 – 95
coffee pot, #5140	$110 – 145
compote, 6"	$15 – 20
creamer, #5140	$30 – 40
cup, #4030	$10 – 15
jewel box, 5"	$25 – 35
jewel box, 2¾"	$20 – 25
pitcher, 2 quart	$75 – 85
pitcher, 1 quart	$50 – 65
pitcher, 1 pint	$20 – 30
plate, 11"	$30 – 35
plate, 8"	$20 – 25
saucer	$10 – 12
sugar, #5140	$30 – 40
teapot	$85 – 110
vase, fan shape	$55 – 65
paper price list	$15 – 20

Stangl's White Grape pattern was loosely based on the Wedgwood Queen's Ware style of decoration. White Grape used a pale blue clay body with grape embellishments cast in white clay. Mr. Stangl had high expectations for this pattern. An extensive advertising campaign was planned and full-color price lists were printed. Unfortunately, White Grape was not adorned with fashion colors, so did not attract the interest of dinnerware retailers at the fall 1966 trade shows. Consequently, White Grape was discontinued on January 1, 1968. Although classically styled and quite attractive, very little White Grape was produced.

Pink Dogwood #5193

Introduced: 1967
Designer: Irene Sarnecki
Shape Style: #3668 Dogwood

Known Pieces:

bowl, lug soup	$15 – 20
bowl, 10" salad	$50 – 65
bowl, 8" vegetable	$30 – 40
creamer	$20 – 25
cup	$10 – 12
plate, 12½" chop	$60 – 75
plate, 10"	$25 – 30
plate, 8"	$15 – 25
plate, 6"	$10 – 15
platter, 14¾" oval	$70 – 85
saucer	$8 – 10
sugar	$20 – 25
tidbit, 10"	$10 – 15
paper napkin, each	$1 – 2
paper price list	$15 – 20

Pink Dogwood was developed with the expectation that it would become as popular as White Dogwood. However, the Pink #193 and Pomona Green colors of this pattern were not fashionable during 1967. For this reason, Pink Dogwood was never a strong seller nor produced in great quantities. The Pink Dogwood pattern became inactive in 1969 so therefore is not very plentiful, but is quite popular now.

Pink Dogwood 10" plate, 8" plate, cup.

Cabbage #5197

Introduced: 1967
Designer: Martin Stangl
Made For: Flemington Outlet
Shape Style: #1800 Cabbage Leaf
Glaze Colors: Chartreuse Green, Dark Green, Canary Yellow, White, Art Ware Green,
  Peach, 22-karat Gold Decorated

Known Pieces:			
bowl, 10" salad	$35 – 50	plate, 8"	$15 – 20
bowl, 9" salad	$25 – 40	plate, 6"	$8 – 10
creamer	$15 – 20	relish, double	$8 – 15
cup	$6 – 10	saucer	$6 – 7
plate, 10"	$20 – 25	sugar	$15 – 20
		teapot	$65 – 80

This re-introduction of the #1800 Cabbage Leaf pattern was updated with 1960s fashion-color glazes or 22-karat gold decoration. This cabbage pattern was treated as a novelty set and sold only at the Flemington Outlet. Only the double relish dish was available nation-wide through Stangl's giftware catalogs. The double relish dishes are the most plentiful pieces of this issue. These pieces nearly always have brass-colored metal handles. Very rarely were the 1960s era solid-color glazed #1800 Cabbage Leaf double relishes produced with pottery handles. Pieces glazed in the Green or White colors are valued at the low end of the range. Pieces glazed with Canary Yellow or Peach are valued at the high end. Items with gold decoration are scarce and valued a little higher than those without gold.

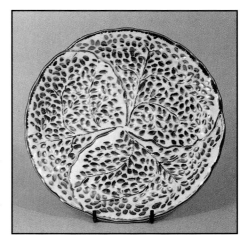

*left:
Cabbage double relish dish, 10" plate, Chartreuse Green; cup & saucer, White.*

*right:
Cabbage 8" plate with 22-karat gold decoration.*

Engobe Decorated Dinnerware "Gingerbread"

Introduced: 1967
Designer: Rose Herbeck
Made For: Flemington Outlet
Glaze Colors: Cobalt Blue, Manganese Brown, Copper Green, Transparent Yellow; Clear Glaze

Known Pieces:	Rim Motifs Simple Florals	Allover Florals	Buildings Birds
bowl, 10" #4062 flared	$35 – 45	$40 – 50	$60 – 75
bowl, 8" #4061 flared	$25 – 35	$30 – 40	$45 – 55
cake stand	$20 – 25	$30 – 40	$40 – 50
creamer	$20 – 30	$30 – 40	$50 – 60
cup	$10 – 15	$15 – 20	$30 – 40
mug, 2 cup	$30 – 40	$40 – 50	$60 – 75
pie plate, 10"	$35 – 45	$50 – 60	$100 – 150
pie plate, 9"	$25 – 35	$40 – 50	$90 – 125
plate, 12½" chop	$45 – 55	$80 – 110	$150 – 200
plate, 10"	$20 – 30	$40 – 50	$75 – 100
plate, 8"	$15 – 20	$25 – 35	$50 – 65
plate, 6"	$10 – 15	$15 – 25	$35 – 50
saucer	$10 – 12	$10 – 15	$15 – 20
sugar	$15 – 20	$20 – 25	$25 – 35
teapot	$80 – 95	$100 – 150	$160 – 200
plate, 12½" chop "Stangl Pottery 1805"	$400 – 500		

Rose Herbeck developed this line of novelty dinnerware specifically for the Flemington Outlet. The motifs and style of decoration were based on antique, peasant-type pottery of Mrs. Herbeck's native Germany. The shapes were decorated with colored engobes using a rubber syringe. Because these pieces resemble icing-decorated cookies, collectors have come to call this line "Gingerbread."

Engobe Decorated items were very popular at the Flemington Outlet and were produced steadily from 1967 until 1972. Rose Herbeck and her assistant were the only people involved in the production of this ware. Because Rose Herbeck was the primary decorator, most of the Engobe Decorated articles will be found with her "HR" cipher.

Engobe Decorated Dinnerware plates and mug with various decorations.

Raised Fruit #1940 Salad Set

Introduced: Late 1960s
Made For: Flemington Outlet
Shape Style: #1940 Raised Fruit

Known Pieces:

bowl, 9" salad . . . . $80 – 95
plate, 14" chop . . . . $85 – 125
plate, 9" . . . . $35 – 45
plate, 8" . . . . $50 – 60

Raised Fruit salad set 8" plate and 14½" chop plate with French Green leaves; 9" plate with Pomona Green leaves.

This pattern was Stangl's final re-introduction of the #1940 salad set. The fruits were decorated in bright, natural colors. Unlike the similar Bountiful pattern made for the Flemington Outlet during the 1940s, the engobe is sprayed on these pieces and the motifs are not carved. The 8" plates, however, were usually cast of white clay, requiring no engobe.

The leaves of this pattern were frequently painted French Green to coordinate with the popular Fruit pattern. To a lesser extent, Pomona Green underglaze color was used to decorate the leaves on these shapes as well.

Flemington Exclusives

Introduced: Late 1960s
Made For: Flemington Outlet

Known Pieces:

canister, concave L. . . . . $35 – 55
canister, concave M . . . . $20 – 35
canister, concave S. . . . . $15 – 25
canister, milk can L . . . . $60 – 75
canister, milk can M. . . . . $40 – 55
canister, milk can S . . . . $25 – 35
deviled egg plate, plain . . . . $25 – 40
deviled egg plate, rooster
   or hen-shape handle . . . . $95 – 130
egg cup, single. . . . . $8 – 15
jar, jam with cover . . . . $8 – 15
jar, relish with cover. . . . . $8 – 15
jar, mustard with cover. . . . . $8 – 15
mold, #1388 with corn . . . . $35 – 45
mold, small with fruit. . . . . $12 – 18
mold, artichoke. . . . . $30 – 40

Flemington items: small concave canister, small lobster mold, Christmas tree 10" tidbit (handle removed), relish jar, Irish Coffee mug, small milk can canister, deviled egg plate with rooster handle.

mold, fish, large . . . . $35 – 45
mold, fish, small. . . . . $12 – 18
mold, lobster, large . . . . $35 – 45
mold, lobster, small . . . . $15 – 20
mold, Turk's cap, 7½". . . . . $25 – 35
mold, fluted, 6". . . . . $20 – 25
mug, Irish Coffee. . . . . $45 – 60
plate, 10" Victorian Lady . . . . $150 – 200
plate, 10" Victorian Man. . . . . $150 – 200
tidbit, 10" Christmas Tree. . . . . $25 – 35

Various dinnerware-related items were produced for the Flemington Outlet during the greater part of the 1960s and 1970s. Most items were novelty pieces, such as the deviled egg plates with chicken handles. Some pieces were quite useful.

The canisters were decorated with several different motifs and color combinations. They were designed to coordinate with nearly any dinnerware pattern or kitchen decor.

The jam and relish jars were actually created to profitably reduce an overstock of Tangerine glazed Toastmaster marmalade jar lids remaining from the 1940s. These jars utilized #4024 shape cups without handles decorated with the appropriate condiment name. These covered jars retailed for $2.00 each at the Flemington Outlet.

Tidbits and tiered servers were exceedingly popular Flemington items. The Christmas Tree 10" tidbits were made on the #3434 rim, #3774 coupe, and #5129 Tiara shapes and were decorated in an assortment of Christmas-type colors. They can be found with either white, gray, or green, and clear or speckled glaze. Most other tidbits and tiered servers are listed with their respective patterns.

Victorian Gentleman 10" plate. The Victorian Lady and Gentleman 10" plates were decorative novelty pieces that are exceptionally difficult to find.

Concave canisters, medium and large with Chartreuse glaze.

Molds, Turk's cap 7½" and fluted 6".

Wedding/Anniversary Plates

Introduced: 1967
Designer: Rose Herbeck

Known Pieces:

plate, 12½" . . . . $180 – 300
plate, 10". . . . . $125 – 200
plate, 12½" with gold trim. . . . . . $225 – 325
plate, 10" with gold trim . . . . $175 – 225
plate, Colonial Couple. . . . . $80 – 130

"Brian and Eve" 12½" Wedding plate, "Golden Anniversary" 10" plate.

Stangl's Wedding and Anniversary plates were produced from 1967 through 1972. These were special-order items available through the Flemington Outlet only. Rose Herbeck was the originator and decorator of the designs used. Nearly all were marked with her "HR" cipher. Wedding plates are more plentiful than Anniversary plates. Gold or silver decorated plates are the least common and very desirable. Rose Herbeck also produced "Colonial Couple" plates. These plates featured the wedding and anniversary motifs, but had stylized borders instead of anniversary names and dates. The "Colonial Couple" plates can be found decorated in full color or simply carved and glazed with no color.

Stardust #5202

Introduced: 1968
Designer: Irene Sarnecki
Shape Style: #3774 Coupe

Known Pieces:

ashtray, 5" fluted . . . . $4 – 6
bowl, cereal . . . . $8 – 10
bowl, fruit . . . . $8 – 10
bowl, coupe soup . . . . $15 – 18
bowl, 12" salad . . . . $45 – 55
bowl, 10" salad . . . . $30 – 40
bowl, 8" vegetable. . . . . $20 – 25
bowl, oval divided vegetable . . . . . . $20 – 25
butter dish. . . . . $25 – 30
casserole, 8" covered. . . . . $45 – 55
coaster/ashtray . . . . $15 – 20
coffee pot, 8 cup . . . . $65 – 80
creamer . . . . $10 – 15
cup. . . . . $6 – 8

egg cup . . . . $8 – 10
gravy boat . . . . $10 – 12
gravy underplate. . . . . $8 – 10
mug, 2 cup. . . . . $25 – 35
pitcher, 2 quart . . . . $45 – 55
pitcher, 1 quart . . . . $30 – 35
pitcher, 1 pint . . . . $25 – 30
pitcher, ½ pint. . . . . $20 – 25
plate, 12½" chop . . . . $45 – 55
plate, 10" . . . . $15 – 20
plate, 8" . . . . $10 – 12
plate, 6" . . . . $7 – 8
platter, 13¾" casual. . . . . $35 – 45
platter, 14¾" oval . . . . $40 – 50
relish dish . . . . $10 – 15
saucer . . . . $4 – 5
salt, pepper; each . . . . $4 – 6
sugar . . . . $10 – 15
teapot. . . . . $55 – 65
tidbit, 10". $10 – 12
paper napkin, each . . . . $1 – 2
paper price list . . . . $10 – 15

The Stardust motif is characterized by Dark Turquoise and Dark Yellow flowers on a dappled background of Dark Turquoise and Art Ware Green. This kaleidoscopic pattern with subtle coloring followed the fashion trends that embraced the use of simplistic daisy motifs. The Star-

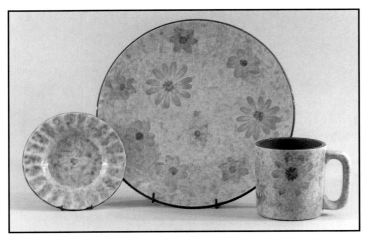

dust pattern failed to gain popularity and was completely discontinued by 1970. This was one of the few Stangl dinnerware patterns never to have been available as an inactive pattern.

Stardust 5" fluted ashtray, 10" plate, #5206 jiggered 2 cup mug.

First Love #5203

Introduced: 1968
Designer: Irene Sarnecki
Shape Style: #3774 Coupe

First Love 6" plate, salt & pepper, 10" plate, cup & saucer.

Known Pieces:

ashtray, 5" fluted . . . . $6 – 8
bowl, cereal . . . . $10 – 12
bowl, fruit. . . . . $8 – 12
bowl, coupe soup. . . . . $15 – 18
bowl, 12" salad. . . . . $40 – 50
bowl, 10" salad. . . . . $25 – 35
bowl, 8" vegetable . . . . $20 – 25
bowl, oval divided vegetable . . . . . . $25 – 30
butter dish. $25 – 30
casserole, 8" covered. . . . . $45 – 55
coaster/ashtray . . . . $10 – 15
coffee pot, 8 cup . . . . $55 – 70
creamer . . . . $10 – 15
cup. . . . . $8 – 12
egg cup . . . . $8 – 12
gravy boat . . . . $15 – 20
gravy underplate. . . . . $8 – 12
mug, 2 cup. $30 – 40
pitcher, 2 quart . . . . $45 – 55
pitcher, 1 quart . . . . $35 – 40
pitcher, 1 pint . . . . $25 – 35
pitcher, ½ pint. . . . . $20 – 25

plate, 12½" chop . . . . $40 – 50
plate, 10" . . . . $15 – 20
plate, 8" . . . . $10 – 12
plate, 6" . . . . $6 – 7
plate, 10" picnic* . . . . $5 – 8
plate, 8" picnic* . . . . $4 – 6
platter, 13¾" casual. . . . . $35 – 45
platter, 14¾" oval . . . . $40 – 50
relish dish . . . . $15 – 20
saucer . . . . $4 – 6
salt, pepper; each . . . . $6 – 8
sugar . . . . $10 – 15
teapot. . . . . $55 – 65
tidbit, 10". . . . . $8 – 12
paper napkins . . . . $1 – 2
paper price list . . . . $10 – 12

First Love featured an attractively designed floral motif decorated with soft browns and greens. This color combination had been recommended by the *House & Garden* color program. The First Love pattern was quite popular during 1968, but not during 1969. Sales dropped significantly enough that this pattern became inactive January 1, 1970.

Inspiration #5204

Inspiration 10" plate, cup & saucer.

Introduced: 1968
Designer: Irene Sarnecki
Shape Style: #5204 Raised Floral

Known Pieces:

bowl, soup	$20 – 25
bowl, 10" salad	$50 – 60
bowl, 8" vegetable	$30 – 35
creamer	$15 – 20
cup	$8 – 12
mug, 13oz.	$35 – 45
pitcher, 1 pint	$50 – 60
plate, 12½" chop	$55 – 70
plate, 10"	$25 – 30
plate, 8"	$15 – 20
plate, 6"	$10 – 12
platter, 14¾" oval	$55 – 65
salt, pepper; each	$8 – 10
saucer	$6 – 7
sugar	$15 – 20
tidbit, 10"	$10 – 15
paper price list	$10 – 15

Inspiration was Stangl's first pattern introduced on the #5204 raised floral coupe shape. The Inspiration blossoms were Tan, Old Gold, and Rust, a muted red underglaze color that was Pink #160 mixed with Tan. The raised motifs were further enhanced with dry-brushed 22-karat gold luster. This added a great deal of richness to the whole pattern. This was one of Stangl's Prestige dinnerware patterns advertised during 1968. Because of the small, painted details and gold luster, Inspiration was a costly pattern that was produced in very limited quantities and was discontinued in 1970.

Treasured #1388

Treasured 10" plate, cup & saucer, 12½" chop plate, teapot.

Introduced: 1968
Designer: Irene Sarnecki
Shape Style: #1388

Known Pieces:

bowl, 12" console, oval	$30 – 40
bowl, soup/cereal	$15 – 18
bowl, 10" salad	$60 – 75
bowl, 8" vegetable	$30 – 40
cake stand, 12"	$25 – 35
cake stand, 10"	$20 – 25
candle, each	$12 – 15
compote, 7"	$15 – 20
creamer	$15 – 20
cup	$10 – 12
plate, 12½" chop	$60 – 70
plate, 10"	$20 – 25
plate, 8"	$15 – 20
plate, 6"	$10 – 15
platter, 14¾" oval	$60 – 75
saucer	$8 – 10
sugar	$15 – 20
teapot	$90 – 110
tidbit, 10"	$10 – 15
paper price list	$10 – 12

The Treasured pattern employed Stangl's #1388 shape, originally introduced in 1931. Each piece of Treasured dinnerware was swirled with Art Ware Green and glazed with Silk glaze before being dry-brushed with 22-karat gold luster. The dry-brushed gold greatly enhanced the modeling of the #1388 shape. Treasured was designed to complement Stangl's very popular Antique Gold artware lines, and was another of the Prestige patterns of 1968. This pattern lasted nearly two years before being discontinued in 1970.

Colonial Dogwood #5205

Introduced: 1968
Designer: Irene Sarnecki
Shape Style: #3668 Dogwood

Known Pieces:

bowl, lug soup	$10 – 12	plate, 8"	$15 – 20
bowl, 10" salad	$45 – 55	plate, 6"	$10 – 12
bowl, 8" vegetable	$25 – 35	platter, 14¾" oval	$60 – 75
creamer	$20 – 25	saucer	$6 – 7
cup	$8 – 12	sugar	$20 – 25
plate, 12½" chop	$50 – 60	tidbit, 10"	$10 – 15
plate, 10"	$20 – 25	paper price list	$15 – 20

Colonial Dogwood was another variation of Stangl's popular raised Dogwood patterns and was part of the 1968 Prestige pattern group. This was a delicate pattern with soft coloring, but never attained the instant appeal of White Dogwood. For that reason, Colonial Dogwood was a slow seller and became inactive on January 1, 1969, one year after introduction.

Colonial Dogwood cup & saucer, 10" plate, 6" plate.

Blossom Ring #5215

Introduced: 1969
Designer: Irene Sarnecki
Shape Style: #5204 Raised Floral

Known Pieces:

bowl, cereal	$10 – 15	creamer	$10 – 15
bowl, 10" salad	$45 – 55	cup	$7 – 8
bowl, 8" vegetable	$20 – 30	mug, 13oz.	$25 – 30
butter dish	$20 – 25	pitcher, 1 pint	$25 – 35
		plate, 12½" chop	$40 – 50

plate, 10"	$12 − 20	salt, pepper; each	$6 − 8
plate, 8"	$10 − 12	sugar	$10 − 15
plate, 6"	$5 − 7	tidbit, 10"	$8 − 10
platter, 14¾" oval	$40 − 50	paper napkin, each	$1 − 2
saucer	$4 − 5	paper price list	$10 − 12

The muted Pomona Green underglaze color used on the Blossom Ring pattern was Willow Green mixed with Walnut Brown. This color was spun over the raised floral band on these shapes, adding depth and dimension to this pattern. The Blossom Ring mug, butter dish, salt, pepper, and pitcher shapes were all cast of white clay. This procedure was used for the production of nearly all of Stangl's Prestige pattern hollow-ware shapes.

Blossom Ring was moderately popular during 1969, but was completely discontinued on June 1, 1970, as per a Stangl memo dated May 12, 1970. Interestingly though, Blossom Ring was reintroduced as an inactive pattern during the late 1970s and was produced occasionally until 1978.

Blossom Ring 13oz. mug, 10" plate, butter dish.

Pie Crust #5216, Sunshine #5217

Introduced: 1969
Designer: Irene Sarnecki
Shape Style: #3506 Pie Crust

Known Pieces:

bowl, 5½" soup	$10 − 15	plate, 6"	$8 − 10
bowl, 10" salad	$45 − 55	saucer	$5 − 6
bowl, 8" vegetable	$25 − 35	salt, pepper; each	$6 − 8
creamer	$15 − 20	sugar, covered	$20 − 25
cup	$8 − 10	sugar, open	$15 − 20
plate, 12½" chop	$50 − 60	tidbit, 10"	$10 − 15
plate, 10"	$20 − 25	paper napkin, each	$1 − 2
plate, 8"	$12 − 15	paper price list	$10 − 12

Pie Crust and Sunshine were Stangl's last additions to the Prestige Dinnerware line. These two patterns utilized the old #3506 Pie Crust shapes and were decorated with a hand-carved floral motif. All the pieces were cast of white-colored clay as it was not worth the added effort to spray the ruffled shapes with engobe. The motifs were carved for additional depth even though there was no red clay to emphasize the carvings.

The Pie Crust pattern was introduced early in 1969 while Sunshine was not introduced until June 1, 1969. Pie Crust was the first of these two patterns to be discontinued on January 1, 1970. Sunshine, however, was produced until June 1, 1970, when it became inactive. It held that status until January 1, 1971, when it too was discontinued.

Pie Crust was decorated with Blue #95 and Dark Turquoise blossoms, French Green leaves, and Black stems. The Ivory Satin glaze was applied to this pattern. The colors used on the Sunshine pattern were Tan and Orange for the flowers, Pomona Green on the leaves, and Walnut Brown for the stems. Sunshine was glazed with clear gloss glaze. There were no #3506 salt and pepper shakers, so #3774 coupe shape shakers were decorated with coordinating bands of color for these two patterns. The covered sugar was produced only in the Sunshine pattern. This shape was not introduced until 1970, shortly before Sunshine became inactive.

Sunshine 6" plate, creamer, 10" plate, open sugar; Pie Crust 10" plate, salt & pepper, cup & saucer.

Colonial Silver #5218

Colonial Silver 10" plate, lug soup, 8 cup coffee pot, 8" plate.

Introduced: June 1, 1969
Designer: Martin Stangl
Shape Style: #5129 Tiara

Known Pieces:

ashtray, 5" fluted	$10 – 15
bowl, lug soup	$8 – 12
bowl, fruit	$8 – 12
bowl, 8" vegetable	$25 – 35
cake stand	$20 – 30
cigarette box, fluted or plain	$60 – 75
coffee pot, 8 cup	$55 – 65
creamer	$10 – 15
cup, after dinner	$12 – 15
cup	$8 – 10
plate, 12½" chop	$45 – 55
plate, 10"	$15 – 20
plate, 8"	$10 – 15
plate, 6"	$8 – 10
platter, 14" oval	$45 – 55
salt, pepper; each	$4 – 6
saucer, after dinner	$5 – 6
saucer	$5 – 6
sugar	$10 – 15
tankard	$25 – 30
teapot	$45 – 55
tidbit, 10"	$10 – 15
warmer	$15 – 20
paper price list	$10 – 15

The Colonial Silver decoration was platinum luster dry-brushed over gray engobe on the #5129 Tiara shape. Although Stangl's dinnerware catalog of July 1969 proudly claimed that Colonial Silver was "the ultimate in sophisticated, beautiful, American created pottery dinnerware," it was not well accepted. The Colonial Silver pattern was completely discontinued on June 1, 1970, exactly one year after introduction.

1970s HAND-CARVED, HAND-PAINTED DINNERWARE

Dahlia #5220, Blue Dahlia

Introduced: 1970
Designer: Irene Sarnecki
Shape Style: #3667 Cosmos

Dahlia 6" plate, creamer, sugar, 10" plate.

Known Pieces:

bowl, lug soup	$10 – 15
bowl, 10" salad	$40 – 50
bowl, 8" vegetable	$25 – 35
cake stand	$20 – 30
creamer	$10 – 15
cup	$8 – 12
plate, 12½" chop	$35 – 45
plate, 10"	$20 – 25
plate, 8"	$12 – 15
plate, 6"	$8 – 10
platter, 14¾" oval	$40 – 50
saucer	$4 – 5
salt, pepper; each	$6 – 8
sugar	$15 – 18
tidbit, 10"	$10 – 15
paper napkin, each	$1 – 2
paper price list	$8 – 12

The #5220 Dahlia pattern was decorated with Blue #95, Dark Turquoise, and French Green underglaze colors and Ivory Satin glaze. These were the identical colors and glaze that had been used on the Pie Crust #5216 pattern. Although this pattern was referred to as Dahlia in all Stangl advertising and records, it was produced with the name "Dahlia" on some pieces while "Blue Dahlia" was stamped on others. This was a popular pattern that continued in active production until mid-1973, at which time it was completely discontinued.

Sierra #5221

Introduced: 1970
Designer: Irene Sarnecki
Shape Style: #5179 Raised Fruit

Known Pieces:

bowl, cereal	$10 – 15
bowl, fruit	$8 – 10
bowl, coupe soup	$15 – 20
bowl, lug soup	$10 – 15
bowl, 10" salad	$35 – 45
bowl, 8" vegetable	$25 – 35
butter dish	$20 – 30
cake stand, 10"	$10 – 15
creamer	$10 – 12
cup	$6 – 8
mug, 13oz	$20 – 30
pitcher, 1 pint	$25 – 35
plate, 12½" chop	$35 – 45
plate, 10"	$15 – 20
plate, 8"	$10 – 15
plate, 6"	$6 – 7
platter, 14¾" oval	$35 – 45
saucer	$5 – 6
salt, pepper; each	$7 – 8
sugar	$10 – 15
tidbit, 10"	$10 – 15
paper napkin	$1 – 2
paper price list	$10 – 12

Sierra was developed in order to take advantage of the great popularity of Stangl's Sculptured Fruit shapes. The Sierra raised fruit motif was decorated in shades of brown under Ivory Satin glaze. This pattern was introduced in 1970 with great fanfare. A Stangl memo describes it as "a frosted finish of real beauty." Sierra, along with three other 1970 introductions Aztec, Monterey, and Galaxy, became inactive on June 1, 1970. After only six months production, these are rather uncommon patterns now.

Sierra 10" plate.

Aztec #5222

Introduced: 1970
Designer: Irene Sarnecki
Shape Style: #5129 Tiara

Known Pieces:

bowl, cereal	$10 – 12
bowl, fruit	$8 – 10
bowl, coupe soup	$10 – 15
bowl, 10" salad	$30 – 40
bowl, 8" vegetable	$20 – 30
creamer	$7 – 10
cup	$6 – 8
mug, 2 cup	$20 – 25
pitcher, 2 quart	$30 – 40
pitcher, 1 quart	$20 – 30
pitcher, 1 pint	$15 – 20
plate, 12½" chop	$30 – 40
plate, 10"	$10 – 15
plate, 8"	$8 – 10
plate, 6"	$6 – 8
saucer	$4 – 6
salt, pepper; each	$5 – 7
sugar	$10 – 15
tidbit, 10"	$10 – 15
paper napkin	$1 – 2
paper price list	$10 – 15

Aztec was based on the same Pomona Green and Old Gold color scheme that had made Sculptured Fruit so popular. Those colors were artistically swirled on each piece, reminiscent of Stangl's Maple Whirl pattern from 1965. The commercial reaction to the Aztec pattern was less than enthusiastic, so it did not share in the popularity of Sculptured Fruit. Aztec became inactive on June 1, 1970, and by 1971 was completely discontinued.

Aztec 10" plate.

Rooster #5223

Introduced: 1970
Designer: Irene Sarnecki
Shape Style: #5129 Tiara

Known Pieces:

bowl, cereal	$20 – 25
bowl, fruit	$15 – 20
bowl, coupe soup	$25 – 35
bowl, 10" salad	$50 – 60
bowl, 8" vegetable	$35 – 45
cake stand	$20 – 30
creamer	$12 – 15
cup	$10 – 15
mug, 2 cup	$40 – 50
pitcher, 2 quart	$85 – 100
pitcher, 1 quart	$65 – 75
pitcher, 1 pint	$30 – 40
plate, 12½" chop	$60 – 70
plate, 10"	$20 – 30
plate, 8"	$15 – 20
plate, 6"	$8 – 12
salt, pepper; each with rooster motif	$12 – 15
salt, pepper; each plain	$8 – 10
saucer	$6 – 8
sugar	$15 – 20
tidbit, 10"	$15 – 25
paper napkin	$2 – 3
paper price list	$15 – 20

The Rooster pattern was inspired by the rooster motif that had been used on the Country Life pattern in 1956. The Rooster motif, however, utilized yellow engobe. This pattern capitalized on the fashionable color scheme of brown and gold during the early 1970s. Rooster was a very popular pattern that was produced until the end of 1974. It is quite popular yet and can be difficult to find but is generally available.

The Rooster 1 quart and 2 quart pitcher shapes and paper napkins were produced only during the first months of 1970 before being dropped from the pattern. Therefore these items are now exceedingly rare.

Rooster 6" plate, 12½" chop plate, creamer, 1 pint pitcher.

Monterey #5224, Galaxy #5225

Introduced: 1970
Designer: Irene Sarnecki
Shape Style: #3434 Rim, #5129 Tiara

Known Pieces:

bowl, cereal	$6 – 8
bowl, fruit	$6 – 8
bowl, coupe soup	$8 – 15
bowl, lug soup	$6 – 8
bowl, 10" salad	$25 – 30
bowl, 8" vegetable	$15 – 20
bowl, divided veg.	$10 – 15
butter dish	$12 – 18
casserole, 8" covered	$20 – 30
creamer	$5 – 6
cup	$5 – 6

gravy boat	$8 – 12	plate, 6"	$5 – 6
gravy underplate	$5 – 7	platter, 14¾" oval	$30 – 40
mug, 2 cup	$15 – 20	saucer	$4 – 5
pitcher, 2 quart	$25 – 35	salt, pepper; each	$4 – 5
pitcher, 1 quart	$15 – 25	sugar	$8 – 10
pitcher, 1 pint	$10 – 15	teapot	$20 – 30
plate, 12½" chop	$30 – 40	tidbit, 10"	$8 – 10
plate, 10"	$10 – 15	paper napkin	$1 – 2
plate, 8"	$7 – 9	paper price list	$10 – 15

Monterey and Galaxy were both sponge-decorated dinnerware patterns advertised as "color variations of the always popular Mediterranean finish." Monterey colors were Tan sponged over Walnut Brown, while Galaxy used Willow Green and Walnut Brown. By 1970, this type of dark, somber color combinations were falling out of favor, so both Monterey and Galaxy became inactive only six months after introduction. They were replaced by the bright and colorful Colonial Rose and Petite Flowers patterns. The Monterey and Galaxy patterns are very hard to find, but Monterey seems much more elusive than Galaxy.

Galaxy 10" plate.

Colonial Rose #5226

Introduced: 1970
Designer: Rose Herbeck; Rudy Kleinebeckel
Shape Style: #5226 Queen Anne

Known Pieces:

bowl, cereal	$20 – 25	plate, 12" chop	$65 – 80
bowl, fruit	$15 – 20	plate, 10"	$25 – 30
bowl, coupe soup	$20 – 30	plate, 8"	$15 – 20
bowl, lug soup	$15 – 20	plate, 6"	$10 – 15
bowl, 10" salad	$50 – 60	plate, soup, 8" oval	$20 – 25
bowl, 8" vegetable	$35 – 45	saucer	$8 – 10
cake plate	$15 – 25	salt, pepper; each	$8 – 10
creamer	$20 – 25	salt, pepper tray	$20 – 25
cup	$10 – 15	sugar	$20 – 25
mug, 2 cup	$35 – 45	teapot	$85 – 110
pitcher, 2 quart	$80 – 95	tidbit, 10"	$10 – 15
pitcher, 1 quart	$45 – 60	paper napkin, each	$1 – 2
pitcher, 1 pint	$25 – 35	paper price list	$10 – 15

The Colonial Rose and Petite Flowers dinnerware patterns were introduced on June 15, 1970. These two colorful patterns were developed in an attempt to recover sales lost by the disastrous introduction of the very drab Sierra, Aztec, Monterey, and Galaxy patterns in January 1970. Martin Stangl instructed Rudy Kleinebeckel to design the #5226 Queen Anne dinnerware shape at Rose Herbeck's insistence. She felt there was a need at that time for fresh new shapes as well as colorful patterns in Stangl's dinnerware lines.

Colonial Rose was the first pattern on the #5226 Queen Anne shape. The bright, unpretentious design was decorated with Pink #193 and Willow Green. This attractive pattern was one of Rose Herbeck's personal favorites, and is avidly desired by collectors.

Colonial Rose 10" plate, cup & saucer, mug.

Petite Flowers #5227

Introduced: 1970
Designer: Irene Sarnecki, Rudy Kleinebeckel
Shape Style: #5226 Queen Anne

Known Pieces:

bowl, cereal	$10 – 15
bowl, fruit	$10 – 15
bowl, coupe soup	$15 – 20
bowl, lug soup	$10 – 15
bowl, 10" salad	$40 – 50
bowl, 8" vegetable	$25 – 35
cake plate	$15 – 20
creamer	$15 – 20
cup	$8 – 10
mug, 2 cup	$25 – 35
pitcher, 2 quart	$60 – 75
pitcher, 1 quart	$45 – 55
pitcher, 1 pint	$20 – 30
plate, 12" chop	$40 – 50
plate, 10"	$15 – 20
plate, 8"	$10 – 15
plate, 6"	$8 – 10

Petite Flowers 6" plate, sugar, 10" plate, cereal bowl, soup plate.

plate, soup, 8" oval	$10 – 15
saucer	$5 – 7
salt, pepper; each	$6 – 8
salt, pepper tray	$10 – 15
sugar	$15 – 20
teapot	$70 – 85
tidbit, 10"	$10 – 15
paper napkin, each	$1 – 2
paper price list	$10 – 12

Petite Flowers was Stangl's only carved pattern on the ivory-colored engobe. Most of the Petite Flowers shapes were decorated with a cheerful design of diminutive Dark Turquoise blossoms with Willow Green and Green #1431 leaves. Items such as bowls were decorated with simple Dark Turquoise bands reflecting the trend at that time of using motifs on primary pieces only. While attractive and well-designed, Petite Flowers is not nearly as desirable at this time as Colonial Rose.

Star Flite

Introduced: 1970
Shape Style: #3434 Rim

Star Flite sugar, 10" plate, coaster/ashtray.

Known Pieces:

cigarette box	$95 – 125
coaster/ashtray	$30 – 40
creamer	$20 – 25
cup	$10 – 15
plate, 10"	$35 – 45
plate, 8"	$20 – 25
plate, 6"	$15 – 20
saucer	$10 – 12
sugar	$20 – 25
teapot	$90 – 125
tidbit, 10"	$15 – 20
tidbit, 2 tier	$25 – 35

The cobalt glazed Star Flite pattern and Jewelled Christmas Tree were the only patterns belonging to Stangl's Classic Ware designation. Both patterns were introduced on July 1, 1970, and were available as special promotional patterns to Stangl's larger, more important retail accounts. Jewelled Christmas Tree, an adaptation of Stangl's earlier Christmas Tree pattern, was immediately successful and sold well through 1974. Unfortunately, Star Flite never caught on as a popular dinnerware pattern. Before the end of 1970, both Star Flite and the vague Classic Ware dinnerware classification were discontinued

The Star Flite pattern was glazed with a simple cobalt-based glaze. On white engobe this glaze was a deep, rich blue. However, on the red clay back of each piece, the cobalt would reduce the red iron oxide of the clay, creating a deep, gloss black. The astral motifs were made in the same manner as the Jewelled Christmas Tree ornaments, with carbide-tipped dentists' drills. The motifs were decorated with 22-karat gold luster, and each piece fired a third time at low temperature to affix the gold.

Morning Blue #5229, Yellow Flower #5230

Introduced: 1971
Designer: Rose Herbeck
Shape Style: #5129 Tiara

Known Pieces:

bowl, cereal	$10 – 12	casserole, 6" covered	$20 – 25
bowl, fruit	$10 – 12	casserole, 4" covered	$10 – 15
bowl, coupe soup	$10 – 15	creamer	$8 – 10
bowl, lug soup	$10 – 12	cup	$5 – 7
bowl, 10" salad	$35 – 45	gravy boat	$10 – 12
bowl, 8" vegetable	$20 – 30	gravy underplate	$10 – 12
bowl, divided veg.	$25 – 35	mug, 2 cup	$15 – 20
butter dish	$25 – 35	mug, stack	$15 – 25
casserole, 8" covered	$35 – 45	pitcher, 2 quart	$30 – 40

pitcher, 1 quart	$20 – 30	saucer	$4 – 5
pitcher, 1 pint	$10 – 15	salt, pepper; each	$4 – 6
plate, 12½" chop	$35 – 45	sugar	$8 – 10
plate, 10"	$12 – 18	tankard	$30 – 35
plate, 8"	$8 – 10	teapot	$40 – 50
plate, 6"	$5 – 7	tidbit, 10"	$8 – 12
platter, 14¾" oval	$35 – 45	paper price list	$10 – 15

Rose Herbeck styled the Morning Blue and Yellow Flower patterns after European peasant-ware designs. These patterns used no engobe, the motifs were decorated directly on the red body of each piece. Morning Blue and Yellow Flower were marked "Red Stoneware." These patterns were Stangl's only patterns stamped with this mark. The Red Stoneware designation was supposed to intone durability, even though all Stangl products were already being fired at stoneware temperatures. Morning Blue and Yellow Flower were the only dinnerware patterns to include the #3434 shape 4" covered casserole. These are both well-executed pleasant patterns, but are not widely collected at this time.

Yellow Flower cup & saucer, 12½" chop plate, 6" covered casserole; Morning Blue 10" plate, 4" covered casserole.

Stangl Stoneware Tiles #5237 – #5240

Introduced: Spring 1971
Designer: Rose Herbeck

Known Pieces:
Square Tiles

#5237 brown glaze, yellow and orange decoration	$30 – 40
#5238 pink and white decoration	$30 – 40
#5239 brown and white heart decoration	$30 – 40
#5240 orange and yellow heart decoration	$30 – 40

Octagonal Tiles

Gray glaze, blue decoration	$30 – 40
Tan glaze, brown decoration	$20 – 30

The Stangl Stoneware tiles #5237 through #5240 were decorated with a glaze-on-glaze treatment. The colored glazes were applied with an ear syringe over the background glaze. The tiles with specifically numbered decorations were produced for only a few weeks because the decorative glaze application was too difficult for economic production.

The 6" octagonal tiles were designed to coordinate with Stangl's Stangl Stoneware dinnerware patterns. They were decorated with various underglaze colors and stoneware styled glazes such as the Tan or Gray dinnerware glazes. The octagonal tiles were decorated with simple geometric motifs and sold primarily at the Flemington Outlet.

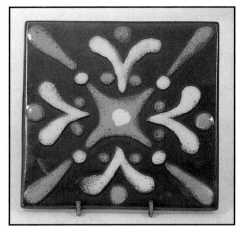

left:
Stangl
Stoneware
Square Tile
#5237.

right:
Stangl
Stoneware
Octagonal Tile
black and
brown abstract
pattern with
Tan glaze.

Stangl Stoneware Patterns:

Antigua #5246, Balboa #5247, Condado #5248, Delmar #5249, Ginger #5250, Montaldo #5251, Trinidad #5252, Kalimar #5255, Brent #5256, Sesame #5257

Introduced: Spring 1971
Designer: Rose Herbeck
Shape Designer: Rudy Kleinebeckel

Known Pieces:

bowl, soup/cereal . . . . $10 – 15	plate, 12½" chop . . . . $30 – 50
bowl, fruit/desert . . . . $8 – 12	plate, 10" . . . . $15 – 30
bowl, 10" salad . . . . $35 – 55	plate, 8" . . . . $8 – 20
bowl, 8" vegetable . . . . $20 – 35	plate, 6" . . . . $5 – 12
butter dish . . . . $20 – 30	salt, pepper; each . . . . $4 – 7
casserole, 8" covered . . . . $40 – 65	saucer . . . . $4 – 5
casserole, 6" covered . . . . $15 – 20	sugar . . . . $10 – 15
coffee pot, 6 cup . . . . $45 – 75	teapot, 6 cup . . . . $40 – 75
creamer . . . . $8 – 15	tidbit, 10" . . . . $10 – 15
cup . . . . $6 – 12	tile . . . . $20 – 30
egg cup . . . . $10 – 12	paper price list . . . . $10 – 15
mug, stack . . . . $15 – 25	dealer sign . . . . $95 – 120

The Stangl Stoneware line of dinnerware was developed as a result of an extensive market analysis conducted by sales manager James Paul. Mr. Paul discovered that the trend in dinnerware styles favored by young couples was toward simple geometric designs in earthtone colors and not fruit or flower motifs, for which Stangl dinnerware was known. The analysis concluded that the primary motif should be on the plates only and the decoration on serving pieces and smaller place setting items should be solid-color glazing or, at most, simple contrasting bands. The preference at that time was to keep the dinnerware shapes unencumbered by superfluous decoration and the design of the shapes themselves should serve as the focal point of the table setting.

In view of this, ten dinnerware patterns and two new dinnerware shapes were designed for the Stangl Stoneware dinnerware line. The #5241 Contempo shape was described as having "the classic simplicity of a modern coupe shape with a graceful turned-up edge." Stangl referred to the #5242 Croyden shape as "an up-to-the-minute variation on the popular pie plate shape with a distinctive raised edge common to each of the pieces."

These ten Stangl Stoneware patterns were introduced on June 1, 1971, and nearly all were decorated with abstract starburst-type motifs. Some of these patterns, namely Balboa, Condado, Kalimar, and Brent were produced in very limited quantities and for such a short time they are now nearly impossible to find. The Delmar, Ginger, and Montaldo patterns are only somewhat more readily available. Antigua, Trinidad, and Sesame are the most common of this group of Stangl Stoneware dinnerware patterns.

Antigua, shape #5241 Contempo — Antigua was originally produced with the Tan glaze over a black and brown "compass point" motif. Later pieces of Antigua will be found on the #3774 coupe shape. Such pieces used white or yellow engobe and were glazed with a clear gloss glaze. Antigua on the Contempo shape with Tan glaze is much more elusive than clear glazed Antigua on the #3774 coupe shape.

Balboa, shape #5129 Tiara — The Balboa pattern was decorated with a stylized starburst motif. This pattern was produced for only a few months, which accounts for its scarcity.

Condado, shape #5241 Contempo — Condado is another Stangl Stoneware pattern that was very short-lived and is rarely seen now.

Delmar, shape #5242 Croyden — Delmar is a simple pattern decorated with a black and brown band on the rim. Tan dinnerware glaze was used directly on the red body with no engobe, Therefore, the Tan glaze appears more brown than yellow, as it would on a pattern with white engobe, such as Antigua.

Ginger, shape #5242 Croyden — The Ginger motif featured conventionalized tulip blossoms in a "compass point" arrangement. As with Delmar, Ginger was glazed with Tan glaze directly on the red body.

Montaldo, shape #5129 Tiara/#5242 Croyden — Montaldo was a stylized starburst pattern in Black underglaze color painted on the red body of the pieces. The Gray dinnerware glaze on the red clay gave this pattern a hazy bluish-brown appearance. Stangl records list this pattern as being on the #5219 Tiara shape, but this pattern is usually found on the #5242 Croyden shape.

Trinidad, shape #5242 Croyden — The Trinidad pattern featured a starburst motif similar to that of Montaldo, but with the underglaze colors Aqua and Rust. Because Trinidad used a white engobe background, Gray dinnerware glaze and contrasting colored motifs, it possessed a vastly different aspect than that of Montaldo.

Brent, shape #5242 Croyden — The underglaze colors Hardened Blue and Black were featured on the simple starburst motif and bands of the Brent pattern. Speckled Gray dinnerware glaze was used on this very short-lived, extremely rare pattern.

Sesame, shape #5242 Croyden — The Sesame motif was a stylized snowflake in shades of brown. This pattern originally used speckled Satin White glaze, but later pieces were produced with a clear gloss glaze. Sesame was more long-lived than most Stangl Stoneware patterns and was produced through 1975.

top:
Stangl Stoneware Antigua 12½"
chop plate with Tan glaze; 10"
plate with yellow engobe and
clear glaze; 8" plate with white
engobe and clear glaze.

middle:
Ginger 6" plate, creamer, Delmar
saucer.

bottom:
Montaldo 8" plate, 10" plate,
butter dish.

top:
Stangl Stoneware Trinidad 10" plate, 8" plate,
cup & saucer.

middle:
Brent 10" plate.

bottom:
Sesame 10" plate with Satin White glaze, 8" plate
with clear gloss glaze.

Adrian #5258

Introduced: 1971
Designer: Rose Herbeck
Made For: Sak's Fifth Avenue
Shape Style: #5242 Croyden

Known Pieces:

bowl, soup/cereal	$10 – 15
bowl, fruit/desert	$8 – 12
bowl, 10" salad	$45 – 55
bowl, 8" vegetable	$25 – 35
butter dish	$25 – 35
casserole, 8" covered	$35 – 45
casserole, 6" covered	$15 – 20
coffee pot, 6 cup	$50 – 60
creamer	$10 – 15
cup	$8 – 10
egg cup	$10 – 15
mug, stack	$20 – 25
plate, 12½" chop	$55 – 65
plate, 10"	$25 – 30
plate, 8"	$15 – 20
plate, 6"	$10 – 15
salt, pepper; each	$6 – 8
saucer	$5 – 7
sugar	$15 – 20
teapot, 6 cup	$50 – 60
tidbit, 10"	$10 – 15
tile	$25 – 30
paper price list	$15 – 20

The floral Adrian pattern used speckled Gray dinnerware glaze. A new underglaze color, Hardened Blue, was used for the motif. This color was similar to Art Ware Blue, only darker, and had less tendency to run or bleed. Adrian was produced exclusively for Sak's Fifth Avenue in limited quantities through the mid-1970s.

Adrian teapot, 10" plate, 6" plate.

Stangl Stoneware Patterns:

Roxanne #5261, Susan #5263, Diana #5264, Rustic Garden #5265

Introduced: 1972
Designers: Rose Herbeck, Irene Sarnecki
Shape Style: #5241 Contempo

Known Pieces:

bowl, coupe soup	$10 – 15
bowl, cereal	$8 – 12
bowl, 10" salad	$40 – 50
bowl, 8" vegetable	$20 – 30
casserole, 8" covered	$35 – 45
casserole, 6" covered	$10 – 15
coffee pot, 6 cup	$50 – 65
creamer	$10 – 15
cup	$6 – 8
egg cup	$10 – 15
mug, stack	$25 – 35
plate, 12½" chop	$55 – 65
plate, 10"	$15 – 20
plate, 8"	$8 – 12
plate, 6"	$5 – 6
salt, pepper; each	$5 – 7
saucer	$5 – 7
sugar	$10 – 15
teapot, 6 cup	$40 – 55
tidbit, 10"	$10 – 15
tile	$25 – 30
paper price list	$10 – 15

Roxanne 10" plate, creamer, sugar.

Martin Stangl felt that the Stangl Stoneware dinnerware line was too dark and formal in appearance and lacked the color and distinction Stangl Pottery was known for. In view of this, he insisted that several Stangl Stoneware patterns be designed "with bright floral motifs and a casual feel." To accomplish the "casual feel," the floral stoneware motifs were all on the #5241 Contempo shape and featured speckled glaze. There were four floral Stangl Stoneware patterns introduced, and all were available for the January 1972 trade shows.

During 1972, most of the ten original geometric Stangl Stoneware patterns introduced during 1971 were discontinued. Only the bestselling patterns continued in production. The remaining geometric patterns were Antigua, Delmar, Sesame, and Trinidad. Added to these were the four floral patterns Roxanne, Susan, Diana, and Rustic Garden to comprise Stangl's "Now! Collection." These eight patterns were advertised as such until the end of 1974 when all Stangl Stoneware patterns were discontinued. All of the Stangl Stoneware patterns are difficult to find, some are nearly impossible.

Roxanne — Designed by Rose Herbeck, this pattern was somewhat similar to the Sak's Fifth Avenue Adrian pattern. The Roxanne colors were Blue #95 and Hardened Blue with speckled Gray dinnerware glaze.

Susan — Rose Herbeck chose Orange and Pomona Green underglaze colors for Susan's bright black-eyed Susan blossoms. Clear glaze was used on this pattern so as not to affect the clarity of the motif.

Diana — Designed by Irene Sarnecki, the Diana pattern was one of the most popular Stangl Stoneware dinnerware patterns. The muted blue and green colors of Diana were further softened by the use of Satin White glaze. Speckled Gray dinnerware glaze was used on undecorated pieces such as the cup, sugar, and creamer shapes. Diana is a very appealing pattern that is easier to find than many Stangl Stoneware patterns.

Rustic Garden — This vibrant Rose Herbeck pattern was decorated with bright Rust blossoms and Dark Pomona Green leaves. The Rustic Garden and Susan patterns are the most difficult of the floral decorated Stangl Stoneware patterns to collect.

Stangl Stoneware patterns: Diana 6" plate, 10" plate, cup & saucer;
Rustic Garden 12½" chop plate; Susan cup, 10" plate, 8" plate.

Flora on Redware

Introduced: 1972
Made For: Flemington Outlet
Shape Style: #5129 Tiara
Glaze Colors: Cobalt Blue, Manganese Brown, Copper Green, Transparent Yellow, Matte Blue

Known Pieces:

bowl, cereal . . . . $8 – 12	plate, 12½" chop . . . . $45 – 60
bowl, fruit . . . . $6 – 8	plate, 10" . . . . $20 – 30
bowl, 10" salad . . . . $40 – 50	plate, 8" . . . . $10 – 20
bowl, 8" vegetable . . . . $20 – 25	plate, 6" . . . . $8 – 10
coffee pot, 6 cup . . . . $55 – 65	salt, pepper; each . . . . $5 – 8
creamer . . . . $10 – 12	saucer . . . . $5 – 7
cup . . . . $6 – 8	sugar . . . . $10 – 15
mug, stack . . . . $25 – 30	teapot, 6 cup . . . . $35 – 50
	tidbit, 10" . . . . $10 – 15

The Flora on Redware pattern was developed to replace the very popular Engobe Decorated "Gingerbread" dinnerware. The two patterns are somewhat similar in appearance and method of decoration. Both were decorated with engobe motifs over red-clay blanks. The Flora on Redware motif was applied by brush whereas Engobe Decorated "Gingerbread" pieces were always decorated with a rubber syringe. Colored transparent glazes were nearly always used on the Flora on Redware shapes.

Usually it is only the Flora on Redware plates that bear the floral motif. The serving pieces were simply glazed with the transparent glazes. The red body of the copper or cobalt glazed pieces will usually have an "almost black" appearance caused by a reduction of the red iron oxide in the clay.

Flora on Redware teapot, Copper Green glaze, 10" plate, Transparent Yellow glaze; 6" plate, Manganese Brown glaze; 10" plate, Copper Green glaze.

Gourmet Ware #5269

Introduced: 1972
Designers: Rudy Kleinebeckel, Irene Sarnecki
Shape Style: #5269 Gourmet
Available Colors: Brown Satin, Gourmet Green, Gourmet Grey

Known Pieces:

au gratin, 6"	$10 – 12
baking dish, 14" x 10"	$25 – 30
baking dish, 11" x 8"	$20 – 25
2½ qt. covered casserole, oval	$35 – 45
40oz. covered casserole, oval	$25 – 35
24oz. covered casserole, oval	$20 – 25
2½ qt. covered casserole, round	$35 – 45
40oz. covered casserole, round	$25 – 35
24oz. covered casserole, round	$20 – 25
creamer	$10 – 12
cruet	$10 – 12
divided vegetable dish	$20 – 25
mug	$25 – 30
plate, 12½" chop	$35 – 45
plate, 10"	$15 – 20
plate, 8"	$8 – 12
plate, 6"	$6 – 8
salt, pepper; each	$6 – 8
soufflé, round 8"	$10 – 15
soufflé, round 7"	$10 – 15
soufflé, round 6"	$8 – 10
soufflé, round 5"	$6 – 8
sugar	$10 – 15
paper price list	$10 – 15

All Gourmet Ware pieces were intended to complement many of Stangl's contemporary dinnerware patterns. All of the Gourmet shapes except the soufflés were newly designed by Rudy Kleinebeckel. The soufflé shapes were simply borrowed from the Cookrite bakeware line and glazed with the Gourmet colors.

Gourmet Ware dinnerware shapes were produced with the Brown Satin finish only. The colors Gourmet Grey and Gourmet Green were on the casseroles, baking dishes, and soufflés. Gourmet Ware met with limited acceptance, so was a very short-lived product.

The Brown Satin finish was a swirl of walnut brown under the Brown Satin glaze. Gourmet Green used a dark green underglaze color on the exterior

Gourmet Ware Brown Satin 10" plate, mug.

of the pieces with Satin White glazed interiors and covers. Pieces with the Gourmet Grey finish were simply glazed with Gray dinnerware glaze. Brown Satin pieces occasionally turn up, but the Gourmet Grey and Gourmet Green colors are seldom seen.

Sgraffito #5275

Sgraffito 10" plate, sugar.

Introduced: 1973
Designer: Sandra Ward
Shape Style: #3774 Coupe

Known Pieces:

bowl, cereal	$10 – 15
bowl, fruit	$10 – 15
bowl, coupe soup	$20 – 25
bowl, lug soup	$10 – 15
bowl, 10" salad	$50 – 60
bowl, 8" vegetable	$25 – 35
bowl, divided veg.	$25 – 35
butter dish	$25 – 30
cake stand	$10 – 20
casserole, 8" covered	$50 – 60
creamer	$10 – 12
cup	$8 – 10
gravy boat	$15 – 20
gravy underplate	$10 – 15
mug, 2 cup	$30 – 35
mug, stack	$25 – 35
napkin ring, each	$15 – 25
pitcher, 2 quart	$50 – 60
pitcher, 1 quart	$35 – 45
pitcher, 1 pint	$20 – 30
plate, 12½" chop	$60 – 75
plate, 10"	$20 – 25
plate, 8"	$15 – 20
plate, 6"	$10 – 12
salt, pepper; each	$6 – 8
saucer	$7 – 8
sugar	$15 – 20
teapot	$60 – 75
tidbit, 10"	$10 – 15
paper napkin, each	$1 – 2
paper price list	$10 – 15

The Sgraffito pattern was in essence the Fruit and Flowers motif without color. The same stencils were used, but the Sgraffito motifs were carved a little deeper to accentuate the workmanship and beauty of the design. This pattern was intended to showcase the talent of Stangl's carving department by emphasizing the sgraffito technique of dinnerware decoration. The Sgraffito dinnerware pattern was popular, but was discontinued when production was shifted from red-bodied to white-bodied wares in 1975.

Grape #5276

Grape 10" plate, stack mug.

Introduced: 1973
Designer: Sandra Ward
Shape Style: #3434 Rim with #5129 Tiara

Known Pieces:

bowl, cereal	$20 – 25
bowl, fruit	$15 – 20
bowl, coupe soup	$25 – 30
bowl, lug soup	$20 – 25
bowl, soup/cereal	$20 – 25
bowl, 10" salad	$65 – 75
bowl, 8" vegetable	$35 – 45

bowl, divided veg.	$40 – 50		pitcher, 1 quart	$40 – 50
butter dish	$45 – 55		pitcher, 1 pint	$25 – 35
cake stand	$15 – 20		plate, 12½" chop	$60 – 75
casserole, 8" covered	$55 – 65		plate, 10" or 10⅝"	$25 – 30
clock, skillet shape	$60 – 75		plate, 8" or 8¼"	$15 – 20
creamer	$15 – 20		plate, 6"	$10 – 15
cup	$10 – 12		salt, pepper; each	$8 – 10
gravy boat	$20 – 25		saucer	$6 – 8
gravy underplate	$10 – 15		sugar	$15 – 20
mug, 2 cup	$35 – 45		teapot	$60 – 75
mug, stack	$35 – 45		tidbit, 10"	$10 – 15
napkin ring, each	$20 – 30		paper napkin, each	$2 – 3
pitcher, 2 quart	$60 – 75		paper price list	$10 – 15

Grape was a bright, bold pattern that featured a stylized cluster of large grapes. Dark Blue was the dominant color, while Victoria Green, Pomona Green, and Black underglaze colors completed the pattern. Grape was very popular throughout the 1970s and was produced in varying quantities until Stangl's close in 1978. For this reason, Grape is available on both white and red-bodied shapes. Although the red-bodied version of the Grape pattern is preferred by most collectors, this pattern has become so coveted that many collectors are searching for white-bodied pieces as well.

Sun Pebbles #5277, New Sun Pebbles

Introduced: 1973
Designer: Sandra Ward
Shape Style: #3774 Coupe with #5129 Tiara

Known Pieces:

bowl, cereal	$10 – 12		mug, stack	$20 – 25
bowl, fruit	$10 – 12		napkin ring, each	$10 – 15
bowl, coupe soup	$12 – 18		pitcher, 2 quart	$35 – 45
bowl, lug soup	$10 – 12		pitcher, 1 quart	$20 – 30
bowl, soup/cereal	$10 – 12		pitcher, 1 pint	$15 – 20
bowl, 10" salad	$35 – 45		plate, 12½" chop	$35 – 45
bowl, 8" vegetable	$20 – 25		plate, 10" or 10⅝"	$15 – 20
bowl, divided veg	$30 – 40		plate, 8" or 8¼"	$8 – 12
butter dish	$20 – 25		plate, 6"	$5 – 7
cake stand	$10 – 15		salt, pepper; each	$6 – 7
casserole, 8" covered	$35 – 45		saucer	$4 – 5
creamer	$8 – 10		sugar	$10 – 15
cup	$5 – 9		teapot	$35 – 45
gravy boat	$10 – 15		tidbit, 10"	$10 – 12
gravy underplate	$8 – 10		paper napkin, each	$1 – 2
mug, 2 cup	$20 – 25		paper price list	$10 – 15

This pattern, with Orange and Tan spots surrounded by Orange and Tan bands, was initially referred to as Sand Pebbles in design notes but was introduced as Sun Pebbles. For its first two

Sun Pebbles 8" plate, 10" plate, gravy boat and underplate, teapot.

years of production, Sun Pebbles used speckled glaze with a carved motif. In 1975, this pattern was converted to white body with no speckles. By 1976, the name was changed to New Sun Pebbles and was produced as such until 1978. Many of the pieces produced after 1976 were decorated simply with bands and no spots. Only the plates continued to have the group of spots in the center.

Cranberry #5278

Cranberry cup & saucer, 10" plate, salt shaker, fruit bowl.

Introduced: 1973
Designer: Sandra Ward
Shape Style: #3774 Coupe

Known Pieces:

bowl, cereal	$20 – 25
bowl, fruit	$20 – 25
bowl, coupe soup	$25 – 30
bowl, lug soup	$20 – 25
bowl, soup/cereal	$20 – 25
bowl, 10" salad	$60 – 75
bowl, 8" vegetable	$35 – 45
bowl, divided veg.	$35 – 45
butter dish	$40 – 50
cake stand	$25 – 35
casserole, 8" covered	$60 – 75
creamer	$20 – 25
cup	$10 – 12
gravy boat	$20 – 25
gravy underplate	$10 – 15
mug, 2 cup	$35 – 45
mug, stack	$35 – 45
napkin ring, each	$20 – 25
pitcher, 2 quart	$60 – 75
pitcher, 1 quart	$40 – 50
pitcher, 1 pint	$20 – 30
plate, 12½" chop	$60 – 75
plate, 10" or 10⅝"	$25 – 30
plate, 8" or 8¼"	$20 – 25
plate, 6"	$10 – 15
salt, pepper; each	$7 – 10
saucer	$6 – 7
sugar	$20 – 25
teapot	$90 – 110
tidbit, 10"	$15 – 20
paper napkin, each	$2 – 3
paper price list	$15 – 20

The very festive Cranberry motif was decorated with Pink #167, Victoria Green, and Willow Green with a wide Pink #167 band. In 1975, Cranberry was adapted to white-bodied shapes; but was discontinued early in 1976. Because of its bright Christmas colors and limited production, Cranberry is now in great demand

Blue Silhouette #5279, Green Silhouette #5280

Introduced: 1973
Designer: Sandra Ward
Shape Style: #3774 Coupe

Silhouette; original black & white promotional photo showing 10" plate, cup & saucer.

Known Pieces:

bowl, fruit/dessert. . . . . $10 − 15
bowl, 10" salad . . . . $40 − 50
bowl, 8" vegetable. . . . . $25 − 35
creamer . . . . $10 − 15
coffee pot. . . . . $50 − 60
cup. . . . . $8 − 10
plate, 12½" chop . . . . $60 − 75
plate, 10". . . . . $30 − 35
plate, 8" . . . . $20 − 25
plate, 6" . . . . $10 − 15   sugar . . . . $15 − 20
saucer . . . . $6 − 7   teapot. . . . . $50 − 60

The dramatic Silhouette patterns featured either a dark blue or dark green arch at the top of each plate. The cups and serving pieces were simply gray with blue or green interiors. The Hardened Blue or Art Ware Green colors were used under the Gray dinnerware glaze to produce the nearly black effect of these motifs.

The plates and bowls were on the #3774 coupe shape. The cup and saucer were on the #5241 Contempo shape, the salt and pepper were #3434. The teapot, coffee pot, creamer, and sugars were all on the #5129 Tiara shape.

The Blue and Green Silhouette patterns were introduced with great fanfare at the spring 1973 Atlantic City trade show, but were eliminated after only a few months of production. These patterns were a little too avant-garde in character so were shunned by Stangl dinnerware buyers.

Oyster Plates

Introduced: 1973

Oyster plate with Dark Turquoise decoration.

Known Pieces:

oyster plate, Dark Turquoise . . . . $250 − 300
oyster plate, Aqua Green . . . . $200 − 250
oyster plate, Pink #193. . . . . $250 − 300
oyster plate, Old Gold . . . . $200 − 250

Stangl produced novelty oyster plates during 1973 and 1974. These plates were decorated with Dark Turquoise, Pink #193, Old Gold, or Aqua Green under-glaze colors. Pink oyster plates were usually produced for the Port Norris Oyster House. These are stamped on the back: "Hand Painted for Port Norris Oyster House, Port Norris, N. J." The blue, gold, and green plates were marked with a typical Stangl mark, sometimes accompanied by the Potters' Union mark. Although not scarce, Stangl's oyster plates are highly collectible.

Flower Pot Patio Ware Salad Set

Introduced: 1973
Designers: Sandra Ward, Rudy Kleinebeckel
Shape Style: #5242 Croyden

Known Pieces:

ashtray, patio	$15 – 25
bowl, 10" salad	$40 – 50
bowl, 6" salad	$10 – 15
cruet, oil	$10 – 15
cruet, vinegar	$10 – 15
mug, flowerpot shape	$15 – 25
plate, 10"	$20 – 25
salt, pepper each	$6 – 10
salad utensils:	
fork	$50 – 60
spade (spoon)	$50 – 60

Original Stangl Flower Pot Patio Ware black & white promotional photo showing 6" salad bowls, 10" salad bowl, salt & pepper, oil & vinegar cruets, and mugs.

Stangl's Flower Pot Patio Ware was developed in response to the outdoor entertaining trend during the early 1970s. These novelty pieces were red clay with gray engobe interiors. This line was produced primarily only during the spring and summer seasons of 1973. A production memo dated February 2, 1973, stated that the daily output of this pattern was 100 – 125 individual salad bowls, 24 – 36 10" salad bowls, and 18 pairs each of salt & peppers and vinegar & oil cruets. This pattern was available through Stangl's catalogs and the Flemington Outlet throughout 1973.

Drabware Patio Ware

Introduced: 1973
Made For: Longenecker Corp.
Designers: Sandra Ward, Rudy Kleinebeckel
Shape Style: #5242 Croyden with #3434 Rim and #5129 Tiara

Known Pieces:

bowl, soup/cereal	$10 – 15
bowl, fruit/dessert	$10 – 15
bowl, 10" salad	$35 – 45
bowl, 8" vegetable	$20 – 30
casserole, 8" covered	$45 – 55
creamer	$10 – 15
cup	$10 – 12
mug, stack	$25 – 30
pitcher, 2 quart	$30 – 40
pitcher, 1 quart	$15 – 25
plate, 12½" chop	$25 – 35
plate, 10"	$15 – 20
plate, 8"	$8 – 10
plate, 6"	$6 – 8
salt, pepper; each	$6 – 8
saucer	$4 – 5
sugar	$10 – 15
teapot	$40 – 50

The Drabware Patio Ware was produced for Longenecker Corp. as a special-order pattern during July 1973. Drabware was based on the same premise as Stangl's Flower Pot Patio Ware, but was not styled on the flowerpot and garden tool forms.

Drabware Patio Ware plate, bowl, and cup and saucer shapes were #5242 Croyden. The pitcher, teapot, creamer, and sugar were the #5129 Tiara shape while the casserole, salt, and pepper were the #3434 shape. The Drabware Patio Ware pieces were red bodied with gray engobe on the exteriors and the edges trimmed to show the red. The teapots and sugars were gray outside, red inside, and had red covers. The salts and peppers were all gray or gray on top with red on the bottoms. Only a few sets of this pattern were produced as Longenecker never ordered more than the initial shipment.

Coffee Mug Assortments, Tulip Snack Set

Introduced: 1973
Designer: Sandra Ward, Rudy Kleinebeckel

Known Pieces:

mug: stripes; blue, purple, pink . . . . . $25 – 35	mug: Blue Flower . . . . $35 – 45
mug: stripes; gold, brown, green . . . . $15 – 20	mug: Forsythia . . . . $35 – 45
mug: sponging; blue or pink. . . . . . . $25 – 35	mug: Cherry. $40 – 50
mug: sponging; gold or green . . . . . . $15 – 20	tulip shape mug . . . . $20 – 25
	tulip snack plate . . . . $10 – 15

Stripe stack mug decorated with Dark Turquoise and Pomona Green; sponged stack mugs decorated with Pink #193, Old Gold, Pomona Green, and Dark Turquoise.

During 1973, Stangl offered a group of coffee mugs in sets of 12 with assorted decorations for $38.70. Initially the assortment was to contain 13 mugs, but that number was reduced to 12. The decorations consisted of vertical stripes, horizontal stripes, sponging in various colors, Sculptured Fruit (with an added Old Gold band), Country Garden, Tulip, Dogwood, and motifs called Blue Flower, Forsythia, and Cherry. The Cherry motif was adapted from the cherries used on the Festival pattern. At this time, stack mugs decorated with blue, purple, pink, or red sponging or stripes are more desirable than those decorated with gold, green, or brown shades. The Blue Flower, Forsythia, and Cherry motifs are the most uncommon of the mug motifs and hardest to come by.

The Tulip Snack Sets each consisted of a tulip-shaped mug on a snack plate decorated with a Pomona green stem and leaves. The original design called for 10" snack plates, but the 8" snack plate was actually used in production. The tulip mugs were decorated with Purple, Pink #193, Dark Turquoise, and Yellow underglaze colors. By 1974, the Stack Mug Assortments and Tulip Snack Sets were discontinued.

Tulip Snack Set mugs; Purple, Dark Turquoise, Yellow, and Pink #193.

Pewter Ware

Pewter Ware 10" plate.

Introduced: 1973
Designer: Sandra Ward, Rudy Kleinebeckel

Known Pieces:

mug	$45 – 55
plate, 10"	$60 – 75

Tentatively called "Revere 1776," the Pewter Ware shapes were styled to look like hand-wrought and aged pieces of pewter. The shapes included such details as dimpling and use dents. The Pewter Ware pieces were sprayed with Satin Gray glaze and covered front and back with satin platinum luster. Because of the clever modeling of the shapes and no clay body showing, Pewter Ware closely resembles actual pewter. The Pewter Ware pattern did not impress department store dinnerware buyers at the January 1973 Atlantic City trade show, so little more than the original dozen trade show samples were produced.

White-Bodied Patterns

Three of the eight patterns introduced during 1974 were produced on shapes sprayed completely inside and out, front and back with white engobe, thus covering all of the red body. These patterns were Town & Country, Blue Melon, and Bamboo. Five patterns with Stangl's traditional white front and red back were also introduced that year. These were Olde Vermont, Posies, Ringles, Wood Rose, and Yankee Doodle. By the end of 1974 all Stangl's dinnerware patterns were converted to white body production.

By 1975 Stangl's standard dinner and salad plate sizes were enlarged from 10" and 8" to 10⅝" and 8¼". For this reason two sizes of dinner and salad plates are listed with several dinnerware patterns.

For most of the patterns introduced in 1974, the napkin ring, 11" oval platter, and coffee pot shapes were only produced for several months during that year. These are some of the more difficult pieces to find in these patterns.

Bamboo #5282

Introduced: 1974
Designer: Sandra Ward
Shape Style: #3774 Coupe

Known Pieces:

Green or Yellow:

bowl, 6" soup/cereal	$10 – 12
bowl, 10" salad	$30 – 40
bowl, 8" vegetable	$20 – 25
cake stand	$10 – 15
coffee pot	$55 – 70
creamer, coupe shape	$10 – 15
creamer, #5129 Tiara	$8 – 10
cup	$5 – 8
mug, stack	$15 – 20
napkin ring, each	$10 – 15
pitcher, 1½" pint	$25 – 30
plate, 12½" chop	$30 – 40
plate, 10" or 10⅝"	$15 – 20
plate, 8" or 8¼"	$8 – 12
plate, 6"	$8 – 10
platter, 14⅜" oval	$35 – 45
platter, 11" oval	$25 – 35
salt, pepper; each	$5 – 6
saucer	$5 – 6
sugar, coupe shape	$15 – 20
sugar, #5129 Tiara	$8 – 10
teapot	$45 – 55
tidbit	$8 – 12
paper price list	$10 – 15

Blue or Brown:

bowl, 6" soup/cereal	$10 – 15
mug, stack	$20 – 30
plate, 8¼"	$15 – 25

Bamboo was an airy, tropical pattern of bright Bamboo Green stalks on white. The Bamboo creamer and sugar shapes with twig handles were newly designed for this pattern, but were replaced in 1976 with the more common #5129 Tiara shape creamer and sugar. The coffee pot, napkin rings, and 11" oval platter were discontinued by 1975. In 1976 the 6" plate was dropped and the 14⅜" oval platter was added.

In 1976, Bamboo was offered as a prepackaged brunch set, which consisted of an 8¼" plate, soup/cereal bowl, and stack mug. These brunch sets were available decorated with green, yellow, brown, or blue. Brown and blue were discontinued before 1977 and are very difficult colors to find. The Bamboo pattern with a yellow motif was available as a full dinner set for a short time as a Flemington Outlet exclusive during 1974 and 1975. By 1976, yellow Bamboo was no longer produced, and only green decorated Bamboo was available from 1976 through 1978.

Bamboo cup & saucer, 10⅝" plate, sugar, creamer, 8¼" plate.

Blue Melon #5283

Introduced: 1974
Designer: Sandra Ward
Shape Style: #3774 Coupe

Known Pieces:

bowl, 6" soup/cereal	$15 – 20	plate, 8"	$15 – 20
bowl, 10" salad	$50 – 60	plate, 6"	$10 – 15
bowl, 8" vegetable	$30 – 40	platter, 11" oval	$55 – 65
coffee pot	$85 – 110	salt, pepper; each	$8 – 10
creamer	$20 – 25	saucer	$10 – 12
cup	$10 – 12	sugar	$20 – 25
napkin ring, each	$15 – 20	teapot	$85 – 110
plate, 12½" chop	$60 – 75	tidbit, 10"	$10 – 15
plate, 10"	$30 – 40	paper price list	$20 – 25

Blue Melon 8" plate, 6" plate drilled for a handle.

Blue Melon featured a stylized motif of Hardened Blue crescents and Bamboo Green spots. Stangl advertising describes the Blue Melon pattern as "an abstract design featuring a leaf green inner band and melon shaped wedges of deep blue. These colors are in perfect harmony against Stangl's white earthenware body." Blue Melon used the #3434 cup shape and #3434 teapot shape with a newly designed ball knob on the lid. Blue Melon was discontinued in March 1974. A memo to all Stangl sales representatives from vice president Michael P. Davis, dated March 14, 1974, declares "Blue Melon and Yankee Doodle will be withdrawn effective immediately." In view of Blue Melon's three-month production run, it is an exceptionally rare pattern.

Olde Vermont #5284

Introduced: 1974
Designer: Sandra Ward
Made For: Tiffany & Co.
Shape Style: #3434 Rim, Hexagon

Known Pieces:

bowl, cereal	$10 – 15	bowl, 10" salad	$35 – 45
bowl, coupe soup	$15 – 20	bowl, 8" vegetable	$20 – 30
bowl, rim soup	$15 – 25	coffee pot, hexagon	$80 – 110
bowl, soup/cereal	$10 – 15	creamer, hexagon	$20 – 25
bowl, 12" salad	$55 – 65	creamer, #5129 Tiara	$10 – 12

cup.	$8 – 10	plate, 6"	$8 – 10
mug, 13oz. coffee	$25 – 30	platter, 14⅜" oval	$40 – 50
pie plate, 11"	$40 – 50	platter, 11½" oval	$30 – 40
pitcher, 1 quart	$35 – 45	salt, pepper; each	$5 – 6
pitcher, 1 pint	$20 – 30	saucer	$5 – 7
pitcher, ½ pint.	$15 – 20	sugar, hexagon shape	$20 – 25
plate, 12½" cheese.	$40 – 50	sugar, #5129 Tiara.	$10 – 15
plate, 12½" chop	$40 – 50	teapot, 6 cup, #5129 Tiara	$40 – 50
plate, 10" or 10⅝"	$15 – 20	tidbit, 10".	$10 – 15
plate, 8" or 8¼"	$10 – 15	paper price list	$10 – 15

The Olde Vermont decoration was a sponged blending of Walnut Brown and Yellow underglaze colors. Olde Vermont was intended to resemble antique Bennington pottery glazes. This pattern was produced on the red body during 1974. Red-bodied pieces sometimes have the engobe trimmed from the edges, allowing the brown rim to show. Beginning in 1975 Olde Vermont was made on the white body with no brown rim.

The original Olde Vermont creamer, sugar, and coffee pot shapes were a newly designed hexagon shape. These were changed in 1975 to the #5129 Tiara shape. Also in 1975, the shape of the cup was changed from #5129 Tiara to the #4024 coupe shape. The 12½" cheese plate, also available with the Caughley and Town & Country patterns, was actually the #5241 Contempo shape 12½" chop plate. Olde Vermont was not produced in great quantities, but was available during most of the late 1970s.

In August 1974, a sponged dinnerware pattern called New Vermont was developed. New Vermont was decorated with Black sponged over Walnut Brown. Only a few sample pieces of this pattern were created before the New Vermont endeavor was halted.

Olde Vermont red-bodied 10" plate, #5129 Tiara cup & saucer; white-bodied sugar and creamer, 10⅝" plate, ½ pint pitcher.

Posies #5285

Introduced: 1974
Designer: Sandra Ward
Shape Style: #3774 Coupe

Known Pieces:

bowl, 6" soup/cereal	$10 – 15	cup.	$6 – 8
bowl, 10" salad	$45 – 55	mug, stack	$30 – 40
bowl, 8" vegetable.	$25 – 30	napkin ring, each	$15 – 20
cake stand	$10 – 15	plate, 12½" chop	$55 – 65
coffee pot.	$70 – 90	plate, 10" or 10⅝"	$25 – 30
creamer	$10 – 15	plate, 8" or 8¼"	$20 – 25
		plate, 6"	$10 – 15

platter, 14⅜" oval . . . . $55 – 65
platter, 11" oval . . . . $35 – 45
salt, pepper; each . . . . $8 – 10
saucer . . . . $7 – 8
sugar . . . . $15 – 20
teapot . . . . $65 – 80
tidbit, 10" or 10⅝" . . . . $10 – 15

paper price list . . . . $10 – 15

During early 1974 the Posies pattern was produced on the red body. By 1975, however, Posies had become a white-bodied pattern. Stangl production notes list Posies as having carved decoration, but no carved Posies pieces have surfaced. The Posies motif was an allover arrangement of simple "lollipop" flowers in bright colors. This pattern was discontinued by fall 1975.

Posies 10⅝" plate, cup & saucer.

Ringles #5286

Introduced: 1974
Designer: Sandra Ward
Shape Style: #5242 Croyden

Known Pieces:

bowl, fruit/dessert . . . . $8 – 10
bowl, 10" salad . . . . $40 – 50
bowl, 8" vegetable . . . . $20 – 25
cake stand . . . . $10 – 15
creamer . . . . $10 – 12
coffee pot . . . . $50 – 65
cup . . . . $7 – 8
mug, stack . . . . $25 – 30
napkin ring, each . . . . $10 – 15
plate, 12½" chop . . . . $45 – 55

plate, 10" or 10⅝" . . . . $15 – 25
plate, 8" or 8¼" . . . . $15 – 20
plate, 6" . . . . $10 – 12
platter, 14⅜" oval . . . . $40 – 50
platter, 11" oval . . . . $20 – 30
salt, pepper; each . . . . $7 – 8
saucer . . . . $7 – 8
sugar . . . . $15 – 20
teapot . . . . $45 – 55
tidbit, 10⅝" . . . . $10 – 15
paper price list . . . . $10 – 15

The Ringles pattern displayed an informal grouping of stylized "lollipop" blossoms and stems. The monochromatic color scheme consisted of Old Gold, Walnut Brown, Tan, and Orange. Ringles pieces originally had white fronts and red clay backs, but were produced for a while on white-bodied shapes during 1975. As with Posies, Ringles was discontinued before the end of 1975.

Ringles coffee pot, sugar, 10⅝" plate.

Town & Country #5287

Introduced: 1974
Designers: Robert Roemer, Rudy Kleinebeckel, and Irene Sarnecki
Shape Style: based on #3434 Rim

Known Pieces:	Blue	Black Crimson	Brown, Green Honey, Yellow
ashtray, bathtub shape	$50 – 60	—	$20 – 30
ashtray, #1953, 4¼"	$25 – 35	—	$15 – 25
ashtray, #3942, 8½"	$35 – 45	—	$20 – 30
baking dish, 9" x 14"	$100 – 125	—	$35 – 45
baking dish, 7" x 10"	$75 – 90	—	$30 – 40
bean pot/cookie jar	$125 – 150	—	$40 – 50
bowl, 12" salad	$110 – 135	—	$55 – 65
bowl, 10" fruit straight sides	$75 – 100	$50 – 60	$40 – 50
bowl, 10" salad rounded shape	$70 – 80	$45 – 55	$35 – 45
bowl, 8" vegetable	$40 – 50	$35 – 45	$25 – 35
bowl, 7½" porridge, straight sides	$30 – 40	$25 – 35	$15 – 25
bowl, 6½" porridge, rounded shape	$25 – 35	—	$15 – 25
bowl, 7½" chili, straight sides	$30 – 40	$20 – 30	$15 – 25
bowl, 6¾" chili, rounded shape	$25 – 35	—	$15 – 20
bowl, 5¾" soup/cereal	$25 – 35	$20 – 30	$15 – 20
bread pan 4¾" x 10"	$90 – 110	—	$25 – 35
butter dish, covered	$60 – 75	—	$25 – 35
cake stand, 10⅝"	$35 – 45	—	$20 – 30
cake stand/chip & dip 12½" round	$110 – 135	—	$50 – 65
candle holder, chamber-stick shape	$45 – 55	—	$25 – 35
candle holder #3410 3" flower shape; each	$25 – 35	—	$10 – 20
candlestick #5299 7½" tall; each	$55 – 65	$45 – 55	$20 – 30
canister, milk can shape with ceramic lid	$125 – 150	—	$65 – 80
canister, #3688 milk can with cork cover	$60 – 70	—	$25 – 35
casserole, 2½ quart	$85 – 100	—	$30 – 50
casserole, 1½ quart	$65 – 90	—	$20 – 40
chamber pot, handled	$90 – 110	—	$40 – 60
citrus juicer with mug	$75 – 100	—	$45 – 65
clock, 10⅝" round	$55 – 75	—	$20 – 35
clock, skillet shape	$70 – 85	—	$30 – 45
coffee pot, 5 cup	$110 – 130	$80 – 100	$40 – 65
cookie jar, 6½" diameter milk can shape	$145 – 175	—	$60 – 75
cornucopia, 10½"	$100 – 125	—	$50 – 60
cornucopia, 7¼"	$65 – 80	—	$30 – 40
creamer	$30 – 40	$15 – 20	$10 – 15
cup	$20 – 25	$15 – 20	$8 – 15
dessert mold, Turk's cap 7½"	$50 – 60	$30 – 40	$25 – 35
dessert mold, fluted 6"	$40 – 50	$25 – 35	$20 – 25
deviled egg plate, 11½" paneled	$130 – 150	—	$50 – 80
flowerpot, 7"	$45 – 55	—	$25 – 35
flowerpot, 5"	$35 – 45	—	$20 – 30

	Blue	Black Crimson	Brown, Green Honey, Yellow
flowerpot, 4"	$25 – 35	—	$15 – 20
flowerpot, 3"	$20 – 25	—	$10 – 15
ginger jar	$110 – 135	—	$60 – 75
gravy boat	$45 – 55	—	$10 – 25
gravy underplate	$25 – 35	—	$10 – 15
lamp, #637 jug shape	$185 – 235	—	$100 – 150
lamp, #9051	$185 – 235	—	$100 – 150
lamp, temple jar shape	$200 – 250	—	$150 – 200
lamp, large square	$175 – 225	—	$100 – 150
mug, 14oz. soup/juicer stand	$50 – 60	—	$20 – 35
mug, 13oz. coffee	$40 – 50	—	$20 – 35
mug, stack	$55 – 65	—	$20 – 35
napkin ring, each	$20 – 25	$20 – 25	$10 – 15
pie plate, 10½"	$55 – 65	$40 – 50	$25 – 40
pitcher, 2½ quart	$100 – 125	$65 – 75	$45 – 60
pitcher, 2½ pint	$80 – 95	$40 – 50	$25 – 40
pitcher, 1½ pint	$60 – 70	$25 – 35	$20 – 30
pitcher & bowl set, large, straight sides	$200 – 225	—	$80 – 150
pitcher & bowl set, small, ribbed sides	$175 – 200	—	$75 – 100
planter, rolling pin	$150 – 165	—	$65 – 75
plate, 12½" cheese	$85 – 110	—	$35 – 55
plate, 12½" chop	$75 – 95	$55 – 70	$30 – 45
plate, 10" or 10⅝"	$35 – 45	$30 – 40	$12 – 20
plate, 8" or 8¼"	$25 – 30	$20 – 25	$8 – 15
plate, 6"	$15 – 20	$10 – 15	$6 – 8
platter, 14⅜" oval	$85 – 110	$50 – 60	$35 – 55
platter, 11½" oval	$60 – 70	$45 – 55	$25 – 40
salad fork	$100 – 125	—	$50 – 60
salad spoon	$100 – 125	—	$50 – 60
salt, pepper; each	$20 – 25	$10 – 15	$8 – 10
salt, pepper with handles; each	$25 – 30	—	$12 – 15
saucer	$12 – 15	$8 – 10	$3 – 6
server, dustpan shape	$75 – 95	—	$40 – 50
server, skillet shape	$60 – 75	—	$25 – 35
server, #3783 pear	$40 – 50	—	$15 – 25
server, #3785 apple	$45 – 55	—	$15 – 25
server, #3857 clover	$40 – 50	—	$15 – 25
shaving mug	$45 – 60	—	$25 – 35
soap dish	$45 – 55	—	$25 – 35
soup tureen, covered	$210 – 245	—	$100 – 150
ladle for tureen	$65 – 80	—	$40 – 60
spoon rest	$45 – 55	—	$25 – 35
sugar	$40 – 45	$25 – 30	$15 – 25
teapot, 5 cup	$130 – 150	$75 – 100	$40 – 65
tray, 8¼" oval	$25 – 35	—	$10 – 15

	Blue	Black Crimson	Brown, Green Honey, Yellow
tray, 7½" square	$35 – 45	$20 – 30	$15 – 25
tidbit, 10⅝"	$30 – 40	$20 – 25	$10 – 15
tile	$30 – 40	—	$10 – 25
tissue box cover	$65 – 80	—	$30 – 60
tumbler, 9oz.	$30 – 40	—	$15 – 25
toothbrush holder	$60 – 70	—	$25 – 35
vase, 6¾" #3981	$75 – 95	—	$25 – 35
vase, 8" #4050	$75 – 95	—	$25 – 35
wall pocket	$80 – 95	—	$20 – 35
dealer sign	$150 – 175	—	$75 – 125

At this time, Blue is the most popular Town & Country color, but Yellow and Green Town & Country are much more popular than Brown or Honey. Brown and Honey items usually sell for approximately half that of Yellow or Green.

Although produced only four years, Stangl's Town & Country was an immensely popular pattern. An excellent advertising program and the straightforward styling of the shapes established Town & Country as Stangl's leading pattern during the late 1970s. Because of this, Town & Country was gradually expanded from seventeen shapes in 1974 to over eighty different shapes by 1978. Just during January 1975, twenty-one shapes were added to the Town & Country line. Some of the shapes added in 1975 were the skillet clock, bread pan, juicer and mug, soup tureen and ladle, and chamber pot. A few shapes considered for the Town & Country line but never produced were canisters in four sizes and three sizes of casseroles with glass covers.

The nostalgic Town & Country shapes and coloring were designed to resemble the enameled kitchenware produced during the late nineteenth and early twentieth centuries. Robert Roemer designed new shapes and effectively adapted items from the #3434 Rim and #5129 Tiara shape lines to achieve the old time styling of Town & Country. The underglaze sponging technique as well as the color selections were developed by designer and decorating supervisor Irene Sarnecki. The colors were sponged under the Silk White glaze to realistically reproduce the look of enamelware.

The original colors available in 1974 were Blue, Black, Yellow, Green, and Crimson, all with black lining on the rims. Crimson was discontinued shortly after introduction; it is exceptionally difficult to find. Black was replaced with brown before January 1975. Black Town & Country is scarce, but can be found now and then. Honey was introduced in January 1977 and was the last color added to the Town & Country assortment. At this time Honey is the least collected Town & Country color. A combination color of brown sponged over black was considered in 1974, but was never produced in quantity.

In 1976 the 7½" straight-sided porridge and chili bowl shapes were replaced with the rounded 6½" porridge and 6¾" chili bowls. Some Town & Country shapes served more than one function. The citrus juicer stand and the 14 ounce soup mug are the same piece, as are the 8¼" oval tray, covered butter bottom, and gravy underplate.

During the latter part of 1976 Stangl's Town & Country Bath Ware line was introduced. This line consisted of milk can canister shapes in two sizes, the ginger jar, pitcher & bowl sets, the chamber pot, bathtub ashtray, flowerpots, soap dish, tissue box cover, shaving mug, tumbler, and toothbrush holder. Also advertised as bath accessories were the 7½" square tray as a vanity tray and the soup/cereal bowl as a sponge bowl.

Town & Country 10⅝" plate, Black; teapot, Yellow; 8" plate, Green; creamer, Brown; 12½" chop plate, Yellow; cup & saucer, Blue; 8¼" plate, Honey; tumbler, Green.

Town & Country bathtub ashtray, Blue; 7½" square tray, Honey; shaving mug, Yellow; 10⅝" plate, Brown; coffee pot, Honey; salt & pepper, Brown; handled salt shaker, Blue; 8¼" plate, Green; #5299 candlestick, Honey.

Town & Country milk can canister, Blue; 6" fluted dessert mold, Yellow; covered butter dish, Brown; 14⅜" oval platter, Honey; spoon rest, Yellow; napkin rings, Blue; 7½" Turk's cap dessert mold, Green.

Wood Rose #5288

Wood Rose 10" plate.

Introduced: 1974
Designer: Sandra Ward
Shape Style: Re-styled #5242 Croyden

Known Pieces:

bowl, fruit/dessert	$10 – 15
bowl, 10" salad	$45 – 55
bowl, 8" vegetable	$25 – 30
cake stand	$10 – 15
creamer	$10 – 15
coffee pot	$60 – 75
cup	$8 – 10
mug, stack	$25 – 30
napkin ring, each	$15 – 20
plate, 12½" chop	$35 – 45
plate, 10" or 10⅝"	$20 – 25
plate, 8" or 8¼"	$15 – 20
plate, 6"	$10 – 12
platter, 14⅜" oval	$45 – 55
platter, 11" oval	$30 – 40
salt, pepper; each	$4 – 6
saucer	$5 – 6
sugar	$10 – 15
teapot	$55 – 65
tidbit, 10" or 10⅝"	$10 – 15
paper price list	$10 – 15

The bold Wood Rose pattern was introduced on Stangl's red body in 1974, but was converted to the white-bodied shapes by 1975. The Rust underglaze color was used on the blossoms while Hardened Blue and Black were on the rims and centers. The Silk White glaze was used to glaze this pattern. Wood Rose was discontinued during 1975, so is somewhat scarce.

Yankee Doodle #5289

Introduced: 1974
Designer: Sandra Ward
Shape Style: Re-styled #5242 Croyden

Known Pieces:

bowl, fruit/dessert	$20 – 25
bowl, 10" salad	$65 – 75
bowl, 8" vegetable	$35 – 45
creamer	$15 – 20
coffee pot	$85 – 135
cup	$10 – 15
napkin ring, each	$25 – 35
plate, 12½" chop	$75 – 90
plate, 10"	$45 – 55
plate, 8"	$20 – 30
plate, 6"	$15 – 20
platter, 11" oval	$65 – 80
salt, pepper; each	$10 – 15
saucer	$8 – 10
sugar	$15 – 25
teapot	$75 – 95
paper price list	$20 – 25

Stangl advertising described Yankee Doodle as "A new hand-carved pattern inspired by the artistry of the Pennsylvania Dutch. It is perfect for casual dining and can be used to accessorize any home. The bright yellow and warm browns of the decoration are truly unique."

Yankee Doodle has the distinction of being Stangl's last hand-carved, red-bodied pattern introduced. The stylized rooster motif was deeply carved through yellow engobe with no additional decoration. A razor knife was used to trim one-fourth of an inch of the engobe from inside the rims of the plates.

Production of Yankee Doodle ended in March 1974, only months after its introduction, making this pattern exceptionally scarce.

Yankee Doodle original Stangl black & white promotional photo showing a 10" plate with a cup & saucer.

Single Tulip

Introduced: 1974
Designer: Sandra Ward
Made For: Flemington Outlet
Shape Style: #5242 Croyden

Single Tulip 10" plate, Blue #95; cup & saucer, 10" plate, Yellow.

Known Pieces:

bowl, soup/cereal	$10 – 15
bowl, fruit/desert	$8 – 12
bowl, 10" salad	$30 – 40
bowl, 8" vegetable	$20 – 25
casserole, 8" covered	$45 – 60
coffee pot, 6 cup	$60 – 75
creamer	$10 – 12
cup	$6 – 8
mug, stack	$20 – 25
plate, 12½" chop	$40 – 50
plate, 10"	$15 – 20
plate, 8"	$10 – 12
plate, 6"	$8 – 10
salt, pepper; each	$6 – 8
saucer	$5 – 6
sugar	$10 – 15
teapot, 6 cup	$40 – 50
tidbit, 10"	$10 – 15

The Single Tulip motif was a streamlined version of Stangl's Early Pennsylvania Tulip design that had been used on artware during the 1940s. Single Tulip was decorated with either Blue #95 or Yellow motifs; the glaze on these patterns was clear and could be either plain or speckled. While not part of the Stangl Stoneware dinnerware line, Single Tulip was on the Stangl Stoneware Croyden shape and marked with the Stangl Stoneware backstamp. Pieces decorated with Blue #95 are more popular at this time than the same pieces decorated with Yellow.

The Single Tulip pattern was available only during the last half of 1974. This same streamlined tulip motif was re-introduced in 1977 on the #3774 Coupe shape as New Tulip #5325.

Decal-Decorated Christmas Patterns

Introduced: Late 1970s
Made For: Flemington Outlet

Known Pieces:	Christmas Tree Father Christmas	Holly and others
ashtray, 8" wind-proof	$30 – 40	$20 – 30
bowl, fruit	$15 – 20	$10 – 15
bowl, cereal	$15 – 20	$10 – 15
bowl, coupe soup	$20 – 30	$15 – 25
bowl, rim soup	$20 – 30	$15 – 25
cake stand	$25 – 35	$20 – 25
candle holder; each	$20 – 25	$15 – 20
cup	$15 – 20	$10 – 15
mug, 2 cup	$35 – 45	$25 – 35
plate, 14" chop	$60 – 75	$40 – 50
plate, 10"	$35 – 45	$30 – 40
plate, 9"	$30 – 40	$25 – 35
plate, 8"	$25 – 35	$20 – 30
plate, 7"	$20 – 25	$20 – 25
plate, 6"	$20 – 25	$10 – 15
saucer	$6 – 8	$6 – 8
tidbit, 10"	$25 – 35	$15 – 25
tidbit, 2 tier	$35 – 45	$25 – 35
tile	$25 – 35	$25 – 30
tray, 7½" square	$30 – 40	$25 – 35

During the 1970s, Stangl produced inexpensive, decal-decorated dinnerware items for holiday sales at the Flemington Outlet. Red-bodied and white-bodied seconds were usually used for these pieces. A quantity of old Scammell's restaurant ware seconds were purchased at a warehouse liquidation and decorated with these decals for the Flemington Outlet as well. The Scammell's pieces are marked with the Stangl backstamp in gold superimposed over the Scammell's trademark.

In November 1975 Stangl introduced a line of better quality china decal-decorated Christmas items. The china blanks were produced by Ridgewood Industries Inc. of Southampton, Pennsylvania. The blanks were made using Stangl molds and were shipped to Stangl's Trenton factory for the application of decals and gold trim.

At least five different decals were used. Holly, Wreath, and Small Tree decals seem to have been applied only to pottery items. The Father Christmas and Christmas Tree decals were used on both pottery and china shapes. China pieces generally had gold trim while white-bodied pottery items were trimmed with dark green.

Decal-Decorated Christmas Patterns: Christmas Tree 6" plate and mug, pottery body; Father Christmas 10" plate; Christmas Tree 9" plate, china body; Holly cup & saucer, pottery body.

These decal motifs were not exclusive to Stangl, and were commercially available to many decorating companies at that time. Because of this, these same decals may also be found on wares other than Stangl.

Flemington Outlet Transfer Plates

Introduced: 1974
Made For: Flemington Outlet

Known Pieces:

plate, 10" or 10⅝"	$130 – 160
plate, 9"	$110 – 135
plate, 8" or 8¼"	$80 – 130

Decorated using an underglaze transfer process, these scenic advertising pieces depict a popular view of the Flemington Outlet building. The underglaze transfer colors used were black, yellow, or blue. A variety of glazes were applied to these plates, including Satin Yellow, Satin Blue, Ivory Satin, and clear gloss. Flemington Outlet Transfer plates are uncommon and quite collectable at this time.

Flemington Outlet Transfer 9" plate, blue design.

Olde Glory #5293

Introduced: 1975
Designers: Sandra Ward and Rudy Kleinebeckel
Shape Style: #5293 Paneled with #3434 Rim

Known Pieces:

bowl, 6" soup/cereal, blue	$15 – 20	plate, 8¼", blue/red	$20 – 25
bowl, 10" salad, blue	$50 – 60	plate, 6", blue/red	$15 – 20
bowl, 8" vegetable, blue/red	$30 – 40	platter, 14⅜" oval, blue/red	$50 – 65
creamer, blue	$20 – 25	saucer, blue/red	$10 – 12
coffee pot, 8 cup, blue, red lid	$85 – 135	salt, red; each	$10 – 15
cup, blue	$12 – 15	pepper, blue; each	$10 – 12
mug, coffee, blue/red	$30 – 40	sugar, blue, red lid	$20 – 30
napkin ring, red; each	$25 – 35	teapot, 6 cup, blue, red lid	$70 – 95
plate, 12½" chop, blue/red	$60 – 75	tidbit, 10⅝", blue/red	$10 – 15
plate, 10⅝", blue/red	$25 – 35	paper price list	$20 – 30

"Olde Glory is fresh and pleasing in shades of Red, White and Blue that symbolize the strength of our great country. By combining sponged and sprayed items in deep Cobalt blue and Olde Glory Red on white, beautifully appropriate dinnerware is achieved. Olde glory by Stangl is perfect for a July 4th cook-out or your most elegant dinner party," so states Stangl's Olde Glory ad copy of 1975.

Olde Glory was originally intended as a patriotic pattern for America's Bicentennial celebration in 1976. The #5293 Paneled shape was unique to this pattern. Initially this pattern was called "Valley Forge" and was to have paneled plates and hollow ware. It was decided, however, to simply use #3434 Rim plates instead. Olde Glory plates were sponged lightly with Pink #160 and Art Ware Blue to create a red, white, and blue effect. The 6" and 10" bowls, coffee pot, teapot, cup, pepper, sugar, and creamer shapes were completely sponged with Art Ware blue. The teapot, coffee pot, sugar bowl lids, and salt shakers were all sprayed with a bright red overglaze color. This color was fired-on over the primary glaze of these pieces. Sadly, the Olde Glory pattern never made it to the Bicentennial. This extremely short-lived pattern was completely discontinued by fall 1975.

Olde Glory covered sugar, 10⅝" plate, 8¼" plate, salt & pepper.

Olde Glory price list, showing some of the pieces available.

Texturware

In 1976, Stangl introduced four new patterns with the Texturware designation. The essence of these patterns were the raised, textured surfaces in decorator colors. Six patterns were designed that emulated coarse-grained fabric texture. Actual fabric was used in the development of the designs. Of the six, only three fabric patterns were chosen for production, these were Burlap, Corduroy, and Shantung. The Verdura Texturware pattern was not fabric inspired but was decorated with a raised vegetable and lattice motif border. Underglaze colors were brushed over the textured areas of each of these patterns, adding depth and dimension to the designs.

Burlap #5295

Introduced: 1976
Designer: Rudy Kleinebeckel
Shape Style: #5295 Rim

Known Pieces:

bowl, 5¾" soup/cereal	$10 – 12	
bowl, 10" salad	$35 – 45	
bowl, 8" vegetable	$20 – 30	
butter dish, covered	$25 – 30	
creamer	$10 – 12	
cup	$6 – 8	
gravy boat	$10 – 15	
gravy underplate	$8 – 12	
pitcher, 1 quart	$30 – 40	

plate, 12" chop . . . . $30 – 40	salt, pepper; each . . . . $5 – 6
plate, 10⅝". $10 – 15	saucer . . . . $5 – 7
plate, 8¼". . . . .$8 – 12	sugar . . . . $10 – 15
plate, 6" . . . .$6 – 8	teapot. . . . . $40 – 50
platter, 15" oval. . . . . $30 – 40	paper price list . . . . $10 – 15

The Burlap pattern was decorated with a coarse, square-weave texture on the rims of the plates and covering the serving pieces. All the shapes were produced through 1978 except the 6" plates, which were discontinued during 1976.

Stangl used several colors and color combinations on the Burlap shapes. For advertising purposes, Texturware colors were given clever names. Sometimes the name of the color was stamped on the backs of Texturware pieces instead of, or in addition to, the pattern name. The Acorn color was dropped from advertising flyers in 1976, while Tangerine was never advertised at all. Following are Stangl's names for the Burlap colors and the underglaze colors used to produce them.

Burlap 10⅝" plate, Lime; cup & saucer, Tangerine; 10⅝" plate, Lemon.

Acorn — Tan used alone on the rims.

Almond — Beige with Walnut Brown edge-lining.

Honey Dew — Bamboo Green with Blue #95 edge-lining.

Lemon — Dark Yellow used alone on the rims.

Lime — Bamboo Green used alone on the rims.

Tangerine — Tan with Walnut Brown edge-lining.

Corduroy #5296

Introduced: 1976
Designer: Rudy Kleinebeckel
Shape Style: #5296 Coupe

Known Pieces:

bowl, 5¾" soup/cereal, rounded sides. $10 – 12	gravy underplate. . . . . $10 – 15
bowl, 5¾" soup/cereal, straight sides. $10 – 12	pitcher, 1 quart . . . . $30 – 40
bowl, 10" salad, rounded sides. . . . . . $35 – 45	plate, 12" chop . . . . $35 – 45
bowl, 8½" salad, straight sides . . . . . . $25 – 30	plate, 10⅝". $10 – 15
bowl, 8" vegetable, rounded sides . . . $25 – 30	plate, 8¼". . . . .$8 – 12
bowl, 7" vegetable, straight sides . . . . $20 – 25	plate, 6" . . . .$6 – 8
butter dish, covered . . . . $20 – 25	platter, 15" oval. . . . . $35 – 45
creamer, rounded side . . . . $10 – 15	salt, pepper; each . . . . $5 – 7
creamer, straight side . . . . $10 – 12	saucer . . . . $5 – 7
cup, rounded side. . . . .$6 – 8	sugar, rounded side. . . . . $10 – 15
cup, straight side. . . . .$6 – 8	sugar, straight side . . . . $10 – 15
gravy boat . . . . $15 – 20	teapot. . . . . $50 – 60
	paper price list . . . . $10 – 15

The Corduroy pattern was decorated with a textured herringbone design covering the entire surface of the plates and exteriors of the serving pieces. The underglaze color Walnut Brown was swirled over textured areas. This finish was described in advertising as Walnut.

Throughout 1976, Corduroy was produced on the same shapes as Burlap and Shantung. For January 1977, Corduroy was totally re-styled. The rounded bowl, cup, creamer, and sugar shapes were replaced with new, straight-sided cylindrical shapes. Also at this time the Corduroy shape assortment decreased. Dropped from the line were the 6" plate, covered butter dish, gravy boat, salt & pepper, pitcher, and teapot shapes. These pieces are rather challenging to find.

The Corduroy pattern was advertised as being available with the Walnut finish only. However, later pieces can be found with the Almond finish, which was Beige with edges lined with Walnut Brown.

Corduroy Almond 8" plate, cup & saucer, 12" chop plate, 10⅝" plate, creamer, sugar; Walnut 6" plate.

Shantung #5297

Shantung teapot, Azure; 10⅝" plate, Celery; soup/cereal bowl, Lavender; 6" plate, Chaff.

Introduced: 1976
Designer: Rudy Kleinebeckel
Shape Style: #5297 Rim

Known Pieces:

bowl, 5¾" soup/cereal	$10 – 12
bowl, 10" salad	$30 – 40
bowl, 8" vegetable	$20 – 30
butter dish, covered	$25 – 30
creamer	$10 – 12
cup	$6 – 8
gravy boat	$10 – 15
gravy underplate	$8 – 12
pitcher, 1 quart	$35 – 45
plate, 12" chop	$30 – 40
plate, 10⅝"	$10 – 15
plate, 8¼"	$8 – 12
plate, 6"	$6 – 8
platter, 15" oval	$30 – 40
salt, pepper; each	$5 – 7
saucer	$5 – 6
sugar	$10 – 15
teapot	$40 – 50
paper price list	$10 – 15

The Shantung motif featured the texture of coarsely woven Shantung silk. As with Burlap, the texture is on the rims of the plates and outside surfaces of the serving pieces. The Azure, Celery, and Chaff colors were available beginning in 1976. Lavender, however, was offered only for a short time during 1977. The Shantung colors were

Azure — Light blue on the texture and rim with deeper blue edge-lining

Celery — A pale beige/green on the rims.

Chaff — Beige used alone on the rims.

Lavender — Lavender with Blue #95 edge-lining.

Verdura #5298

Introduced: 1976
Shape Style: #5298 Rim

Known Pieces:

bowl, 5¾" soup/cereal	$10 – 15
bowl, 10" salad	$35 – 45
bowl, 8" vegetable	$25 – 35
butter dish, covered	$25 – 35
creamer	$10 – 15
cup	$8 – 10
gravy boat	$15 – 20
gravy underplate	$10 – 15
pitcher, 1 quart	$45 – 55
plate, 12" chop	$45 – 55
plate, 10⅝"	$15 – 20
plate, 8¼"	$10 – 15
plate, 6"	$8 – 10
platter, 15" oval	$45 – 55

Verdura covered sugar, manganese brown glaze; 8¼" plate, Blue #95; cup & saucer, Dark Yellow; 10⅝" plate, Tan.

salt, pepper; each	$6 – 7
saucer	$5 – 7
sugar	$15 – 20
teapot	$50 – 60
paper price list	$15 – 20

The short-lived Verdura pattern was decorated with bright colors on the rims, as well as entirely glazed with a rich, manganese brown glaze. Both decorations are equally rare. Although Verdura is usually stamped with the Texturware mark, this pattern was not promoted with Burlap, Corduroy, or Shantung. Verdura was discontinued before 1977, so is not easily found.

New Tulip #5325

Introduced: 1977
Shape Style: #3774 Coupe

Known Pieces:

bowl, brunch	$10 – 15	mug, stack	$20 – 25
bowl, fruit/dessert	$10 – 12	pitcher, 1½ pint	$30 – 40
bowl, 5¾" soup/cereal	$10 – 15	plate, 12" chop	$35 – 45
bowl, 10" salad	$35 – 45	plate, 10⅝"	$15 – 20
bowl, 8" vegetable	$20 – 30	plate, 8¼"	$10 – 15
canister, hexagon, large, 9"	$35 – 45	plate, 6"	$10 – 12
canister, hexagon, medium, 8"	$20 – 25	salt, pepper; each	$6 – 8
canister, hexagon, small, 5"	$15 – 20	saucer	$5 – 7
clock, round	$35 – 45	sugar	$10 – 15
clock, skillet shape	$50 – 60	teapot	$45 – 55
creamer	$10 – 15	tidbit	$8 – 12
cup	$8 – 10	tumbler	$10 – 12
		paper price list	$10 – 15

The New Tulip pattern used the same stencils as the Single Tulip pattern during 1974. New Tulip, when decorated with Dark Yellow, was distributed throughout the nation, while New

Tulip decorated with Blue #95 or Pink #160 were sold only at the Flemington Outlet. The blue and pink are more popular at this time than yellow New Tulip.

Indian Summer #5326

Introduced: 1977
Designer: Roy Hamilton
Made For: Tiffany & Co.
Shape Style: #5326 High-Rim

New Tulip tumbler, 10⅝" plate, 8¼" plate, cup & saucer, sugar, hexagon canisters medium and small.

Known Pieces:

bowl, soup/cereal 15oz.	$10 – 15
bowl, coupe soup	$10 – 12
bowl, 12" salad	$50 – 60
bowl, 10" salad	$30 – 40
bowl, 8" vegetable	$20 – 30
casserole, 5½qts.	$50 – 60
casserole, 3qts.	$35 – 45
creamer	$10 – 12
cup, 8oz.	$7 – 8
mug, 14oz.	$25 – 35
pitcher, large 48oz.	$35 – 45
pitcher, small 24oz.	$20 – 30
plate, 12" chop	$45 – 55
plate, 10½".	$20 – 25
plate, 7"	$10 – 15
saucer	$5 – 6
sugar, open	$10 – 15
teapot/beverage server	$45 – 60
dealer sign	$85 – 135
paper price list	$10 – 15

Indian Summer 12" chop plate, Blue Earth; creamer, Sand, 10½" plate, Earth; large pitcher, White Earth.

Tiffany supplied Stangl with Roy Hamilton's design for the Indian Summer pattern. Stangl then produced this pattern according to Tiffany's specifications. Indian Summer was available in two basic colors: Sand, a warm beige color, and Earth, a dark chocolate brown. These colors were applied as engobe to the white-bodied Indian Summer shapes. Certain pieces of Earth Indian Summer were available with either black and white or light blue and dark blue underglaze decoration. The decorated pieces were referred to as White Earth or Blue Earth. The decorated shapes were the plates, soup/cereal bowl, cup, mug, and large pitcher. Decorated pieces are relatively uncommon, and are usually priced a bit higher than plain Indian Summer pieces.

Maize-Ware #5327

Introduced: 1978
Designer: Rudy Kleinebeckel
Glaze Colors: Pioneer-Brown, Summer-Green, Harvest-Yellow, Winter-Tan

Maize-Ware #5327 (continued)

Known Pieces:

bowl, soup/cereal 15oz.	$10 – 15	plate, 10⅝".	$15 – 20
bowl, 8" vegetable	$20 – 30	plate, 8¼".	$10 – 15
bowl, 7½" brunch	$15 – 20	salt, pepper, corn; each	$8 – 12
butter dish, covered	$15 – 20	saucer	$5 – 6
creamer	$10 – 15	sugar	$20 – 25
cup, 8oz.	$8 – 12	tile, 7½" round	$15 – 20
mug, 16oz.	$20 – 30	dealer sign	$80 – 110
plate, 12" chop	$40 – 50	paper price list	$10 – 15

Stangl's corn-shaped Maize-Ware pattern was decorated with solid-color glazes in decorator shades popular during the late 1970s. These glazes enhanced the well-executed modeling of this pattern.

Maize-Ware was advertised as an informal dinnerware suitable for outdoor or casual dining. This colorful pattern was becoming popular and would have been very successful had Stangl continued in business beyond 1978.

*Maize-Ware soup/cereal bowl, Summer-Green; 10⅝"
plate, Pioneer-Brown; cup, Winter-Tan; butter dish, Harvest-Yellow; 8¼" plate, Winter-Tan; mug, Pioneer-Brown.*

Kiddieware Patterns 1941 – 1978

Stangl began advertising children's patterns during the 1950s as "Kiddieware," and "Kiddie Sets." The term "baby set" was frequently used by Stangl employees when referring to these items. Today the name "Kiddieware" is collectively used for this group of Stangl products.

Stangl's first Kiddieware sets were introduced during the early 1940s and were produced exclusively for Frederik Lunning. Each set included a plate, cereal bowl, and cup. In 1950, two-piece sets consisting of a three-part divided dish and cup were introduced.

Stangl began producing Kiddieware bearing the Stangl trademark in 1953 after the Lunning contract ended. Throughout the 1950s and 1960s, Stangl Kiddieware was exceptionally popular and new patterns were introduced on a regular basis. During the 1960s, non-carved items with Kiddieware motifs were made specifically for the tourist business at the Flemington Outlet.

Nearly all of Stangl's Kiddieware was produced on the characteristic red-clay body until the end of 1974, at which time Stangl's dinnerware body was changed to white-colored clay. Although carving was tried on the white-bodied pieces, many of the Kiddieware patterns did not adapt well without the underlying red clay to give depth to the designs. Subsequently, by January 1975 all but four Kiddieware patterns were discontinued. The remaining four patterns were produced on the white body until Stangl's close in 1978.

To illustrate the development of Stangl's Kiddieware patterns, they are presented in their order of introduction.

1941 Patterns

"Lunning Dog"
10" plate.

Made For: Frederik Lunning, Inc.

"Lunning Dog"

bowl, cereal	$300 − 350
cup	$200 − 225
plate, 10"	$350 − 450

The "Lunning Dog" pattern seems to have been Stangl's first Kiddieware pattern. The use of the #1902 shape is unusual because this shape was normally reserved for Della-Ware patterns made for Fisher, Bruce & Company. "Lunning Dog" is an extremely rare pattern.

1942 Patterns

Designer: Kay Hackett
Made For: Frederik Lunning, Inc.

Little Bo Peep		*Peter Rabbit*	
bowl, cereal	$110 − 130	bowl, cereal	$110 − 130
cup, #3434	$80 − 110	cup, #3434	$80 − 110
plate, 9"	$100 − 145	plate, 9"	$100 − 145

These two patterns were produced exclusively for Frederik Lunning until 1953. During that year the Lunning contract ended and some of the Lunning patterns were slightly redesigned and re-introduced bearing the Stangl trademark. The shapes used for these, and nearly all subsequent Kiddieware patterns, were #3434 9" plate, cereal bowl, and baby cup shapes. The #3434 baby cup shape was used until 1953 when it was replaced with the #3826 straight-sided baby cup shape.

The original colors used on Lunning's Little Bo Peep were Blue #95 and Yellow. Pennsylvania Dutch Green was the predominant color on the rim of Peter Rabbit. As with all patterns made for Lunning, seconds usually had the Lunning mark blacked out.

Little Bo Peep, Lunning 9" plate, #3434 baby cup;
Peter Rabbit, Lunning 9" plate, #3434 baby cup.

1946 Patterns

Designers: Cleo Salerno, Bea Jackson
Made For: Frederik Lunning, Inc.

Goldilocks #3764		*Little Boy Blue #3765*	
bowl, cereal	$200 – 250	bowl, cereal	$120 – 140
cup, #3434	$175 – 200	cup, #3434	$80 – 110
plate, 9"	$200 – 250	plate, 9"	$110 – 135

Goldilocks (Bea Jackson) and Little Boy Blue (Cleo Salerno) were both originally Frederik Lunning exclusives. These patterns were decorated primarily with French Green, which makes them quite dark when compared to Stangl's later Kiddieware patterns.

Goldilocks' appearance is that of typical 1940s teenagers. Her hair style, jumper, and bobby-socks certainly link her to that era. The Little Boy Blue pattern was based on the familiar nursery rhyme of the same name. In 1946 both these patterns retailed for $2.25 per three-piece set.

In 1953 Little Boy Blue was re-designed, brightened with Blue #95 and offered under the Stangl trade-mark. Unfortunately, Goldilocks appeared too dated for the 1950s and was discontinued in 1952.

Goldilocks, Lunning 9" plate, cereal bowl; Little Boy Blue, Lunning 9" plate, cereal bowl.

1949 Patterns

Designer: Kay Hackett
Made For: Frederik Lunning, Inc.

Musical Mugs #3807 without music box:		*Musical Mugs #3807 with music box:*	
Mary Had a Little Lamb	$150 – 225	Mary Had a Little Lamb	$300 – 350
Jack and Jill	$150 – 225	Jack and Jill	$300 – 350
Toy Soldiers	$150 – 225	Toy Soldiers	$300 – 350
Peter Rabbit	$300 – 400	Peter Rabbit	$500 – 600

Stangl's Kiddieware musical mugs were made for Frederik Lunning only and were produced from 1949 until 1952. Lunning installed the music box movements in New York then distributed these items to various gift and jewelry stores around the country. Therefore, red-bodied mugs can be found with either hand-brushed or sprayed engobe. Kay Hackett designed the motifs and the unique mug shape as well. The Peter Rabbit motif was discontinued early, and is quite rare.

During 1953 Stangl produced #3807 Musical Mugs on both a vitreous china body and white earthenware body. The Mary Had a Little Lamb, Jack and Jill, and Toy Soldiers motifs were used on these mugs. The designs, however, were decorated in pastel, over-glaze colors instead of Stangl's usual underglaze colors. White-bodied and china-bodied #3807 Musical Mugs are far more difficult to find than red-bodied musical mugs.

The #3807 Musical Mugs are unmarked, as the music box in the bottom would have hidden any markings. Many of these mugs found today no longer contain the music box. Mugs with the original music box still intact are rare but available. The tunes they play are Mary Had a Little Lamb, Jack and Jill, and March of the Toys.

Lunning Musical Mugs; Toy Soldiers, Jack and Jill, and Mary Had a Little Lamb.

1950 Patterns

Designer: Kay Hackett
Made For: Frederik Lunning, Inc.

Bluebird #3827
cup, #3826 . . . . $200 – 225
divided dish . . . . $300 – 350

Our Barnyard Friends #3828
cup, #3826 . . . . $45 – 55
divided dish . . . . $80 – 95

Mealtime Special #3829
cup, #3826 . . . . $45 – 55
divided dish . . . . $75 – 95

Bluebird cup and divided dish.

In 1950 the three-section #3819 divided dish and #3826 straight-sided baby cup shapes were introduced and sold together as two-piece sets. The three motifs introduced on these shapes were made for Frederik Lunning until 1953. During 1953 the Bluebird pattern was discontinued and Our Barnyard Friends and Mealtime Special became Stangl patterns. The pieces made for Lunning usually have brushed engobe and the Lunning trademark.

Our Barnyard Friends was available until the late 1960s. Mealtime Special continued in production on the red body until 1974, and was made on the white body for a very short time afterward. Mealtime Special was discontinued by 1975.

Bluebird divided dish; Our Barnyard Friends cup, divided dish; Mealtime Special cup, divided dish.

1953 Patterns

Designer: Kay Hackett

Peter Rabbit #3882
bowl, cereal . . . . $110 – 130
cup, #3826 . . . . $75 – 90
plate, 9" . . . . $150 – 175

Little Bo Peep #3883
bowl, cereal . . . . $90 – 110
cup, #3826 . . . . $60 – 70
plate, 9" . . . . $80 – 100

Little Boy Blue #3765
bowl, cereal . . . . $80 – 95
cup, #3826 . . . . $50 – 65
plate, 9" . . . . $75 – 90

Once Stangl no longer produced patterns for Frederik Lunning, these three Kiddieware designs were re-worked and offered as Stangl patterns. The principal changes made to these patterns were the colors and the shape of the cups. The original #3434 baby cup shape was replaced with the streamlined #3826 baby cup shape.

The colors were brightened and the wide bands on the rims were narrowed and moved to the shoulders of the plates. A narrow Orange stripe was put on the edges of the bowls and plates. Peter Rabbit's Pennsylvania Dutch Green was changed to Willow Green, and the Blue #95 on Little Bo Peep was replaced with the more feminine Pink #193. All of the French Green on Little Boy Blue was changed to Light Blue and Blue #95. These simple modifications gave the designs a cheery aspect that was lacking in the Lunning versions. As a result of the changes, these three patterns became very popular throughout the 1950s and 1960s.

Peter Rabbit was discontinued in 1959, but Little Bo Peep and Little Boy Blue were both produced through 1974. Since neither of these motifs readily adapted to production on the white body, they were discontinued early in 1975.

Little Boy Blue cereal bowl, 9" plate, cup; Peter Rabbit cup, 9" plate;
Little Bo Peep cereal bowl, 9" plate, cup.

1955 Patterns

Designer: Kay Hackett

Indian Campfire #3916
bowl, cereal . . . . $125 – 145
cup . . . . $80 – 95
plate, 9" . . . . $180 – 200
plate, grill 9" . . . . $375 – 400

Pony Trail #3917
bowl, cereal . . . . $125 – 145
cup . . . . $80 – 95
plate, 9" . . . . $180 – 200

Ranger Boy #3918

bowl, cereal . . . . $125 – 145
cup . . . . $75 – 95
plate, 9" . . . . $180 – 200

Kitten Capers #3919

cup . . . . $50 – 60
divided dish . . . . $100 – 125

Playful Pups #3920

cup . . . . $50 – 60
divided dish . . . . $80 – 110

The Western television shows so popular during the mid-1950s were the inspiration for the Indian Campfire, Pony Trail, and Ranger Boy patterns. The antics of household pets were the basis for Kitten Capers and Playful Pups. All of these patterns were quite popular throughout the 1950s and 1960s. Ranger Boy and Pony Trail were produced through the 1960s. Indian Campfire and Playful Pups were discontinued on May 8, 1968. Kitten Capers was the only pattern of this group produced after 1968, but it, too, was discontinued in 1974. During the 1960s, grill plates with the Indian Campfire motif were produced for the Flemington Outlet.

*Indian Campfire cup, 9" plate, cereal bowl; Pony Trail cup, 9" plate, cereal bowl;
Ranger Boy cup, 9" plate, cereal bowl.*

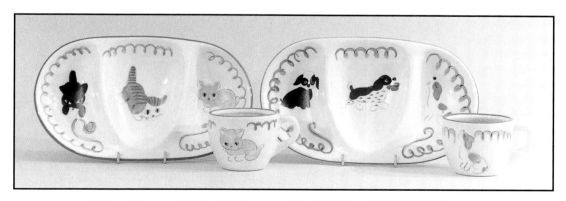

Kitten Capers divided dish, cup; Playful Pups divided dish, cup.

1956 Patterns

Designer: Kay Hackett

ABC #3947

cup . . . . $50 – 60
divided dish . . . . $80 – 95

Five Little Pigs #3948

cup . . . . $140 – 155
divided dish . . . . $210 – 250

Cat and the Fiddle #3949

bowl, cereal	$210 – 250
cup	$185 – 210
plate, 9"	$250 – 300

Woman in the Shoe #3950

bowl, cereal	$210 – 250
cup	$185 – 210
plate, 9"	$250 – 300

Mary Quite Contrary #3951

bowl, cereal	$140 – 155
cup	$100 – 125
plate, 9"	$185 – 230

Nursery rhymes and letters of the alphabet were the basis for the 1956 Kiddieware patterns. Five Little Pigs, Cat and the Fiddle, and Woman in the Shoe were all discontinued by 1963, making these patterns particularly difficult to find. Mary Quite Contrary was advertised as late as 1968, but still is not a common pattern.

ABC was in constant production from 1956 through 1978. White-bodied versions produced after 1974 were produced on the straight-sided #5287 Town & Country cup shape that was used with Kiddieware patterns at that time.

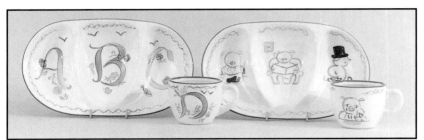

ABC divided dish, cup; Five Little Pigs divided dish, cup.

Cat and the Fiddle cup, 9" plate; Woman in the Shoe cereal bowl, 9" plate, cup; Mary Quite Contrary cereal bowl, 9" plate, cup.

1957 Patterns

Designer: Kay Hackett

Ginger Boy #3958

bowl, cereal	$165 – 185
cup	$110 – 135
plate, 9"	$200 – 250

Ginger Girl #3959

bowl, cereal	$165 – 185
cup	$110 – 135
plate, 9"	$200 – 250

Cookie Twins #3960

cup	$140 – 150
divided dish	$200 – 250

The cookie-like motifs of these three patterns were similar to a motif that had been designed for a tidbit cookie plate made for Nieman-Marcus. When originally introduced, Ginger Boy and Ginger Girl were decorated with 22 karat gold luster accents in the manner of Jewelled Christmas Tree. These patterns with gold trim retailed for $10.00 per three-piece set. There was no demand for gold decorated Kiddieware at such a high price, so by the end of 1957, these patterns were produced without gold decoration. Ginger Boy and Ginger Girl without gold trim then retailed for $5.00 per set, which was the standard price for Stangl's Kiddieware sets during the late 1950s.

Although appealing, Ginger Boy, Ginger Girl, and Cookie Twins were discontinued by 1963 and are now difficult to find.

Ginger Boy cup, 9" plate; Ginger Girl cereal bowl, 9" plate, cup; Cookie Twins divided dish, cup.

1958 Patterns

Designer: Kay Hackett

Pink Fairy #4044
bowl, cereal . . . . $130 – 150
cup . . . . $120 – 130
plate, 9" . . . . $150 – 175

Blue Elf #4045
bowl, cereal . . . . $200 – 225
cup . . . . $150 – 165
plate, 9" . . . . $200 – 225

Little Quackers #4046
bowl, cereal . . . . $110 – 135
cup . . . . $70 – 95
plate, 9" . . . . $110 – 130

Ducky Dinner #4047
cup . . . . $80 – 100
divided dish . . . . $115 – 140

Bunny Lunch #4048
cup . . . . $150 – 165
divided dish . . . . $180 – 220

Inspired by children's poetry, Kay Hackett's Blue Elf and Pink Fairy patterns portray these fantasy characters seeking shelter from a shower. The Blue Elf pattern was discontinued shortly after introduction, and is now extremely rare. Pink Fairy was in production through the late 1960s and is also not easy to find.

The Little Quackers, Ducky Dinner, and Bunny Lunch patterns feature baby duck and rabbit motifs. Bunny Lunch was a very short-lived pattern and is as uncommon as Blue Elf. Little Quackers and Ducky Dinner were evidently more popular. Ducky Dinner was in production through 1968; while Little Quackers continued to be available until the close of Stangl in 1978.

Pink Fairy cup, 9" plate, cereal bowl; Blue Elf cup, 9" plate; Little Quackers cup, 9" plate, cereal bowl.

Ducky Dinner divided dish, cup; Bunny Lunch divided dish.

1960 Patterns

Flying Saucer #5018	*Pink Carousel #5020*
bowl, cereal . . . . $275 – 300	bowl, cereal . . . . $100 – 120
cup . . . . $225 – 250	cup . . . . $80 – 110
plate, 9" . . . . $375 – 410	plate, 9" . . . . $125 – 140
Blue Carousel #5019	*Carousel (Gold)*
bowl, cereal . . . . $100 – 120	bowl, cereal . . . . $150 – 175
cup . . . . $80 – 110	cup . . . . $120 – 140
plate, 9" . . . . $125 – 140	plate, 9" . . . . $225 – 250

Flying Saucer was a lively design that featured a juvenile astronaut piloting a cup and saucer through space. This pattern was certainly reflecting the nation's eye on the space program at that time. The skillful use of the colors Blue #95, Pink #160, and Orange give a balanced effect to the Flying Saucer motif. The Flying Saucer pattern was discontinued in 1963 and is quite uncommon.

The bright Blue Carousel and Pink Carousel patterns were designed by Shirley Thatcher Spaciano. These patterns were decorated with bands of Dark Turquoise and Pink #193 respectively. In 1966, as a cost-saving measure, the Pink and Blue Carousel patterns were replaced with a single pattern decorated with bands of Old Gold. This Old Gold decorated pattern was simply called Carousel, and was discontinued altogether on May 8, 1968.

Flying Saucer cereal bowl, 9" plate, cup.

Blue Carousel cereal bowl, 9" plate, cup; Pink Carousel cereal bowl, 9" plate, cup; Carousel (gold) 9" plate, cereal bowl.

1961, Warming Dish Patterns

Alphabet #5085. . . . . $325 – 375
Duck #5090 . . . . $325 – 375
Rabbit #5091 . . . . $350 – 400

The warming dish shape was introduced in May of 1961. The decorations used were based on previously popular Kiddieware motifs. Usually, Stangl cruet stoppers are found with these dishes, but plastic stoppers were available as well. The warming dish shape was unpopular and too costly so very few were produced.

Alphabet warming dish; Duck warming dish.

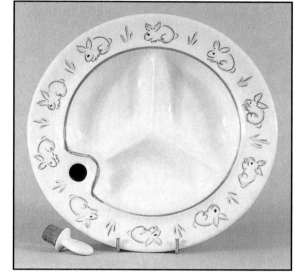

Rabbit warming dish.

1962 Patterns

Humpty Dumpty #5118 (Pink)
bowl, cereal . . . . $180 – 210
cup . . . . $130 – 150
plate, 9" . . . . $225 – 250

Humpty Dumpty #5118 (Blue)
bowl, cereal . . . . $125 – 145
cup . . . . $90 – 110
plate, 9" . . . . $180 – 200

Humpty Dumpty #5118 (Green)
bowl, cereal . . . . $110 – 130
cup . . . . $80 – 100
plate, 9" . . . . $135 – 150

Mother Goose #5119 (Pink)
bowl, cereal . . . . $180 – 210
cup . . . . $160 – 180
plate, 9" . . . . $275 – 300

Mother Goose #5119 (Blue)
bowl, cereal . . . . $180 – 210
cup . . . . $160 – 180
plate, 9" . . . . $275 – 300

These nursery rhyme patterns were originally available in pink or blue. Humpty Dumpty was decorated with dark Pink #167, Mother Goose with Pink #193. Dark Turquoise was the color used on the blue versions of both Mother Goose and Humpty Dumpty. In 1966, the pink and blue Humpty Dumpty patterns were replaced with non gender-specific Victoria Green decorated Humpty Dumpty. The green Humpty Dumpty pattern was available until the early 1970s. The Mother Goose pattern was discontinued shortly after introduction and is particularly difficult to find.

Humpty Dumpty (pink) 9" plate; Humpty Dumpty (blue) cup, cereal bowl; Humpty Dumpty (green) 9" plate; Mother Goose (pink) 9" plate; Mother Goose (blue) 9" plate.

1963 Patterns

Bunny #5128		cup	$125 – 150
bowl, fruit	$125 – 150	plate, 8"	$220 – 265

Bunny 8" plate, cup, fruit bowl.

Bunny was an inexpensive adaptation of the earlier Peter Rabbit pattern. The decoration was simplified and the colors were brightened by making Orange the primary rim color. The Bunny motif was adapted to the smaller fruit bowl and 8" plate shapes so that this pattern could retail for $3.45 per set. The retail price for a standard size Kiddieware set with a cup, 9" plate, and cereal bowl was $4.95 in 1963. Bunny is a scarce pattern with plates seemingly the most difficult to find.

1964 Patterns

Designer: Beatrice Grover
Made For: Tiffany & Co.

Tiffany Wildlife #5150		cup	$180 – 220
bowl, coupe soup	$260 – 300	plate, 9"	$300 – 350

Tiffany supplied Stangl with Beatrice Grover's designs for the Wildlife pattern. The colorful, hand-painted animal motifs are highly detailed. Particularly novel is the Victoria Green frog hand painted in the bottom of each cup. This frog was very important to Tiffany and was integral to the development of the pattern. The intricate motifs required the decorators to be much more exacting than what was required on most Kiddieware patterns. Because of the added labor, Wildlife was quite costly.

As with Tiffany's Caughley pattern, all Wildlife pieces were covered entirely with engobe. Tiffany desired that none of Stangl's red-clay body to show. Tiffany also required the coupe soup shape be used instead of the cereal bowl shape in order to accommodate all of the Wildlife motif without alterations.

Due to Stangl's contract with Tiffany, Wildlife was the first Kiddieware pattern produced after the fire in 1965. Although Wildlife continued in active production until 1970, since it was much more expensive, very little Wildlife was actually produced during that time.

Tiffany Wildlife coupe soup bowl, 9" plate, cup.

Tiffany Wildlife interior of cup showing hand-painted frog motif.

1965 Patterns

Wizard of Oz #5159
bowl, cereal . . . . $600 – 650
cup . . . . $400 – 450
plate, 9" . . . . $850 – 1000

Circus Clown #5175
bowl, cereal . . . . $130 – 150
cup . . . . $100 – 125
plate, 9" . . . . $165 – 180

Ginger Cat #5176
bowl, cereal . . . . $180 – 200
cup . . . . $160 – 180
plate, 9" . . . . $200 – 250
plate, grill 9" . . . . $400 – 450

Stangl's Wizard of Oz Kiddieware pattern was developed in response to the tremendous popularity of the yearly television telecasts of MGM's 1939 musical *The Wizard of Oz*. Stangl's Dorothy and Scarecrow motifs were based loosely on the Judy Garland and Ray Bolger characters. The Cowardly Lion and Tin Woodsman, however, more closely resemble the W. W. Denslow illustrations used in L. Frank Baum's original book version, *The Wonderful Wizard of Oz*.

Wizard of Oz was a very short-lived Kiddieware pattern. At this time, Stangl's Wizard of Oz pieces are in great demand.

The Circus Clown and Ginger Cat patterns were introduced on August 1, 1965. Both of these were designed by Kay Hackett. Circus Clown and Ginger Cat were produced for several years before being discontinued in 1974. Circus Clown was re-introduced on the white body in 1975. Instead of having a green rim, the white-bodied Circus Clown was available decorated with either Pink #193 or Dark Turquoise rims.

top left: Wizard of Oz 9" plate, cup, cereal bowl.

top right: Ginger Cat 9" grill plate.

left: Circus Clown cup, 9" plate, cereal bowl; Ginger Cat 9" plate, cup.

1968 Patterns

Woman-in-the-Shoe #5208	
bowl, cereal	$130 – 150
cup	$100 – 125
plate, 9"	$180 – 220

Mother Hubbard #5209	
bowl, cereal	$125 – 150
cup	$80 – 100
plate, 9"	$175 – 200

Jack-in-the-Box #5210	
bowl, cereal	$125 – 150
cup	$80 – 100
plate, 9"	$175 – 200

Woman-in-the-Shoe, Mother Hubbard, and Jack-in-the-Box were the last hand-carved Kiddieware patterns introduced by Stangl. The #5208 Woman-in-the-Shoe pattern is vastly different from the #3950 Woman in the Shoe pattern introduced in 1956. The Mother Hubbard pattern depicts scenes of the Mother Hubbard nursery rhyme, while Jack-in-the-Box shows a comical Jack-in-the-box toy. These three patterns were actively produced until they were discontinued in 1974.

Woman-in-the-Shoe cup, 9" plate, cereal bowl; Mother Hubbard cup, 9" plate, cereal bowl; Jack-in-the-Box cup, 9" plate, cereal bowl.

Flemington Exclusives

Introduced: Late 1960s
Made For: Flemington Outlet

Known Pieces:			
feeding dish	$250 – 300	grill plate, 9"	$300 – 400
		tile, 5½"	$150 – 185

The Flemington grill plates and feeding dishes were decorated with various motifs designed to complement several Kiddieware patterns. Grill plates with Lamb and Indian Campfire motifs are the most commonly found. Ginger Cat grill plates are much more elusive and desirable. Grill plates and feeding dishes with the Lamb decoration were available with Victoria Green, Pink #160, or Blue #95 bands on the rims. As with most Flemington Exclusives, these were red-bodied items, but the motifs were not carved.

The 5½" tiles were actually made from damaged plates that had the rims cut away and edges glazed. Similar items were made with standard dinnerware patterns.

Lamb Feeding Dishes with Pink #160, Victoria Green, and Blue #95 bands.

Ginger Cat Grill plate.

1970 Personalized Kiddie Set Patterns

Blocks pattern		*Ducks pattern*	
bowl, cereal	$150 – 200	bowl, cereal	$150 – 200
cup	$100 – 150	cup	$100 – 150
plate	$150 – 200	plate	$150 – 200

The Personalized Kiddie Sets were marketed through the infants and juvenile departments of many leading department stores, with some orders generating at the Flemington Outlet. These sets were produced at the Trenton factory then shipped to the store from whence the order originated. Throughout their production, personalized sets retailed for $1.25 to $1.50 more than standard Kiddieware three-piece sets.

The motifs offered were Blocks or Ducks. Both patterns were available decorated with either Blue #95 or Pink #193. The Personalized Kiddie Sets were advertised as having the child's name on the plate only. The cup was decorated with "All mine!" and the cereal bowl with "All gone!" The set in the photo with the name "Alaina Christine" on all three pieces is very unusual.

When originally introduced in 1970, the Personalized Kiddieware patterns were furnished on 8" plates and Ducks was the only motif offered. The Blocks pattern was introduced in 1972. During 1973 the Personalized Kiddieware plate became 9" but returned to 8" again in 1974. In 1975 with the introduction of white-bodied ware, the plate size was changed to 8¼".

Personalized Kiddie Sets; Ducks "Elsie Alexandre" 8¼" plate; boy Blocks "Kris" cereal bowl and 8" plate; girl Blocks "Alaina Christine" cup, 8" plate and cereal bowl.

1975 White-Bodied Patterns

Circus Clown (Blue)
bowl, soup/cereal . . . . $75 – 90
cup . . . . $50 – 70
plate, 8¼" . . . . $100 – 125

Circus Clown (Pink)
bowl, soup/cereal . . . . $75 – 90
cup . . . . $50 – 70
plate, 8¼" . . . . $100 – 125

ABC
cup . . . . $50 – 70
divided dish . . . . $80 – 100

Little Quackers
bowl, soup/cereal . . . . $75 – 90
cup . . . . $50 – 70
plate, 9¼" . . . . $80 – 100
plate, 8¼" . . . . $80 – 100

Between the end of 1974 and the beginning of 1975, Stangl began to produce all dinnerware patterns, including Kiddieware, on a white stoneware body. For several months during that time, the following patterns were made on the white body: ABC, Circus Clown, Ginger Cat, Humpty Dumpty, Jack-in-the-Box, Kitten Capers, Little Bo Peep, Little Boy Blue, Little Quackers, Mealtime Special, Mother Hubbard, Woman-in-the-Shoe, and Personalized Kiddieware. By January 1975 nearly all of those patterns were discontinued. The only Kiddieware patterns remaining in production on the white body until 1978 were ABC, Circus Clown, and Little Quackers.

Several changes were made to some of the shapes of the 1975 introductions. The cup was changed from the old #3826 rounded Kiddieware cup to the straight-sided #5287 Town & Country cup shape. The cereal bowl was changed to the 20 ounce soup/cereal bowl shape. The Little Quackers pattern was available on 8¼" and 9¼" rim, and 8¼" coupe shape plates. Circus Clown was produced on the 8¼" coupe shape plate.

In production for three years, the later white-bodied Kiddieware patterns are not very common but not avidly collected at this time either.

Circus Clown (blue) cup; Circus Clown (pink) 8¼" plate; Circus Clown (blue) soup/cereal bowl; Little Quackers 9¼" plate; ABC divided dish; ABC cup.

Kiddieware Samples

As with Stangl's dinnerware lines, samples of Kiddieware trial patterns were frequently produced. Samples of familiar patterns can be found with variations in color or motif. Samples of patterns never produced, however, are usually the most interesting.

Sample pieces were sometimes marked "Sample," marked with the designer's initials, or not marked at all. A standardized value structure for Kiddieware samples is nearly impossible to determine. The value of Kiddieware and dinnerware samples rests solely on the desirability of the motifs depicted. Some samples may fetch hundreds at auction, while others may not be salable at fifty dollars.

right: Kay Hackett's Circus Clown sample with Dark Turquoise band; Kay Hackett's Porpoise sample cup and 9" plate.

below right: Bowl with Wolf at the Door motif; bowl with Fox motif.

below left: Kay Hackett's samples for Ginger Cat with dark Turquoise Bands.

Kiddieware Paper Price Lists

Kiddieware paper price list. . . . . $40 – 75

Price lists for the Kiddieware patterns were printed from the 1950s through the 1970s. The price lists were usually full color and ranged from 7" x 9" single sheets to 8½" x 11" bi-fold sheets. Kiddieware price lists rarely listed single patterns but usually showed all Kiddieware patterns available at the time the list was printed. Stangl's Kiddieware price lists are very collectible. Values for these price lists vary, depending on the patterns listed and size of the sheet.

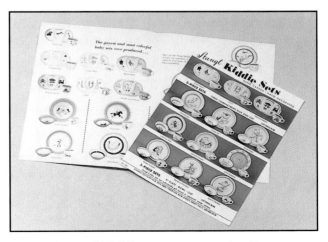

Several Kiddieware paper price lists.

Samples and Test Pieces

Color and Glaze Tests

One to Nine Colors Tested		Ten or More Colors Tested	
plate, 10"	$45 – 100	plate, 12½"	$200 – 250
plate, 9"	$35 – 70	plate, 11"	$200 – 250
plate, 8"	$35 – 55	plate, 10"	$100 – 200
plate, 6"	$10 – 20	plate, 9"	$80 – 125
saucer	$8 – 15		

Stangl's lab produced color tests as quality control devices to determine whether new batches of underglaze color would match colors already in use. Color tests were usually done on saucers or 6" plates, although larger plates and hollow ware pieces were also used. Color test pieces were decorated with swirls, bands, or abstract brush strokes and always had information on the front or back pertaining to the glaze or color being tested. An "S" on the front of some pieces indicated a test sample. Larger sized glaze and color tests with interesting designs or multiple colors are always valued higher than small single-color pieces.

Stangl's glaze tests were similar in appearance and function to the color tests. Glaze tests were often marked with the date and glaze identification numbers or a "Lab Test" backstamp.

top left: Group of color tests 8" 3-color test, saucer 1-color test, 9" 2-color test, saucer 4-color test, 8" 3-color test.

top right: Typical color test markings.

above: Color test 10" plate with 31 colors.

right: Lab test rubber-stamp mark.

Carvers' and Decorators' Samples

Carvers' samples and decorators' samples were another quality control device utilized by Stangl. Carvers' samples were carved but undecorated examples of each piece in each active pattern and were used in the carving department as a guide to double check the work of the carvers. Decorators' samples served the same function, but were accurately decorated and were employed in the decorating department. These samples will have the words "Sample," "Carvers' Sample," or "Carving Sample" and the name or number of the pattern carved on the front or side of the piece.

For most patterns, carvers' sample coffee pots, teapots, and sugar bowls had no lids. Carvers' sample lids were made only if the lid had carved decoration. By the mid-1950s, holes were drilled in the smaller sample pieces in an effort to prevent theft.

Carvers' samples are generally valued at up to double the value of the same piece in the pattern represented, while decorator's samples have sold for many times the retail value of the represented production item.

Carvers' samples; Fruit ½ pint pitcher, Wildwood 10" plate, Golden Harvest/Pink Lily coffee pot.

Decorators' samples; Blueberry teapot, Mountain Laurel 12" chop plate, Jonquil 6" plate.

Prototype Samples

In order to keep abreast of decorating trends and popular taste, Stangl was constantly developing new dinnerware patterns and motifs. There was at least one designer employed at the pottery at all times. Stangl's more leading designers from the 1930s – 1970s were Gerald Ewing, Cleo Salerno, Ethel Kennedy, Kay Hackett, Irene Sarnecki, Rose Herbeck, and Sandra Ward.

The designer's primary duty was to develop new dinnerware patterns, always keeping abreast of trends in popular taste. Days were spent developing rough drafts in pencil, ink, and tempera paints. Once a promising prototype motif was worked out, it was tried on a 9" or 10" sample plate and shown to Martin Stangl for approval. Cleo Salerno and Rose Herbeck have each stated that they were required to furnish two prototype sample plates per week for Mr. Stangl. Nearly 90 percent of these sample patterns were never produced. Unused samples were not thrown out, however. Any item not necessary for daily production was packed and sent to the Flemington Outlet to be sold. Consequently, many of Stangl's prototypes and tests are able to be preserved at this time.

During the few times there were no designers employed, Martin Stangl held design contests. All Stangl employees were given the opportunity to develop dinnerware designs. These were usually submitted as sketches or watercolors. If a design proved promising it was made into a 9" or 10" sample plate. Employees that developed designs that qualified for production, were rewarded whatever prize Mr. Stangl deemed suitable.

Often design samples were not marked. Occasionally sample plates have the word "sample" carved or painted on the back. A "SAMPLE" rubber stamp was available but was generally used on production pieces for the sales representatives to show to prospective buyers, not on prototype samples.

Designers occasionally identified their samples with their own unique initials. Kay Hackett used a lower case "k"; Rose Herbeck marked her pieces with "HR"; Irene Sarnecki used "ImS" on her samples; and Sandra Ward pieces are marked "WARD," "W," or "S. W."

A standardized value structure for prototype samples is nearly impossible to determine. The value of dinnerware prototype samples rests solely on the desirability of the motifs depicted. While one sample piece may reach a high bid in the hundreds at auction, another may be nearly unsalable due to the poor design portrayed. Even though many sample plates are one of a kind, they generally do not command very high prices.

Sample underglaze stamp, late 1940s – early 1950s.

1940s sample plates, Ethel Kennedy.

1940s sample plates, unknown designers.

Kay Hackett's "k." initial.

1950s sample plates, Kay Hackett.

282

1960s sample plates, Irene Sarnecki.

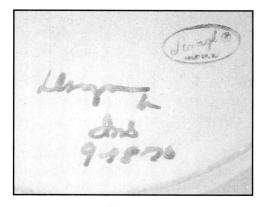

Irene Sarnecki's "ImS" signature.

1970s sample plates, Rose Herbeck.

Rose Herbeck's "HR" cipher.

1970s sample plates, Sandra Ward.

1970s sample plates: 9" plate with fired-on overglaze transfer motif; 10⅝" plate with silk-screen and hand-painted decoration; 10⅝" plate with underglaze transfer decoration.

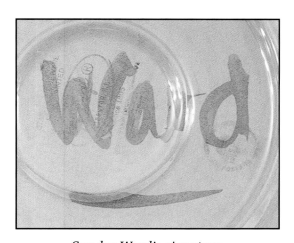

Sandra Ward's signature.

Novelty Salt and Pepper Shakers

Beginning in 1939 Stangl produced various salt and pepper shakers in novelty shapes. Most were glazed with the solid-color or Terra Rose glazes used at that time. Some shakers, however, were hand painted to coordinate with certain dinnerware patterns. In 1942 the cowboy and sailor salt and pepper shapes were dubbed Ranger Dudes and Jolly Tars and advertised independently from the Ranger and Newport dinnerware patterns

In 1943, two more novelty salt and pepper sets were introduced. One set was shaped like a Pennsylvania Dutch boy and girl and the other set was tulips. These were available with solid-color glazes, Terra Rose glazes, or hand-painted decoration.

The next novelty shakers came about during the early 1950s when the Golf Ball shakers were made for the Flemington Outlet. Golf Ball shakers were created from the same golf ball shape that decorated the Golfer Sportsman ashtrays.

In spring 1965, apple-shape salt and pepper shakers were introduced with the Apple Delight dinnerware pattern and the #3298 Daisy salt and pepper shakers were re-introduced decorated to match the Blue Daisy pattern. The Apple and Daisy shakers were both short-lived products; neither were produced after the fire in August 1965.

During the late 1960s, the Hen, Rooster, and Pig novelty salt and pepper shaker shapes were produced for the Flemington Outlet. The 1960s Hen and Rooster shakers used less color than the 1939 versions. Only the base (Pomona Green), eyes (Black), beak (Orange), and comb (Pink #167) were decorated. The Pigs were decorated with either Black or Pink #160 spots. Often the Pig, Hen, and Rooster shakers were not marked. These pieces relied on the "Stangl" rubber stopper to identify them as Stangl products.

The last figural-novelty salt and pepper shakers introduced by Stangl were the corn-shaped shakers that were part of the Maize-Ware dinnerware pattern. Introduced in 1978, these shakers were available in the solid-color glazes Pioneer-Brown, Summer-Green, Harvest-Yellow, and Winter-Tan.

1939 Introductions:	Solid Color	Hand Painted
Rooster #3285, pepper, each	$50 – 65	$90 – 125
Hen #3286, salt, each	$50 – 65	$90 – 125
Lemon #3290, pepper, each	$20 – 25	$40 – 50
Lemon #3291, salt, each; matches dinnerware pattern	$20 – 25	$40 – 50
Tropic #3338.		

Rooster #3285 and Hen #3286 with hand-painted colors, Rooster #3285 in Persian Yellow glaze.

1939 Introductions (continued):   *Solid Color*   *Hand Painted*

Fish #3292, pepper, each . . . . $25 – 35 . . . . $50 – 65

Fish #3293, salt, each; matches dinnerware . . . . $25 – 35 . . . . $50 – 65
    pattern Galley #3336.

Cowgirl #3294, pepper, each . . . . $145 – 165 . . . . $300 – 350

Cowboy #3295, salt, each; matches dinnerware pattern . . . $145 – 165 . . . . $300 – 350
    Ranger #3304.

Sailor Girl #3296, pepper, each . . . . $145 – 165 . . . . $200 – 250

Sailor Boy #3297, salt, each; matches dinnerware pattern . $145 – 165 . . . . $200 – 250
    Newport #3333.

Daisy #3298, salt or pepper, each; matches dinnerware . . . . . $30 – 35 . . . . $45 – 60
    patterns Field Daisy #3306, Brown-Eyed Daisy #3345,
    Blue Mountain Daisy #3346, or Pink Mountain Daisy #3347.

Blue Bell #3290, salt, pepper, each; matches dinnerware . . . . $25 – 35 . . . . $50 – 65
    patterns Blue Bell #3334 and Sunflower #3340.

Lemon salt & pepper #3291, #3290 with Persian Yellow glaze.

Fish salt & pepper #3293, #3292 with Silver Green glaze.

1943 Introductions: *Solid Color*   *Hand Painted*

Pennsylvania Dutch Boy #3718, salt . . . . $110 – 145 . . . . $150 – 175

Pennsylvania Dutch Girl #3719, pepper . . . . $110 – 145 . . . . $150 – 175

Tulip #3721, salt or pepper, each . . . . $30 – 40 . . . . $50 – 65

1950s Introductions: *Solid Color*

Golf Ball, salt or pepper, each . . . . $20 – 35

Golf Ball salt & pepper.

right: Pennsylvania Dutch Boy #3718 and Girl #3719, Colonial Blue glaze.

1960s Introductions: *Solid-Color*

Apple, salt or pepper, each; matches dinnerware. . . . . $35 – 45
    pattern Apple Delight #5161.

Daisy #3298, salt or pepper, each; matches dinnerware. . . . . $50 – 60
    pattern Blue Daisy #5131.

Pig, salt or pepper, each . . . . $65 – 80
Rooster #3285, pepper, each . . . . $70 – 95
Hen #3286, salt, each . . . . $70 – 95

Pig salt & pepper.

1978 Introductions:
Corn, salt or pepper, each; matches dinnerware
    pattern Maize-Ware #5327 . . . . $8 – 12

Dealer Signs

    From the 1920s through the 1970s Stangl produced dealer signs for retailers to use with Stangl displays. The signs were always decorated to match the Stangl products advertised at that time. Signs from the 1920s and 1930s were glazed with solid-color glazes, later signs were produced with hand-painted motifs. Most dealer signs had a simple bracket stand. Beginning in the late 1960s, some dealer signs were produced with a pocket on the back for holding dinnerware price lists.

Fulper Fayence dealer sign, 1924 – 1929. . . . . $800 – 950
Fulper/Stangl dealer sign, 1926 – 1929 . . . . $750 – 900
Stangl dealer sign, jar shape solid-color glazes, late 1920s . . . . $350 – 500
Stangl dealer sign, vase motif, deco letters solid-color glazes, late 1920s – 1930s . . . . $350 – 500
Stangl dealer sign, vase motif, deco letters black or ivory with gold or
    silver luster, 1934 . . . . $400 – 550
Stangl Pottery individual display letters solid-color glazes, mid-1930s; per
    complete set. . . . . $850 – 1,200
Stangl Rainbow Sets dealer sign, solid-color glazes, 1937 – 1940 . . . . $600 – 750
Stangl dealer sign, vase motif, hand painted, 1938 – 1945 . . . . $400 – 550
Della-Ware dealer sign, palette shape, 1940 – 1950. . . . . $300 – 400
Stangl Terra Rose dealer sign, rose shape, 1940 – 1950s. . . . . $250 – 350
Stangl Terra Rose dealer sign, oval, 1940 – 1950s . . . . $300 – 400
Stangl Dinnerware dealer sign, hand-carved Tulip and Garden
    Flower motifs, 1945 – 1950s . . . . $300 – 400
Stangl Dinnerware dealer sign, hand-carved Thistle and Blueberry
    motifs, 1950 – 1960s. . . . . $300 – 400

Stangl dealer sign, hand carved, green letters, 1950 – 1960s . . . . $175 – 200
Antique Gold dealer sign, 1957 – 1970s. . . . . $75 – 100
Granada Gold dealer sign, 1963 – 1970s . . . . $75 – 100
Tiffany Caughley dealer sign, 1964 – 1978, blue . . . . $350 – 450
Tiffany Caughley dealer sign, 1964 – 1978, brown, green. . . . . $150 – 200
Caughley dealer sign, 1964 – 1978, blue . . . . $250 – 350
Caughley dealer sign, 1964 – 1978, brown, green, yellow . . . . $100 – 150
Stangl dealer sign, raised lettering with floral and cherry motifs, late 1960s – 1978 . . $200 – 275
Stangl Stoneware dealer sign, 1971 – 1973 . . . . $90 – 120
Stangl Stoneware hand painted dealer sign, 1971 – 1973. . . . . $95 – 120
Stangl Stoneware Dinnerware dealer sign, 1971 – 1973 . . . . $95 – 120
Town & Country dealer sign, 1974 – 1978, blue . . . . $150 – 175
Town & Country dealer sign, brown, green, yellow. . . . . $75 – 125
Indian Summer dealer sign, 1977 – 1978. . . . . $85 – 135
Maize-ware dealer sign, 1978 . . . . $80 – 110
Dainty-Ware dealer sign, late 1970s . . . . $70 – 95

*Fulper/Stangl dealer sign, late
1920s, Persian yellow glaze.*

*Stangl dealer sign, 1930s, vase motif,
Oxblood glaze.*

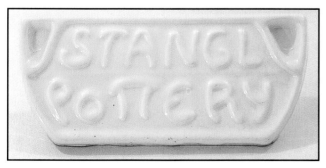

*Stangl dealer sign, late 1920s, jar shape, Persian
yellow glaze.*

*Stangl dealer sign, 1934, vase motif with
black glaze and 22-karat gold luster.*

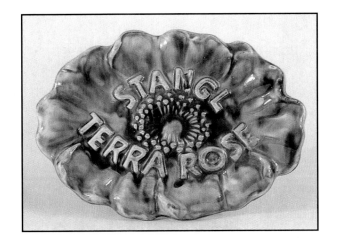

top left: Stangl dealer sign, 1938, vase motif, hand painted with Satin Blue glaze.

middle left: Terra Rose dealer sign, rose shape, mauve.

bottom left: Terra Rose dealer sign, oval shape, blue.

top right: Della-Ware dealer sign, palette shape.

middle right: Stangl Dinnerware dealer sign, Garden Flower and Tulip motifs.

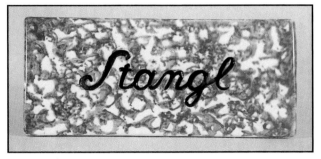

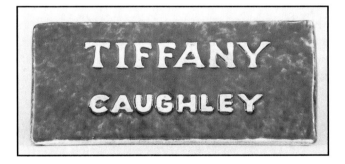

Clockwise beginning at top left:

Stangl Dinnerware dealer sign, Thistle and Blueberry motifs.

Stangl dealer sign, hand-carved lettering.

Antique Gold dealer sign.

Tiffany Caughley dealer sign, blue.

Stangl dealer sign, raised lettering, floral and cherry motif.

Stangl Stoneware dealer signs, redware with dark turquoise and yellow lettering to coordinate with the Morning Blue and Yellow Flower dinnerware patterns.

Stangl Stoneware dealer sign, Hardened Blue lettering with Satin Gold glaze.

Town & Country dealer sign, blue.

Paper Products, Advertising & Premiums

As with many companies, Stangl printed a wide assortment of price lists, catalogs, booklets, and other paper items. Price lists for open stock dinnerware patterns were given to customers at department stores and the Flemington Outlet. Catalogs showing Stangl's general line of merchandise were usually available only to retailers or wholesale distributors. Booklets, pamphlets, and advertising novelties were nearly always available only at the Flemington Outlet. Stangl's paper napkins and placemats were sold at department stores as well as the Flemington Outlet.

Paper Napkins and Placemats

Stangl's first paper napkins were produced for a short time during the mid-1950s. These were dinner- and cocktail-sized napkins printed with motifs matching a few of the more popular dinnerware patterns. These napkins had a scalloped edge and were packed 100 to a pasteboard box or 25 in a cellophane package. This style of napkin was discontinued by the late 1950s. Stangl did not offer paper napkins again until the late 1960s.

Paper placemats were produced only during the mid-1950s. The placemats measure 14" x 10" and were sold in pasteboard boxes of 100. Paper placemats were available with the same motifs as the scalloped edge paper napkins.

Blueberry and Thistle dinner napkins, Thistle cocktail napkin, pasteboard napkin box, cocktail size.

Paper placemats with Thistle motif and pasteboard box.

The paper napkins Stangl marketed during the 1960s and 1970s had straight edges instead of scalloped, and were sold in cellophane packs of 50. There is continuing collector interest in many of Stangl's paper napkin patterns. Paper napkin values are listed with their respective dinnerware patterns.

Dinnerware Price Lists

Price lists were usually printed for Stangl's most popular patterns only. Stangl rarely, if ever, made price lists available for private label patterns, salad sets or Flemington patterns.

Several of the paper napkin patterns available during the late 1960s to mid-1970s.

During the 1930s, price lists for hand-painted dinnerware patterns were usually 8½" x 11" mat-finish, four-color single sheets. Beginning in 1942, hand-carved dinnerware pattern price lists were mat-finish, four-color 3½" x 6¼" bi-fold sheets. From the 1950s through the 1970s, Stangl used glossy, full-color bi-fold, tri-fold, and single sheet price lists ranging from 3½" x 6¼" to 8½" x 11". Known values for price lists are listed with each dinnerware pattern.

Various Stangl price lists.

Booklets and Handouts

Several different booklets were printed from the 1940s through the 1970s describing Stangl's history, manufacturing processes, and decorative attributes. These items were usually distributed at department store demonstrations and the Flemington Outlet.

Attractive Settings for Your Table, 1946; 6 pages 7" x 8½" . . . . $50 – 60
Stangl Dinnerware and How They Do It, 1948; 2½" x 5¼" . . . . $20 – 25
History of Stangl Pottery, 1964; 8 pages 3½" x 5½" . . . . $25 – 35
Facts About Stangl, 1965. . . . . $10 – 15
Stangl, A Portrait of Progress in Pottery, 1965; 32 pages . . . . $40 – 50

*Stangl, A Portrait of Progress in Pottery
and History of Stangl Pottery.*

*Several Flemington Outlet fliers and promotional
leaflets.*

Flemington Outlet Advertising and Novelties

From the 1930s onward, Stangl sent fliers listing sales, weekly specials, and upcoming events to patrons on the Flemington Outlet mailing list. These were usually 8½" x 11" or 8½" x 14" sheets with mimeograph printing.

In addition to promoting the Flemington Outlet with fliers and local newspaper ads, Stangl used assorted advertising give-away items. These were usually small and inexpensively produced.

bridge tally, 1940s; paper with tassel. $15 – 20
canasta tally, 1940s; paper . . . . $20 – 25
litter bag, 1970s; printed vinyl . . . . . . $20 – 25
Fulper matchbook, 1930s . . . . $50 – 75
Stangl matchbooks, 1930s – 1950s. . . $15 – 25
Stangl matchboxes, 1960s . . . . $15 – 20
memorandum booklet, 1970s;
   printed vinyl with calendar. . . . . . $10 – 15
memorandum booklet, 1940s
   and 1950s; printed paper. . . . . $20 – 25

pen, 1950s – 1970s; ball point . . . . . . $10 – 20
pencil, 1950s; mechanical . . . . $15 – 25
pencil, 1950s; wood . . . . $5 – 10
postcard, 1960s; Flemington Outlet
   building . . . . $10 – 15
ruler, 1950s; 6" with calendar, paper . $15 – 20
ruler, 1950s; 18" metal . . . . $25 – 35
tumbler, 1976 employee Christmas
   party souvenir, glass . . . . $35 – 45
Flemington Outlet flyers, mailers, ea. $20 – 35

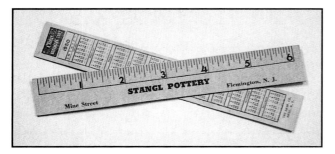

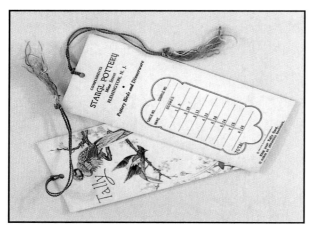

Clockwise beginning at top left:

Stangl 6" calendar rulers.

Stangl matchbooks and matchbox, Fulper matchbook.

Paper and vinyl memo booklets and wood pencil.

Bridge tally, front and back.

Stangl 1976 Christmas party tumbler.

Because Martin Stangl was producing a product with a known reputation for high quality, he felt that every piece sold should bear a recognizable trademark. This was accomplished with paper labels and indelible markings.

The earliest Fulper Fayence and Fulper/Stangl pieces usually had only the shape number cast into the bases. Because these numbers were part of the mold and were attained during the casting process they were known as "in-mold" numbers. During the late 1920s and early 1930s, a steel die was used to impress the Fulper/Stangl or Stangl name into the base alongside the in-mold shape number. Paper labels were always used in conjunction with these marks.

When Stangl began mass producing underglaze decorated articles, rubber stamped underglaze marks began to be used. Variations of underglaze backstamps were in use from 1937 until the close of the factory. The only exception to this was for a short time between 1946 and 1949 when underglaze decal marks were used.

During the 1950s, Stangl used rubber stamp marks with a date code. The code was basically a Roman numeral system. Beginning in 1953, three small slashes were used in conjunction with the oval backstamp. The three slashes represented 1953. In 1954 there were four slashes, and five slashes during the first half of 1955. By the end of 1955, the five slashes were replaced with the Roman numeral V. During the last half of the 1950s, Roman numerals represented the date for each year. The Roman numeral X represented 1960, which was the last year that a date code backstamp was used.

During the 1960s, various logos were added to the trademark, such as: "Hand Painted," "Dura-Fired," and "Oven Proof." After the fire in 1965, the trademark was significantly modified. The word "Pottery" was removed, and the oval became somewhat flattened. The words "Since 1805" were added at this time.

Stangl Marks and Labels

Fulper Fayence paper label, 1924 – 1930.

In-mold shape number, 1924 – 1970s.

Fulper/Stangl paper label, 1926 – 1930.

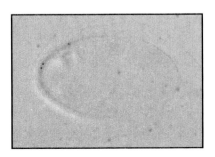

Fulper/Stangl die-pressed mark, 1926 – 1930.

Stangl Pottery paper label, 1929 – early 1930s.

Stangl die-pressed mark, 1929 – 1940s.

Paper label, vase motif,
1930 – 1940s.

Underglaze stamp, block letters,
1937 – 1939.

Underglaze stamp, vase
motif, dark letters,
1937 – 1939.

Underglaze stamp, vase motif,
light letters, 1937 – 1939.

Hand Painted dinnerware mark,
1938 – 1940.

Underglaze stamp,
Handpainted,
1938 – 1940s.

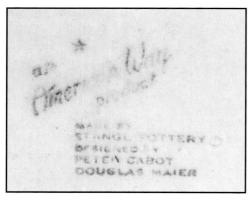

American Way underglaze stamp,
1940 – 1942.

Della-Ware underglaze stamp,
1940 – 1953.

Carole Stupell Ltd. underglaze
stamp, 1940 – 1945.

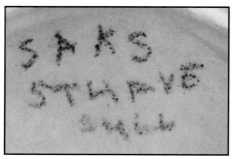

Sak's Fifth Avenue
mark, 1940 – 1945.

Frederik Lunning, Inc.
underglaze stamp,
1940 – 1942.

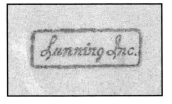

Lunning, Inc. underglaze stamp, 1942 – 1953.

Terra Rose underglaze stamp, block letters, 1940 – 1950.

Terra Rose paper label, early 1940s.

Terra Rose underglaze stamp, script letters, mid-1940s.

Terra Rose underglaze decal, 1946 – 1949.

Stangl Pottery paper label, late 1940s – 1978.

Stangl Pottery underglaze decal, 1947 – 1949.

Stangl Pottery underglaze stamp, 1949 – 1953.

Underglaze stamp, dated 1954.

150th Anniversary underglaze stamp, 1955.

American Bone China gold luster stamp, 1955.

Gold luster stamp, dated
1958.

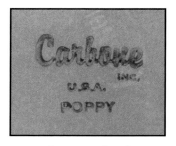

Carbone underglaze
stamp, 1959 – 1963.

Oven Proof underglaze stamp, early
1960s.

Made For Jordan Marsh underglaze
stamp, early 1960s.

Made For Bloomingdales underglaze
stamp, early 1960s.

Henri Bendel underglaze
stamp, early 1960s.

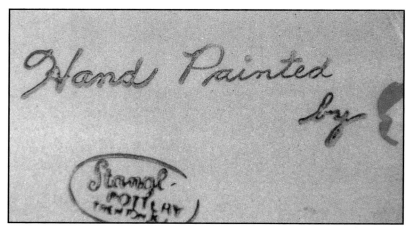

Hand Painted By… underglaze stamp, early 1960s.

Dura-Fired underglaze
stamp, 1963 – 1965.

Hand Painted Since
1805 underglaze stamp,
1965 – 1978

Large Hand Painted underglaze stamp, late 1960s.

Carole Stupell LTD gold luster stamp, 1970 – 1974.

Potter's Association under-glaze stamp, early 1970s.

Hand Painted by Experi-enced Artists underglaze stamp, early 1970s.

Large Stangl Stoneware underglaze stamp, 1971 – 1974.

Small Stangl Stoneware underglaze stamp, 1971 – 1974.

TO oven… underglaze stamp, late 1977 – 1978.

Genuine Handcrafted under-glaze stamp, late 1977 – 1978.

Micro - Oven - Table - Dishwasher underglaze stamp, 1978.

Maize-Ware underglaze stamp, 1978.

Seconds Marks

Stangl marked second-quality items with special seconds marks for several reasons. Primarily, to prevent seconds purchased at the Flemington Outlet from being returned to department stores as firsts. This was why Lunning's contract with Stangl required that all Lunning seconds have the Lunning mark obliterated in some way. The Lunning marks were at first obliterated by grinding them with a grinding wheel. Beginning in 1942, the mark on Lunning seconds was covered with black glaze and the whole piece re-fired. This added considerable cost and labor to second quality merchandise.

Pieces that were determined to be seconds before glaze was applied were marked with one of several underglaze second rubber-stamps. Until the early 1950s, there was no truly effective way to permanently mark glazed pieces as second quality. By 1953 a sandblast marking system was developed which enabled the word "Stangl" to be indelibly etched into the glaze, indicating the piece as second quality.

Until the late 1960s, seconds were sold only at the Flemington Outlet. During the late 1960s and early 1970s, however, Stangl began selling "nearly perfect" seconds to discount stores at reduced prices. This group of seconds was called the "A" Line or "A" Ware. Each piece was marked with a sandblasted "A" within a circle.

Frederik Lunning, Inc. obliterated underglaze stamp, 1940 – 1942.

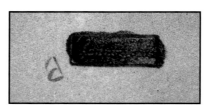

Lunning, Inc. blacked-out underglaze stamp, 1942 – 1953.

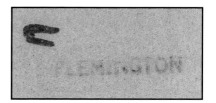

Flemington second underglaze stamp, mid-1940s.

Flemington "F" second underglaze stamp, mid-1940s.

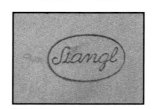

Oval Stangl second underglaze stamp, late 1940s – 1978.

Stangl Sec. second underglaze stamp, 1950s – 1960s.

Sandblasted second mark, 1953 – 1978.

Sandblasted "A" Ware mark, late 1960s – early 1970s.

Sandblasting machine in use at the Trenton factory marking seconds in 1954.

Solid-Color Dinnerware Glazes

These brief descriptions of Stangl's early, solid-color dinnerware glazes are intended to assist in identifying colors and to give a general idea of the time-period each glaze was used.

Blue

Alice Blue — mid 1930s
A transparent light blue that intensifies in the crevices of the shapes. This was an artware glaze not usually used on dinnerware.

Aqua Blue — 1937 to mid-1940s
This is a transparent glaze, lighter and more blue than turquoise. Aqua Blue is thicker in the crevices of the pieces and thinner on the raised portions.

Blue-of-the-Sky — early 1930s
An opaque light blue. This glaze was primarily used on Stangl's artware shapes. In rare instances, however, Blue-of-the-Sky was applied to certain dinnerware lines.

Colonial Blue — 1924 to mid-1940s
Semi-opaque medium blue. Good quality versions of Colonial Blue glaze are very heavy, and have tiny dark blue flecks in the glaze. Lesser quality versions are usually lighter and thinner.

Satin Aqua — late 1930s
A bright, opaque aqua-turquoise color with a mat finish.

Satin Blue — 1937 to late 1940s
Transparent mat light blue. This glaze was used alone as a solid-color glaze and with under-glaze decorations.

Turquoise — 1930 to 1936
A semi-opaque soft blue-green. This glaze was generally used to line Tangerine glazed cups, teapots, and pitchers.

Brown

Satin Brown — 1937 to 1938
Very dark, warm chocolate brown. Very little of this glaze was used on dinnerware.

Rust — 1928 to 1943
A textured, mat red-brown that could range from almost a coppery gold to dark, warm brown. Stangl catalogs describe this glaze as "a variegated color, sometimes orange and sometimes a golden-brown as in autumn leaves."

Grey, Black

Grey — late 1920s
Thin, glossy light gray with flecks of dark gray and dark blue. A very rarely used glaze.

Black — 1929 to mid-1930s
> High gloss, semi-transparent black. This glaze was seldom used alone, but was used in conjunction with the Sunburst glaze finish and as a base for platinum luster during the early 1930s.

Green

Apple Green — 1930 to mid-1930s
> A semi-mat, medium gray-green with silvery flecks. This glaze was very popular during the 1930s and is most evident on Stangl's handmade lines.

Bronze Green — 1937
> Medium satiny green with random areas of copper sheen. This was a short-lived dinnerware glaze.

Dark Green — 1935 to 1936
> Dark, semi-mat green. This was used only in conjunction with the Tropical glaze treatments during 1935 – 1936.

Green Matte — 1930 to 1937
> A mat, medium green resembling Apple Green but less glossy and without the silvery flecks. Like Apple Green, this glaze was used primarily on handmade articles. Green Matte was sometimes referred to as Matte Green.

Leaf Green — mid 1930s
> A transparent dark to medium green, used primarily on the #1800 cabbage shapes.

Satin Green — 1937 to late 1940s
> A light, semi-mat green. This glaze was used alone as a solid-color glaze and with underglaze motifs.

Silver Green — 1924 to mid-1940s
> Heavy, semi-opaque, gloss light green. On quality glazed pieces, this glaze is quite heavy and almost shades toward gray. Stangl described this glaze as "a light, cool refreshing green."

Pink, Purple

Eggplant — 1935 to 1936
> Very dark, nearly black, high gloss purple. This glaze was used only in conjunction with the Tropical glaze treatments during 1935 – 1936.

Lavender — 1930 to early 1930s
> Opaque, semi-gloss orchid-pink. This glaze was seldom used on dinnerware shapes. Stangl described this glaze in 1931 as "a perfect blend of red and blue."

Plum — 1937
> An semi-transparent, gloss brownish purple. This glaze was almost always applied only to lamps.

Rose — 1928 to 1930
> A glossy dark rose pink. Generally used as a Fulper Fayence artware glaze, Rose was applied to certain dinnerware shapes.

Violet — 1930 to early 1930s
An opaque, gloss violet. This is a very rare dinnerware glaze.

Red, Orange
Oxblood — 1928 to early 1936
Very dark, gloss, maroon-red. This was an expensive glaze that was usually special-ordered, so it is quite rare.

Tangerine — 1929 to 1943
Semi-mat, opaque, orange-red. Developed by Henry Below, this uranium based glaze was discontinued when the U. S. government took control of all commercial grade uranium oxide in 1943.

Tangerine, Oxblood, and Rust were more costly than other glazes. Wholesale prices for pieces glazed with these three colors were always between 25% and 50% higher than other glazes as a result of higher production costs.

White
Chinese Ivory — 1924 to 1926
Heavy, gloss white with bluish tones. Very rare dinnerware glaze, used primarily on Fulper Fayence artware.

Ivory — 1931 to late 1930s
Transparent, gloss, warm ivory. This glaze was nearly always used in conjunction with platinum luster overglaze decoration.

Oyster White — 1935 to 1936
A pearly satin white. This glaze was used only with the Tropical glaze treatments during 1935 – 1936.

Satin White — 1933 to late 1970s
Transparent mat white. This glaze was used both alone as a solid-color glaze and with underglaze decorations. Variations of this glaze were produced until Stangl closed. Another name is White Satin.

Surf White — 1930 to 1937
An opaque, flat white, used on both artware and dinnerware. The name Surf White was used again in 1940 to describe a blue and white artware treatment.

Yellow
Maize — 1935 to 1936
A satin pale yellow. Very little of this glaze was used on dinnerware or artware.

Persian Yellow — 1924 to mid-1940s
A very bright, semi-opaque gloss yellow. Occasionally this glaze can be thin and pale, especially on pieces produced during the 1940s.

Satin Yellow — 1939 to late 1940s
> A transparent, mat gold. This glaze was used on artware alone as a solid-color glaze, but on dinnerware it was used only with underglaze decorated motifs.

Underglaze Colors

Following is a list of some of Stangl's more prominent underglaze colors, with a few examples of patterns where each color was used.

Black

Eye Black
> This color was used on the eyes of the pottery bird figurines and some dinnerware accents. This was a very thin transparent color.

Lyric Black, Black #92
> The black on Lyric, a very deep, opaque color and ultimately came to be called simply "Black."

Blue

Art Ware Blue
> The deep cobalt based blue used on Mediterranean and Caughley. Also used under the silk glaze on Terra Rose artware and dinnerware.

Blue #95
> The predominant dark blue used throughout Stangl's underglaze-decorated dinnerware production. This color is best seen on early pieces of the Blueberry pattern.

Dark Blue
> A somewhat darker color than Blue #95, used during the late 1950s through the 1970s.

Delphinium Blue, Blue #8B
> The medium blue used on the bands of American Garden.

Hardened Blue
> A very dark blue used during the 1970s. Similar to Art Ware blue, but does not become watery under the glaze. This color can best be seen on Wood Rose and Blue Silhouette.

Light Blue
> Originally a light application of Blue #95, this color was used primarily on the blue stripe on the rim of Fruit and Flowers and the lighter blue on Blue Tulip.

Terra Rose Blue
> Another term for Art Ware Blue.

Dark Turquoise, Turquoise #4A-5360
> The Iris and stripe on the rim of Country Garden.

Turquoise #4673
The "water" on Waterlily.

Brown

Pomona Brown Light, Pomona Brown Dark
These two neutralized values of muted brown were created by mixing Carnival Green with Walnut Brown. The Pomona series of colors was first developed for the Pomona dinnerware pattern.

Saddle Brown, Brown #81
The brown on Bachelor's Button, Blue Daisy, and Fig.

Tan, Brown #4044
The orange color in Bittersweet, and the light colored leaves on Amber Glo.

Terra Rose Mauve
A transparent, purplish manganese brown, used under the silk glaze on the Terra Rose artware and dinnerware.

Walnut Brown, Brown #4528
Very dark, opaque brown, usually the stems on Fruit and the dark leaves and bands on Golden Harvest.

Gray

Amber Grey
This color was actually standard gray engobe applied by brush, most evident as the wide gray bands on Amber Glo chop plates.

Green

Art Ware Green
The green copper oxide used under the Silk glaze on the Terra Rose artware and dinnerware lines.

Aqua
A combination of French Green and Dark Turquoise, the Aqua color was used on green Oyster plates and the lighter leaves of the Bella Rosa pattern.

Bamboo Green
A bright green somewhat darker than Victoria Green, used during the 1970s on Bamboo.

Carnival Green
A mixture of Olive Green and Victoria Green that was used on the Carnival dinnerware pattern.

Fathom Green
Another name for Art Ware Green; used under the Silk glaze as a seconds treatment, and on a dinnerware pattern of the same name for Jordan Marsh.

French Green, Green #4055
    The dark blue/green on the bands and leaves of the Fruit and Garden Flower patterns.

Frosted Fruit Green
    A light version of Art Ware Green, used primarily under the Satin White glaze. This color produced the pale blue/green on the Frosted Fruit and Florentine dinnerware patterns.

Grass Green, Green #4815
    An early medium green, thinner than Pennsylvania Dutch Green, used during 1949 and 1950 on the leaves of Kumquat, Lime, and Prelude.

Green #1431
    A light green having more substance than Victoria Green. This color was used during the 1960s on the Florette and Caughley patterns.

Medium Green
    A bright green used on certain Della-Ware patterns during the early 1950s to replace Grass Green.

Olive Green
    A very soft gray/green used on the bands of olive.

Pennsylvania Dutch Green, Green #4055
    The only dark green, other than French Green, used throughout the 1940s. It can be seen on the rims of the Della-Ware patterns Laurita, El Rosa, and Festival, and had a tendency to run and blur.

Pomona Green Light, Pomona Green Dark
    These neutralized shades of green were mixtures of Willow Green and Walnut Brown. Originally developed for Pomona, these colors were used extensively during the 1960s and were featured on patterns such as Golden Grape and Sculptured Fruit.

Terra Rose Green
    Another term for Art Ware Green.

Victoria Green, Green #4309 (old), Green #B-204 (new)
    A chartreuse green, used on the stems of Wild Rose and the accent leaves of Tulip.

Willow Green, Green #F3683X
    Very smooth, opaque, dark green. Found on Thistle and Jewelled Christmas Tree. This color replaced Pennsylvania Dutch Green during the early 1950s.

Purple

Lavender
    Used on the plums on Fruit, the Canterbury Bells on Garden Flower, and the asters on Fruit and Flowers. During the 1960s, this color was improved and renamed Purple.

Orchid #1032X
    The understrokes on Thistle blossoms.

Purple
>   The same color as lavender.

Terra Rose Amethyst
>   A violet color, used under the Silk glaze on a dinnerware and artware line made exclusively for American Way during 1941.

Pink, Red

Alpine Rose
>   The original name for Pink #193, used during the late 1930s.

Crimson
>   The original name for Pink #160, last used during the late 1930s.

Pink #193
>   The light pink on Wild Rose and Thistle. Initially called Alpine Rose during the late 1930s.

Pink #160
>   This color was the truest red Stangl had available during the 1940s and 1950s. It decorated the dark starbursts of Carnival and the blossoms of Magnolia as well as the cherries on Fruit and Festival. Pink #160 was known as Crimson during the late 1930s.

Pink #167
>   This color, darker than Pink #160, was as near to red as possible. Introduced in the 1960s, it was used on some of the later Festival motifs and the bands and fruits of Cranberry.

Rust
>   This color was a mixture of Tan and Pink #160. It is best seen as the large blossom on the Wood Rose pattern.

White

White #10
>   The flowers on Star Flower and the white areas on Bella Rosa and Magnolia. A very opaque color used wherever white details were needed on darker backgrounds.

Yellow

Dark Yellow, Yellow #4893
>   This color is somewhere between Yellow and Orange. It was used on the rims of Flora.

Gold
>   The gold color used during the 1940s on the rims of Red Cherry.

Golden Harvest Yellow
>   A mixture of Yellow and White #10. This was a heavy, opaque color so that the dark background of colored engobes would not show through. This color was used primarily on Golden Harvest.

Light Yellow
A medium yellow used for a short time during the early 1940s.

Old Gold
This mixture of Walnut Brown and Yellow was the gold color used during the 1960s on Sculptured Fruit and Golden Blossom. By the late 1960s, the color name was shortened to simply Gold.

Orange
The dark yellow on the rims of Fruit and Garden Flower.

Yellow, Yellow #4034
This color was lighter than Orange, and was used on Waterlily, and the apple and pear motifs on Fruit and Festival.

Post Stangl

Royal Cumberland

After closing Stangl Pottery in 1978, Frank Wheaton, aware of the popularity of certain Stangl patterns, continued to manufacture adaptations of Stangl dinnerware and Kiddieware motifs during the early 1980s at his Royal Cumberland plant in Millville, New Jersey.

Some of the Stangl-inspired dinnerware patterns produced with the Royal Cumberland mark were Holly, Pine Cone, Grape, Fruit, and Town & Country. The Grape and Fruit bands were hand painted but the motifs were overglaze decals. The Holly, Pine Cone, and Town & Country patterns were completely hand painted.

Royal Cumberland Fruit 8" plate, 10" plate, cup; Grape cup.

Royal Cumberland Holly vase, 8"
plate, cup & saucer.

Stangl designer Irene Sarnecki created several new motifs and adaptations of Stangl designs for the Royal Cumberland Kiddieware line. Royal Cumberland Kiddieware sets consisted of a 9" plate, cereal bowl, and cup. These pieces were made from the same molds that had been used for the Stangl white-bodied Kiddieware.

Royal Cumberland Kiddieware patterns.

Although the quality of the Royal Cumberland Town & Country and Kiddieware is comparable to Stangl, nearly all Royal Cumberland pieces are well marked with Royal Cumberland backstamps.

"New Stangl"

During 1991 and 1992, there was an attempt to re-establish the manufacturing of Stangl products at the Royal Cumberland plant in Millville. These articles were cast using original Stangl molds. Town & Country, Kiddieware, and several novelty items were included in this line of New Stangl. A few of the Kiddieware motifs were older Stangl designs, but most were newly created for this venture.

While the shapes and patterns resembled original Stangl products, the body, colors, and glazes did not approximate Stangl quality. The colors lacked brilliance and usually did not match Stangl's original colors. The glaze often possessed

Royal Cumberland mark.

a milky, pink tint and frequently exhibited crazing. The mark used on the New Stangl products was a variation of the script Stangl trademark. Occasionally, pieces were stamped "Millville."

The blue Town & Country dealer sign seems to be the only New Stangl piece to cause trouble. Neither Stangl nor New Stangl dealer signs were marked. Original Stangl blue Town & Country dealer signs are more brilliantly colored and better glazed than the New Stangl signs.

By 1993, the high cost of skilled labor and difficulties encountered in producing a quality, hand-crafted product precipitated the end of New Stangl.

New Stangl brown mug, blue flowerpot, yellow flowerpot, green creamer.

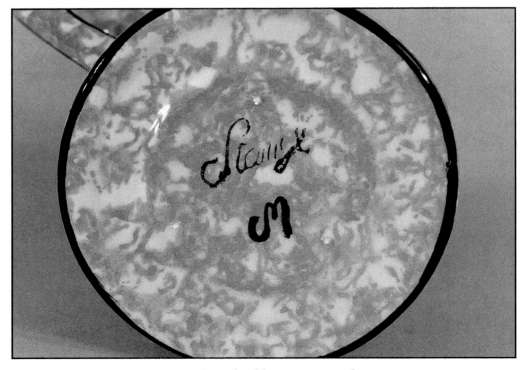

New Stangl rubber stamp mark.

Bibliography

Cameron, Elisabeth
Encyclopedia of Pottery and Porcelain: 1800 – 1960
 copyright 1986, Cameron Books
 2a, Roman Way, London N7 8XG

Chappell, James
The Potter's Complete Book of Clay and Glazes
 copyright 1977, Watson-Guptill Publications
 1515 Broadway, New York, New York

Evans, Paul
Art Pottery of the United States
 Feingold & Lewis Publishing
 1088 Madison Avenue
 New York, New York

Gray, Gordon W.
Fulper! Form, Function & Finance
 copyright 1992
 Clinton Historical Museum
 P.O. box 5005 56 Main St.
 Clinton, New Jersey

Hennessey, William J.
Russel Wright: American Designer
 copyright 1983, MIT Press

Lee, Warren F.
Down Along the Old Bel-Del
 copyright 1987, Bel-Del Enterprises, Ltd.
 Albuquerque, New Mexico

Parmelee, Cullen W.
Ceramic Glazes
 copyright 1951, Industrial Publications, Inc.
 Chicago, Illinois

Shuman, Eleanor Nolan
The Trenton Story
 copyright 1958
 Eleanor Nolan Shuman

An Inventory of Historic Engineering and Industrial Sites;
Trenton, New Jersey
copyright 1975
Trenton, New Jersey

Business Executives of America
copyright 1950
Institute for Research Biography, Inc.
New York 7, New York

New Jersey: Life, Industries & Resources of a Great State
copyright 1928
New Jersey State Chamber of Commerce
Newark, New Jersey

Raritan Township, Flemington and Environs
copyright 1976
Raritan Township, New Jersey

Industrial Trenton and Vicinity
copyright 1900
George A. Wolf
Wilmington, Delaware

250th Anniversary of the Settlement of Trenton
copyright 1929
Trenton Chamber of Commerce
Trenton, New Jersey

Haeger, the Craftsmen for a Century
copyright 1971, Haeger Potteries, Inc.
Dundee, Illinois

Stangl, A Portrait of Progress in Pottery, booklet
copyright 1965, Stangl Pottery
Trenton, New Jersey

History of Stangl Pottery, booklet
copyright 1964, Stangl Pottery
Trenton, New Jersey

Bucks County Traveler, periodical
November 1957

China, Glass & Tablewares, periodical
Summer supplement, 1955

Crockery and Glass Journal, periodical
Summer supplement, 1955

Enamel - Glass - Whiteware, periodical
May 1955

Hunterdon County Democrat, newspaper
September 19, 26, 1929; October 10, 1929; November 7, 1929; August 24, 1951
Flemington, New Jersey

The Trentonian, newspaper
August 30, 1965
Trenton, New Jersey

Hunterdon Historical Newsletter
Winter 1973
Hunterdon county Historical Society
Flemington, New Jersey

American Way, Regional Handcraft Program
sales catalog, 1940

Fulper Pottery
sales catalogs, advertising, company records

Stangl Pottery
sales catalogs, dinnerware price lists, company records

Martin Stangl's personal notebooks
1927 – 1978, handwritten
Martin Stangl; Anne Pogranicy

Interviews and conversations with former Stangl employees
conducted 1989 – 1999

Author Rob Runge with Stangl's top three designers,
left to right: Irene Sarnecki, Rose Herbeck, and Kay Hackett.

Known to champion the cause of historic preservation, Rob Runge is fondly referred to as "Mr. Stangl." He is universally respected as the one person who possesses a "textbook" knowledge of the history, operation, and products of the Stangl Pottery company.

Through his tireless research efforts, Rob has delved into company files, as well as public and museum records. He has access to Martin Stangl's personal production notebooks and a wealth of file memos. He conducted countless interviews with former Stangl company employees. Martin Stangl's own daughter and son-in-law, Christl Stangl Bacheler and Merrill Bacheler, often quip that Rob knows more about the company than "Pop" Stangl himself!

Rob's Stangl work has spanned a 20-year period although his very first attraction to Stangl's bright primary colors occurred when he was but six months old. He had pulled an entire stack of Stangl Fruit dinner plates off the table and sent them crashing to the floor while visiting his great-grandmother in Florida, a story that the Runge family enjoys retelling even now!

Rob Runge was born, raised, and educated in the Hunterdon County/Trenton, New Jersey area. He follows closely in his father Robert Sr.'s footsteps in that they share a love of local New Jersey history. His involvement with the Runge family-owned Delaware Valley Nursery segued into a fascination with the industrial growth and importance that the Trenton ceramics industry had in the economic structure of the state of New Jersey.

There began the thirst and quest for knowledge as well as the desire to preserve Stangl history. Recently, top Stangl designer Rose Herbeck was quoted as saying of Rob, "For many years, a Stangl museum has been on Rob's 'wish list' of things to get done. I know Rob; he gets what he wants. Stangl is not just for yesterday, it is for tomorrow as well."

Rob Runge has been intensely involved with many civic activities aimed at advancing the interests of collectors of today. He has organized major events which honored former Stangl employees. He was instrumental in having historic markers erected in Flemington to designate important Fulper and Stangl sites. The most important feat was when Rob rescued the original Stangl molds from a building slated for demolition. Today, they sit safely in storage as a result of his efforts. Always interested in sharing his knowledge, he has been responsible for presenting many exhibits and programs.

He has been instrumental in establishing a pottery museum in the Flemington, New Jersey, area to house a Fulper and Stangl collection. Rob has been working on this for more than 10 years, initially acquiring examples of the Stangl Company's products from the mundane to the fanciful. He is currently working on the acquisition of two sites to house a display spanning the years of Stangl's manufacturing from 1924 to 1978. Fulper products representing the years prior to 1935 will also be showcased.

Another source of a museum-ripe collection is the original Stangl archival material that was stored when the facility closed in Flemington. This collection will be made available to the general public on loan after a permanent museum is established.

On a personal note, Rob is one of the most genuinely sincere people I know. He unselfishly shares his knowledge with new collectors and anyone interested in spending a moment or an hour discussing the intricate points of Stangl collecting.

This book is exciting and represents the span of many years of research plus hundreds of photos which accurately portray the color and quality of these wonderful items. Rob is once again entrenched in newly discovered research material for a book on Stangl artware. This future book will be a real surprise package of wondrous things. From mundane utilitarian ware in the Stangl Pottery Company's infant years, it will lead the reader through the years and the kaleidoscope of colors, unique shapes, and sizes that made this pottery company different from all the others!

— Diana E. Bullock